The Repo and Reverse Markets

The Repo and Reverse Markets

MARCIA STIGUM

DOW JONES-IRWIN™
Homewood, Illinois 60430

© RICHARD D. IRWIN, INC., 1989

Dow Jones-Irwin is a trademark of
Dow Jones & Company, Inc.

Project editor: Jean Roberts
Production manager: Bette Ittersagen
Jacket design: Ray Machura
Compositor: Bi-Comp, Inc.
Typeface: 10/12 Helvetica Light
Printer: Arcata Graphics/Kingsport

Library of Congress Cataloging-in-Publication Data

Stigum, Marcia L.
    The repo and reverse markets.

    Bibliography: p.
    Includes index.
    1. Money market.   I. Title.
HG226.S75   1989   332.63′2   88–7145
ISBN 0-87094-988-8

Printed in the United States of America

1 2 3 4 5 6 7 8 9 0   K   5 4 3 2 1 0 9 8

To my good friend,
David Shay,
with many thanks for many things

Preface

THIS BOOK PROVIDES a comprehensive description of the *repo* and *reverse repurchase* (*reverse* for short) markets. In particular, the book describes in detail the history of these markets, current practices in these markets, the use of these markets by the Federal Reserve in its open market operations, and the use of these markets by private parties—dealers, banks, investors, and others.

To those who are encountering the repo and reverse markets for the first time, these markets appear complex. In fact, the adjective *complex* is inevitably applied to these markets by lawyers, regulatory examiners, congressmen, and others who are trying to unravel trades done by various parties in these markets—for example, repo and reverse trades done by some dealer who went bankrupt and in the process caused losses to some of its repo and reverse customers.

Actually, the apparent complexity of repo and reverse transactions derives mostly from the unfamiliarity of the observer with these transactions. In truth, nothing could be simpler than a repo or reverse transaction.

*Aside: Just as one man's buy is another man's sell, one man's repo is another man's reverse; so in speaking of repos and reverses, we are really speaking of just **one** type of transaction.*

In every repo or reverse, what goes on is actually extremely *simple*: To do a repo, one merely agrees to buy something today at one price and to sell it some time in the future at some other price—maybe the original price plus some accrued repo interest. The person on the other side of the transaction does a reverse. That's repos and reverses in a nutshell.

Note, in the money market, it is money market securities—governments, agencies, and other securities—that are repoed. One could, however, repo (in theory at least) any asset that is liquid and has value. Gold is repoed in the gold market, and there's no reason why soybeans could not be repoed if a cheap delivery mechanism were available.

Having said that a repo is a simple trade, we must hasten to add that there is complexity in the repo-reverse market. It derives from the not–intuitively-obvious uses to which such trades have been put: reverses to maturity, the creation of vast matched books by dealers, arbitrages that require financing, and so on. In later chapters of this book, we talk about such transactions, which, if worked through step-by-step, are not that hard to follow.

This book should be of use to new entrants to the money market who need to understand how repos and reverses are, in their full bloom, used by dealers, banks, and others. Also, any investor who does not fully understand repos and reverses and who is thinking of doing such a transaction should read this book carefully. Many investors have lost money—millions upon millions of dollars—in the repo and reverse markets; all were investors who did not sufficiently understand these transactions to take simple steps to protect themselves against credit risk (the essence of a repo transaction is that it is a secured loan—more about that later).

This book should also be useful to a host of others: lawyers, accountants, and regulators who, although they will never do a repo themselves, need to have a handle on what such transactions are.

It is expected that many readers of this book will be new to the money market. Part One provides background that should help such readers understand the rest of the book. It describes clearly the instruments traded in the money market, how yields and prices of such securities are calculated, and how money market dealers and brokers operate. Part Two describes in detail all aspects of the repo and reverse markets: the history, current practices, brokering, and clearing. There is a separate chapter by attorney Lee Stremba on the history of repo litigation.

In every area of life, people develop special terms or give common terms special meanings to communicate precisely and concisely with each other their particular interests and activities; hence *jargon*. The money market is no exception, and this book uses money market jargon extensively. To aid the reader, each piece of jargon used is carefully defined the first time it appears in the text. Also, at the end of the book is a Glossary in which a wide range of money and bond market terms are defined.

People who become fascinated by the money market may find it useful to read any and/or all of the following books:

Marcia Stigum, *The Money Market, Revised Edition* (Homewood, Ill.: Dow Jones-Irwin, 1983).

Marcia Stigum and Rene O. Branch, Jr., *Managing Bank Assets and Liabilities* (Homewood, Ill.: Dow Jones-Irwin, 1983).

Marcia Stigum, *Money Market Calculations: Yields, Break-Evens, and Arbitrage* (Homewood, Ill.: Dow Jones-Irwin, 1981).

Marcia Stigum, *After the Trade* (Homewood, Ill.: Dow Jones-Irwin, 1988).

The pronoun *he* is used frequently through this book. This pronoun has long been used in English to mean *person*. Any attempt to avoid this use of *he* leads, in my opinion, to nothing but bad and awkward English. I, therefore, make no such attempt.

In conclusion, I would like to thank the many people—dealers, brokers, bankers, traders, investors, and others—who have answered with patience and grace my multifarious queries about repos and reverses. A special thanks to Lee Stremba for contributing Chapter 19.

Marcia Stigum
Quechee, Vermont

Acknowledgments

THERE WAS ONLY ONE WAY research for this book could be conducted. That was by interviewing market participants at length. To the following people, I would like to express a very heartfelt thanks for the patient and thoughtful answers they proferred to my many questions. A particular thank you also goes to those listed below, who volunteered to read and criticize those chapters that covered their area of specialty. Needless to say, the author bears full responsibility for any remaining errors of fact, which I hope are few.

My thanks also to the many people, not mentioned below, who spoke to me about the repo market in years past, long before I thought of writing a book on this topic.

Tim Anderson
John Astrino
Robert Beehler
Al Clark
Peter Clark
Mary Clarkin
Frank Elleo
Bruce English
Kenneth Entler

Michael Farrell
Michael Friband
Patricia Gaus
Raymond Gottardi
Gregory Gnall
William Hubard
Margaret Kelly
James Killeen
Joan Lovett

Steve Magacs
Bruce Maxwell
Charles Morton
James Pauline
Thomas Pankosky
John Perini
Ralph Peters
Robert Portnoy

Dennis Phalon
Donald Ringsmuth
Gerard M. Reilly
Tom Smith
Kevin Sullivan
Mary Sue Sullivan
Sheila Tschinkel

Abbreviations

EXAMPLES AND QUOTES in this book often contain "Street" abbreviations of the names of various institutions. The most common are:

Bank of America. . . . . .B of A
Bank of New York. . . . . .BONY
Chase Manhattan Bank . . . . .Chase
Citibank. . . . . .Citi
Goldman Sachs. . . . . .Goldman
Irving Trust Company . . . . .Irving
Merrill Lynch . . . . .Merrill
Manufacturers Hanover Trust Co. . . . . .Manny
Morgan Guaranty Trust Co. . . . . .Morgan
Salomon Brothers. . . . . .Sali
Security Pacific. . . . . .Sec Pac

Contents

Chapter 1

Introduction

THIS IS A BOOK ABOUT THE REPO AND REVERSE MARKETS. Repos and reverses are strictly money market transactions, typically big ones: single repos for 500, even 800 million occur daily in the money market. Rather few people work in and thus know much about the money market: there are far more farmers, doctors, lawyers, and Indian chiefs than there are money market pros. Consequently, to most people, the term *repo* is incomprehensible jargon—a term that sounds as if it might perchance have something to do with an auto dealer repossessing a car.

Since this book is written partly for people new to the money market, it calls for *two* introductions, one to the money market and one to repos and reverses. People who know the money market should skip to the second introduction.

THE MONEY MARKET

The U.S. money market is a huge and significant part of the nation's financial system in which banks and other participants trade hundreds of billions of dollars every working day. Where those billions go and the prices at which they are traded affect how the U.S. government finances its debt, how business finances its expansion, and how consumers choose to spend or save.

The money market is a wholesale market for low-risk, highly liquid, short-term IOUs. It is a market for various sorts of debt securities rather than equities. The stock-in-trade of the market includes a large chunk of the U.S. Treasury's debt and billions of dollars worth of federal agency securities, negotiable bank certificates of deposit, bankers' acceptances, municipal notes, and commercial paper. Within the confines of the money market each day, banks—domestic and foreign—actively trade in multimillion-dollar blocks billions of dollars of Federal funds and Eurodollars, and banks and nonbank dealers are each day the recipients of billions of dollars of secured loans through what is called the "repo market." State and municipal governments also finance part of their activities in this market.

The heart of the activity in the money market occurs in the trading rooms of dealers and brokers of money market instruments. During the time the market is open, these rooms are characterized by a frenzy of activity. Each trader or broker sits in front of a battery of direct phone lines linking him to other dealers, brokers, and customers. The phones never ring, they just blink at a pace that makes, especially in the brokers' market, for some of the shortest phone calls ever recorded. Despite the lack of ringing phones, a dealing room is anything but quiet. Dealers and brokers know only one way to hang up on a direct-line phone; they BANG the off button. And the more hectic things get, the harder they bang. Banging phones, like drums in a band, beat the rhythm of the noise generated in a trading room. Almost drowning that banging out at times is the constant shouting of quotes and tidbits of information.

Unless one spends a lot of time in trading rooms, it's hard to get a feel for what is going on amid all this hectic activity. Even listening in on phones is not very enlightening. One learns quickly that dealers and brokers swear a lot (it's said to lessen the tension), but the rest of their conversations is unintelligible to the uninitiated. Money market people have their own jargon, and until one learns it, it is impossible to understand them.

Once adjusted to their jargon and the speed at which traders converse, one observes that they are making huge trades—$5, $50, $250 million—at the snap of a finger. Moreover nobody seems to be particularly awed or even impressed by the size of the figures. A Fed funds broker asked to obtain $100 million in overnight money for a bank might—nonchalant about the size of the trade—reply, "The buck's yours from the B of A," slam down the phone, and take another call. Fed funds brokers earn only $1 per $1 million on overnight funds, so it takes a lot of trades to pay the overhead and let everyone in the shop make some money.

Despite its frenzied and incoherent appearance to the outsider, the money market efficiently accomplishes vital functions everyday. One is shifting vast sums of money between banks. This shifting is required because major money market banks all need a lot more funds than they obtain in deposits, while many smaller banks have more money deposited with them than they can profitably use internally.

The money market also provides a means by which the surplus funds of cash-rich corporations and other institutions can be funneled to banks, corporations, and other institutions that need short-term money. In addition, in the money market the U.S. Treasury can fund huge quantities of debt with ease. And the market provides the Fed with an arena in which to carry out open market operations destined to influence interest rates and the growth of the money supply. The varied activities of money market participants also determine the structure of short-term interest rates, for example, what the yields on Treasury bills of different maturities are and how much commercial paper issuers have to pay to borrow. The latter rate is an important cost to many corporations, and it influences in particular the interest rate that a consumer who buys a car on time will have to pay on the loan. Finally, one might mention that the U.S. money market is increasingly becoming an international short-term capital market. In it, the oil imports of the nationalized French electric company, Electricite de France, as well as those of Japan—and a lot of other non-U.S. trade too—are financed. Also, foreign investors, in particular, Japanese institutions, have become increasingly important as dealers and investors in this market.

Anyone who observes the money market soon picks out a number of salient features. First and most obvious, it is not *one* market but a *collection* of markets for several distinct and different instruments. What makes it possible to talk about *the* money market is the close interrelationships that link all these markets. A second salient feature is the numerous and varied cast of participants. Borrowers in the market include foreign and domestic banks, the Treasury, corporations of all types, the Federal Home Loan Banks and other federal agencies, dealers in money market instruments, and many states and municipalities. The lenders include almost all of the above plus insurance companies, pension funds—public and private—and various other financial institutions. And often standing between borrower and lender is one or more of a varied collection of brokers and dealers.

Another important characteristic of the money market is that it is a *wholesale* market. Trades are big, and the people who make them are almost always dealing for the account of some substantial institution. Because of the sums involved, skill is of the utmost importance, and money market participants are skilled at what they do. In effect the market is made by extremely talented specialists in very narrow professional areas. A bill trader extraordinaire may have only vague notions as to what the Euromarket is all about, and the Euro specialist may be equally vague on other sectors of the market.

Another key characteristic of the money market is *honor.* Every day traders, brokers, investors, and borrowers do hundreds of billions of dollars of business over the phone, and however a trade may appear in retrospect, people rarely renege. The motto of the money market is: *My word is my bond.* Of course, because of the pace of the market, mistakes do occur, but, typically, no one assumes that they are intentional, and they are ironed out in what seems the fairest way for all concerned.

They say exceptions prove the rule. A few bad-apple dealers have caused a number of too-trusting, money market investors to lose hundreds of millions of dollars. Perhaps, these dealers were able to do so not, principally, because the investors they defrauded were too naive, but rather because the market was too accustomed to operating in an atmosphere of honor and trust: my word is my bond.

The most appealing characteristic of the money market is innovation. Compared with our other financial markets, the money market is lightly regulated. If someone wants to launch a new instrument or to try brokering or dealing in a new way in existing instruments, he does it. And when the idea is good, which it often is, a new facet of the market is born.

THE REPO AND REVERSE MARKETS

In this section, we present a brief introduction to the repo and reverse markets.

Definitions: Repo and reverse

Repurchase agreements (repos for short) are contracts involving the *simultaneous sale and future repurchase* of an asset, most often Treasury securities. Typically, the seller buys back the asset at the same price at which he sold it; also, on the buy-back date, the original seller pays the original buyer *interest* on the implicit *loan* created by the transaction. Interest due on a repo at maturity is at the stated *repo rate* for the stated maturity of the repo.

Whenever a repo is structured so that a dealer, a bank, or another party that normally uses the repo market to *fund* (finance) itself is cast in the role of securities purchaser and money lender, the resulting transaction is known as a *reverse repurchase or simply as a reverse.* Dealers often cover shorts by reversing in securities. Also, every large dealer currently does reverses to create one side of a huge matched book that he runs as a profit center. Whenever a dealer reverses in securities as part of his matched-book operation, he "hangs out" those same securities on the other side—repos them to obtain money equal to or exceeding the amount he has lent to the party with whom he has done a reverse.

In "Street-speak," the Federal Reserve (the *Fed* to those who know her well) is said to be "doing repos" when, to add to bank reserves, it lends against bank and dealer collateral. Conversely, the Fed is said to be "doing *matched sale/purchases*" (Fed jargon for reverses) when, to drain reserves, it borrows from banks and dealers against securities in its portfolio.

Market practices in brief

Later in this book, we will say a lot about market practices in the repo and reverse markets. Here, we present, as preface to later chapters, thumbnail sketches of key practices in these markets.

The agreement. In brief, repos (and reverses) are structured as follows. Normally, the two parties to the transaction sign some sort of repo agreement; the latter may be a bare-bones description of the nature of the trade or it may contain lots of legal bells and whistles that one or both parties think necessary to protect their interests under all contingencies. Occasionally, two parties will do a repo but sign *no* agreement; they may be just sloppy, but more likely, party A's lawyer doesn't like party B's agreement and vice versa. The *Public Securities Association (PSA),* which is the dealers' trade association, has recently created a standard repo agreement that most dealers now use (Chapter 14).

Term. The maturity (term) of a repo, time between sale and repurchase, may be of any length: overnight, one week, several weeks, one month, or some number of months. In terms of volume done, short-dated repos, overnight out to several weeks, are by far the most common. Thirty-day repos are also done, but less frequently than short-dated repos; occasionally, repos are done for as long as 6 months; rarely, they are done for as long as a year.

Overnight repos are often done on what is in effect a *demand* or *open* basis, the contract being understood by both parties to be renewable or cancelable daily. In such cases, the repo rate paid may vary from day to day.

Return on a repo. For a borrower of money, a repo always begins with a sale of securities and ends with the repurchase of those same securities. All terms of that repurchase are set at the start date of the repo. Both parties understand that the lender of money expects to earn on the transaction a short-term rate of interest on the money he puts up during the period he puts it up. This return can be incorporated into the transaction in either of several ways. The securities traded may be first sold and then repurchased at identical prices; in this case, the investor is paid an explicit repo rate on the money he invests. Alternatively, the repurchase price may be set above the purchase price, far enough above so that the investor earns the return due him.

Repo rates. The rate of interest paid on a particular repo depends principally on what interest rates prevail in the maturity range of the repo—overnight, one week, or whatever; the rate does *not* depend on the yield offered by the underlying security. For example, the yield on an overnight repo of 30-year Treasury bonds relates to the overnight Fed funds rate, not to the yield on the government long bond. Normally, the overnight repo rate is a spread *below* the overnight Fed funds rate.

Credit risk. A repo is structured as a buy and a *forward* sale (a sale that settles at a *future* date) of securities. As such, a repo creates *credit risk,* risk of a sort that would not be created by a simple, cash-market buy, for immediate settlement, of securities. Credit risk arises for both parties in a repo because each party commits to doing a forward trade with the other, and each party's ability to honor its forward commitment depends on its continued solvency.

Collateral. Everyone in the repo and reverse markets always refers to the securities that change hands in such transactions as *collateral.* Also, it has always been thought—believed—that, if the borrower of money in a repo should default on his obligation to repay at the term of the repo, then the holder of collateral (the giver of money) would have the right to make himself whole by selling the collateral he'd received.

Margin. To ensure that the lender of money could, under *all* circumstances, get back at least as many dollars as he had lent, the common practice became that the securities that passed hands in a repo and that served as collateral for the repo loan were to be *priced* for purposes of the repo *at market*; also, *margin* was to be given to the lender of money. For example, the borrower of money might give the lender of money securities that were trading at 100 and borrow from him not 100, but only 98. Margin, particularly on a term repo transaction, assured the lender of money that the market value of the securities he'd taken in as collateral could bounce around a bit without impairing the protection that the collateral he had accepted gave him against credit risk.

The right of substitution. On a term repo, a borrower of money often would like to be able to substitute one batch of collateral for another. Maybe the borrower is a dealer who's financing inventory for some number of days; if so, he'd like to be able to sell from his inventory; and to do so, he must be able to give the lender of money new collateral for the old collateral he's sold and wants to deliver out. For a slightly sweeter repo rate, a number of investors will grant a borrower in the repo market *the right of substitution.*

The economic significance. While a repo (or a reverse) is structured like a pair of securities trades, the essence of the transaction is, as we've suggested, that it is a hybrid form of *collateralized loan.* Certainly, people who take in money in the repo market think of themselves as borrowers of money and as givers of collateral, not as sellers of securities; similarly, repo investors think of themselves as lenders of money, not as buyers of securities.

Legal significance. To ask, What is the economic significance of a repo transaction? is one question. A wholly different question is, What is the legal standing of a repo: is a repo a securities trade or is it a collateralized borrowing? On the latter question, there are various positions. In some dealer bankruptcy cases, the courts have ruled, narrowly always, that repo was to be deemed a securities trade; in other cases, the courts have ruled that repo was to be deemed a collateralized borrowing. Participants in the repo market, each of whom has his own ax to grind, take varying positions on just what the courts should take repo to be. In particular, the Fed has, in amicus briefs, argued in various court cases that repo is a securities transaction; the Fed's reasoning is that it does lots of repo (Chapter 8) even though it has no authority to make secured loans to dealers in governments. Dealers, on the other hand, will say, "Sure, we *fund* our securities positions with repo, *but* for purposes of the law, repo should be taken to be a securities trade." Dealers want borrowings in the repo market to be deemed securities trades because, in the *Lombard-Wall* case, the court ruled that repo was a secured lending and forbade holders of collateral on defaulted repo loans from immediately selling their collateral to make themselves whole. This ruling created risk for dealers who do not only lots of repos, but lots of reverses as well (see Chapter 16 on dealers' matched books).

Size and function of the repo market

The U.S. repo market is not, as one new to the money market might guess, a minor and obscure financial market. Quite to the contrary, it is the single most important short-term credit (debt) market in the United States.

The size of the U.S. repo market must be "guesstimated" because the only statistics on this market are those that the Fed publishes on two classes of borrowers, primary dealers (dealers whom the Fed recognizes and with whom it does business) and commercial banks. There are several problems with the Fed's figures. First, a number of primary dealers are commercial banks, so adding the Fed's figures for repo borrowings by commercial banks to its figures for repo borrowings of primary dealers would involve some *double counting.* A second problem with the Fed's figures is that they are *incomplete*: they omit the repo borrowings of many institutions, including secondary dealers, thrifts, and other institutional investors.

In May 1987, the primary dealers were borrowing, on an average daily basis, $290 billion in the repo market and lending $273 billion in the reverse market. The sum of these figures is roughly $560 billion. Probably, the gross size of the repo market is at least that large or larger, since the *double counting* (Salomon Brothers reverses in securities from Goldman Sachs) that results from adding primary dealer lendings and borrowings in the repo and reverse markets is likely to be more than offset by the omission from this figure of a large fraction of the borrowings that non–primary-dealer commercial banks and other institutions do in the repo market to fund both their dealer and portfolio positions. Also omitted from this figure are the investments foreign central banks make in repos with the Fed.

Five hundred billion plus, even $400 billion, is a big number relative to other money market numbers. In May 1987, commercial paper outstanding totaled $354 billion; bankers' acceptances outstanding totaled $68 billion; and U.S. Treasury bills and other Treasury securities maturing in a year or less totaled $39 billion. At the same time, commercial banks held $304 billion of demand deposits and $366 billion of large-denomination (over $100,000) time deposits.[1]

STRUCTURE OF THE BOOK

Since a number of the people who read this book are likely to be new to the money market, we wanted this to be a *stand-alone* book in the sense that it would neither confuse nor lose a lay reader. We have, therefore, broken the book into two parts. In Part One, we describe some money market fundamentals: what instruments are traded in the money market, what money market dealers and brokers do, and how discount and interest-bearing instruments tick.

Readers familiar with this material should skip to Part Two, which tells the story this book was written to tell. We begin Part Two with the early

---

[1] The source of all statistics cited above is the statistical section of the *Federal Reserve Bulletin* for September 1987. This bulletin is published monthly by the Board of Governors of the Federal Reserve System, Washington, D.C.

history of the repo and reverse markets. We then describe the use of repos and reverses by the Fed post–World War II as well as the revival and growth of private repos during this period. Next, we focus on current practices in the repo and reverse markets: the brokering of repos and reverses, the use of reverses as a substitute for the borrowing of securities, the doing of reverses to maturity, the running of matched books, and the clearing of repo and reverse trades. Finally, we talk about a much discussed, much litigated, and perennially unanswered question: What is this thing called repo? Is repo a secured lending or is it a securities transaction? To be specific, is repo, for the lender of money, a *spot* buy of a security combined with a *forward* sale of that same security, or is it a secured lending?

Before beginning, we remind the reader of something we said in the Preface. This book uses money market jargon extensively. To aid the reader, each piece of jargon used is carefully defined the first time it appears in the text. Also, at the end of the text, there is a Glossary in which a wide range of money market and bond market terms are defined.

We end the book with a Bibliography for what it is worth; unfortunately, much of the material that has been written about the repo market is dated and/or fails to describe market practices in any detail. Also, some of this material is just plain incorrect because it was written by market outsiders who did not do their homework before they put pen to paper.

THE NEXT CHAPTER

For the benefit of readers new to the money market, we present in the next chapter brief descriptions of the various instruments traded in the money market.

Part one

Some fundamentals

Chapter 2

The instruments in brief

HERE'S A QUICK RUNDOWN of the major money market instruments. Don't look for subtleties; just enough is said to lay the groundwork for later chapters.

DEALERS AND BROKERS

The markets for all money market instruments are made in part by brokers and dealers. *Brokers* bring buyers and sellers together for a commission. By definition, brokers never position securities. Their function is to provide a communications network that links market participants who are often numerous and geographically dispersed. Most brokering in the money market occurs between banks that are buying funds from or selling funds to each other and between dealers in money market instruments.

Dealers make markets in money market instruments by quoting bid and asked prices to each other, to issuers, and to investors. Dealers buy and sell for their own accounts; thus, assuming positions—long and short—is an essential part of a dealer's operation.

U.S. TREASURY SECURITIES

To finance the U.S. national debt, the Treasury issues several types of securities. Some are nonnegotiable, for example, savings bonds sold to consumers and special issues sold to government trust funds. The bulk of the securities sold by the U.S. Treasury are, however, negotiable.

What form these securities take depends on their maturity. Those with a maturity at issue of a year or less are known as *Treasury bills, T bills* for short or just plain *bills.* T bills bear no interest. An investor in bills earns a return because bills are issued at a discount from face value and redeemed by the Treasury at maturity for face value. The amount of the discount at which investors buy bills and the length of time bills have to be held before they mature together imply some specific yield that the bill will return if held to maturity.

T bills are currently issued in 3-month, 6-month, and 1-year maturities.[1] In issuing bills, the Treasury does not set the amount of the discount. Instead, the Federal Reserve auctions off each new bill issue to investors and dealers, with the bills going to those bidders offering the highest price, that is, the lowest interest cost to the Treasury. By auctioning new bill issues, the Treasury lets currently prevailing market conditions establish the yield at which each new issue is sold.

The Treasury also issues interest-bearing *notes.* These securities are issued at or very near face value and redeemed at face value. Notes have an *original maturity* (maturity at issue) of 2 to 10 years.[2] Currently, the Treasury issues 2-, 3-, 4-, 5-, 7-, and 10-year notes on a regular cycle. Notes of other maturities are issued periodically depending on the Treasury's needs. Interest on Treasury notes is paid semiannually. Notes, like bills, are sold through auctions held by the Federal Reserve. In these auctions participants bid yields, and the securities offered are sold to those dealers and investors who bid the lowest yields, that is, the lowest interest cost to the Treasury. Thus, the coupon rate on new Treasury notes, like the yield on bills, is determined by the market. The last exception was a 1976 subscription offering in which the Treasury sold the famed 8s of 86.

In addition to notes, the Treasury issues interest-bearing negotiable *bonds* that have a maturity at issue of 10 years or more. The only difference between Treasury notes and bonds is that bonds are issued in longer maturities. In recent years the volume of bonds the Treasury can issue has been limited because Congress has imposed a 4.25% ceiling

---

[1] For tactical debt management purposes, the Treasury occasionally meets cash flow gaps by issuing very short-term "cash management bills."

[2] A 5-year note has an *original maturity* at issue of 5 years. One year after issue it has a *current maturity* of 4 years.

on the rate the Treasury may pay on bonds. Since this rate has for years been far below prevailing market rates, the Treasury is able to sell bonds only to the extent that Congress authorizes it to issue bonds exempt from the ceiling; the current exemption, which has been successively raised, is $270 billion. Treasury bonds, like notes, are normally sold at yield auctions.

Banks, other financial institutions, insurance companies, pension funds, and corporations are all important investors in U.S. Treasury securities. So, too, are some foreign central banks and other foreign institutions. The market for government securities is largely a wholesale market, and especially at the short end, multimillion-dollar transactions are common. However, when interest rates get extremely high, as they did in 1974 and again in 1978 to 1982, individuals with small amounts to invest are drawn into the market.

Because of the high volume of Treasury debt outstanding, the market for bills and short-term government securities is the most active and most carefully watched sector of the money market. At the heart of this market stands a varied collection of dealers who make the market for *governments* (market jargon for government securities) by standing ready to buy and sell huge volumes of these securities. These dealers trade actively not only with investors but with each other. Most trades of the latter sort are carried out through brokers.

Governments offer investors several advantages. First, because they are constantly traded in the *secondary market* in large volume and at narrow spreads between the bid and asked prices, they are highly *liquid*. Second, governments are considered to be free from credit risk because it is inconceivable that the government would default on these securities in any situation short of destruction of the country. Third, interest income on governments is exempt from state taxation. Because of these advantages, governments normally trade at yields below those of other money market instruments.

Generally, yields on governments are higher the longer their *current maturity,* that is, time left to maturity. The reason, explained in Chapters 3 and 4, is that the longer the current maturity of a debt security, the more its price will fluctuate in response to changes in interest rates and therefore the greater the *price risk* to which it exposes the investor. There are times, however, when the yield curve *inverts,* that is, yields on short-term securities rise above those on long-term securities. This, for example, was the case during much of the period 1979 to 1981. The reason for an inverted yield curve is that market participants anticipate, correctly or incorrectly, that interest rates will fall. As a result, borrowers choose to borrow short-term while investors seek out long-term securities; the result is that supply and demand force short-term rates above long-term rates.

The 30-year bill, alias STRIP

Recently, the Treasury has permitted the creation, out of standard T bonds, of what amount to T bills with distant maturities. Here's the story.

The Treasury once issued, upon request, notes and bonds in bearer form. Some dealers came up with the idea of *stripping*—clipping off coupons from—bearer bonds and selling, at discounted prices, the resulting pieces. Each such piece was a *non-interest-bearing security with a fixed maturity and a fixed value at maturity*. Such securities are known generically as *zero-coupon securities* or simply as *zeros*.

Dealers could make money stripping bearer Treasuries because demand for the pieces was so great that the sum of the values of the pieces exceeded the value of the whole bond. Unfortunately, the Treasury and the Fed opposed, for various reasons (including possibilities for tax evasion), the stripping of bearer Treasuries.

To satisfy investors' desire for long-term zeros, Merrill got a bright idea: It bought Treasuries, placed them with a custodian in a special trust, and then sold to investors participations in its trust. Under the Merrill scheme, each such participation sold was a *zero-coupon security,* backed by unstripped Treasuries. Merrill named its product TIGRs. Soon, every other major dealer was offering its addition to the zoo. Sali sold CATs; Lehman, LIONs; and so on. Also, some dealers sold plain vanilla TRs (trust receipts).

The new "zoo" zeros sold extremely well to institutional investors and even to individuals. The Treasury, eyeing this success, said, "There's money to be made in stripping, let *us* earn it." So in 1985, the Treasury introduced, for certain new T bond issues, an additional feature: Any owner of such a bond, Merrill, a small dealer, or even an individual, can ask the Treasury to cut that bond into pieces, provided it is in book-entry (electronic-record-keeping) form. Each such piece corresponds to a different payment due on the bond, and each carries its own CUSIP (ID) number.[3] On a 30-year bond, there are 61 such payments: 60 semiannual interest payments and 1 payment of *corpus* (principal) at maturity. Stripped Treasuries created in the manner we've just described were dubbed *STRIPs*.

Today on Wall Street, STRIPs are a popular item, actively traded by the same dealers who make markets in regular Treasury notes, bonds, and bills.

---

[3] The terms *CUSIP number* and *book-entry* are precisely defined in Chapter 12.

Internationalization of the market for Treasuries

A decade ago, when one spoke of *the* market for Treasuries, one was referring to a market that was almost exclusively domestic. The borrower, of course, was domestic and so too were most of the investors, except for a few foreign central banks. Today, that situation has changed dramatically. Foreigners, and most importantly Japanese investors, have become big buyers of Treasury securities.

Not surprisingly, there are now active markets for Treasuries in Tokyo, in London, and, to a lesser extent, in certain other foreign financial centers. Today, reflecting in part the fact that foreigners currently own approximately 16% of all outstanding marketable Treasuries, the market for these securities has in truth become a 24-hour, international market.

The dealers who make this round-the-globe market are of two sorts: big American dealers, such as Merrill and Sali, who have opened offices in major financial centers around the globe, and foreign dealers, particularly Japanese dealers, who have opened offices in the U.S. and become big factors in the domestic trading of Treasury securities.

FINANCIAL FUTURES AND OPTIONS MARKETS

In discussing the market for governments, we have focused on the *cash market,* that is, the market in which existing securities are traded for same- or next-day delivery. In addition, there are markets in which Treasury bills, Treasury notes, Treasury bonds, bank CDs, and other money market instruments are traded for *future* delivery. The futures contracts in Treasuries that are most actively traded are for 3-month bills with a face value of $1 million at maturity and for notes and long bonds with a par value of $100,000.

Interest rate futures markets offer institutions that know they are going to borrow or lend in the future a way to *hedge* that future position, that is, to lock in a reasonably fixed borrowing or lending rate. They also provide speculators with a way to bet money on interest rate movements that provides greater leverage—bang for the buck—than going short or long in cash securities.

Since being introduced in 1976, futures markets for financial instruments have grown at an unforeseen and astonishing rate. In fact, futures contracts for Treasury bills and bonds have been among the most successful contracts ever launched on commodities exchanges. Their success has led to the introduction of trading of like contracts on a number of commodity exchanges in foreign financial centers.

The rapid growth and internationalization of markets for financial futures has, not surprisingly, created situations in which the relationship between the rates on different futures contracts or between the rates on a futures contract and the corresponding cash instrument get, as the Street would say, "out of sync," that is, out of synchronization or line. Thus, yet another major class of traders in financial futures has been arbitrageurs who seek to establish positions from which they will profit when a reasonable relationship between the out-of-line rates is inevitably reestablished.

Another recent innovation in the money market is the introduction of trading in *options,* rights to buy or to sell at a fixed price over a preset period, certain money market securities and futures contracts for such securities. Options, like futures, are actively traded by hedgers, speculators, and arbitrageurs.

FEDERAL AGENCY SECURITIES

From time to time Congress becomes concerned about the volume of credit that is available to various sectors of the economy and the terms on which that credit is available. Congress's usual response is to set up a federal agency to provide credit to that sector. Thus there are the Federal Home Loan Bank System, which lends to the nation's savings and loan associations as well as regulates them; the Government National Mortgage Association, which funnels money into the mortgage market; Banks for Cooperatives, which make seasonal and term loans to farm cooperatives; Federal Land Banks, which give mortgages on farm properties; Federal Intermediate Credit Banks, which provide short-term financing for producers of crops and livestock; and a host of other agencies.

Initially, all the federal agencies financed their activities by selling their own securities in the open market. Today, all except the largest borrow from the Treasury through an institution called the Federal Financing Bank. Those agencies still borrowing in the open market do so primarily by issuing notes and bonds. These securities (known in the market as *agencies*) bear interest, and they are issued and redeemed at face value. Instead of using the auction technique for issuing their securities, federal agencies look to the market to determine the best yield at which they can sell a new issue, put that yield on the issue, and then sell it through a syndicate of dealers. Some agencies also sell short-term discount paper that resembles commercial paper (see below).

Normally, agencies yield slightly more than Treasury securities of the same maturity for several reasons. First, agency issues are smaller than Treasury issues and are therefore less liquid. Second, while all agency issues have de facto backing from the federal government (it's inconceivable that the government would let one of them default on its obligations), the securities of only a few agencies are explicitly backed by the full faith and credit of the U.S. government. Third, interest income on some federal agency issues is subject to state taxation.

The market for agencies, while smaller than that for governments, has, in recent years, become an active and important sector of the money market. Agencies are traded by the same dealers that trade governments and in much the same way.

FEDERAL FUNDS

All banks and other *depository institutions* (savings and loan associations, savings banks, credit unions, foreign bank branches, and so on) are required to keep reserves on deposit at their district Federal Reserve Bank.[4] The reserve account of a depository institution (*DI* for short) is much like an individual's checking account; the DI makes deposits into its reserve account and can transfer funds out of it. The main difference is that, while an individual can let the balance in his checking account run to zero and stay there, each DI is required by law to maintain some *minimum* average balance in its reserve account over the week— Wednesday to Wednesday. Under *contemporaneous reserve accounting,* introduced by the Fed in February 1984, that minimum average balance is based on the total deposits of various types held by the DI during the current settlement week.

The category of DIs that holds by far the largest chunk of the total reserves that all DIs together maintain at Federal Reserve Banks is commercial banks. Funds on deposit in a bank's reserve account are referred to as *Federal funds* or *Fed funds.* Any deposits a bank receives add to its supply of Fed funds, while loans made and securities purchased reduce that supply. Thus, the basic amount of money any bank can lend out and otherwise invest equals the amount of funds it has received from depositors minus the reserves it is required to maintain.

For some banks, this supply of available funds roughly equals the amount they choose to invest in securities plus that demanded from them by borrowers. But for most banks it does not. Specifically, because the nation's largest corporations tend to concentrate their borrowing in big money market banks in New York and other financial centers, the loans and investments these banks must fund exceed the deposits they re-

---

[4] The Federal Reserve System, which comprises 12 district Federal Reserve Banks, is the United States's central bank, and as such it is responsible for the implementation of domestic monetary policy. [See Marcia Stigum, *The Money Market,* Revised Edition (Homewood, Ill.: Dow Jones-Irwin, 1983), chap. 8, "The Fed."] Prior to passage of the Monetary Control Act of 1980, only *member banks* in the Federal Reserve System were required to hold reserves at the Fed.

ceive. Many smaller banks, in contrast, receive more money from local depositors than they can lend locally or choose to invest otherwise. Because large banks have to meet their reserve requirements regardless of what loan demand they face and because excess reserves yield no return to smaller banks, it was natural for large banks to begin borrowing the excess funds held by smaller banks.

This borrowing is done in the *Federal funds market.* Most Fed funds loans are overnight transactions. One reason is that the amount of excess funds a given lending bank holds varies daily and unpredictably. Some transactions in Fed funds are made directly, others through New York brokers. Despite the fact that transactions of this sort are all loans, the lending of Fed funds is referred to as a *sale* and the borrowing of Fed funds as a *purchase.* While overnight transactions dominate the Fed funds market, transactions for longer periods also occur there. Fed funds traded for periods other than overnight are referred to as *term* Fed funds.

DIs other than domestic commercial banks also participate in the Fed Funds market. Foreign banks are particularly active buyers and sellers of funds.

The rate of interest paid on overnight loans of Federal funds, which is called the *Fed funds rate,* is a key interest rate in the money market; all other short-term rates relate to the funds rate. This rate used to be closely pegged by the Fed, but starting in October 1979, the Fed allowed the Fed funds rate to fluctuate over a wide band; more recently, the Fed has reversed this policy.

EURODOLLARS

Many foreign banks will accept deposits of dollars and grant the depositor an account *denominated in dollars.* So, too, will the foreign branches of U.S. banks. The practice of accepting dollar-denominated deposits outside of the United States began in Europe, so such deposits came to be known as *Eurodollars.* The practice of accepting dollar-denominated deposits later spread to Hong Kong, Singapore, the Mideast, and other centers around the globe. Consequently today a *Eurodollar deposit is simply a deposit denominated in dollars in a bank or bank branch outside the United States,* and the term *Eurodollar* has become a misnomer. To make things even more confusing, in December 1981, domestic and foreign banks were permitted to open *international banking facilities (IBFs)* in the United States. Dollars deposited in IBFs are also Eurodollars.

Most Eurodollar deposits are for large sums. They are made by corporations—foreign, multinational, and domestic; foreign central banks and other official institutions; U.S. domestic banks; and wealthy individuals.

With the exception of *call money*,[5] all Eurodeposits have a fixed term, which can range from overnight to 5 years. The bulk of Euro transactions are in the range of 6 months and under. Banks receiving Eurodollar deposits use them to make loans denominated in dollars to foreign and domestic corporations, foreign governments and government agencies, domestic U.S. banks, and other large borrowers.

Banks that participate in the Eurodollar market actively borrow and lend Euros among themselves, just as domestic banks borrow and lend in the Fed funds market. The major difference between the two markets is that in the market for Fed funds, most transactions are on an overnight basis, whereas in the Euromarket, interbank placements (deposits) of funds for longer periods are common.

For a domestic U.S. bank with a reserve deficiency, borrowing Euro-dollars is an alternative to purchasing Fed funds. Also, for a domestic bank with excess funds, a *Europlacement* (i.e., a deposit of dollars in the Euromarket) is an alternative to the sale of Fed funds. Consequently, the rate on overnight Euros tends to closely track the Fed funds rate. It is also true that, as one goes out on the maturity scale, Euro rates continue to track U.S. rates, though not so closely as in the overnight market.

Currently, futures for 3-month Eurodollar deposits are actively traded in Chicago and abroad as well.

CERTIFICATES OF DEPOSIT

The maximum rate banks may pay on savings deposits and time deposits (a time deposit is a deposit with a fixed maturity) used to be set by the Fed through *Regulation Q.* Essentially, what Reg Q did was to make it impossible for banks and other depository institutions (who were each subject to their own versions of Reg Q) to compete with each other for small deposits by offering depositors higher interest rates.[6] One exception to Reg Q was that, on large deposits, $100,000 or more, banks used to be able to pay any rate they chose so long as the deposit had a minimum maturity of 14 days. This exception led, so to speak, to the invention in 1961 of negotiable certificates of deposit.

There are many corporations and other large investors that have hundreds of thousands, even millions, of dollars they could invest in bank time deposits. Few do so, however, because they lose liquidity by mak-

---

[5] Call money is money deposited in an interest-bearing account that can be called (withdrawn) by the depositor on a day's notice.

[6] The rates banks and thrifts may pay depositors were gradually deregulated under the Monetary Control Act (MCA) of 1980. Also the Banking Act of 1982 permitted depository institutions to begin offering unregulated rates on super-NOW and money market deposit accounts.

ing a deposit with a fixed maturity. The illiquidity of time deposits and their consequent lack of appeal to investors led banks, who were free to bid high rates for large deposits, to begin to offer big investors *negotiable certificate of deposit,* or *CD* for short.

CDs are normally sold in $1 million units. They are issued at face value and typically pay interest at maturity. CDs can have any maturity longer than 14 days, and some 5- and even 7-year CDs have been sold (these pay interest semiannually). Most CDs, however, have an *original maturity* of 1 to 6 months.

The quantity of CDs that banks have outstanding depends largely on the strength of loan demand. When demand rises, banks issue more CDs to fund the additional loans they are making. The rates banks offer on CDs depend on the maturity of the paper they write, on how bad the banks want to write new CDs, and on the general level of short-term interest rates.

Most bank CDs are sold directly by banks to investors. Some, however, are issued through dealers for a small commission. The same dealers make an active secondary market in CDs.

Yields on CDs exceed those on bills of similar maturities by varying spreads. One reason for the higher yield on CDs is that buying a bank CD exposes the investor to some credit risk—would he be paid off if the issuing bank failed? A second reason CDs yield more than bills is that they are less liquid.

A futures market for 3-month CDs was started in Chicago. For various reasons, including differences in the credit ratings of the top banks whose paper could be delivered by sellers of the contract, the CD contract proved unsuccessful.

Eurodollar CDs

A Eurodollar time deposit, like a domestic time deposit, is an illiquid asset. Since some investors in Eurodollars wanted liquidity, banks in London that accepted such deposits began to issue *Eurodollar CDs.* These resemble domestic CDs except that, instead of being the liability of a domestic bank, they are the liability of the London branch of a U.S. bank, of a British bank, or of some other foreign bank with a branch in London.

Many of the Eurodollar CDs issued in London are purchased by other banks operating in the Euromarket. A large proportion of the remainder are sold to U.S. corporations and other U.S. institutional investors. Many Euro CDs are issued through dealers and brokers who also make a secondary market in these securities.

The Euro CD market is younger and smaller than the market for domestic CDs, but it has grown rapidly since its inception. For the investor, a key advantage of buying Euro CDs is that they offer a higher return than do domestic CDs. The offsetting disadvantages are that they are less liquid and expose the investor to some extra risk because they are issued outside of the United States.

The most recent development in the Eurodollar CD market is that some large banks have begun offering such CDs through their Caribbean branches. Note that a CD issued, for example, in Nassau is technically a Euro CD because the deposit is held in a bank branch outside the United States.

Yankee CDs

Foreign banks issue dollar-denominated CDs not only in the Euromarket but also in the domestic market through branches established there. CDs of the latter sort are frequently referred to as *Yankee CDs;* the name is taken from Yankee bonds, which are bonds issued in the domestic market by foreign borrowers.

Yankee, as opposed to domestic, CDs expose the investor to the extra (if only in perception) risk of a foreign name; they are also less liquid than domestic CDs. Consequently, Yankees trade at yields close to those on Euro CDs. The major buyers of Yankee CDs are corporations that are yield buyers and that "fund to dates" (that is, invest in short-term securities maturing on the date funds will be needed).

COMMERCIAL PAPER

While some cash-rich industrial firms participate in the bond and money markets only as lenders, many more must, at times, borrow to finance either current operations or expenditures on plant and equipment. One source of short-term funds available to a corporation is bank loans. Large firms with good credit ratings, however, have an alternative source of funds that is cheaper, namely, the sale of commercial paper.

Commercial paper is an unsecured promissory note issued for a specific amount and maturing on a specific day. All commercial paper is negotiable, but most paper sold to investors is held by them to maturity. Commercial paper is issued not only by industrial and manufacturing firms but also by finance companies. Finance companies normally sell their paper directly to investors. Industrial firms, in contrast, typically issue their paper through dealers. Recently, foreign bank holding companies, municipalities, and municipal authorities have joined the ranks of commercial paper issuers.

The maximum maturity for which commercial paper may be sold is 270 days, since paper with a longer maturity must be registered with the Securities and Exchange Commission (SEC), a time-consuming and costly procedure. In practice, very little 270-day paper is sold. Most paper sold is in the range of 30 days and under.

Since commercial paper has such short maturities, the issuer rarely will have sufficient funds coming in before the paper matures to pay off his borrowing. Instead, he expects to *roll* his paper, that is, sell new paper to obtain funds to pay off his maturing paper. Naturally the possibility exists that some sudden change in market conditions, such as when the Penn Central went "belly up" (bankrupt), might make it difficult or impossible for him to sell paper for some time. To guard against this risk, commercial paper issuers back all or a large proportion of their outstanding paper with lines of credit from banks.

The rate offered on commercial paper depends on its maturity, on how much the issuer wants to borrow, on the general level of money market rates, and on the credit rating of the issuer. Almost all commercial paper is rated with respect to credit risk by one or more of several rating services: Moody's, Standard & Poor's, and Fitch. While only top-grade credits can get ratings good enough to sell paper these days, there is still a slight risk that an issuer might go bankrupt. Because of this, and because of illiquidity, yields on commercial paper are higher than those on Treasury obligations of similar maturity.

BANKERS' ACCEPTANCES

Bankers' acceptances (BAs) are an unknown instrument outside the confines of the money market. Moreover, explaining them isn't easy because they arise in a variety of ways out of a variety of transactions. The best approach is to use an example.

Suppose a U.S. importer wants to buy shoes in Brazil and pay for them four months later after he has had time to sell them in the United States. One approach would be for the importer to borrow from his bank; however, short-term rates may be lower in the open market. If they are, and if the importer is too small to go into the open market on his own, then he can go the bankers' acceptance route.

In that case, he has his bank write a letter of credit for the amount of the sale and sends this letter to the Brazilian exporter. Upon export of the shoes, the Brazilian firm, using this letter of credit, draws a time draft on the importer's U.S. bank and discounts this draft at its local bank, thereby obtaining immediate payment for its goods. The Brazilian bank, in turn, sends the time draft to the importer's U.S. bank, which then stamps "accepted" on the draft (that is, the bank guarantees payment on the draft and thereby creates an *acceptance*). Once this is done, the draft becomes an irrevocable primary obligation of the accepting bank. At this point, if the Brazilian bank did not want cash immediately, the U.S. bank would return the draft to that bank, which would hold it as an investment and then present it to the U.S. bank for payment at maturity. If, on the other hand, the Brazilian bank wanted cash immediately, the U.S. bank would pay it and then either hold the acceptance itself or sell it to an investor. Regardless of who ends up holding the acceptance, it is the importer's responsibility to provide its U.S. bank with sufficient funds to pay off the acceptance at maturity. If the importer fails to do so, the bank is still responsible for making payment at maturity.

Our example illustrates how an acceptance can arise out of a U.S. import transaction. Acceptances also arise in connection with U.S. export sales, trade between third countries (e.g., Japanese imports of oil from the Middle East), the domestic shipment of goods, and domestic or foreign storage of readily marketable staples. Currently, most BAs arise out of foreign trade; they may be in manufactured goods but more typically are in bulk commodities, such as cocoa, cotton, coffee, and crude oil. Because of the complex nature of acceptance operations, only large banks with well-staffed foreign departments act as accepting banks.

Bankers' acceptances closely resemble commercial paper in form. They are short-term, non–interest-bearing notes sold at a discount and redeemed by the accepting bank at maturity for full face value. The major difference is that payment on commercial paper is guaranteed only by the issuing company. In contrast, bankers' acceptances, in addition to carrying the issuer's pledge to pay, are backed by the underlying goods being financed and also carry the guarantee of the accepting bank. Consequently, bankers' acceptances are less risky than commercial paper and thus sell at slightly lower yields.

The big banks through which bankers' acceptances are originated generally keep some portion of the acceptances they create as investments. The rest are sold to investors through dealers or directly by the bank itself. Major investors in BAs are other banks, foreign central banks, money market funds, corporations, and other domestic and foreign institutional investors. BAs have liquidity because dealers in these securities make an active secondary market in those that are eligible for purchase by the Fed. Today, Japanese banks are major issuers of BAs in the U.S. domestic money market.

REPOS AND REVERSES

A variety of bank and nonbank dealers act as market makers in governments, agencies, CDs, and BAs. Because dealers, by definition, buy and sell for their own accounts, active dealers inevitably end up holding some securities. They will, moreover, buy and hold substantial positions if they believe that interest rates are likely to fall and that the value of these securities is therefore likely to rise. Speculation and risk taking are an inherent and important part of being a dealer.

While dealers have large amounts of capital, the positions they take are often several hundred times that amount. As a result, dealers have to borrow to finance their positions. Using the securities they own as collateral, they can and do borrow from banks at the dealer loan rate. For the bulk of their financing, however, they resort to a cheaper alternative, entering into *repurchase agreements* (*repos*, for short) with investors.

Much repo financing done by dealers is on an overnight basis. It works as follows: The dealer finds a corporation, money fund, or other investor who has funds to invest overnight. He sells this investor, say, $10 million of securities for roughly $10 million, which is paid in Federal funds to his bank by the investor's bank against delivery of the securities sold. At the same time, the dealer agrees to repurchase these securities the next day at a slightly higher price. Thus, the buyer of the securities is in effect making the dealer a one-day loan secured by the obligations sold to him. The difference between the purchase and sale prices on the repo transaction is the interest the investor earns on his loan. Alternatively, the purchase and sale prices in a repo transaction may be identical; in that case, the dealer pays the investor some explicit rate of interest.

Often a dealer will take a speculative position that he intends to hold for some time. He might then do a repo for 30 days or longer. Such agreements are known as *term* repos.

From the point of view of investors, overnight loans in the repo market offer several attractive features. First, by rolling overnight repos, investors can keep surplus funds invested without losing liquidity or incurring a price risk. Second, because repo transactions are secured by top-quality paper, investors expose themselves to little or no credit risk.

The overnight repo rate generally is less than the Fed funds rate. The reason is that the many nonbank investors who have funds to invest overnight or very short term and who do not want to incur any price risk, have nowhere to go but the repo market because (with the exception of S&Ls) they cannot participate directly in the Fed funds market. Also, lending money through a repo transaction is safer than selling Fed funds because a sale of Fed funds is an unsecured loan.

On term, as opposed to overnight, repo transactions, investors still have the advantage of their loans being secured, but they do lose some liquidity. To compensate for that, the rate on a repo transaction is generally higher the longer the term for which funds are lent.

Banks that make dealer loans fund them by buying Fed funds, and the lending rate they charge—which is adjusted daily—is the prevailing Fed funds rate plus a one-eighth to one-quarter markup. Because the overnight repo rate is lower than the Fed funds rate, dealers can finance their positions more cheaply by doing repos than by borrowing from banks.

A dealer who is bullish on the market will position large amounts of securities. If he's bearish, he will *short* the market, that is, sell securities he does not own. Since the dealer has to deliver any securities he sells whether he owns them or not, a dealer who shorts has to borrow securities one way or another. The most common technique today for borrowing securities is to do what is called a *reverse repo,* or simply a *reverse.* To obtain securities through a reverse, a dealer finds an investor holding the required securities; he then buys these securities from the investor under an agreement that he will resell the same securities to the investor at a fixed price on some future date. In this transaction, the dealer, besides obtaining securities, is extending a loan to the investor for which he is paid some rate of interest.

A repo and a reverse are identical transactions. What a given transaction is called depends on who initiates it; typically, if a dealer hunting money does, it's a repo; if a dealer hunting securities does, it's a reverse.

A final note: The Fed uses reverses and repos with dealers in government securities to adjust the level of bank reserves.

MUNICIPAL NOTES

Debt securities issued by state and local governments and their authorities are referred to as *municipal securities.* Such securities can be divided into two broad categories: bonds issued to finance capital projects and short-term notes sold in anticipation of the receipt of other funds, such as taxes or proceeds from a bond issue.

Municipal notes, which are an important money market instrument, are issued with maturities ranging from a month to a year or more. They bear interest, and minimum denominations are highly variable ranging anywhere from $5,000 to $5 million.

Most muni notes are general obligation securities; that is, payment of principal and interest is secured by the issuer's pledge of its full faith, credit, and taxing power. This sounds impressive, but as the spectacle of New York City tottering on the brink of bankruptcy brought home to all, it is possible that a municipality might default on its securities. Thus, the investors in evaluating the credit risk associated with publicly offered muni notes rely on ratings provided principally by Moody's and by Standard & Poor's.

The major attraction of municipal notes to an investor is that interest income on them is exempt or at least partially exempt from federal taxation and usually also from any income taxes levied within the state in which they are issued. The value of this tax exemption is greater the higher the investor's tax bracket, and the muni market thus attracts relatively highly taxed investors—commercial banks, cash-rich corporations, and wealthy individuals.

Large muni note issues are sold to investors by dealers who obtain the securities either through negotiation with the issuer or through competitive bidding. The same dealers also make a secondary market in muni notes.

The yield a municipality must pay to issue notes depends on its credit rating, the length of time for which it borrows, and the general level of short-term rates. It used to be that a good credit risk could normally borrow at a rate well below the yield on governments of equivalent maturity because of the value to the investor of the tax exemption on municipal securities. Currently, numerous complex changes and proposed changes in the federal tax code have lessened the value of the tax exemption attached to municipal securities. As a result, muni securities have, at times, actually traded at rates above Treasuries, which is precisely where they would trade were it not for the tax advantages they offer. Because of the ever-changing federal tax code and the consequent changing nature of the spread of Treasury to muni yields, some municipal bodies have begun, in recent times, to issue fully taxable securities and even to tap the Euromarket for money. Today, the muni market is an innovative place, and some muni issuers have even experimented with issuing zero-coupon securities.

MORTGAGE-BACKED, PASS-THROUGH SECURITIES

Mortgage-backed, pass-through securities are a hybrid debt instrument, one that has correctly been called the most complex security ever traded on Wall Street. Strictly speaking, pass-throughs are not a money market instrument, since their average life, a variable number at best, exceeds by far that of true money market instruments. Nonetheless, because pass-throughs are so actively traded, we introduce such securities here and describe in Chapter 11 how trades in them are cleared.

The securities

Total residential mortgage debt outstanding is roughly $1.5 trillion, a sum far greater than total Treasury and federal agency debt outstanding. About a fifth of total residential mortgage debt has been used to back various types of negotiable securities, which in turn have been sold to investors. Of the more than $300 billion of mortgage-backed securities outstanding, all but about $20 billion are pass-throughs.

Pass-through securities are formed when mortgages are pooled and undivided interests in the pool are sold. *Pass-through* means that the cash flow from the underlying mortgages is *passed through* to the holders of the securities via *monthly payments of interest and principal.*

Undivided means that each security holder has a proportionate interest in each cash flow generated by the pool. Payments of principal on a pass-through include *prepayments;* the latter occur when a mortgage holder prepays the remaining principal on his mortgage because he moves, refinances his mortgage, or less commonly, dies.

Pass-throughs have existed for decades, but they first made sense on a broad scale when several federal credit agencies began to provide credit guarantees and standards of uniformity for pass-throughs issued through them. This made pools of mortgages underlying pass-throughs readily marketable; in particular, the standardization of mortgage characteristics within pools made the resulting securities easier to analyze and, thus, more suitable for nontraditional mortgage investors. Also, the credit guarantee by a federal agency lessened investor concerns about collection of amounts due.

Mortgage originators such as savings and loans, commercial banks, and mortgage companies are active in pooling mortgages to back pass-throughs. An originator can either issue a private pass-through or file the necessary documents with a guarantor to issue a pass-through backed by the latter. The sale of a pass-through security represents a sale of assets; thus a pass-through is not a debt obligation of the originator.

The issuers

Pass-throughs come in four flavors: there are Ginnie Mae, Freddie Mac, and Fanny Mae pass-throughs issued by federal or quasi-federal credit agencies; also, there are private pass-throughs. All pass-throughs are structured similarly, but differences exist among the four types with respect to the nature of the credit guarantee, if any; the size of the pools used; and the nature of the underlying mortgages. Because of these, different types of pass-throughs trade at varying spreads to each other.

Ginnie Mae pass-throughs are guaranteed by the *Government National Mortgage Association (GNMA),* known to the Street as Ginnie Mae. The mortgage pools underlying GNMA pass-throughs are made up of mortgages that are either insured by the Federal Housing Administration (FHA) or guaranteed by the Veterans Administration (VA). GNMA pass-throughs are backed by the full faith and credit of the U.S. government. Pass-throughs issued by GNMA are fully modified: regardless of whether mortgage payments are received, the holders of GNMAs receive full and timely payment of principal and interest due them.

The *Federal Home Loan Mortgage Corporation (FHLMC),* created by the Federal Home Loan Banks, also issues pass-throughs. These pass-throughs, the second largest class of pass-throughs, have been dubbed *Freddie Macs.* Freddie Macs are based on *conventional mortgages:* single-family residential mortgages that are neither guaranteed by the

VA nor insured by the FHA. Whereas GNMA and FNMA (discussed next) guarantee the timely payment of interest and principal, FHLMC guarantees only the timely payment of interest and the ultimate payment (within a year) of principal. Because of the difference in guarantee, Freddie Macs trade at a spread above Ginnie Maes.

A third type of pass-through, *Fannie Maes,* is issued by the *Federal National Mortgage Association (FNMA).* Fannie Maes are similar to Freddie Macs except that they carry a guarantee like the one on GNMAs.

The fourth type of pass-through security is private pass-throughs. In terms of volume outstanding, this type pass-through is the least important of the four types discussed.

Pass-throughs are based on mortgages with a 30-year life, but due to prepayments, they have, in normal times, if such exist, an expected life of only 12 years. Prepayments rates on pass-throughs vary with the level of mortgage rates. In years when mortgage rates are high, people choose not to move or to refinance, which cuts prepayment rates sharply. In contrast, low mortgage rates in 1986 brought forth a flood of refinancings of existing high-rate mortgages. The resulting high rate of prepayment on some high-coupon Ginnies caused these securities to be viewed and traded as odd-ball, short-term (2-year in some cases) Treasuries.

Pass-throughs are attractive to investors; they carry little or no credit risk but yield more than Treasuries of approximately similar maturity. Pass-throughs are bought by banks, savings and loan associations, GNMA mutual funds, and a range of other investors.

THE NEXT CHAPTER

In the next chapter, we discuss, with a little simple math, non–interest-bearing IOUs, T bills, and other short-term paper, which the Street refers to as discount securities or *discount paper.*

Chapter 3

Discount paper

THE MONEY MARKET DEALS IN TWO TYPES of instruments, *interest-bearing securities* and *discount paper.* Yields on these two types of instruments are calculated and quoted in quite different ways. Thus, a discussion of the clearing of money market securities should be prefaced by some simple math that shows how yields and prices on these different instruments are calculated. We start with discount securities.[1]

TREASURY BILLS

To illustrate how a discount security works, we assume that an investor who participates in an auction of new Treasury *year bills* picks up $1 million of them at 10%. What this means is that the Treasury sells the investor $1 million of bills maturing in one year at a price approximately 10% below their face value. The "approximately" qualifier takes a little explaining. Offhand, one would expect the amount of the discount to be the face value of the securities purchased times the rate of discount times the *fraction of the year* the securities will be outstanding. In our

---

[1] For a complete description, see Marcia Stigum in collaboration with John Mann, *Money Market Calculations: Yields, Break-Evens, and Arbitrage* (Homewood, Ill.: Dow Jones-Irwin, 1981).

example, the discount calculated this way would equal $1 million times 10% times one full year, which amounts to $100,000. That figure, however, is incorrect for two reasons. First, the year bill is outstanding not for a year but for 52 weeks, which is 364 days. Second, the Treasury calculates the discount as if a year had only 360 days. So the fraction of the year for which the security is outstanding is 364/360, and the true discount on the security is:

$$\binom{\text{Discount on \$1 million of}}{\text{year bills issued at 10\%}} = \$1{,}000{,}000 \times 0.10 \times \frac{364}{360}$$
$$= \$101{,}111.11$$

Because the Treasury calculates the discount as if the year had 360 days, our investor gets his bills at a discount that exceeds $100,000 even though he invests for only 364 days. The price he pays for his bills equals *face value minus the discount,* that is,

$$\binom{\text{Price paid for \$1 million of}}{\text{year bills bought at 10\%}} = \$1{,}000{,}000 - \$101{,}111.11$$
$$= \$898{,}888.89$$

Generalizing from this example, we can construct formulas for calculating both the discount from face value and the price at which T bills will sell, depending on their current maturity and the discount at which they are quoted. Let

D = Discount from face value
F = Face value
d = Rate of discount
t = Days to maturity
P = Price

Then

$$D = F\left(\frac{d \times t}{360}\right)$$

and

$$P = F - D = F\left(1 - \frac{d \times t}{360}\right)$$

EQUIVALENT BOND YIELD

If an investor lent $1 million for one 365-day year and received at the end of the year $100,000 of interest plus the $1 million of principal invested, we would—calculating yield on a *simple interest basis*—say that he had earned 10%.[2] Using the same approach—return earned divided by principal invested—to calculate the return earned by our investor who bought a 10% year bill, we find that, on a simple interest basis, he earned significantly *more than* 10%. Specifically,

$$\left(\begin{array}{c} \text{Return on a simple interest basis on} \\ \text{\$1 million 10\% year bills held to maturity} \end{array} \right) = \frac{\$101,000.11}{\$898,888.89} \div \frac{364}{365}$$

$$= 11.28\%$$

In this calculation, because the bill matures in 364 days, it is necessary to divide by the fraction of the year for which the bill is outstanding to annualize the rate earned.

Treasury notes and bonds, which—unlike bills—are *interest bearing,* pay the holder interest equal to the face value times the interest (i.e., *coupon*) rate at which they are issued. Thus, an investor who bought $1 million of Treasury notes carrying a 10% coupon would receive $100,000 of interest during each year the securities were outstanding.

The way yields on notes and bonds are quoted, 10% notes selling at *par* (i.e., face value) would be quoted as offering a 10% yield. An investor who bought these notes would, however, have the opportunity to earn *more than* 10% simple interest. The reason is that interest on notes and bonds is paid in semiannual installments, which means that the investor can invest, during the second six months of each year, the first semiannual interest installment.

To illustrate the effect of this on return, consider an investor who buys at issue $1 million of 10% Treasury notes. Six months later, he receives $50,000 of interest, which we assume he reinvests at 10%. Then at the end of the year, he receives another $50,000 of interest plus interest on the interest he has invested; the latter amounts to $50,000 times 10% times the one-half year he earns that interest. Thus, his total dollar return over the year is:

$$\$50,000 + (0.10)(\$50,000)(0.5) + \$50,000 = \$102,500$$

and the percentage return that he earns, expressed in terms of simple interest, is

$$\frac{\$102,500}{\$1,000,000} = 10.25\%$$

Note that what is at work here is *compound interest;* any quoted rate of interest yields more dollars of return, and is thus equivalent to a higher

---

[2] By *simple interest* we mean interest paid once a year at the end of the year. There is no compounding as, for example, on a savings account.

simple interest rate, the more frequently interest is paid and the more compounding that can thus occur.

Because return can mean different things depending on the way it is quoted and paid, an investor can meaningfully compare the returns offered by different securities only if these returns are stated on a comparable basis. With respect to *discount* and *coupon* securities, the way yields are made comparable in the money market is by restating yields quoted on a *discount basis*—the basis on which T bills are quoted—in terms of *equivalent bond yield*—the basis on which yields on notes and bonds are quoted.

We calculated above that an investor in a year bill would, on a simple interest basis, earn 11.28%. This is slightly higher than the rate he would earn measured on an equivalent bond yield basis. The reason is that equivalent bond yield understates, as noted, the true return on a simple interest basis that the investor in a coupon security would earn if he reinvested interest. When adjustment is made for this understatement, the equivalent bond yield offered by a 10% year bill turns out to be something less than 11.28%. Specifically, it is 10.98%.

The formula for converting yield on a bank discount basis to equivalent bond yield is complicated for discount securities that have a current maturity of longer than six months, but that is no problem for investors and other money market participants because bill yields are always restated on dealers' quote sheets in terms of equivalent bond yield at the *asked* rate (Table 3–1).

On bills with a current maturity of six months or less, equivalent bond yield is the simple interest rate yielded by a bill. Let

$$d_b = \text{Equivalent bond yield}$$

TABLE 3–1
Selected quotes on U.S. Treasury bills, June 22, 1987

Billions outstanding	Days to maturity	Maturity	Discount (%)		Dollar price	Equivalent bond yield
			Bid	Asked		
14.2	1	6/25/87	4.80	4.76	99.987	4.840
13.6	29	7/23/87	5.40	5.36	99.568	5.473
13.0	64	8/27/87	5.50	5.46	99.029	5.605
6.4	92	9/24/87	5.66	5.62	98.564	5.797
6.6	120	10/22/87	5.76	5.72	98.093	5.928
6.4	148	11/19/87	5.85	5.81	97.611	6.051
9.75	183	12/24/87	5.95	5.93	96.986	6.216
9.50	239	2/18/88	6.07	6.05	95.983	6.361
9.75	267	3/17/88	6.13	6.11	95.468	6.441
9.75	351	6/9/88	6.25	6.23	93.926	6.638

Source: The Morgan Bank.

Then, on a security quoted at the discount rate d, equivalent bond yield is given by

$$d_b = \frac{365 \times d}{360 - (d \times t)}$$

For example, on a 3-month bill purchased at 8%, equivalent bond yield is

$$d_b = \frac{365 \times 0.08}{360 - (0.08 \times 91)} = 8.28\%$$

From the examples we have considered, it is clear that the yield on a discount security is *significantly less* when measured on a discount basis than when measured in terms of equivalent bond yield. The absolute divergence between these two measures of yield is, moreover, not constant. As Table 3–2 shows, the greater the yield and the longer the maturity of the security, the greater the divergence.

TABLE 3–2
Comparisons, at different rates and maturities, of rates of discount and equivalent bond yields

Yields on a discount basis (%)	Equivalent bond yields (%)		
	30-day maturity	182-day maturity	364-day maturity
4	4.069	4.139	4.183
6	6.114	6.274	6.375
8	8.166	8.453	8.639
10	10.227	10.679	10.979
12	12.290	12.952	13.399
14	14.362	15.256	15.904

MONEY MARKET YIELD

Equivalent bond yield on a bill is calculated on the basis of a 365-day year. Bill rates are—to make them directly comparable to rates on CDs and other interest-bearing, money market instruments—often converted to a simple interest rate on a 360-day-year basis. That number, dubbed *money market yield,* is obtained by substituting 360 for 365 in the above equation for equivalent bond yield; specifically,

$$\left(\begin{array}{c}\text{Money market yield} \\ \text{on a bill}\end{array}\right) = \frac{360 \times d}{360 - (d \times t)}$$

FLUCTUATIONS IN A BILL'S PRICE

Normally, the price at which a bill sells will rise as the bill approaches maturity. For example, to yield 9% on a discount basis, a 6-month bill must be priced at $95.45 per $100 of face value. For the same bill three months later (three months closer to maturity) to yield 9%, it must have risen in price to $97.72. The moral is clear: If a bill always sold at the same yield throughout its life, its price would rise steadily toward face value as it approached maturity.

A bill's yield, however, is unlikely to be constant over time; instead, it will fluctuate for two reasons: (1) changes may occur in the general level of short-term interest rates, and (2) the bill will move along *the yield curve.* Let's look at each of these factors.

Short-term interest rates

T bills are issued through auctions in which discounted prices (yields) are bid. The rate of discount determined at auction on a new bill issue depends on the level of short-term interest rates prevailing at the moment of the auction. The reason is straightforward. Investors who want to buy bills at the time of a Treasury auction have two alternatives—to buy new bills or to buy existing bills from dealers. This being the case, investors will not bid for new bills at a rate of discount lower than that available on existing bills. If they did, they would be offering to buy new bills at a price higher than that at which they could buy existing bills. Also, investors will not bid substantially higher rates of discount (lower prices) than those prevailing on existing bills. If they did, they would not obtain bills, since they would surely be underbid by others trying to get just a slightly better return than that available on existing securities. Thus, the prevailing level of short-term rates determines, within a narrow range, the discount established on new bills at issue.

However, the going level of short-term rates is not constant over time. It rises and falls in response to changes in economic activity, the demand for credit, investors' expectations, and monetary policy as set by the Federal Reserve System. Figure 3–1, which plots auction rates on 6-month T bills for the period January 1981 to February 1987, portrays vividly the volatility of short-term interest rates. It shows both the sharp ups and downs that occurred in these rates as the Fed successively eased and tightened and the myriad of smaller fluctuations over the period in response to short-lived changes in other determinants of these rates.

If the going level of short-term rates (which establishes the rate at which a bill is initially sold) falls after a bill is issued, then this bill—as long as its price doesn't change—will yield more than new bills. There-

FIGURE 3–1
Average auction rate on 6-month T bills (*week averages*)

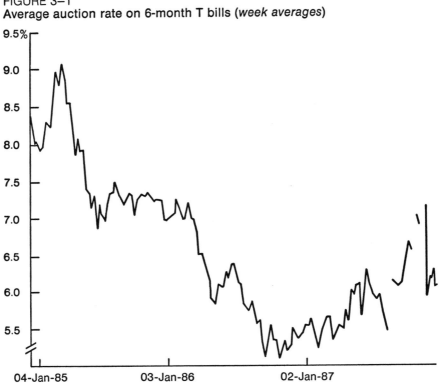

04-Jan-85   03-Jan-86   02-Jan-87

Breaks in date due to disruptions in Treasury's auction schedule due to failure of Congress to make
a timely increase in statutory ceiling on federal debt.
Source: J. P. Morgan Securities.

fore, buyers will compete for this bill, and in doing so, they will drive up
its price and thereby force down its yield until the bill sells at a rate of
discount equal to the new, lower going interest rate. Conversely, if short-
term rates rise after a bill is issued, the unwillingness of buyers to purchase any bill at a discount less than that available on new issues will
drive down its price and thereby force up its yield.

The yield curve

Even if the going level of short-term interest rates does not change
while investors hold bills, it would be normal for the rate at which they
could sell their bills to change. The reason lies in the *yield curve*. How
this works is a function of several factors, described next.

Price risk. In choosing among alternative securities, an investor considers three things: risk, liquidity, and return. Purchase of a money market instrument exposes an investor to two sorts of risk: (1) *credit risk:* Will the issuer pay off at maturity? and (2) *price risk:* If the investor later sold the security, might he have to do so at a loss because interest rates had subsequently risen? Most money market investors are risk averse, which means that they will accept lower yields to obtain lower risk.

The price risk to which bills and other money market instruments expose the investor is *larger* the *longer* their current maturity. To see why, suppose that short-term interest rates rise a full percentage point across the board; then the prices of all bill issues will drop, *but the price drop will be greater, the longer an issue's current maturity.* For example, a 1 percentage point rise in market rates would cause a 3-month bill to fall only $2,500 in price per $1 million of face value, whereas the corresponding price drop on a 9-month bill would be $7,600 per $1 million of face value.

The slope of the yield curve. Because a 3-month bill exposes the investor to less price risk than a 9-month bill does, it will normally yield less than a 9-month bill. In other words, the bill market yield curve, which shows the relationship between yield and current maturity, normally slopes upward, indicating that the longer the time to maturity, the higher the yield. We say "normally" because other factors, such as the expectation that interest rates are going to fall, may, as explained below, alter this relationship.

To illustrate the concept of the yield curve, we have used the bid quotes in Table 3–1 to plot a yield curve in Figure 3–2; each dot is one quote. Our results show a normal upward-sloping yield curve. Lest you try doing the same and be disappointed, we should admit that we cheated a bit in putting together our demonstration yield curve. On April 27, 1987, there were many more bill issues outstanding than those quoted in Table 3–1. Had we plotted yields on all of these in Figure 3–2, we would have found that yield did not rise quite so consistently with maturity; the points plotted for some bill issues would have been further off a smooth yield curve. Yields may be out of line for various reasons. For example, a bill issue maturing around a tax date might be highly desired by investors who had big tax payments to make and, for this reason, trade at a yield that was relatively low compared to yields on surrounding issues.

While the yield curve for short maturities normally slopes upward, its shape and slope vary over time. Thus, it is difficult to pinpoint a "normal" spread between, say, 1-month and 6-month bills.

Yield spreads between different securities are always measured in terms of basis points. *A basis point is 1/100 of 1 percentage point.* Thus,

FIGURE 3–2
Yield curve for Treasury bills—April 27, 1987

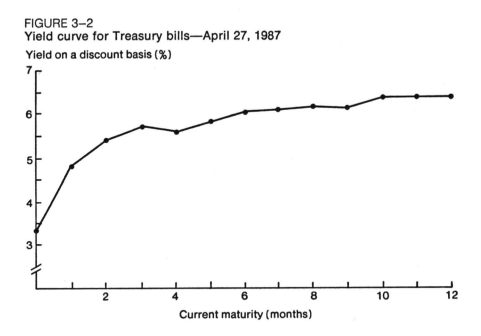

Yield on a discount basis (%)

Current maturity (months)

if 5-month bills are quoted at 10.45 and 6-month bills at 10.56, the spread between the two is said to be 11 basis points. A yield spread between two securities of 100 basis points would indicate a full 1% difference in their yields. A basis point is also frequently referred to as an 01 (pronounced oh one).

BANKERS' ACCEPTANCES AND COMMERCIAL PAPER

In talking about discount securities, we have focused on bills since they are the most important discount security traded in the money market. All we have said about yields on bills is, however, equally applicable to yields on BAs and commercial paper, both of which are sold on a discount basis with the discount being calculated on a 360-day year.

THE NEXT CHAPTER

In the next chapter, we shift our focus to interest-bearing notes and bonds. We also introduce several key concepts: (1) the relationship, for a bond, of current maturity and coupon to price volatility, and (2) the yield curve as measured in the Treasury market.

Chapter 4

Interest-bearing securities

THE STOCK-IN-TRADE OF THE MONEY MARKET includes, besides discount securities, a variety of *interest-bearing* instruments: Treasury and federal agency notes and bonds, municipal notes and bonds, and bank certificates of deposit. Notes, bonds, and other interest-bearing debt securities are issued with a fixed *face value;* they mature at some specified date and carry a *coupon rate,* which is the annual interest rate the issuer promises to pay the holder on the security's face value while the security is outstanding.

Some notes and bonds are issued in *registered* form; that is, the issuer keeps track of who owns its outstanding IOUs, just as a corporation keeps track of who owns its common stock. Most notes and bonds, however, are issued in *bearer* form. To prove ownership of a bearer security, the owner must produce or bear it. An issuer with $50 million of bearer bonds outstanding does not know where to send interest when a payment date comes along. Consequently, such securities carry *coupons,* one for each interest date. On the interest date, the investor or his bank clips the appropriate coupon from the security and sends it to the issuer's paying agent, who, in turn, makes the required payment.[1] Gener-

---

[1] The procedure is different on Treasury and agency securities, which are now being issued in *book-entry* form; computerized records of ownership maintained by the Fed and banks have been substituted for actual securities.

ally, interest payments are made semiannually on coupon securities. Because notes and bonds carry coupons, the return paid on face value is called the *coupon rate* or simply the *coupon.*

Notes and bonds with a short current maturity are referred to as *short coupons,* those with an intermediate current maturity (two to seven years) as *intermediate coupons,* and those with a still longer current maturity as *long coupons.*

CALL PROVISIONS

Once a bond issue is sold, the issuer might choose to redeem it early. For example, if interest rates fell, the borrower could reduce his interest costs by refunding his loan: paying off outstanding high-coupon bonds and issuing new lower-coupon bonds.

For the investor, early repayment on a bond is almost always disadvantageous because a bond issuer will rarely be tempted to repay early when interest rates are rising, a time when it would be to the bondholder's advantage to move funds out of the issuer's bonds into new, higher-yielding bonds. On the other hand, early payment looks attractive to the issuer when interest rates are falling, a time when it is to the investor's advantage to keep funds invested in the issuer's high-coupon securities.

To protect investors making long-term commitments against frequent refundings by borrowers out to minimize interest costs, most bonds contain call provisions. A bond issue is said to be *callable* when the issuer has the option to repay part or all of the issue early by paying some specified redemption price to bondholders. Most bonds offer some call protection to the investor. Some are noncallable for life; others, for some number of years after issue. Thirty-year Treasury bonds are callable by the Treasury only during the final five years of their life.

Call provisions usually specify that the issuer who calls a bond must pay the bondholder a price above face value. The call premium frequently equals the coupon rate on early calls and then diminishes to zero as the bond approaches maturity.

PRICE QUOTES

Note and bond prices are quoted in slightly different ways depending on whether they are selling in the new issue or the secondary market. When notes and bonds other than governments are issued, the price at which they are offered to investors is normally quoted as a percentage of face value. To illustrate, the two Fannie Mae bond issues announced in Figure 4–1 were offered at prices of 100% and 99.875%, respectively, which means that the investor had to pay $100 for each $100 of face value on the 8.55% debentures and $99.875 for each $100 of face value

FIGURE 4–1
Pricing announcement for two new Fannie Mae debentures

Source: *The Wall Street Journal.*

on the 9.20% debentures. This percentage price is often called the bond's *dollar price*. The securities described in Figure 4–1 happened to be offered at par, so the actual yields offered by these securities equaled their respective coupon rates. Often on a new offering this is not the case.

Once a note or bond issue is distributed and trading in it moves to the secondary market, prices are also quoted on a percentage basis but always, depending on the security, in 32nds, 8ths, 4ths, or halves. Table 4–1 reproduces, by way of illustration, a few quotes on Treasury notes and bonds posted by a dealer on April 27, 1987. The first bid is 101–4, meaning that this dealer was willing to pay $101–4/32, which equals $101.125 per $100 of face value for that issue. One advantage of dollar pricing of notes and bonds is that it makes the prices of securities with different denominations directly comparable.

TABLE 4–1
Quotations for selected Treasury notes—April 27, 1987

Millions of $s publicly held	Coupon rate	Maturity	Bid*	Asked	Yield to maturity	Yield value of 1/32	Issue date
9250	8⅞	10/31/87	101–4	101–5	6.511	.0631	10/31/85
9500	8½	11/30/87	101–0	101–1	6.645	.0542	12/2/85
9500	7⅞	12/31/87	100–20	100–21	6.815	.0478	12/31/85
9750	6⅝	4/30/88	99–17	99–18	7.066	.0328	4/30/86
3381	10⅜	11/15/09–04†	111–26	111–30	9.007	.0033	11/15/79

* Prices quoted in 32nds.
† Issue matures in 2009 but is callable in 2004.
Source: The Morgan Bank.

Treatment of interest in pricing

There's another wrinkle with respect to note and bond pricing. Typically, interest on notes and bonds is paid to the holder semiannually on the coupon dates. This means that the value of a coupon security rises by the amount of interest accrued as a payment date approaches and falls thereafter by the amount of the payment made. Since notes and bonds are issued on every business day and consequently have coupon dates all over the calendar, the effect of accrued interest on the value of coupon securities would, if incorporated into the prices quoted by dealers, make meaningful price comparisons between different issues difficult. To get around this problem, the actual prices paid in the new issue and secondary markets are always the quoted dollar price *plus* any accrued interest. For example, if an investor—three months before a coupon date—bought $100,000 of 12% Treasury notes quoted at 104, he would pay $104,000 plus $3,000 of accrued interest:

$$\$104,000 + 0.5 \left[\frac{(0.12)(\$100,000)}{2} \right] = \$104,000 + 0.5(\$6,000)$$
$$= \$107,000$$

where (0.12)($100,000)/2 represents the $6,000 semiannual interest due on the notes.

FLUCTUATIONS IN A COUPON SECURITY'S PRICE

When a new note or bond issue comes to market, the coupon rate on it is, with certain exceptions, set so that it equals the yield prevailing in the market on securities of comparable maturity and risk. This permits the new security to be sold at a price equal or nearly equal to par.

The price at which the security later trades in the secondary market will, like that of a discount security, fluctuate in response to changes in the general level of interest rates.

Yield to maturity

To illustrate, let's work through a simple example. Suppose a new 6-year note with an 8% coupon is issued at par. Six months later, the Fed tightens, and the yield on comparable securities rises to 8.5%. Now what is this 8% security worth? Since the investor who pays a price equal to par for this "seasoned issue" is going to get only an 8% return, while 8.5% is available elsewhere, it is clear that the security must now sell at *less* than par.

To determine how much less, we have to introduce a new concept— *effective yield.* When an investor buys a coupon security at a *discount* and holds it to maturity, he receives a two-part return: the promised interest payment *plus* a capital gain. The capital gain arises because the security that the investor bought at less than par is redeemed at maturity for full face value. The investor who buys a coupon issue at a *premium* and holds it to maturity also receives a two-part return: interest payments due plus a capital *loss* equal to the premium paid.

For dollars invested in a coupon issue that sells at a discount or premium, it is possible to calculate the overall or effective rate of return received, which is the rate that the investor earns on his dollars when both interest received *and* capital gains (or losses) are taken into account. Naturally, an investor choosing between securities of similar risk and maturity will do so not on the basis of coupon rate but on the basis of effective yield, referred to in the financial community as *yield to maturity.*

To get back to our example, it is clear that once rates rise to 8.5% in the open market, the security with an 8% coupon has to be priced at a discount sufficiently great so that its yield to maturity equals 8.5%. Figuring out how many dollars of discount this requires involves complicated calculations. Dealers used to use bond tables, but all have now switched to bond calculators. A trader can thus determine in a few seconds that, with interest rates at 8.5%, a $1,000 note with an 8% coupon and a 3½-year current maturity must sell at $985.13 (a discount of $14.87) to yield 8.5% to maturity.

Current maturity and price volatility

A capital gain of $14.87, which is what the investor in our discounted 8% note would realize if he held it to maturity, will raise effective yield more the faster this gain is realized (the shorter the current maturity of the security). Conversely, this capital gain will raise effective yield less the more slowly it is realized (the longer the current maturity of the security).[2]

But if this is so, then a one-half percentage point rise in the yield on comparable securities will cause a larger fall in price for a security with a long current maturity than for one with a short current maturity. In other words, the discount required to raise a coupon security's yield to maturity by one-half percentage point is *greater* the *longer* the security's maturity.

By reversing the argument above, it is easy to see that if six months after the 6-year, 8% note in our example was issued, the yield on comparable securities *fell* to 7.5%, the value of this note would be driven to a *premium;* that is, it would sell at a price above par. Note also that a one-half percentage point *fall* in the yield on comparable securities would force an outstanding high-coupon security to a *greater* premium the *longer* its current maturity.

As these observations suggest, when prevailing interest rates change, prices of long coupons respond more dramatically than prices of short coupons. Figure 4–2 shows this sharp contrast. It pictures, for a $1,000 note carrying an 8% coupon, the relationship between *current* maturity and the discount that would prevail if the yield on comparable securities rose to 8.5% or to 10%. It also plots the premium to which a $1,000 note with an 8% coupon would, depending on its current maturity, be driven if the yield on comparable securities fell to 6%.

---

[2] If you don't see this, just think—somewhat imprecisely—of the capital gain as a certain number of dollars of extra interest paid out in yearly installments to the investor as his security matures. Clearly, the shorter the security's current maturity, the higher these extra annual interest installments will be and, consequently, the higher the overall yield to the investor.

FIGURE 4–2
Premiums and discounts at which a $1,000 note with an 8% coupon would
sell, depending on current maturity, if market yields on comparable
securities were 6%, 8.5%, and 10%

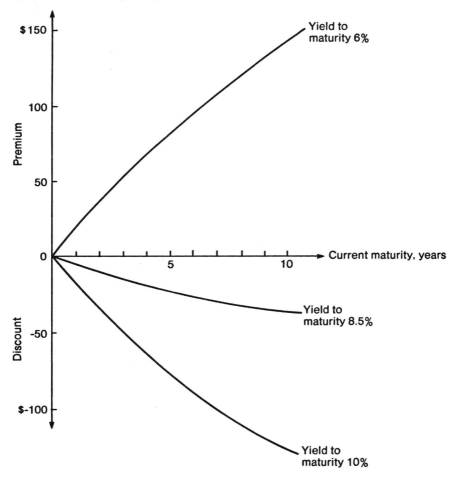

Coupon and price volatility

The volatility of a note or bond's price in the face of changing interest
rates also depends on its coupon; the *lower* the coupon, the *greater* the
percentage change in price that will occur when rates rise or fall. To
illustrate, consider two notes with four-year current maturities. Note A
has an 8% coupon and note B a 6% coupon. Both are priced to yield 8%.

Suppose now that interest rates on comparable securities rise to 10%. Note A will fall in price by $6.46; since it was initially priced at $100, that works out to a 6.46% fall in value. Note B's dollar price drops from $93.27 to $87.07—a $6.20 fall, which equals a 6.64% loss of value. The reason for the greater percentage fall in the price of the low-coupon note is that capital appreciation represents a greater proportion of promised income (capital appreciation plus coupon interest) on the low coupon than on the high coupon. Therefore, for the low-coupon note's yield to maturity to rise two percentage points, its price has to fall relatively *more* than that of the high-coupon note.

Zeros.   As the reasoning in the preceding paragraph suggests, *zero-coupon* securities (securities with a zero coupon) are far more volatile in price than securities paying even as low a coupon as 6%.

Yield value of 1/32.   Prices of government and federal agency securities are quoted in 32nds. The greater the change in yield to maturity that results from a price change of 1/32, the less volatile the issue's price will be in the face of changing interest rates. As a result, dealers include on their quote sheets for such securities a column titled *Yield value of 1/32.* Looking back at Table 4–1, we see that the yield value of 1/32 on the 8⅞s Treasury notes maturing on 10/31/87 was .0631, which means that a fall in the asked price on this security from 101– 5 to 101– 4 (a 1/32 fall) would have raised yield to maturity by 0.0631%, from 6.511 to 6.572. The yield value of 1/32 drops sharply as current maturity lengthens. Thus, on the 10⅜s Treasury bonds maturing on 4/30/88 (the next to last line of the table), the yield value of 1/32 was only .0328, indicating that these notes would have had to fall in value by approximately 30.5/32 (almost a point) for their yield to rise 1%.

Current yield

So far we have focused on yield to maturity, which is the yield figure always quoted on coupon securities. When the investor buys a note or bond, he may also be interested in knowing what rate of return interest payments per se will give him on the principal he invests. This measure of yield is referred to as *current yield.*

To illustrate, consider our earlier example of a note with an 8% coupon selling at $985.13 to yield 8.5% to maturity. Current yield on this note would be: ($80/$985.13) × 100, or 8.12%. On a discount note or bond, current yield is always less than yield to maturity; on a premium bond it exceeds yield to maturity.

THE YIELD CURVE

From the examples we have worked through, it is clear that investors in notes and bonds expose themselves, like buyers of discount securities, to a *price risk*. Moreover, even though longer-term rates fluctuate less violently than do short-term rates (Figure 4–3), the price risk associated with holding debt securities tends to be greater the longer the current maturity. Thus, one would expect the yield curve to slope upward over the full maturity spectrum. And often it does.

FIGURE 4–3
U.S. government security yields (*month averages*)

Source: J. P. Morgan Securities.

Price risk, however, is not the only factor affecting the shape of the yield curve. Borrowers' and investors' *expectations* with respect to future interest rates are also an important—at times dominant—factor.

If the general expectation is that interest rates are going to rise, investors will seek to keep their money in short coupons to avoid getting locked into low-yield, long coupons. Borrowers, on the other hand, will try to lengthen the maturity of their outstanding debt to lock in prevailing low rates for as long as possible. Both responses tend to force short-term rates down and long-term rates up, thereby accentuating the upward slope of the yield curve. The expectation that interest rates would rise is one reason that the December 11, 1987, yield curve sloped steeply upward (see Figure 4–4).

FIGURE 4–4
Three upward-sloping yield curves at different points in time

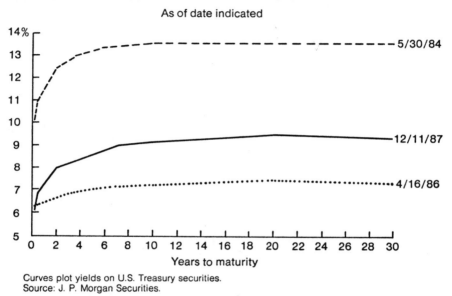

As of date indicated

Curves plot yields on U.S. Treasury securities.
Source: J. P. Morgan Securities.

People, of course, may expect interest rates to fall. When this is the case, investors respond by buying long coupons in the hope of locking in a high yield. In contrast, borrowers are willing to pay extremely high short-term rates while they wait for long rates to fall so that they can borrow more cheaply. The net result of both responses is that, when interest rates are expected to fall, the yield curve (or at least some part of it) may be *inverted,* with short-term rates above long-term rates. Figure 4–5 pictures the yield curve on February 4, 1980, when people antici-pated a fall in rates. Note that after a current maturity of one month, the slope of this curve becomes negative.

If, inspired by our yield curves, you start pouring over dealer quote sheets on governments, you are bound to discover some out-of-line yields. The reasons are varied.[3] For one thing, sale of a large new issue

---

[3] One trivial reason may be a mistake in the quote sheet. These are typically compiled daily in great haste with the result that errors creep in. For this reason, such sheets often carry a footnote stating that the quotes are believed to be reliable but are not "guaranteed."

FIGURE 4–5
Two yield curves that are downward sloping over at least some
maturity span

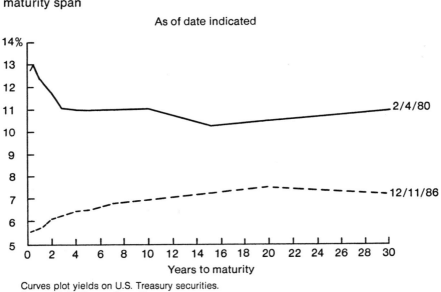

As of date indicated

Curves plot yields on U.S. Treasury securities.
Source: J. P. Morgan Securities.

may cause a temporary upward bulge in the yield curve in the maturity range of the new issue. Also, a security with an out-of-line yield may have some special characteristic. Some government bonds (*flower bonds* to the Street) are acceptable at par in payment of federal estate taxes when owned by the decedent at the time of death. These bonds, which all sell at substantial discounts, have yields to maturity much lower than those on straight government bonds.

Yields are not always directly comparable

In calculating the yield on discount securities, we found a considerable discrepancy between yield measured on a discount basis and equivalent bond yield. There are also many discrepancies—albeit smaller ones—between the ways that interest is measured and quoted on different interest-bearing securities. For example, interest on Treasury notes is calculated for actual days on the basis of a 365-day year, while interest on CDs is calculated for actual days on the basis of a 360-day year. Thus, a 1-year CD issued at 10% would yield a higher return than a 10% year note selling at par. Partially offsetting this advantage, however, is the fact that a 1-year CD would pay interest only at maturity, whereas a

1-year note would pay it semiannually. The latter disadvantage disappears, however, on CDs with a maturity longer than one year, since such CDs pay interest semiannually.

Another discrepancy: When government notes and bonds are sold, accrued interest is calculated between coupon dates on the basis of actual days passed since a coupon date, while on agency securities it accrues as if every month had 30 days. Thus, for example, agency securities accrue no interest on October 31, but they do accrue interest on February 30!

These and the many other minor discrepancies among yields on interest-bearing securities have little importance for understanding the workings of the money market, but they are important to the market participant out to maximize return.

THE NEXT CHAPTER

In the next chapter, we turn to *dealers,* those key players who make the markets that together comprise the money market.

Chapter 5

The market makers: Dealers

THAT A COLLECTION OF MARKETS is called *the* money market suggests that the participants in this market trade in a single market where at any time one price reigns for any one instrument. This description is accurate, but that is startling. Money market instruments, with the exception of futures contracts, are traded not on organized exchanges but strictly over the counter. Moreover, money market participants, who vary in size from small to gargantuan, are scattered over the whole United States—*and* throughout Canada, Europe, the Middle East, and the Far East. Thus, one might expect fragmentation of the market, with big New York participants dealing in a noticeably different market from their London or Wichita counterparts. However, money market lenders and borrowers can operate almost as well out of Dearborn, Michigan, Washington, Singapore, or Tokyo as they can from Wall Street. Wherever they are, their access to information, bids, and offers is (time zone problems excepted) essentially the same. That the money market is a single market is due largely to the activities of the dealers and brokers who weld the market's many participants into a unified whole and to the modern communication techniques that make this possible.

THE DEALERS

Money market dealers are a mixed bag. Some are tiny; others are huge. Some specialize in certain instruments; others cover the waterfront. One is also tempted to say that some are immensely sharp and others are not so sharp, but the not-so-sharp players tend to lead short lives. Despite dealers' diversity, one can generalize about their operations.

Activities

The hallmark of a dealer is that he buys and sells for his own account, that is, trades with retail and other dealers off his own position. In addition, dealers engage in various activities that come close to brokering.

The prime example of the latter is commercial paper dealers. Each day they help their customers borrow hundreds of millions of dollars from other market participants. Commercial paper dealers' responsibilities are: (1) to advise their clients on market conditions, (2) to ensure that their clients post rates for different maturities that give them the lowest possible borrowing costs but are still high enough to get their paper sold, and (3) for a one-eighth commission, to show and sell that paper to retail. Positioning is part of a commercial paper dealer's operation but only marginally so. Paper dealers will position any of their clients' paper that goes unsold, but that amounts to little. One reason is that dealers are careful to ensure that their clients post realistic rates. A second reason is that commercial paper dealers as a group feel that it is not in their best interest or in that of their clients for them to position large amounts of paper. Commercial paper dealers do, however, stand ready to bid for paper bought from them by retail and thus make a secondary market in paper. Such activity leads them at times to position paper, but the amounts are small because the secondary market in commercial paper is inactive. Thus, dealers in commercial paper act more like brokers than like true dealers.

Dealers also act at times like brokers in the CD market. A bank that wants to do a large program in one fast shot may call one or more dealers and offer them several basis points on any CDs they can sell to retail. Finally, smaller dealers who are hesitant about the market or who are operating outside their normal market sector at times act more or less as brokers, giving a firm bid to retail only if they can cross the trade on the other side with an assured sale.

As noted, however, brokering is not what dealing is all about. *The crucial role dealers play in the money market is as market makers, and in performing that role, they trade off their own positions.*

Part of the dealers' role as market makers involves underwriting new issues. Most large municipal note issues are bought up at issue by dealers or syndicates of them who take these securities into position and sell them off to retail. In the market for governments there is also underwriting, though of a less formal nature; frequently dealers buy large amounts of new government issues at auction and then distribute them to retail.

In the secondary market, dealers act as market makers by constantly quoting bids and offers at which they are willing to buy and sell. Some of these quotes are to other dealers. In every sector of the money market, there is an *inside market* between dealers. In this market, dealers quote price *runs* (bids and offers for securities of different maturities) to other dealers, often through brokers. Since every dealer will *hit* a bid he views as high or *take* an offering he views as low, trading in the inside market creates at any time for every security traded a prevailing price that represents dealers' consensus of what that security is worth.

Dealers also actively quote bids and offers to retail. In doing so they consistently seek to give their customers the best quotes possible because they value retail business and they know that other shops are competing actively with them for it. This competition between dealers ensures that dealers' quotes to retail will never be far removed from prices prevailing in the inside market. Thus, all the money market's geographically dispersed participants can always trade at close to identical bids and offers.

As the above suggests, through their trading activities, the dealers give the secondary market for money market instruments two important characteristics. First, they ensure that at any moment a single price level will prevail for any instrument traded in it. Second, by standing ready to quote firm bids and offers at which they will trade, they render money market instruments liquid.

Profit sources

Dealers profit from their activities in several ways. First, there are the 05s and ⅛s (less today) that they earn selling CDs and commercial paper. Particularly for firms that are big commercial paper dealers, these commissions amount to a substantial sum, but in total they represent only a small part of dealers' profits.

A second source of dealers' profits is *carry*. As noted below, dealers finance the bulk of their long positions (muni notes excepted) in the repo market. Their repo borrowings are of shorter maturity than the securities they position. Thus, their financing costs are normally less than the yields on the securities they finance, and they profit from *positive* carry.

Carry, however, is an undependable source of profit because, when the yield curve inverts, carry turns negative.[1] As one dealer commented, "Back in 1974 when Fed funds were 10 to 14%, there was nothing you could position at a positive carry. You might position because you thought rates were going to fall, but not for carry. And you knew *ex ante* that, if you positioned and the market did not appreciate, you would lose money on two levels: carry and depreciation of values. This led to the phenomenon of the Friday night bill trader. At one point, to carry bills over the weekend cost 5 basis points. So traders would attempt on Friday to sell the 90-day bill for cash settlement and buy it back for regular settlement." The late 1970s and early 1980s were also characterized often by negative carry.

A third source of dealer profits is what might be called day-to-day trading profits, buying securities at one price and reselling them shortly at a slightly higher price, or shorting securities and covering in at a slightly lower price. How traders seek to earn 02s and 32nds from such trading is discussed later.

The sources of profit mentioned so far suffice to pay dealers' phone and light bills—to cover their overhead. Dealers earn really big money on position plays, that is, by taking into position huge amounts of securities when they anticipate that rates will fall and securities prices will rise or by shorting the market when they are bearish.

Being willing to position on a large scale is characteristic of all dealers, although the appetite of some shops for such *speculation* is stronger than that of others.[2] One might argue that positioning done specifically to speculate as opposed to the positioning that arises out of a dealer's daily trading activities with retail and other dealers is not an inherent part of being a market maker. But such speculation serves useful functions. It guarantees that market prices will react rapidly to any change in conditions, economic or in demand, supply, or rate expectations. Also, and more important, the profits dealers can earn from correct position plays are the prime incentive they have for setting up the elaborate and expensive operations they use daily to trade with retail and each other. Position profits help to oil the machinery that dealers need to be effective market makers.

---

[1] The yield curve is said to be *inverted* when short-term rates exceed long-term rates. For an inverted yield curve, see Figure 4–5.

[2] The term *speculation* as used here and throughout the book is *not* meant to carry pejorative connotation. *Speculation is taking an unhedged position, short or long.* A homeowner who buys a house financed with a mortgage is assuming a speculative, levered position in real estate. A dealer who buys governments with repo money is assuming a speculative, levered position in governments. The only difference between the two is that the dealer knows he's speculating; the homeowner used not to think of it that way.

Dealers possess no crystal balls enabling them to perfectly foresee the future. They position on the basis of carefully formulated expectations. When they are right, they make huge profits; however, when they are wrong, their losses can be staggering. Thus, the successful shops and the ones that survive are those that are right on the market more often than wrong.

DEALER FINANCING

The typical dealer runs a highly levered operation in which securities held in position may total a large multiple of their capital. Some dealers rely heavily on dealer loans from New York banks for financing, but as one dealer commented, "The state of the art is that you don't have to." Repo money is cheaper, and sharp dealers rely primarily on it to meet their financing needs. For such dealers the need to obtain repo money on a continuing basis and in large amounts is one additional reason for assiduously cultivating their retail customers. The money funds, corporations, state and local governments, and other investors that buy governments and other instruments from them are also big suppliers of repo money to the dealers.

Much of the borrowing dealers do in the repo market is done on an overnight basis. The overnight rate is typically the lowest repo rate. Also, securities "hung out" on repo for one night only are available for sale the next day. Nonbank dealers have to clear all their repo transactions through the clearing banks, which is expensive. As a result, they also do a lot of *open repos* at rates slightly above the overnight rate. Open or demand repos have an indefinite term; either the borrower or the lender can each day choose to terminate the agreement.

The financing needs that nonbank dealers do not cover in the repo market are met by borrowing from banks at the dealer loan rate. Even dealers who look primarily to the repo market for financing will use bank loans to finance small pieces they hold in inventory. A typical nonbank dealer commented, "The smallest repo ticket I will write is 2 [million]. On a transaction of less than 2, writing the tickets and making deliveries is not worth the cost and trouble. I can combine small pieces, but generally I let such junk just sit at the bank."

In financing, bank dealers have one advantage over nonbank dealers—they can finance odd pieces they do not repo by buying Fed funds.

While much dealer financing is done using open or very short repos, dealers will sometimes finance speculative positions they anticipate holding for some time with term repo, taking in money for 30, 60, or 90 days, or even longer.

Fails and the fails game

If, on the settlement date of a trade, a seller does not make timely delivery of the securities purchased, delivers the wrong securities, or fails in some other way to deliver in proper form, the trade becomes a *fail*. In that case the buyer does not have to make payment until proper delivery is made, presumably the next day; *but* he owns the securities as of the initially agreed-upon settlement day. Thus, on a fail the security buyer (who is *failed to*) receives, overnight, a free loan equal to the amount of the purchase price, that is, one day's free financing. And if the fail persists, the free loan continues. Fails occur not only in connection with straight trades but in connection with repos; on a repo the lender has to make timely return of the collateral he is holding to unwind the transaction and get his money back.

Dealers often play some portion of their financing needs for a fail; that is, they estimate on the basis of past experience the dollar amount of the fails that will be made to them and reduce their repo borrowing accordingly. If their estimate proves high, more securities will end up in their box at the clearing bank than they had anticipated, and that bank will automatically grant them a box loan against that collateral. On such last-minute loans the clearing banks charge the dealer a rate that's a margin above their posted dealer loan rate to encourage dealers to track their positions and run an orderly shop. A dealer who plays the *fails game* is in effect using his clearing bank as a lender of last resort.

INTEREST RATE PREDICTIONS

The key rate in the money market is the Fed funds rate. Because of the role of this rate in determining dealers' cost of carry (the repo rate is usually slightly below the funds rate), the 90-day bill rate settles close to the Fed funds rate, and other short-term rates key off this combination in a fairly predictable way (Figure 5–1). Thus when a dealer positions, he does so on the basis of a strongly held view with respect to where money supply numbers and Fed policy are headed; and *every long position he takes is based on an implicit prediction of how high Fed funds and other money market instruments might trade* within the time frame of his investment. In formulating expectations about short-term interest rates, dealers engage in constant and careful Fed watching.

CONFIDENCE LEVEL IN POSITIONING

Positioning is a form of gambling, and the dealers most skilled in this art attempt, first, to express their expectations about what might occur in terms of probabilities of various outcomes and, second, to estimate the

FIGURE 5–1
Other short-term money rates key off the Fed funds rate (*month averages*)

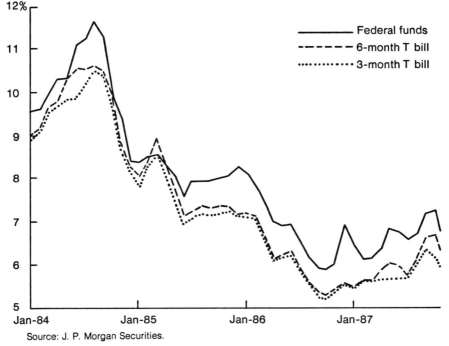

Source: J. P. Morgan Securities.

payoff or loss that a given strategy would yield if each of these outcomes were to occur. Then on the basis of these numbers, they decide whether to bet and how much to bet.

Probabilists who have theorized about gambling like to talk about a fair gamble or a *fair game*. A fair game is one that, if played repeatedly, will yield the player neither net gains nor losses. For example, suppose a person plays the following game: A coin is flipped; if it lands heads up, he wins $1; if it lands heads down, he loses $1. The probability that the coin will land heads up is one-half. So half the time he bets our player will lose $1; half the time he will win $1; and his *expected winnings* or *return,* if he plays the game repeatedly, is *zero*.

There is nothing in it for a dealer to make a fair bet. What he looks for is a situation in which expected return is *positive;* and the more positive it is, the more he will bet. For example, if a dealer believed (1) that the probabilities that the Fed would ease and tighten were 60 percent and 40 percent, respectively, and (2) that a given long position would return him $2 if the Fed eased and would cause him to lose $1 if the Fed tightened, then his *expected* winnings would be

$$0.6 \times \$2 - 0.4 \times \$1 = \$0.80$$

In other words, the gamble is such that, if the dealer made it 10 times, his expected winnings would be $8. That degree of favorableness in the bet might suffice to induce the dealer to position.

If the game were made still more favorable, for example by an improvement in the odds, then he would gamble still more.

All this may sound a bit theoretical, but it is the way good dealers think, explicitly or intuitively; and such thinking disciplines them in positioning. Noted one dealer, "The alternative is a sloppy operation in which a dealer runs up his position because he sort of likes the market now or runs it down because he doesn't like the market."

Quantifying his thinking about the market also helps a dealer provide retail with useful suggestions. Most customers can find fair bets on their own. What they appreciate is a dealer who can suggest to them a favorable bet.

In quantifying expectations and payoffs and acting on them, fleet-footedness is essential since everyone on the Street is playing the same game, and the market therefore frequently anticipates what the Fed is going to do.

THE MATURITY CHOICE

We suggested that the more favorable the gamble a dealer faces, the more securities he's likely to position. There is one more wrinkle to the dealer's positioning decision. A classic part of a bullish strategy is for a dealer to extend to longer maturities. The reason he is tempted to extend is that the longer the maturity of the securities he positions, the more price play he will get—and the more risk.

Dealers are very conscious that extending to longer maturities exposes them to greater *price risk*. They also tend to think that extending to longer maturities exposes them to greater risk for another reason; namely, the predictability of long-term rates is less than that of short-term rates. Short rates relate directly to Fed policy; long rates do so to a much lesser extent because they are also strongly influenced by the *slope* of the yield curve. Thus the dealer who extends must be prepared not only to predict Fed policy but to predict shifts in the slope of the yield curve— an art that is separate from and, in the eyes of many dealers, more difficult than successful Fed watching.

To protect against the risks posed by extending maturity, some dealers confine their unhedged positions largely to securities of short current maturity. A dealer typical of this group noted, "We are accused of being an inch wide and a mile deep—the mile deep being in securities with a maturity of a year and under. There are various arts in this business: predicting spreads, predicting the yield curve, predicting the trend in interest rates. You go with the learning curve of the organization you have, and ours is strong in predicting short-term spreads and yields."

Other dealers are more willing to extend maturity to reach for gains, but in doing so they seek to control carefully the price risk they assume. The guidelines used to control price risk—frequently they take the form of smaller position limits on longer maturities—vary considerably from shop to shop. One reason is that there is no objective way a dealer can compare the risk he assumes in holding 6-year notes to that he assumes in holding 6-month bills. Another is that in establishing position limits by instrument and maturity, a dealer is inevitably making subjective judgments about the ability of each of his traders.

SHORTING

When money market dealers are bullish, they place their bets by positioning securities; when they are bearish, they do so by shorting. One might expect that the quantity of securities a dealer would short, if he were confident that securities prices would fall, would be as great as the quantity of securities he would position if he were confident that securities prices would rise. But in fact, dealers will, at a given confidence level, short smaller amounts of securities than they would position. There are several reasons. First, the only instruments dealers can short are governments and agencies; other instruments, such as commercial paper, BAs, CDs, and muni notes, are too heterogeneous with respect to name, maturity, and face amount to short. Second, shorting securities tends to be more cumbersome and expensive than going long because the short seller must find not only a buyer, but—since the shorted securities must be delivered—a source of these securities.

In recent years it has become increasingly common for dealers to *reverse in* securities shorted rather than to borrow them. One reason is that the reverse may be cheaper. When a dealer borrows securities, he gives up other securities as collateral and pays the lender a borrowing fee, which typically equals ½ of 1% but may be more if many people want to short an issue at once. On a reverse the dealer obtains the securities shorted by buying them from an investor with an agreement to repurchase. In effect the dealer is extending a collateralized loan to the owner of these securities. The owner takes the loan because he needs cash or, more typically, because he can reinvest the loan proceeds at a higher rate, and the reverse thus becomes to him part of a profitable arbitrage.

Whether a dealer borrows securities or reverses them in, he must make an *investment*—in the first case in collateral, in the second case in a loan to the institution on the other side of the reverse. To figure which investment would yield more, he compares the rate he could earn on the collateral *minus* the borrowing fee with the reverse rate. For example, suppose a dealer has some short-dated paper yielding 9.25% he could use as collateral. If he did so, he would own that paper at 9.25% minus the 0.5% borrowing fee, that is, at an effective rate of 8.75%. If the reverse rate were 9%, he would do better on the reverse.

A dealer's overall cost on a short is (1) the interest that accrues on the securities shorted (rise in value in the case of a discount security) over the period the short is outstanding, *minus* (2) the yield on the offsetting investment he makes. If the reverse rate exceeds the net rate he could earn on collateral backing a borrowing, reversing will be the cheaper way to support his short.

A dealer who borrows securities to support a short can never know with certainty how long he can have those securities because borrowed securities can be called by the lender on a day's notice. If, alternatively, a dealer reverses in securities for a fixed period, he knows he will have the securities for that time. Thus a dealer who anticipates maintaining a short for some time may choose to cover through a reverse rather than a borrowing partly because a reverse offers him certainty of availability.

REPO AND REVERSE BOOK

A large dealer who is known to the Street can borrow more in the repo market and at better rates than can a small dealer or a corporate portfolio manager. Thus, a large dealer finds knocking at his doors not only customers who want to give him repo money but would-be borrowers who want to reverse out securities to him because that is the cheapest way they can borrow. In response to the latter demand, large dealers have taken to doing repos and reverses not just to suit their own needs but as a profit-making service to customers. In providing that service, the dealer takes in securities on one side at one rate and hangs them out on the other side at a slightly more favorable (lower) rate; or to put it the other way around, the dealer borrows money from his repo customers at one rate and lends it to his reverse customers at a slightly higher rate. In doing so, the dealer is acting like a bank, and dealers know this well. As one noted, "This shop *is* a bank. We have customers lining up every morning to give us money. Also we are in the business of finding people who will give us securities at a little better rate than we can push them out the repo door. So we are a bank taking out our little spread, acting—if you will—as a financial intermediary."

A dealer who seeks to profit by borrowing in the repo market and lending in the reverse market ends up in effect running a *book* in repo. And he can mismatch that book to increase his profit, that is, borrow short and lend long.

POSITIONING AND PROFITS

Ever since the Fed turned monetarist with a vengeance in October 1979, interest rates—short- and long-term—have displayed a degree of volatility far exceeding anything experienced in past years (Figure 5–1).

The recent volatility in interest rates has altered both the relative importance that many dealers assign to positioning as a source of profits and also the size and ways in which they are willing to position. Prior to the big run up in interest rates that began in 1979, it was hard to find a big dealer who did not claim to make his real profits from big position plays that were on the mark. There are still shops that operate this way: They might be satisfied to lose money for four months in small amounts and then to make it big in the fifth month.

Among dealer shops today, however, a more typical attitude is that the first step in building a successful, long-term operation is to establish a mix of dependable profit sources that can be counted on to be there in good markets and bad. For such a shop, position profits are icing on the cake, not the cake itself. Typical of this attitude is a bank dealer who noted, "Our focus has changed from one where we were always trying to make large amounts of money from guessing right the big swings in the market to one where we are trying to develop in our department a base of operations that makes money day in and day out. If you can build a business that makes money consistently, then you can afford to speculate with money that you have made as a department, as opposed to speculating with the bank's capital."

One base for earning consistent profits that is getting much attention from dealers these days is retail business. In describing operations, one dealer after another will stress the importance they place on building a solid retail business by providing good markets to retail. Noted one manager, "For us to make money, we had to focus on the real nuts and bolts of the business—service. We look at our business as one in which we provide our clients access to the market, investment advice, risk transfer, and execution."

No dealer can stand ready to make markets with customers without holding inventory and being willing to take securities into position on which customers want to bid. Shops that stress making markets to retail realize this and emphasize techniques to minimize the risks inherent in being a market maker. One technique is hedging. Hedging, which used to be a sometimes affair, now gets a lot of attention especially with the development in Chicago of large and liquid futures markets in governments and other securities. Using these markets, a dealer can transfer the risk generated by customer business back into the markets a lot faster than formerly, and agile shops do just that.

Dealers trying to make money regularly on retail business also strive to develop techniques to anticipate order flow. Said one dealer, "We put a lot of effort into developing relations with major buyers and sellers of securities so that they will give us the inquiry. When we look at the brokers' screens and there is a lot of activity in a sector, we want to know who is participating and what they are doing. This is a crucial part of our business. Now we *all* know what the Fed is doing. What is really tough is to keep on top of and anticipate what retail is or will be doing."

Arbitrage is another base that more dealers are seeking to develop as a source of consistent profits—not spectacular gains but 10 basis points here and 30 there earned by observing an anomaly in the market, taking a position against it, and then having the patience to wait until natural market forces eliminate that anomaly and permit the arbitrage to be unwound at a profit.

ARBITRAGES

Pure *arbitrage* means to buy at a low price in one market and simultaneously resell at a higher price in another market. Money market participants use the term *arbitrage* to refer not only to pure arbitrage, but to various transactions in which they seek to profit by *exploiting anomalies* either in the yield curve or in the pattern of rates established between different instruments. Typically, the anomaly is that the yield spread between two similar instruments is too wide or too narrow: one instrument is priced too generously relative to the other. To exploit such an anomaly, the arbitrager *shorts* the expensive instrument and goes *long* in its underpriced cousin.

If the arbitrager is successful, he will be able to unwind his arbitrage at a profit because the abnormal yield spread will have changed in one of several ways: (1) the security shorted will have fallen in price and risen in yield, (2) the security purchased will have risen in price and fallen in yield, or (3) a combination of the two will have occurred.

In the money market, yield spread arbitrages are often done (1) between identical instruments of similar maturity (one government is priced too generously relative to another of similar maturity) and (2) between different instruments of the same maturity (an agency issue is priced too generously relative to a government issue of the same maturity).

In a strictly defined yield spread arbitrage (the long and the short positions in similar maturities), the arbitrager exposes himself to *no mar-*

ket risk. If rates rise, the resulting loss on his long position will be offset by profits on his short position; if rates fall, the reverse will occur. Thus the arbitrager does not base his position on a prediction of the direction of market rates; he is concerned about a possible move up or down in interest rates only insofar as such a move might alter yield spreads in the money market.

A pure arbitrage involves *no* risk, since the sale and purchase are assumed to occur simultaneously or almost so. An arbitrage based on a yield spread anomaly involves no market risk, but it does involve risk of another sort: The arbitrager is speculating on a yield spread. If he bets that a given spread will narrow and it widens instead, he will lose money. Thus, even a strictly defined yield spread arbitrage offers no locked-in profit.

Most money market dealers, with the exception of commercial paper and muni note dealers, actively play the arbitrage game. They have input to a computer all sorts of information on historical yield spreads and have programmed the computer to identify anomalies in prevailing spreads as they feed into it data on current yields. Dealers used the resulting "helpful hints to the arbitrager" both to set up arbitrages themselves and to advise clients of arbitrage opportunities.

Generally in a dealer shop, arbitrage is done in an account that is separate from the *naked trading* account. Arbitrage and naked trading are distinctly different lines of business. The trader who seeks to profit from a naked position long or short is a specialist in one narrow sector of the market, and the positions he assumes are based on a prediction of interest rate trends and how they are likely to affect yields in his sector of the market. The arbitrager, in contrast, has to track yields in a number of market sectors, and if he engages in strictly defined yield-spread arbitrage, he is not much concerned with whether rates are likely to rise or fall.

Anomalies in yield spreads that offer opportunities for profitable arbitrage arise due to various temporary aberrations in market demand or supply. For example, if the Treasury brings a big 4-year note issue to market, it might trade for a time at a higher rate than surrounding issues because investors were loath to take the capital gains or losses they would have to in order to swap into the new issue. In this case, the cause of the out-of-line yield spread would be, for the time it persisted, that the new issue had not been fully distributed. Alternatively, an anomaly might be created by a particular issue being in extremely scarce supply.

Bull and *bear market arbitrages* are based on a view of where interest rates are going. A bull market arbitrager anticipates a fall in interest rates and a rise in securities prices. Thus, he might, for example, short 2-year Treasuries and go long in 10-year Treasuries on a one-for-one basis, hoping to profit, when rates fall, from the long coupon appreciating more than the short coupon. If, alternatively, the arbitrager were bearish, he would do the reverse: short long governments and buy short ones.

An arbitrage can also be set up to profit from an anticipated change in the slope of the yield curve. For example, an arbitrager who anticipated a flattening of the yield curve might buy notes in the 7-year area for high yield and short notes in the 2-year area not necessarily on a one-to-one basis. If the yield curve flattened with no change in average rate levels, the 7-year note would appreciate, the 2-year note would decline in price, and the arbitrage could be closed out at a profit.

Money market practitioners are wont to call any pair of long and short positions an arbitrage; as the maturities of the securities involved in the transaction get further and further apart, however, price risk increases, and at some point the "arbitrage" becomes in reality two separate speculative positions, a naked long and a naked short.

Money market arbitragers normally put on both sides of an arbitrage simultaneously, but they rarely take them off simultaneously. As one dealer noted, "The compulsion to *lift* a leg [unwind one side of an arbitrage before the other] is overwhelming. Hardly anyone ever has the discipline to unwind both sides simultaneously. Instead they will first unwind the side that makes the most sense against the market. If, for example, the trader thinks the market is going to do better, he will lift a leg by covering the short."

RELATIVE VALUE

We have said that a dealer will position securities if he is bullish. In choosing which securities to buy, he considers relative value.

Every rational investor is interested in risk, liquidity, and return. Specifically he wants maximum return, maximum liquidity, and minimum risk. When he shops for securities, however, he finds that the real world presents him with nothing but trade-offs; securities offering higher returns tend to be riskier or less liquid than securities offering lower returns. That is as true in the money market as elsewhere, and it is the reason money market dealers think first of *relative* value when they decide to position.

If the spread at which one security is trading relative to another more than adequately compensates for the fact that the high-yield security is riskier or less liquid than the low-yield security, the high-yield security has greater relative value and should be bought in preference to the low-yield security. If, alternatively, the spread is inadequate, then the low-yield security has greater relative value and should be bought in preference to the high-yield security. When dealers talk about relative value, they are really talking about the management of credit risk, market risk, and liquidity.

How relative value considerations affect a dealer's decisions as to what to position was put rather nicely by one dealer, "When we are all bullish, my bill trader, my CD trader, and my BA trader all want to take on stuff, and my reverse trader wants to take on 90-day collateral. At that point we have to sit down and get our heads together about relative value theory. Say we want to position $100 million in 6 months and under. Our most obvious options are CDs and bills. If, because of unusual supply conditions in the CD market, CDs are trading at a narrow spread—8 basis points—to bills, we are not going to buy CDs. Now picture a slightly different situation. Loans are not increasing at major New York banks, and additionally CDs are trading in the 6-month area 35 basis points off bills. We expect market rates to fall, and we also expect the spread between CDs and bills to narrow. In this situation CDs have greater relative value, so we will buy some. *But* putting all our eggs in one basket might be terribly unwise because we can only make an intelligent guess about supply in the CD market. Morgan might do a large Euro loan and fund the first 6 months with domestic CDs. If so, bing, we get knocked out of the water. We do not get the price action we expected out of the CD market even though the market as a whole rallies. Because that's possible, we might go 60% CDs and 40% bills—hedge our bets by diversifying. That way we will not miss the entire flip. I have seen it happen on numerous occasions, when we have done half bills and half CDs, that bills rallied 30 basis points—a nice flip we had anticipated—and CDs just sat there like a rock."

Relative value considerations arise not only in choices between different instruments but in choices between different maturity sectors of the same market. A dealer might ask whether he should position 6-month or 1-year bills. If the yield curve were unusually steep out to one year and the dealer expected it to flatten, then the year bill would have more relative value than the 6-month bill.

THE NEXT CHAPTER

In the next chapter, we turn to the *brokers* and other communications networks that enable each of the decentralized, over-the-counter sectors of the money market to operate in truth as a single, competitive, and efficient market.

Chapter 6

The market makers:
Brokers and other
information networks

FOR A MARKET OR SET OF MARKETS TO BE COMPETITIVE, a key requisite is that information on market prices be widely disseminated among market participants. In the money market, this condition is more than met; throughout the day, money market brokers and other vendors of information busily beam into trading rooms current money market prices as well as a wealth of other information: prices in related markets, latest values of economic indicators, money supply numbers, and so on.

THE BROKERS

A broker is a firm that brings buyers and sellers together for a commission. Unlike dealers, brokers by definition do not position. Brokers are everywhere in the money market. They are active in the *interdealer* markets in governments, agencies, CDs, bankers' acceptances, repo, and reverse, and in the *interbank* markets for Fed funds and Euro time deposits.[1]

---

[1] Some people call money market brokers *brokers' brokers* in order to distinguish them from stock brokers. This cumbersome bit of jargon is not needed in the money market, since no one there would confuse a broker of governments with Merrill Lynch, the parent of Merrill Lynch's GSI (Government Securities Inc.).

Volume and commissions

The volumes of funds and securities that are brokered each business day are staggering. Unfortunately, because statistics on brokered trades are not collected in most sectors of the market, it is impossible to put precise dollar figures on these amounts. Currently, almost all interdealer trades in governments and agencies are done through brokers.

Brokers could not survive without a huge volume of trades because the commissions they receive per $1 million of funds or securities brokered are small. In the bill market, brokerage on 90-day bills works out to $12.50 per $1 million; in the Fed funds market, on overnight trades it's only $0.50 per $1 million. In some sectors of the market (Fed funds and Euros) brokerage is paid by both the buyer and the seller; in others (governments and agencies), it is paid only by the dealer who initiates a trade by either hitting a bid or taking an offer quoted by the broker.

The service sold

Much of what a broker is selling his clients is a fast information service that tells the trader where the market is—what bids and offers are and how much they are good for. Speed of communication is thus crucial to a money market broker, and each has before him a board of direct phone lines through which he can contact every important trader he services by merely punching a button. Over those lines brokers constantly collect bids and offers throughout the day. They pass these on to other traders either by phone calls or more commonly over display screens, referred to throughout the industry as *CRTs*—short for cathode ray tubes.

In many sectors of the market (governments, Euro time deposits) the broker gives runs: bids and offers for a number of issues or maturities. In others (the market for overnight Fed funds), just one bid and offer are quoted. In some sectors of the market, bids and offers are good until withdrawn; in others they are understood to be good for only a few minutes.

The pace at which brokering is done in all sectors of the money market is hectic most of the time and frantic at certain crucial moments—in the Fed funds market on Wednesday afternoon when the banks settle with the Fed, in the government market on Thursday afternoon after the Fed announces money supply figures.

Brokerage operations vary a lot in size. Since shops dealing in CDs have a single CD trader, CDs can be brokered by just a couple of people sitting in a small room with a battery of direct phone lines. Brokering governments or Euros takes more personnel because there are many more traders to be covered and many more bids and offers to be quoted. Some brokerage outfits are large because they broker a number of different instruments. A Euro broker, for example, often brokers foreign exchange, and some firms that broker Fed funds also broker a potpourri of other instruments.

A broker has to be not only quick but *careful* because he is normally expected to substantiate any bid or offer he quotes. This means that, if he quotes a market inaccurately to a trader, he must either (1) pay that trader an amount equal to the difference between the price he quoted and the price at which the trade can actually be got off or (2) buy securities from or sell securities to that trader at the quoted price and then cover, typically at a loss, his resulting long or short position.

The ethics of brokering are strict in all sectors of the money market. A broker is not supposed to and never will give up the names of the dealers or banks that are bidding or offering through him. He simply quotes prices and size. However, in certain markets, once a bid is hit or an offer taken, names are given up. In the Fed funds market, for example, before the seller can agree to a trade, he must know to whom he is selling because he has to check that he has a line to the buyer and that that line is not full. Also, the buyer has to know who the seller is because the two institutions clear the transaction directly with each other over the Fed wire. In many brokered securities trades, in contrast, the seller never knows who the buyer is, and vice versa.

There are certain rules of ethics that brokers' clients are expected to observe. In particular, in markets in which names are given up, the customer is not supposed to then go around the broker and do the trade direct. Also, brokers feel it is unfair of a trader to use them as an information service and just do small trades through them. Traders who make a practice of this get to be known and ignored by brokers.

Usefulness of brokers

In recent years, brokerage has been introduced to almost every sector of the money market; and in those market sectors where it did exist, the use of brokers has increased dramatically. One reason is that in all sectors of the market the number of dealers has expanded sharply; as a result, it has become increasingly difficult for a trader to know where other traders are quoting the market and to rapidly disseminate his own bids and offers other than through the communications network provided by the brokers. In the government market, there are 40 primary dealers, and no bill trader can possibly keep in touch with his counterparts at other shops by talking directly to each of them.

Another reason brokers are used is anonymity. A big dealer may operate in such size that simply by bidding or offering, he will affect either market quotes or the size for which they are good. A trader who would be willing to buy $15 million in bills through a broker might, for example, be leery of buying the same amount at the same price from a big position house like Salomon Brothers for fear that Sali might have a lot more of these bills to sell.

A second reason anonymity is valued by traders is the "ego element." In the words of one dealer, "Anonymity is very important to those giant egos on Wall Street. When they make a bad trade, they just do not want the whole world to watch them unwind it at a loss."

Still another reason the brokers are used is because many traders literally hate each other, usually because of some underlying ethical issue, real or perceived. As one trader noted, "There are guys I would not deal with personally, but if it happens through a broker, well OK. Money is green whatever the source."

A final reason brokers are used, particularly in the government market, is that the brokers' screens provide an arena in which a trader can paint pictures and play other trading games.

Agent or principal?

All brokers of governments claim that, whenever they broker a trade in governments, they are acting *not as a principal, but as an agent for undisclosed principals.* Some dealers on the Street and certain lawyers take the position that any entity that acts in a transaction as an agent for an undisclosed third party assumes in that transaction—like it or not—the role of principal.

So long as all goes smoothly, whether a broker of governments or of other securities is acting as agent or principal has no impact on the outcome of the transaction. Where the legal position of the broker does matter is if the principal on one side of a brokered trade or other transaction—a reverse, a borrowing of securities or whatever—fails to fulfill its obligation under that transaction and, as a result, the principal on the other side stands to lose money. As noted, if the amount of the loss is small and the problem has perhaps arisen out of a misunderstanding, the broker will absorb the loss in the interests of customer relationships. But if the foul-up is not the broker's fault and if making the "injured party" whole would cost the broker hundreds of thousands of dollars or more, the broker is likely to go to court and have his lawyer argue, "Broker XYZ has *no* responsibility for any losses incurred by one party to a trade brokered by XYZ because the second party to that trade failed to live up to his side of the bargain. Broker XYZ was acting solely as *agent,* not principal."

Personnel

Brokering is much more than quoting rates. As brokers are wont to note, it's a highly professional business. The broker is often required to make split-second decisions about difficult questions. If a trader offers at a price and the broker has x bids at that price on his pad, with which buyer does he cross the trade? Technically, he attempts to decide who was there first, but the choice is often complicated by the fact that the offer is for one amount, the bids for others.

Also, in some sectors of the money market, a broker does more than quote rates. The buyer or seller may look to him for information on the tone of the market, and it's the broker's job to sense that tone and be able to communicate it—to say, for example, to a bidder, "The market's $5/16$–$3/8$, last trade at 5, but I think it could be worth $3/8$."

Being a broker is also part salesmanship, to get a buyer or seller who has done one trade to let the broker continue to work for him. This is especially the case in markets, such as those for Fed funds and Euros, where a dealer who does a trade is likely to have a lot more business to do in the same direction during the day. In one area of brokering, the reverse market, salesmanship is crucial. To get a bank or an S&L to reverse out securities, the broker almost always has to point out a profitable arbitrage and then sell the institution on doing that arbitrage.

Being a good broker requires a special mix of talents. Salesmanship is one. In addition, a broker must be able to listen with one ear on the phone and keep the other tuned to bids and offers coming in around him, to maintain a feel for his own market and for other related markets as well. A good broker also must be able to think on his feet and often use his own personality to put trades together. As one broker noted, "Brightness is not enough; anyone can quote a market."

Many brokers are ex-traders, people who have the advantage when they come to brokering of knowing a market and how traders in it operate. One reason traders become brokers is the pressure under which traders operate. Another is their own inability to do what many good traders do, forget their position when they go home. Said one successful broker, "Trading is a problem. You track the things you think might impact the market and then buy. All too often the unexpected—war in the Middle East—happens and you end up being right for the wrong reason, or vice versa. Once as a trader, I was down three-quarters of a million. I made 2 million the next month, but accepting the fact that I had done something stupid at one point in time was too much. It's part of the reason I became a broker."

Consolidation of brokers

In recent years there has been a strong tendency for brokers to merge. The reasons are various. For a big broker, a marriage that adds to capital can look extremely attractive. A second reason for broker mergers is that a shop that handles a wide menu of securities has a better chance of getting its foot into a dealer's door and, once there, can better service the dealer's needs. Institutions that reverse out securities often do so, for example, as part of an arbitrage in which they invest in another security; a broker that offers one-stop shopping can put together the whole arbitrage package.

In Euro and foreign exchange brokering, both cross-market and transatlantic mergers made sense. The foreign exchange and Euromarkets could not be separated, and no broker could provide an international service without having an office or tie of some sort in at least both New York and London.

The advent of Liberty

The major brokers of governments, of which there are six or seven, show their quotes to and do business with only the big primary dealers recognized by the Federal Reserve Bank of New York. These brokers form what economists would call an oligopoly. It's possible to enter their business, but it's expensive and tough enough to discourage most people from trying. All this means that, until recently, brokers of governments were nicely insulated from price competition.

Over the last decade, several developments occurred that tended to increase brokers' profits. First, there were technological changes that lowered the cost of brokering. Second, huge increases occurred in the average size and number of brokered interdealer trades; brokers could, moreover, accommodate this extra business at limited additional cost to themselves. Despite these developments, no broker cut his rates; interbroker price competition was nil. The upshot was that brokers earned increasingly high profits, profits that dealers finally came to regard as absurd. A dealer's definition of what constituted an absurd level of brokers' profits was simple: at the old brokerage rates ($78 per million on a trade of government bonds), a big broker who assumed *no risk* was earning, on an $80 billion–volume day, more profit than was the average dealer who—to make any money—had to assume *a great deal of risk*.

To introduce some price competition to the world of government brokering, in 1986 Salomon Brothers, together with a group of 30 other dealers, formed a new government bond broker, Liberty Brokerage, Inc. The advent of Liberty caused brokerage rates on government notes and bonds to fall immediately by 50%, and then yet more.

Forcing a cut in brokerage rates was not the sole objective of the dealers who formed Liberty. Another was to create the possibility for more netting of interdealer trades at the broker level, a change that would decrease the volume of trades that dealers must clear through their clearing banks. Doing the latter, not an easy task, would offer dealers two advantages: it would cut their normal operating costs, and it would decrease the opportunities for the costly, occasional mistakes that inevitably creep into any clearing operation.

Who may tune in

Most brokers of governments will accept as clients only *primary dealers* (dealers with whom the Fed does business) and *"aspiring" dealers* (dealers who report to the Fed and are seeking primary-dealer status).[2] The exception is Cantor Fitzgerald, who has opened its screens to other dealers and major investors who meet its credit standards. Dealers denied access to the market that the activities of the principal brokers of governments and the primary dealers create have criticized this "inside market" as monopolistic; and one nonprimary dealer, Lazard Freres & Co., is suing to end what it terms the "private club approach" to the dissemination of bond price information. The U.S. General Accounting Office, in consultation with the Fed, the Treasury, and the SEC, is also looking into the question of whether access to brokers' electronic screens should be widened.

Naturally, the primary dealers oppose the giving by the brokers of wider access to their screens. In doing so, the primary dealers argue that widening access to the brokers' screens would reduce liquidity in the government market.

COMMUNICATIONS

In a discussion of the makers of the money market, ignoring the phone company, Telexes, CRTs, computers, and other communications facilities would be a serious omission. Without Ma Bell and her foreign counterparts, the money market would be utterly different. That the money

---

[2] In May 1987, there were 40 primary dealers, including several Japanese dealers, and 13 aspiring dealers.

market is a single market that closely approaches the economist's assumption of perfect information is currently due in no small part to the fact that New York brokers and traders are one push of a direct-phone-line button away from the B of A and often only a four-digit extension from London, Singapore, and other distant spots. All this is extremely expensive. Banks spent well over half a billion dollars on phone bills; and the nonbank dealers and brokers spend huge amounts in addition to that. To cut costs, the banking industry has considered setting up a private interbank phone network, which would be the most ambitious private phone network in the country.

The phone bill is one reason for the concentration of the money market in New York. The brokers in particular have to be there to minimize communications costs. It is cheaper to be in New York with one direct phone line to the B of A than to be in San Francisco with 30 direct lines to New York.

Phones, while ubiquitous, are not enough. Giving and receiving quotes over the phone takes more time than money market participants have; thus the growing role of CRTs.

Years ago, the only way money market participants could get current quotes was by calling brokers and dealers. Moreover, to get a range of quotes they had to make several calls because no quote system covered the whole market. In 1968, a new organization, *Telerate,* began to remedy this situation by quoting commercial paper rates on a two-page, CRT display system; it then had 50 subscribers. From this modest start, the system was quickly expanded because people wanted more information.

Today, several hundred pages of information on credit market quotes and statistics are available to Telerate subscribers; the subscriber gets the page he wants by pressing a series of numbered buttons. Information on current quotes, offerings, and bids are inputted into the system through computers around the country, and the system is dynamically updated; that is, if GMAC changes its posted rate while a viewer is looking at the commercial paper quotes, the quotes change as GMAC inputs its new rates into the system. A wide range of institutions now use Telerate; its advent has not only eliminated a lot of phone calls but vastly improved communications within the money market. On the international scene, there is a similar *Reuters* system that flashes information on the Euromarket, the foreign exchange market, and other related markets into foreign countries and the United States. Since the money market is international in scope, it was to be expected that both Telerate and Reuters invaded each others' turf both geographically and in terms of information provided.

Many brokers in the government and other markets have also replaced endless phone quotes with CRTs that they have placed before the traders at dealer shops. Today every trading room is literally strewn with CRTs.

Deathknell of the dumb terminal?

When Telerate and other quote systems first hit money market trading rooms with their CRTs, the latter were regarded as incredibly useful, *high-tech* gadgets—a paradigm of the marvels that modern technology could produce. Alas, no love affair is forever.

With the advent of the IBM PC in 1981, the CRTs of information vendors began to be described disparagingly as "dumb" terminals. A dumb terminal gives you quotes but that's it; to massage a quote, you must copy it down from your CRT. From there on in, you're on your own.

The power and the cheapness of the IBM PC, combined with the fact that most young people today feel as comfortable with a computer as secretaries of yore felt with a typewriter, created a need and niche for a new sort of information system: one that fed quotes into a smart terminal. With such a system, for a tidy annual fee, the customer gets an IBM PC, current quotes, access to a database of past quotes, and an analytic software package all in one fell swoop.

For investors, traders, and arbitragers, this innovation offers the opportunity to do a lot of analysis that's highly useful, especially if doing it doesn't require much time and effort. For example, if a user sees an instrument whose price looks attractive, he can, using his smart terminal, calculate the instrument's yield on any of a variety of bases, its duration, its past spread to some other instrument. The possibilities are endless. The computer's response time is, of course, rapid. This is a crucial advantage to a user because markets move so fast today that a trader or investor can't wait long for analysis, lest he find that the quote that interested him is history before he's set to act.

Smart terminals have even permitted some traders to change their lifestyles outside of business hours. For example, if a user likes to look at technical charts, he can pick the technical indicators that he wants to follow and then instruct, as often as he wants, his computer to update and to print these indicators. Said one trader, "I live in Jersey but used to sleep weeknights in New York, so I'd have time to do my charts. Now, a machine does them for me, and I see my wife seven nights a week." That's one guy who doesn't decry the onward march of technology.

Our remarks on smart terminals are not meant to indicate that the days of dumb terminals are necessarily numbered. Users of smart terminals often like to have an old, read-only Telerate sitting around for various reasons—they need other information it provides or they feel that, when markets move fast, Telerate's quotes stay more current.

The black box

While impressive, the various present CRT systems are not the ultimate state of the art. In the view of some participants, the money market is on the threshold of a communications revolution. One London dealer noted, "We are working on a system by which we will show our offerings and rates on a CRT. Say Ford in Dearborn, Michigan, hits our code. They will be able to type on a machine, like a Telex, a message that will come up on our CRT in London: 'Want to buy your 5 million Chases, Oct. 17th, bid you 7/8.' We are offering at 13/16 and decide to hit their bid. So we type in, 'OK, done.' Then they type in, 'Deliver to Morgan,' and the confirmations come out of the machine. We are going to put on the screen actual offerings; Cantor Fitzgerald already does that in governments, but they do not trade off the machine."

Said another dealer, envisioning much the same sort of development, "The firms like us without branch offices will introduce machines to the world to undercut the branch office franchisees of the Merrills and the Salis. It is clear that for firms like us that lack branch offices, this is the cost-effective way to compete. We will trade off those machines; the *black box* is coming, and when it does, the market will go central marketplace."

THE NEXT CHAPTER

In the next chapter, we begin the heart of this book's story about the repo and reverse markets. Chapter 7 describes the origins of the repo market.

Part two

The repo and reverse markets

Chapter 7

Origins of the repo market

IN THIS CHAPTER, WE DESCRIBE BRIEFLY the origins of the repo market.

EARLY USE OF REPO BY THE FED[1]

The beginnings of repo as a modern money market instrument can be traced to the birth of the Federal Reserve System[2] (established by act of Congress in 1913) and to the inception of the bankers' acceptance (BA) market at the close of World War I.

Repos against BAs and Treasuries

Before the formation of the Federal Reserve System, BAs created to finance the export of U.S. commodities, such as cotton, were discounted

---

[1] This section and later sections that deal with the revival of the repo market post–World War II are based partly on information obtained from an interesting and well-researched thesis by Ralph Peters. At the time he wrote his thesis, Peters, now chairman of Discount Corporation of New York, had been working for some time at Discount; consequently, parts of his thesis are based on first-hand knowledge. See Ralph F. Peters, "The Repurchase Agreement: Its Position in Today's Market" (Thesis, Stonier School of Banking, 1962).

[2] For a detailed description of how the Fed operates, see Marcia Stigum, *The Money Market,* Revised Edition (Homewood, Ill.: Dow Jones-Irwin, 1983), chap. 8.

(sold at a discount to obtain immediate cash) in the London market. Users of domestic BA financing thought that their paper would be discounted at a lower rate if a domestic market in BAs were developed. Thus, one of the three paramount objectives of the Federal Reserve System, as outlined in the Federal Reserve Act, was to foster the development of a domestic BA market. Once the Fed was formed, it encouraged the creation of new dealers to trade BAs; also, some existing dealers in U.S. government securities began to trade BAs. The Fed had hoped that the New York clearing banks would provide, at favorable rates, the credit needed by BA dealers to support their positions. These banks did not do so, however, and the Fed immediately found it necessary to provide BA dealers with supplementary financing. The Fed provided such financing by offering in 1918 to do with dealers, at a publicly quoted rate of discount, "resale agreements" (repos) against BAs.

Initially, to create bank reserves, the Fed bought short-term, loan notes from banks. This practice created a situation in which the Fed, to collect its money, had, as each note it bought matured, to collect money from a private borrower. To get out of the private-loan-collection business, the Fed, in the early 1920s, switched from buying notes outright to discounting notes at the discount window. Banks borrow at the window at their volition, not the Fed's. Consequently, this policy change left the Fed in need of a tool for making volitional short-term adjustments in bank reserves. The Fed could have attempted to effect such changes by varying its outright purchases of government securities. However, it feared that frequent outright buys and sells of governments by it would churn the market for governments. Consequently, the Fed began, in 1923, to use short-term repos against governments as a tool for altering bank reserves. By 1929, the Fed had on its books $23 million of repos against governments (see column 3, Table 7–1).

Repo agreements

In the early repo market, the mechanics of putting on repos were quite simple. The method first used, and the one still used by the Federal Reserve Bank of New York (FRBNY), was for the two parties to exchange a letter that spelled out the terms of the simultaneous sale and repurchase (Figure 7–1).[3] These terms include the following:

1. The names of both parties.
2. A description of the asset traded.
3. The pricing of the asset.

---

[3] The Federal Reserve Bank of New York is one of 12 district Federal Reserve banks.

FIGURE 7–1
Specimen contract letters on repurchase agreement

REPURCHASE AGREEMENT

_____
(date)

Federal Reserve Bank of New York,
        New York 45, N. Y.

Gentlemen:

        We hand you herewith United States Government securities (with
all unmatured coupons, if any, attached), having a total par value of
$_____, listed below, which we have today sold to you for
$_____. In consideration of the purchase by you of such secu-
rities, we hereby agree to repurchase them from you at any time at your
or our option on or before_____, at the same price plus
interest thereon at the rate of ___% per annum for the number of days
that said securities are held by you. It is understood that, if any of
the attached coupons mature before we repurchase the securities as provided above, you will, upon notice by us, deliver such coupons to us or
collect them for our account. Our obligations hereunder are secured by
and subject to the terms and conditions of our general collateral agreement with you.

                         Very truly yours,

                         _____
                               (Name of dealer)

                    By_____
                               (Signature)

                         _____
                               (Title)

          SCHEDULE OF SECURITIES COVERED BY ABOVE AGREEMENT

Description of Issue	Maturity	Amount (Par Value)

Source: Federal Reserve Bank of New York.

TABLE 7-1

Fed portfolio and other factors supplying bank reserves*

Millions of dollars

	Factors supplying reserve funds *										
	Federal Reserve Bank credit outstanding									Spe-cial draw-ing rights certif-icate ac-count	Trea-sury cur-rency out-stand-ing
Period	U.S. Treasury and federal agency securities			Loans	Float	All other	Other Federal Reserve assets	Total	Gold stock		
	Total	Bought out-right	Held under repur-chase agree-ment								
1918	239	239	0	1,766	199	294	0	2,498	2,873	. . .	1,795
1919	300	300	0	2,215	201	575	0	3,292	2,707	. . .	1,707
1920	287	287	0	2,687	119	262	0	3,355	2,639	. . .	1,709
1921	234	234	0	1,144	40	146	0	1,563	3,373	. . .	1,842
1922	436	436	0	618	78	273	0	1,405	3,642	. . .	1,958
1923	134	80	54	723	27	355	0	1,238	3,957	. . .	2,009
1924	540	536	4	320	52	390	0	1,302	4,212	. . .	2,025
1925	375	367	8	643	63	378	0	1,459	4,112	. . .	1,977
1926	315	312	3	637	45	384	0	1,381	4,205	. . .	1,991
1927	617	560	57	582	63	393	0	1,655	4,092	. . .	2,006
1928	228	197	31	1,056	24	500	0	1,809	3,854	. . .	2,012
1929	511	488	23	632	34	405	0	1,583	3,997	. . .	2,022
1930	739	686	43	251	21	372	0	1,373	4,306	. . .	2,027
1931	817	775	42	638	20	378	0	1,853	4,173	. . .	2,035
1932	1,855	1,851	4	235	14	41	0	2,145	4,226	. . .	2,204
1933	2,437	2,435	2	98	15	137	0	2,688	4,036	. . .	2,303
1934	2,430	2,430	0	7	5	21	0	2,463	8,238	. . .	2,511
1935	2,431	2,430	1	5	12	38	0	2,486	10,125	. . .	2,476
1936	2,430	2,430	0	3	39	28	0	2,500	11,258	. . .	2,532
1937	2,564	2,564	0	10	19	19	0	2,612	12,760	. . .	2,637
1938	2,564	2,564	0	4	17	16	0	2,601	14,512	. . .	2,798
1939	2,484	2,484	0	7	91	11	0	2,593	17,644	. . .	2,963
1940	2,184	2,184	0	3	80	8	0	2,274	21,995	. . .	3,087
1941	2,254	2,254	0	3	94	10	0	2,361	22,737	. . .	3,247
1942	6,189	6,189	0	6	471	14	0	6,679	22,726	. . .	3,648
1943	11,543	11,543	0	5	681	10	0	12,239	21,938	. . .	4,094
1944	18,846	18,846	0	80	815	4	0	19,745	20,619	. . .	4,131
1945	24,252	24,262	0	249	578	2	0	15,091	20,065	. . .	4,339
1946	23,350	23,350	0	163	580	1	0	24,093	20,529	. . .	4,562
1947	22,559	22,559	0	85	535	1	0	23,181	22,754	. . .	4,562
1948	23,333	23,333	0	223	541	1	0	24,097	24,244	. . .	4,589
1949	18,885	18,885	0	78	534	2	0	19,499	24,427	. . .	4,598
1950	20,778	20,725	53	67	1,368	3	0	22,216	22,706	. . .	4,636
1951	23,801	23,605	196	19	1,184	5	0	25,009	22,695	. . .	4,709
1952	24,697	24,034	663	156	967	4	0	25,825	23,187	. . .	4,812
1953	25,916	25,318	598	28	935	2	0	26,880	22,030	. . .	4,894
1954	24,932	24,888	44	143	808	1	0	25,885	21,713	. . .	4,985
1955	24,785	24,391	394	108	1,585	29	0	26,507	21,690	. . .	5,008
1956	24,915	24,610	305	50	1,665	70	0	26,699	21,949	. . .	5,066
1957	24,238	23,719	519	55	1,424	66	0	25,784	22,781	. . .	5,146
1958	26,347	26,252	95	64	1,296	49	0	27,755	20,534	. . .	5,234
1959	26,648	26,607	41	458	1,590	75	0	28,771	19,456	. . .	5,311
1960	27,384	26,984	400	33	1,847	74	0	29,338	17,767	. . .	5,398
1961	28,881	30,478	159	130	2,300	51	0	31,362	16,889	. . .	5,585
1962	30,820	28,722	342	38	2,903	110	0	33,871	15,978	. . .	5,567
1963	33,593	33,582	11	63	2,600	162	0	36,418	15,513	. . .	5,578
1964	37,044	36,506	538	186	2,606	94	0	39,930	15,388	. . .	5,405

TABLE 7–1 (*concluded*)

Millions of dollars

	Factors supplying reserve funds									Spe-cial draw-ing rights certif-icate ac-count	Trea-sury cur-rency out-stand-ing
	Federal Reserve Bank credit outstanding										
	U.S. Treasury and federal agency securities						Other Federal Reserve assets	Total	Gold stock		
Period	Total	Bought out-right	Held under repur-chase agree-ment	Loans	Float	All other					
1965	40,768	40,478	290	137	2,248	187	0	43,340	13,733	. . .	5,575
1966	44,316	43,655	661	173	2,495	193	0	47,177	13,159	. . .	6,317
1967	49,150	48,980	170	141	2,576	164	0	52,031	11,982	. . .	6,784
1968	52,937	52,937	0	186	3,443	58	0	56,624	10,367	. . .	6,795
1969	57,154	57,154	0	183	3,440	64	2,743	64,584	10,367	. . .	6,852
1970	62,142	62,142	0	335	4,261	57	1,123	67,918	10,732	400	7,147
1971	70,804	69,481	1,323	39	4,343	261	1,068	76,515	10,132	400	7,710
1972	71,230	71,119	111	1,981	3,974	106	1,260	78,551	10,410	400	8,313
1973	80,495	80,395	100	1,258	3,099	68	1,152	86,072	11,567	400	8,716
1974	85,714	84,760	954	299	2,001	999	3,195	92,208	11,652	400	9,253
1975	94,124	92,789	1,335	211	3,688	1,126	3,312	102,461	11,599	500	10,218
1976	104,093	100,062	4,031	25	2,601	991	3,182	110,892	11,598	1,200	10,810
1977	111,274	108,922	2,352	265	3,810	954	2,442	118,745	11,718	1,250	11,331
1978	118,591	117,374	1,217	1,174	6,432	587	4,543	131,327	11,671	1,300	11,831
1979	126,167	124,507	1,660	1,454	6,767	704	5,613	140,705	11,172	1,800	13,083
1980	130,592	128,038	2,554	1,809	4,467	776	8,739	146,383	11,160	2,518	13,427
1981	140,348	136,863	3,485	1,601	1,762	195	9,230	153,136	11,151	3,318	13,687
1982	148,837	144,544	4,293	717	2,735	1,480	9,890	63,659	11,148	4,618	13,786
1983	160,795	159,203	1,592	918	1,605	418	8,728	172,464	11,121	4,618	15,732
1984	169,627	167,612	2,015	3,577	833	0	12,347	186,384	11,096	4,618	16,418
1985	191,248	186,025	5,223	3,060	988	0	15,302	210,598	11,090	4,718	17,075
1986	221,459	205,454	16,005	1,565	1,261	0	17,475	241,760	11,084	5,018	17,567

* Reserve funds are bank reserves.
Source: 73rd Annual Report, 1986, Board of Governors of the Federal Reserve System.

4. The rate of interest to be paid by the buyer to the seller upon repurchase of the asset.
5. The length of the agreement: demand (open) basis or for a specific term (from start date X to end date Y).
6. The place of delivery.

A sample repo agreement is given in Figure 7–1. This letter, which is addressed to the Federal Reserve Bank of New York (FRBNY) and has been used for decades by the FRBNY, confirms a repo between a dealer and the Fed in which the Fed lends to the dealer money against collateral *on a demand basis* for some maximum number of days. Note that the agreement provides for the pass-through of coupon interest. Demand repos, which may be terminated at any time by either party, are today referred to as "open repos."

Term of repos done

During the 1920s, the Fed did mostly short-term (five days on average) repos against both BAs and government collateral.

Pricing and margin

In 1921, the Fed stated that it would ask for margin on its repo lendings equal to 1% of the face amount of the underlying collateral. In practice, the Fed priced securities provided to it as repo collateral an average of half a point below their market value if they were selling below par; it priced the securities at par, if they were selling at or above par. From the inception of the repo market, the need for adequate margin was officially recognized. Also, the Fed followed another banking maxim—"know thy customer"; it granted repos only to dealers it had approved.

The repo rate

The rate at which the Fed offered to do repos against BAs was related to, but not always equal to, its discount rate; at that time, this rate was quoted on a *discount basis,* as opposed to a *simple-interest (add-on) basis.*[4] Depending on the structure of short-term rates and the needs of BA dealers for financing, the Fed offered at times to do dealer repos against BAs at a rate slightly above the dealer bid rate for 90-day BAs (a rate also quoted on a discount basis).

Legality of repos

The Federal Reserve Act is mute on the question of whether it is permissible for the Fed to use repos to extend credit to nonmember institutions. During congressional hearings in 1925, the Fed stated that it felt that the legality of its doing so was established under Sections 4 and 14 of the Federal Reserve Act, which deal with loans to nonmember banks.

References made during this period in Federal Reserve Board annual reports to "authority" to do repo refer to the internal authority granted by

---

[4] If a lender quotes a *discount rate* of 5%, this means that, if he makes a one-year loan of $100, he will give the borrower only $95 but will require the latter to pay him, at the end of one year, the full $100. If a lender quotes a *simple-interest, add on rate* of 5%, this means that, if he makes a one-year loan of $100, he will lend the borrower the full $100 and will require the latter to pay him, at the end of one year, $100 of principal *plus* $5 of interest.

the Board to Reserve Banks or to the Federal Open Market Committee (FOMC) to do repo.[5]

Private lenders in the repo market

During the 1920s, corporations, seeking to earn a return on idle funds, bought short-term Treasuries. To secure needed maturities, corporations also invested as much or more funds in repos with dealers, who needed, sometimes more than others, to supplement the ongoing credit the Fed provided them by doing repos.

USE OF REPOS DURING THE 1930s

During the 1930s, the Fed and private lenders continued to do repos with dealers. However, demand for such credit was limited because the decline in world trade reduced substantially the volume of BAs outstanding. Also, domestic public debt had not yet begun the explosive growth later caused by World War II. Consequently, demands for short-term credit were far less than those that developed subsequently, and Fed repos tailed off (Table 7–1).

THE REPO AND REVERSE MARKETS: POST–WORLD WAR II

In the decades following World War II, the repo market was revived. Repo came to be relied on extensively by the Fed to implement open market operations, by private parties to borrow. Repo proved, in the hands of securities dealers, to be an especially versatile tool: dealers used repo to borrow vast sums; they used the flip side of the trade, a reverse, to cover their short positions. And—by establishing huge matched books of repos and reverses—dealers *(a)* entered the profitable business of credit intermediation and *(b)* turned collateral into a new trading vehicle for making considered, often highly profitable, bets on trends in short-term interest rates.

THE NEXT CHAPTER

The next chapter describes in detail how the Fed has, since the end of World War II, gradually incorporated repos and reverses into the open market operations it undertakes to achieve its policy goals.

---

[5] The Fed's FOMC is described in Figure 8–1.

Chapter 8

Fed use of repos and reverses post–World War II

ONLY AFTER WORLD WAR II did Fed use of repos achieve prominence not only as a mechanism for extending credit, but as a means of implementing monetary policy.

THE PERIOD OF PEGGED RATES

To finance fighting World War II, the U.S. Treasury had to sell what then seemed like a vast amount of debt. Accordingly, the Fed adopted in April 1942 an official rate, 3⁄8%, at which it stood ready to buy T bills. By pegging the bill rate, the Fed prevented the Treasury's large sales of new debt from driving up interest rates. The Fed ceased to peg bill rates in July 1947.

During wartime, the Fed did no repos against governments, because the Fed's willingness to buy any bills offered to it at a pegged rate and its commitment to maintain a fixed pattern of rates on government coupons created an environment in which banks could create, at their own volition, any amount of reserves they wanted by selling governments to the Fed (columns 2 and 3 of Table 7–1, pp. 84–85).

Revival of Fed use of repos

Repos by the Fed began to grow in importance after the 1951 Treasury-Fed *accord* (column 2 of Table 7–1). That accord signaled the end of a period during which the Fed had, in response to pressure from the Treasury, pegged yields on government bonds at artificially low levels. To declare and protect its right to let yields on government bonds fluctuate freely and to pursue an independent monetary policy, the Fed announced at the time of the accord that henceforth it would buy "bills only."

In this initial period of the revival of Fed use of repo, the Fed was permitted to do repos only against short-term Treasuries and only for a maximum of 15 days. The rate at which the Fed first did repos was the discount rate; later, the Fed was given leeway to do repos at a rate as low as the current issuing rate on 3-month bills. The Fed was to use the repo mechanism only to make *temporary* adjustments in bank reserves.

FED USE OF REPOS AND REVERSES TODAY

From insignificant beginnings, repos and reverses have grown in the post–World War II period, to be a key part of Fed open market operations. We describe below their current use by the Fed.

The tools of open market operations

Whenever it buys securities or does repos, the Fed adds to bank reserves and that is so regardless of who its counterparty in the trade is. Conversely, whenever the Fed sells securities or does reverses, it drains bank reserves.

Loans extended by the Fed at the discount window also add to bank reserves. However, such loans are made at the volition of the banks, not the Fed. Thus, the Fed lacks close control over day-to-day changes in loans at the discount window. The Fed does, however, impose an upper limit on the amount banks may borrow there. It does so by strongly stating that banks are to view borrowing at the discount window as a privilege, one they should use only sparingly and temporarily.

The New York open market desk

The Federal Open Market Committee (FOMC) in Washington sets, at its eight meetings per year, the targets to be pursued by the Fed in its open market policy. Money supply is to grow within a specified percentage band; or in the old days, Fed funds were to trade at such and such a rate.[1] The FOMC's directive is today carried out by the open market desk of the New York Fed.

Over time, the Fed has accumulated a portfolio of over $205 billion of government and federal agency securities through outright purchases of securities designed to create permanent bank reserves. The Fed at the end of 1986 also had on its books $16 billion of repos it had done to create temporary bank reserves (Table 8–1, pp. 92–93).

Authorization for open market operations

What actions the desk may take to effect the FOMC's directive to it are determined by the Federal Reserve Act and by the Fed's interpretation of it. Simply put, the Federal Reserve Act authorizes the Fed to buy and sell securities and to lend against collateral at the discount window. The act does not authorize the Fed to make other sorts of collateralized loans to banks and dealers, nor does it authorize the Fed to borrow on a collateralized basis either from banks or from nonbank dealers. The FOMC directs the open market desk of the FRBNY to buy and sell securities for the System's account under what it calls the "authorization for domestic open market operations." This authorization is published in "The Annual Report of the Board of Governors of the Federal Reserve System" at the end of the March directive given by the FOMC to the desk (see Figure 8–1 for partial authorization).

Since the Fed is not authorized to borrow or lend, except at the discount window, the Fed consistently takes the position that, when the desk does repos, it is doing first a purchase and then a sale of a security, and that, when the desk does a reverse, it is doing first a sale and then a purchase of a security. The Fed is adamant about this. To gain authority to do collateralized lending and borrowing, the Fed would have to ask Congress to amend the Federal Reserve Act.

Influencing bank reserves

In implementing the FOMC's directive, the desk has two jobs. First, as the economy grows over time, a secular increase in bank reserves is required to prevent upward pressure on interest rates and to permit adequate growth of money supply. One job of the desk is thus to add

---

[1] This statement reflects the Street's oversimplified interpretation of what the Fed's binding guidelines currently are. In fact, the Fed always couches its guidelines in terms of a number of economic variables, which are subject to change over time.

TABLE 8–1
Fed balance sheet, December 31, 1986

1. Detailed Statement of Condition of All Federal Reserve Banks Combined, December 31, 1986[1]

Thousands of dollars

ASSETS

Gold certificate account			**11,083,947**
Special drawing rights certificate account			**5,018,000**
Coin			**485,827**
Loans and securities			
Loans to depository institutions		**1,564,797**	
Federal agency obligations			
Bought outright		**7,829,312**	
Held under repurchase agreement		**2,313,535**	
U.S. Treasury securities			
Bought outright			
Bills	103,774,920		
Notes	68,125,600		
Bonds	25,723,814		
Total bought outright		197,624,334	
Held under repurchase agreement		13,691,465	
Total securities		**211,315,799**	
Total loans and securities			**223,023,443**
Items in process of collection			
Transit items		8,063,084	
Other items in process of collection		2,211,741	
Total items in process of collection			**10,274,825**
Bank premises			
Land		105,638	
Buildings (including vaults)	452,363		
Building machinery and equipment	157,448		
Construction account	127,236		
Total bank premises		737,047	
Less depreciation allowance		182,516	554,531
Bank premises, net			**660,169**
Other assets			
Furniture and equipment		515,885	
Less depreciation		249,460	
Total furniture and equipment, net		266,425	
Denominated in foreign currencies[2]		9,474,797	
Interest accrued		2,601,442	
Premium on securities		1,206,675	
Due from Federal Deposit Insurance Corporation		2,904,299	
Overdrafts		190,096	
Prepaid expenses		26,159	
Suspense account		17,483	
Real estate acquired for banking-house purposes		6,368	
Other		126,488	
Total other assets			**16,820,232**
Total assets			**267,366,443**

Source: 73rd Annual Report of the Board of Governors of the Federal Reserve System, 1986.

TABLE 8–1   (*concluded*)

LIABILITIES

Federal Reserve notes
Outstanding (issued to Federal Reserve Banks) 231.612.805
Less held by Federal Reserve Banks 36,252,042

    Total Federal Reserve notes, net **195,360,763**

Deposits
Depository institutions **48,107,361**
U.S. Treasury, general account **7,587,759**
Foreign, official accounts **286,709**

Other deposits
Officers' and certified checks 54.673
International organizations 198,757
Other[3] 669,890

    Total other deposits **923,320**
Deferred credit items **9,012,278**

Other liabilities
Discount on securities 2.247.837
Sundry items payable 49.437
Suspense account 30.228
All other 14,121

    Total other liabilities **2,341,623**

    Total liabilities **263,619,813**

CAPITAL ACCOUNTS

Capital paid in **1,873,315**
Surplus **1,873,315**
Other capital accounts[4] **0**

    Total liabilities and capital accounts **267,366,443**

1. Amounts in boldface type indicate items in the Board's weekly statement of condition of the Federal Reserve Banks.
2. Of this amount $3,028.1 million was invested in securities issued by foreign governments, and the balance was invested with foreign central banks and the Bank for International Settlements.

3. In closing out the other capital accounts at year-end, the Reserve Bank earnings that are payable to the Treasury are included in this account pending payment.
4. During the year, includes undistributed net income, which is closed out on Dec. 31; see table 8.

FIGURE 8–1
Federal Reserve Authorization for Open Market Operations

**Authorization for Domestic
Open Market Operations**

In Effect January 1, 1986

1. The Federal Open Market Committee authorizes and directs the Federal Reserve Bank of New York, to the extent necessary to carry out the most recent domestic policy directive adopted at a meeting of the Committee:
   (a) To buy or sell U.S. Government securities, including securities of the Federal Financing Bank, and securities that are direct obligations of, or fully guaranteed as to principal and interest by, any agency of the United States in the open market, from or to securities dealers and foreign and international accounts maintained at the Federal Reserve Bank of New York, on a cash, regular, or deferred delivery basis, for the System Open Market Account at market prices, and, for such Account, to exchange maturing U.S. Government and Federal agency securities with the Treasury or the individual agencies or to allow them to mature without replacement; provided that the aggregate amount of U.S. Government and Federal agency securities held in such Account (including forward commitments) at the close of business on the day of a meeting of the Committee at which action is taken with respect to a domestic policy directive shall not be increased or decreased by more than $6.0 billion during the period commencing with the opening of business on the day following such meeting and ending with the close of business on the day of the next such meeting;
   (b) When appropriate, to buy or sell in the open market, from or to acceptance dealers and foreign accounts maintained at the Federal Reserve Bank of New York, on a cash, regular, or deferred delivery basis, for the account of the Federal Reserve Bank of New York at market discount rates, prime bankers acceptances with maturities of up to nine months at the time of acceptance that (1) arise out of the current shipment of goods between countries or within the United States, or (2) arise out of the storage within the United States of goods under contract of sale or expected to move into the channels of trade within a reasonable time and that are secured throughout their life by a warehouse receipt or similar document conveying title to the underlying goods; provided that the aggregate amount of bankers acceptances held at any one time shall not exceed $100 million;
   (c) To buy U.S. Government securities, obligations that are direct obligations of, or fully guaranteed as to principal and interest by, any agency of the United States, and prime bankers acceptances of the types authorized for purchase under 1(b) above, from dealers for the account of the Federal Reserve Bank of New York under agreements for repurchase of such securities, obligations, or acceptances in 15 calendar days or less, at rates that, unless otherwise expressly authorized by the Committee, shall be determined by competitive bidding, after applying reasonable limitations on the volume of agreements with individual dealers; provided that in the event Government securities or agency issues covered by any such agreement are not repurchased by the dealer pursuant to the agreement or a renewal thereof, they shall be sold in the market or transferred to the System Open Market Account; and provided further that in the event bankers acceptances covered by any such agreement are not repurchased by the seller, they shall continue to be held by the Federal Reserve Bank or shall be sold in the open market.
2. In order to ensure the effective conduct of open market operations, the Federal Open Market Committee authorizes and directs the Federal Reserve Banks to lend U.S. Government securities held in the System Open Market Account to Government securities dealers and to banks participating in Government securities clearing arrangements conducted through a Federal Reserve Bank, under such instructions as the Committee may specify from time to time.
3. In order to ensure the effective conduct of open market operations, while assisting in the provision of short-term investments for foreign and international accounts maintained at the Federal Reserve Bank of New York, the Federal Open Market Committee authorizes and directs the Federal Reserve Bank of New York (a) for System Open Market Account, to sell U.S. Government securities to such foreign and international accounts on the bases set forth in paragraph 1(a) under agreements providing for the resale by such

Source: 73rd Annual Report of the Board of Governors of the Federal Reserve System, 1986.

slowly to the permanent supply of reserves available to banks. Doing that job alone would not require that the Fed be in the market often.

However, bank reserves are influenced not only by the Fed's actions, but by various "operating factors" such as the size of Treasury balances at the Fed, the amount of currency in circulation, Federal Reserve float, and the size of foreign central bank balances at the Fed. These operating factors, which are outside the control of the Fed, constantly fluctuate by sizable sums. If the Fed did nothing to offset them, the amount of reserves available to banks would also fluctuate, often unpredictably, and this in turn would cause random, short-term movements in the monetary base and in interest rates.

The Fed wants to prevent this, so it tries to offset fluctuations in the operating factors, and thereby to keep bank reserves reasonably stable over the short run. For example, if the Fed forecasts that tax collections will cause Treasury balances to rise X billion the following week, and that the net change in other operating factors will be small, it will plan to take some offsetting action.

An increase in certain operating factors (e.g., Treasury balances at the Fed, currency in circulation) *drains* bank reserves, whereas an increase in other of these factors (e.g., float) *adds to* bank reserves. Thus, to offset the impact on bank reserves of a rise in Treasury balances, the Fed might do billions of repos. Conversely, to offset the impact on bank reserves of a rise in float or of a seasonal decline in currency in circulation, the Fed might do reverses.

The advantages of doing repos and reverses

To offset fluctuations in operating factors, the Fed needs to take temporary, tactical actions. We emphasize "temporary," because most changes in operating factors that affect bank reserves are short-lived. It snows; planes do not fly; checks do not move and clear; and float rises. The weather improves, and float falls.

In theory, the Fed could offset the impact on bank reserves of all short-term changes in the operating factors by doing *outright* purchases and sales of Treasury bills or coupons. The Fed, however, does not do this; instead, to make temporary adjustments in bank reserves, it uses repos and what it calls "matched/sale purchases" *(MSPs);* the latter transactions resemble reverses. Repos and MSPs have proved to be much more versatile tools than outright trades for the Fed to use for temporarily adjusting bank reserves. There are several reasons.

First, there is the question of where the securities would come from if the Fed did outright buys, and of where the securities would go if the Fed did outright sales. Frequent purchases and sales of securities by the Fed on the scale required might disrupt the flows in the market or the implementation by dealers of their strategies with respect to positioning securities. This would be especially true if the Fed sold tomorrow what it bought today.

Repos, in contrast to outright sales, are nondisruptive. Dealers are always looking to finance their positions, and because dealers may deliver to the Fed, as collateral against a repo, any securities *eligible* for purchase by the Fed, the impact of repos by the Fed is spread over the whole of the markets for Treasuries and federal agency securities.[2]

A second advantage to the Fed of doing repos and MSPs is that repos and MSPs are self-liquidating. To offset a three-day drain on reserves, the Fed, if it bought bills, would have to sell those same bills or other securities three days later. In contrast, when the Fed does a 3-day repo, that transaction matures and rolls off its books without the Fed having to take additional action. Thus, repos permit the Fed to tailor the duration of its injection of reserves.

A third advantage of repos is that the Fed can do them in such a way that they are self-correcting. When the Fed does repos, it usually gives dealers the right to withdraw collateral during the life of the repo; the Fed expects dealers to exercise that right, and they regularly do so. This can work to the Fed's advantage. The Fed carries out open market operations on the basis of its forecast as to what the *net* impact of changes in *all* operating factors will be on bank reserves. Such forecasts are subject to big errors. If the Fed does $5 billion of 4-day repos on the basis of a forecast that bank reserves will be down $5 billion due to changes in its operating factors, and reserves are down only $4 billion, there will be excess reserves in the banking system. This will cause the Fed funds rate and the repo rate in the national market to fall. This weakening of overnight rates will in turn cause dealers, bank and nonbank, who always seek to finance their positions at the least cost possible, to pull collateral to finance it more cheaply elsewhere. To the extent that they do so, the Fed's error will self-correct.

A fourth advantage to the Fed of doing repos and MSPs is that the Fed, as explained below, can do repos and MSPs faster and with less effort than it can do outright purchases and sales.

The beginning: Matched-sale/ purchase transactions

The Fed has been doing repos since the 1920s. In contrast, it devised MSPs only in the late 1960s. Someone on the desk described the Fed's

---

[2] Obligations currently *eligible* for purchase by the Fed comprise U.S. government securities, and obligations that are direct obligations of, or fully guaranteed as to principal and interest by, any agency of the United States. Prime bankers' acceptances once were, but since July 1984 no longer are, eligible collateral.

first matched sale/purchase as follows: "The Fed did its first MSP because it anticipated an airline strike. A strike would cause bank reserves to rise, since checks, to be delivered by air, would not move and consequently would not clear. We tried to devise a transaction that would permit us to drain reserves on a temporary basis. We could not do what the market called a reverse repo because it looked too much like a borrowing. We had to do an outright sale of securities we owned. So we came up with MSPs, which we book as a sale of securities out of our portfolio."

Fed MSPs resemble, but are not identical to, Street reverses.

Getting bids and offers: A "go-around"

The way the Fed does outright purchases of securities is to call all the dealers and say, "We want to buy securities [bills or coupons]; make us some offers for delivery on date X." Each dealer responds, after due consideration, by saying, "We offer to sell you, the Fed, so much of issue X at such and such a price, so much of issue Y at such and such a price, and so on." Since each dealer may offer the Fed several or more of a wide range of securities, the Fed has many offerings to cope with when it seeks to do outright purchases.

Whenever the Fed enters the market, it has decided what dollar total it wants to do: $1 billion, $2 billion, or whatever. The dealers, in bidding or offering to the Fed, compete with each other for the Fed's business. In response, the Fed ranks the dealers' bids or offerings and takes those that are most favorable, subject to the constraint that the Fed wants to maintain what it deems an appropriate mix of issues (Treasuries and agencies) and of maturities in its portfolio.

The process by which the Fed solicits bids and offers from dealers and decides with which of them it will do business is known as a *go-around*. The Fed still posts price and yield quotations for securities on one of the few remaining chalk boards on the street. It also ranks by hand the offers and bids it collects from dealers in the course of a go-around. Thus, when the Fed goes into the market to do outright purchases, its go-around is time-consuming. This is something that the Fed can live with, since it does outright purchases in the market only about five times a year. Also, when it is buying, it does bill purchases on one day, coupons on another. The Fed has never sold coupons in the market.

A repo go-around.   When the Fed does a go-around for repos, the process is simpler. The Fed asks the dealers to bid a repo rate: to say, "We bid to do X million of repo with you at rate Y." Dealers, besides bidding for financing for their own positions, may also pass along to the Fed bids of their customers for repo money. Once the Fed has the dealers' bids, it "hits," starting with the highest bid, however many bids it must to do the total of repos it wants to do. The lowest bid rate that the Fed accepts is known as the "stop-out" rate.

The Fed accepts propositions stated in terms of face amounts of securities. Consequently, it doesn't actually know the precise amount of reserves it has provided as a result of a repo go-around until the dealers indicate what collateral they will deliver. At that time, the Fed prices at the market all collateral delivered to it, takes its margin, and then figures how many dollars [of financing] it will pay each dealer with whom it has struck a deal. When the Fed agrees to do $500 million of repos with a dealer, it might actually pay [lend to] that dealer only $495 million.

An MSP go-around.   When the Fed does a go-around for MSPs, it offers to sell to dealers one or several bill issues at the rates at which these issues are trading in the market. It then asks the dealers to offer a rate at which they will resell these bills to the Fed. The Fed expects the dealers to set the buy-back (repurchase) rates they offer so that they earn some reverse rate on the money they lend to the Fed. In doing MSPs, the Fed hits those bids that give it the lowest implied reverse rate. Remember, the Fed in this transaction is borrowing from the dealers.

MSPs versus Street reverses

The substance of Fed MSPs is the same as that of Street reverses. However, the mechanics of the trades differ. Normally, dealers do reverses at a reverse rate they quote to customers. In contrast, the Fed does MSPs at the rate implied by those dealer bids of buy-back rates that it accepts.

MSPs, unlike repos done by the Fed, are not subject to withdrawal since they are literally outright sales from the Fed's portfolio matched by specified *forward* purchases to be added to that portfolio.

CHARACTERISTICS OF FED REPOS

The agreement

In doing repos and MSPs with dealers, the Fed still uses a letter of agreement similar to the one in Figure 7–1, p. 83.

Term of Fed repos

The desk may do repos up to 15 calendar days in length. In practice, it rarely does repos with a term of over seven days. Most often, the Fed does overnight repos, but on a Thursday, it may do 4-day, over-the-weekend repos or, on a Friday, it may do 3-day, over-the-weekend repos.

The reason that the Fed does such short repos, and short MSPs as well, is that short repos and MSPs are the most flexible tools the Fed can use to deal with a highly variable and often difficult-to-forecast situation, namely the ever-changing level of bank reserves.

When it does multiday repos, the Fed will often do more than it really needs to because it anticipates that, before the repos mature, dealers will withdraw some of the collateral they delivered to the Fed at the start of the repo.

Margin

The Fed always takes margin when it does repos. It won't publicly state how much except to say that it takes 2½ to 3 points on longer issues. The Street thinks that the margins the Fed takes are "biggies."

The Fed reprices each day the collateral dealers give it when it does repos with them. The reason that the Fed takes big margins is that it wants sufficient margin on repos so that it will not be required by any likely rise in market rates to call for additional margin. Apparently the Fed succeeds; it has never happened, in the memory of people currently at the desk, that the Fed has had to call for additional margin.

Right of substitution

When it does a repo for several days, the Fed permits the dealers to substitute collateral on the first day of the repo. The Fed realizes that the dealers may sell, unexpectedly, securities that they had said they would deliver to it, and the Fed wants to ensure that it does, regardless of such sales, the volume of repos it contracted to do in the go-around. After the first day, the Fed does not permit substitution on repos done with it.

Counterparties

We have spoken about the Fed doing repos and reverses with dealers in governments. Dealers in fact are not the only counterparties that the Fed has in such transactions. As noted below, the Fed does a lot of MSPs with foreign central banks. Also, since the mid-1970s, the Fed has permitted dealers to show customer money to it when it was doing reverses and customer collateral to it when it was doing repos. Many dealers' customers, however, are unaware that this possibility exists. One commercial paper issuer observed, "Sometimes on a Wednesday commercial paper issuers post attractive rates to get money, then rates start to sag in the money market, collateral dries up, and all of a sudden they get hit with money. In this sort of situation—the market falling apart—the Fed will generally come in and do reverse repurchase agreements. A paper issuer with excess funds can at that point call a primary dealer and ask them to show, say, $20 million for him into the Fed. I do it, but I don't see many others doing it." The Fed rarely intervenes anymore on a Wednesday afternoon, but dealers can and still do show customer securities (money) into the Fed when the Fed is doing repos (reverses) as part of its normal daily open market operations.

Fed accounting for repos and for MSPs

The Fed records on its balance sheet its holding of securities delivered to it as collateral for repos as securities "Held under repurchase agreement" (Table 8–1). Such securities are not comingled with portfolio holdings that the Fed creates through outright purchases.

MSPs are a different matter. The Fed treats leg one as a sale of securities out of its portfolio and leg two as a purchase of securities that adds to its portfolio. Specifically, when the Fed sells bills as part of an MSP, it records as a capital gain (or loss) the difference between the book value of the bills sold and the price at which it sells these securities. When it repurchases the bills, it bases their new book value on the repurchase price it has paid for them.

TRANSACTIONS FOR THE ACCOUNTS OF FOREIGN CENTRAL BANKS

Foreign central banks hold short-term balances of dollars for a number of reasons. One is that the dollar is a reserve currency, a currency that foreign central banks hold, instead of or in addition to gold, as part of their foreign exchange reserves. Sweden is an example of a country that pegs the value of its currency to the dollar and must therefore hold dollars with which to buy krona should the krona start to weaken against the dollar.

The Fed offers to invest, in either bills or repos, any dollar balances that foreign central banks hold with it. The Fed does so for several reasons. Its service is a convenience to foreign central banks. Also, by providing this service, the Fed gets to know firsthand what is happening to foreign-central-bank dollar balances.

Foreign central banks with long-term dollar balances often invest these balances in Treasury bills. Thus, the Fed sometimes sells to or buys from foreign central banks Treasury securities. Such transactions are in addition to its normal purchases of securities *in the market* (i.e., from dealers).

Normally, foreign central banks will have at least some temporary balances sitting at the Fed: funds just received, funds that they will need in several days to make a payment. Naturally, foreign central banks want to earn a return on such balances. To permit them to do so, the Fed offers foreign central banks an investment facility: it permits them to invest dollars short term in a *pool of funds* that it in turn invests in the repo market by doing System MSPs with dealers; foreign-central-bank investments in the pool pay a return determined by the current level of repo rates.

In determining what reserves it needs to provide to the banking system, the Fed takes the expected size of the foreign-central-bank repo (MSP to the Fed) pool to be an operating factor, like currency in circulation or Treasury balances. If the pool turns out to be larger than anticipated, that drains bank reserves and vice versa. Either eventuality may put the Fed in a position where it must take additional action to achieve its reserves target.

Normally, when a foreign central bank requests that the Fed purchase or sell Treasuries for it, the Fed does the resulting outright transaction in the market. However, if it suits the Fed's purpose to effect a change in reserves, the Fed may do such a transaction internally with its own portfolio. For example, an inflow of money into a foreign central bank's account at the Fed has no impact on bank reserves if it is immediately used to purchase bills from the Street, but it drains bank reserves if it is used to purchase securities from the Fed's portfolio.

Suppose, for example, that a foreign central bank receives a payment of 100 million from Morgan and that it uses those funds to purchase securities from the Fed's portfolio; in that case, Morgan's reserves, a Fed liability, fall by 100 million and so, too, do the Fed's holdings of governments (a Fed asset). Were the foreign central bank, in contrast, to use the 100 million it received to immediately purchase securities from, say, the dealer operation of Citibank, the whole transaction—inflow and outflow of 100 million from the foreign central bank's deposit account at the Fed—would be, with respect to its impact on domestic bank reserves, a wash.[3]

As the above remarks suggest, internal transactions between the Fed's portfolio and those of foreign central banks can be a substitute for Fed action in the open market. Occasionally, it serves the Fed's purposes to be able to carry out foreign-central-bank investment requests through internal transactions with its own portfolio rather than to show that business to the Street. By doing such a transaction, the Fed may be able to avoid giving an incorrect signal to the market—for example, it

---

[3] Note that it makes no difference, with respect to the ultimate impact on bank reserves, whether the foreign central bank purchases its bills from Citibank or from a nonbank dealer. Had the foreign central bank purchased its bills from, say, Merrill, its payment for these bills would have immediately added 100 million to the reserves of Merrill's clearing bank.

may be able to avoid, when it was in fact easing, doing visible-to-the-market MSPs to offset a reserve rise caused by a change in its operating factors.

We have said that, when a foreign central bank requests the Fed to buy or to sell Treasuries for it, the Fed can do such a transaction in the market or against its own portfolio. In addition, the Fed is sometimes able to offset buy and sell orders from different foreign central banks against each other.

Most typically, foreign central banks make overnight investments in the Fed's pool of MSPs. The Fed, however, invests funds in this pool not only in overnight repos, but in repos of longer maturities. On an average day, foreign central banks currently invest 3½ to 5 billion in MSPs with the Fed.

Looking at Table 8–1, we see that, at the end of 1986, foreign central banks had uninvested deposit balances of $286.7 million at the Fed (Table 8–1, under "Deposits: Foreign-official accounts"). Foreign official investments in MSPs with the Fed do not appear (as either an asset or a liability) on the Fed's balance sheet because the Fed treats MSPs as a sale of securities. Elsewhere, however, the Fed does publish figures on the amounts of such MSPs (see, in particular, footnote 1 to H.4.1, published by the Federal Reserve each Thursday).

VOLUME OF FED OPEN MARKET OPERATIONS

Outrights

The Fed uses outright purchases of government and agency securities to make permanent additions to bank reserves. To offset the impact on bank reserves of the maturing of securities in its portfolio, the Fed rolls its maturing securities, except when it wants to drain reserves. The Fed never sells coupons, and it sells bills only infrequently (Table 8–2). Over the last decade, the Fed has added roughly $13 billion a year to bank reserves through increases in its portfolio (Table 7–1). To do that amount of business, the Fed need not do outrights often, and it does not. It's in the market no more than half a dozen times a year.

Repos

Repos are by far the most frequent transaction the Fed does in connection with open market operations. This is so because doing repos is really the only way that the Fed can offset temporary drains on bank reserves. These drains occur frequently, but according to no set pattern.

Thus, the Fed, during a given reserve period, may be in the market day after day doing repos, or it may be out of the market for days.

At any time, the Fed has only a notion of what it needs to do because it is operating on the basis of an error-prone forecast of where bank reserves are going and an estimate of what bank reserves actually are. Consequently, the Fed is often sparked into action by market conditions. It will say: "Gee, we thought we had added enough bank reserves, but things look tight in the market; overnight rates on funds and repos are going up; maybe we ought to add more reserves by doing repos."

Figures on what open market operations the Fed did over the year don't tell about the interplay between what the Fed does for its own account and what it does for the accounts of foreign central banks. Still, it's revealing to note that in 1986 the Fed bought outright $24 billion of Treasuries, of which $1 billion covered redemptions. The Fed bought no agencies outright, but did take them in under repos. In contrast, the Fed, during the same year, did $201.5 billion of repos for its own account, and it had on its books at the end of the year $16 billion of governments and agencies held under repurchase agreements (Tables 7–1 and 8–2). Since the Fed, when it goes into the market to do repos, typically does a total of $2.5 billion to $5 billion, the above figures indicate that the Fed must be in the market quite often to do repos for its own account. The Fed is also in the market some days solely to do customer-related repos for foreign accounts.

MSPs

When the Fed wants to drain reserves temporarily, it can do so by doing MSPs with the Street. Because the Fed must secularly raise bank reserves, it finds that the occasions on which it wants to do MSPs with the Street are far fewer than the occasions on which it wants to do repos with the Street.

Fed statistics on MSPs are misleading. In 1986, the Fed sold, under MSPs, $930 billion of securities (Table 8–2). This makes MSPs sound as if they must be, by far, the tool most frequently used by the Fed in carrying out open market operations. In fact, someone at the desk guessed that MSPs represent no more than 10% of the open market operations carried out by the Fed with the Street. The vast bulk of the MSPs that the Fed does are the counterpart of the repos that foreign central banks do with it.

Neither the MSPs that the Fed does with the Street nor those it does with foreign central banks show up on its balance sheet. When the Fed does net new MSPs, the impact on the asset side of its balance sheet is a decrease in the size of its securities holdings; the offset to this, on the

TABLE 8–2
Fed open market operations, 1986

Federal Reserve Open Market Transactions, 1986[1]

Millions of dollars

Type of transaction	Jan.	Feb.	Mar.	Apr.
U.S. TREASURY SECURITIES				
Outright transactions (excluding matched transactions)				
Treasury bills				
Gross purchases	286	0	396	2,988
Gross sales	225	2,277	0	0
Exchange	0	0	0	0
Redemptions	0	1,000	0	0
Others within 1 year				
Gross purchases	0	0	0	0
Gross sales	0	0	0	0
Maturity shift	725	4,776	1,152	447
Exchange	−596	−2,148	−1,458	−1,129
Redemptions	0	0	0	0
1 to 5 years				
Gross purchases	0	0	0	0
Gross sales	0	0	0	0
Maturity shift	−703	−4,776	−1,152	−447
Exchange	596	1,548	1,458	1,134
5 to 10 years				
Gross purchases	0	0	0	0
Gross sales	0	0	0	0
Maturity shift	−22	0	0	−5
Exchange	0	350	0	0
More than 10 years				
Gross purchases	0	0	0	0
Gross sales	0	0	0	0
Maturity shift	0	0	0	0
Exchange	0	250	0	0
All maturities				
Gross purchases	286	0	396	2,988
Gross sales	225	2,277	0	0
Redemptions	0	1,000	0	0
Matched transactions				
Gross sales	63,109	90,459	88,917	109,253
Gross purchases	61,156	94,368	88,604	103,957
Repurchase agreements[2]				
Gross purchases	24,257	0	6,748	21,156
Gross sales	24,699	3,087	6,748	13,634
Net change in U.S. Treasury securities	−2,335	−2,456	83	5,214
FEDERAL AGENCY OBLIGATIONS				
Outright transactions				
Gross purchases	0	0	0	0
Gross sales	0	0	0	0
Redemptions	0	40	0	0
Repurchase agreements[2]				
Gross purchases	5,384	0	1,821	3,387
Gross sales	6,454	623	1,821	1,955
Net change in agency obligations	−1,070	−663	0	1,432
Total net change in System Open Market Account	**−3,405**	**−3,119**	**83**	**6,647**

*Less than $500,000 in absolute value.
1. Sales, redemptions, and negative figures reduce holdings of the System Open Market Account; all other figures increase such holdings. Details may not add to totals because of rounding.

2. In July 1984 the Open Market Trading Desk discontinued accepting bankers acceptances in repurchase agreements.

Source: 73rd Annual Report of the Board of Governors of the Federal Reserve System, 1986.

May	June	July	Aug.	Sept.	Oct.	Nov.	Dec.	Total
3,196	1,402	867	2,940	861	928	3,318	5,422	22,602
0	0	0	0	0	0	0	0	2,502
0	0	0	0	0	0	0	0	0
0	0	0	0	0	0	0	0	1,000
0	0	0	0	0	0	190	0	190
0	0	0	0	0	0	0	0	0
1,847	1,152	579	1,715	1,053	974	2,974	1,280	18,673
−1,819	−1,957	−1,253	−4,087	−1,892	−529	−1,810	−1,502	−20,179
0	0	0	0	0	0	893	0	893
0	0	0	0	0	0	0	0	0
−1,532	−1,152	−386	−1,194	−1,053	−969	−2,414	−1,280	−17,058
1,019	1,957	1,253	2,587	1,892	529	1,510	1,502	16,984
0	0	0	0	0	0	236	0	236
0	0	0	0	0	0	0	0	0
−315	0	−193	−520	0	−5	−560	0	−1,620
500	0	0	1,000	0	0	200	0	2,050
0	0	0	0	0	0	158	0	158
0	0	0	0	0	0	0	0	0
0	0	0	0	0	0	0	0	0
300	0	0	500	0	0	100	0	1,150
3,196	1,402	867	2,940	861	928	4,795	5,422	24,078
0	0	0	0	0	0	0	0	2,502
0	0	0	0	0	0	0	0	1,000
62,663	80,219	70,928	60,460	73,179	77,262	60,146	91,404	927,997
67,147	80,674	69,659	60,011	70,817	81,892	60,232	88,730	927,247
12,395	5,640	18,657	0	14,717	5,670	16,888	44,303	170,431
19,917	5,640	18,657	0	8,403	11,984	15,471	32,028	160,268
158	1,857	−403	2,491	4,814	−756	6,298	15,023	29,989
0	0	0	0	0	0	0	0	0
0	0	0	0	0	0	0	0	0
50	0	*	90	*	93	125	0	398
3,135	1,691	4,984	0	2,678	952	1,622	5,488	31,142
4,567	1,691	4,984	0	869	2,761	1,274	3,522	30,522
−1,482	0	*	−90	1,809	−1,902	223	1,965	222
−1,324	**1,857**	**−403**	**2,401**	**6,623**	**−2,658**	**6,522**	**16,988**	**30,211**

liability side of its balance sheet, is a decrease either in foreign official or in member bank deposits at the Fed. When the Fed rolls existing MSPs, there is no impact on its balance sheet (except for minor changes caused by the roll in the book value of certain bills it holds).

Bankers' acceptances

Today, the BA market is well-established in the United States, and the Fed no longer feels the need to buy BAs, even occasionally, to support this market. The Fed, however, did, until July 1984, repos against BAs; its motive for doing so was to add to bank reserves, not to supply—as in the early days of the BA market—supplementary financing to BA dealers. While it was still doing repos against BAs, the Fed, when it did a repo go-around, always included BA dealers, some of whom were not primary dealers, but rather specialty shops.

THE NEXT CHAPTER

In the next chapter, we turn to some interesting tales about the post–World War II development of private (dealer-to-customer, bank-to-customer) trades in repo and reverse: the rebirth of private repos, the creation of tails, and the birth of private reverse repurchase agreements.

OTHER SOURCES ON FEDERAL RESERVE
OPEN MARKET OPERATIONS

Meek, Paul. *U.S. Monetary Policy and Financial Markets.* New York: Federal Reserve Bank of New York, 1982; see in particular Chapter 7.

Melton, William. *Inside the Fed, Making Monetary Policy.* Homewood, Ill.: Dow Jones-Irwin, 1985; see in particular Chapter 7.

Chapter 9

The revival and growth of private repos

DURING THE 1950s, the use by private borrowers of the repo market was revived. First a story, perhaps apocryphal, of how the first all-private repo trade was done. Then a description of the forces that led to the revival of private borrowing in the repo market.

THE BEGINNING: ALL-PRIVATE REPOS

One bright day back in the early 1950s, the General Motors portfolio manager said to Discount Corporation, a respected primary dealer: "We've got Y million of cash that we want to invest to a specific date. The money is earmarked for paying our next quarterly dividend, so we don't want market risk. No maturing bill issue fits our date, and we can't do a collateralized loan. What do you suggest?"

To which Discount replied: "We've got something for you. We will sell you T bills at a discount slightly below the rate at which they are trading in the market. The dollar purchase price will equal Y million. At the same time, we will contract to repurchase from you X days hence, when you need funds, those same bills at the rate at which we sold them to you.

"The deal's good for both of us. You'll get a *certain* return and *no* market risk. Also, you'll have *no* credit risk, since we will deliver to your custodial bank all bills we sell to you. We, on the other hand, will get a fixed-rate loan at an attractive rate. Let's do it."

GM did do the trade with Discount, and together they set an example of creative dealer financing and corporate investing. Soon other dealers and corporate investors were striking similar deals. The private repo market was not only reborn, but grew with vigor.

As we noted in Chapter 1, the essence of a repo, despite the fact that it begins with a purchase of securities and ends with a sale of securities, is that it is a hybrid collateralized loan. This being the case, it's natural to ask: Why didn't dealers arrange to do plain-vanilla collateralized borrowings from investors instead of doing with them repos and the attendant hocus pocus of buys and sells of securities? One answer is that many, probably most, potential investors in repo were not empowered to make collateralized loans, but they could buy and sell all the securities they needed to stay fully invested.

THE BACKGROUND

Even if GM and Discount were not the first entities to do in the 1950s a private-on-both-sides repo, the above story bears telling. Like a parable, it suggests important truths: That dealers were searching for cheaper financing and that corporations needed an investment instrument that would permit them to invest, with no market risk, an amount of their choosing to a date of their choosing.

The midwife to, if not the father of, the reborn private repo market was the lids imposed in the 1930s on the rates banks were permitted to pay on deposits. The Banking Act of 1933 prohibited banks from paying interest on *demand deposits.* This act also gave the Fed the authority to impose lids on the rates that member banks might pay on *time deposits.* The Fed imposed such lids under Regulation Q. Reg Q ceilings were later applied by the Federal Deposit Insurance Corporation (FDIC) to all banks whose deposits it insured. Note prohibiting banks from paying interest on demand deposits amounted to imposing a 0% ceiling on the rate that banks might pay on such deposits. The notion behind imposing ceilings on the bank deposit rates was that such regulation would protect banks from excessive price (rate) competition with other banks; bankers were regarded as too irresponsible and incompetent to survive the rigors of a free market in deposits.

The upshot of deposit-rate ceilings was that many money market participants were barred from doing economically sensible things. Big money market banks were losing deposits to suburban banks at the same time that they faced an increasing demand for medium-term loans from major U.S. corporations, which were expanding rapidly. Meanwhile, smaller banks were flush with funds but lacked an investment instrument that would permit them to utilize these funds efficiently. A natural solution to everyone's problem—including what corporate America was to do with its short-term, cash balances—would have been for big New York and any other large, deposit-poor banks to pay interest on call and short-term deposits; by doing so, big banks would have been able to bid away, from country banks, corporations, and other cash-rich institutions, their surplus funds. The big New York and other money center banks could have used such deposits to fund their growing commercial and industrial loans (C&I), and additional dealer loans as well. Rate ceilings made this impossible with the result that New York and certain other banks lost out on potentially profitable growth.

Rate ceilings, an American regulatory aberration, were indefensible in a non–Islamic country that had no religious prohibition against the payment by banks of interest; but they would not go away. Consequently, money market participants had to find ways to adjust to rate ceilings or, in the case of banks, to evade them. This everyone did quite well. In fact, adjustments to and evasions of rate ceilings explain a great deal about how the U.S. money market evolved from the 1950s to the present.

To evade rate ceilings, banks revived the Fed funds market in which deposit-rich banks "sold" reserve dollars (more accurately, lent reserve dollars on an unsecured basis) to deposit-poor banks at a market rate of interest. Later, deposit-poor banks followed the lead of dealers and began to buy, in the repo market, short-term money from cash-rich institutions, including the same corporations from whom they were forbidden to take short-term (less than 30-day) interest-bearing deposits. Big banks also bought, from just about everyone, money in the Euro time deposit market, a market that big banks and their customers invented—albeit in a stumbling fashion—partly to evade domestic rate lids.

Rate lids stimulated rapid growth not only of the repo, the Fed funds, and the Euro time deposit markets, but of the commercial paper and BA markets as well. Probably all those markets would be with us, with or without rate lids, but some portion of the rapid growth of these markets, post–World War II, was surely a substitute for a more rapid expansion of domestic banking, one that would have occurred had banks been free to pay market rates on their deposits.

GROWTH AND DEVELOPMENT OF THE EARLY REPO MARKET

Against this background, it is easy to understand why different repo market participants came to play the roles they did in the early repo market.

The dealers

Dealers, at the time that they began to borrow repo money from corporations, were already getting repo financing from the Fed. However, the timing and amount of such financing was set by the Fed; a dealer could not take the initiative and ask the Fed to do repos with it when it wanted to take on a big position. Dealers needed private funding—and lots of it—to supplement the credit extended to them by the Fed.

Dealers had available one ready source of private credit; they could borrow overnight from the New York banks at the dealer call loan rate against New York Stock Exchange collateral, but the rate New York banks charged dealers for such loans became increasingly unattractive. The deposit-poor New York banks had more attractive things to do with their money than lend it to dealers who, unlike corporations, never gave them big deposits.

The corporate investors

Meanwhile, corporations with money to invest for short periods were barred by rate lids from making interest-bearing deposits at banks. Also, because they are not exempt lenders, corporations were barred from selling Fed funds to banks. "Fed funds purchased," an unsecured loan, are a *nonreservable* liability for the purchasing bank only if the seller of funds is an *exempt* lender. Other banks, certain bank subsidiaries, and certain other financial institutions are, under Fed regulations with respect to reserve requirements, classified as exempt lenders; corporations are not.

The natural outcome of dealers' and corporations' offsetting balance-sheet needs—dealers needed more and cheaper financing, while corporations needed a flexible, short-term instrument on which they could earn interest—was that private repo transactions should be revived, specifically, that dealers should begin borrowing from corporations using the repo mechanism. Precisely this occurred. A few dealers started to borrow and a few corporations to lend by doing short-term repos; the lead of these pioneers was quickly followed by other dealers and by numerous cash-rich corporations.

The out-of-town banks

Banks in the United States operate under either a state or a federal charter. Thanks to restrictions imposed by federal and state laws on branch banking, the number of banks operating in the United States, currently over 15,000, is huge compared to the number in any other country. A few U.S. banks are large, world-class, money market banks.

Most of the rest are small, rural, or suburban banks. Middle-sized regional banks used to fall between these two groups, but some *super regionals* are now in the process, due to mergers, of becoming top-size U.S. banks.

Because nationally-chartered banks are permitted to extend to any one borrower loans equal to no more than 10% of their capital plus surplus, large corporate borrowers have always centered their banking relationships and their borrowing on the large money center banks. Country banks, in contrast, get most of the deposits—demand and time—of consumers, of unincorporated businesses, of small corporations (financial and nonfinancial), and of municipal bodies, of which tens of thousands are scattered across the land. Because of the above factors, large U.S. banks, with the exception of the Bank of America, which operates in a state that permits branch banking, are chronically deposit poor, whereas smaller banks are deposit rich.

For U.S. banks to utilize efficiently the aggregate reserves provided them by the Fed, reserves must be transferred by some means from the nation's many deposit-rich country banks to its fewer in number, but larger in size, money market banks. Thus, one natural trade for banks to do, from the early 1950s on, was for small banks to sell to large banks Fed funds (reserve dollars) overnight or for some short period. This was done, with NYC banks in particular becoming massive net buyers of funds. The Fed funds market, which grew rapidly, became a source of liquidity to both large and small banks; small banks could vary from day-to-day the amount of excess reserves they invested through the sale of Fed funds, whereas large banks could vary from day-to-day the reserve deficiency that they covered through the purchase of Fed funds. (The terms *purchase* and *sale* of Fed funds are misleading. Buyers of Fed funds are borrowers, sellers are lenders; the lending of Fed funds is done on an unsecured basis, and most typically the term is overnight or over the weekend. When both parties are members of the Fed, Fed funds bought are moved over the Fed wire.)

In the early days of the Fed funds market, a problem for sellers of funds was that such sales were subject to bank lending limits. This meant that a nationally-chartered bank with many reserve dollars to sell might, to stay within its lending limits, have to sell funds to several banks. No restriction has ever existed on the amount of Treasury securities a nationally-chartered bank may acquire. Banks took the view that, in doing repos against governments, they were buying Treasuries, and therefore they were permitted to do with any counterparty as large a repo as they chose. For a bank with large excess reserves, it was more convenient to do one big repo than to scramble around the market selling small amounts of Fed funds to each of several buyers. Consequently, repo with NYC dealers in governments became an attractive investment for out-of-town banks, who began, once the NYC dealers started to borrow in the repo market, to lend large amounts to these dealers.

In seeking loans from out-of-town banks, NYC dealers were competing with NYC banks for the excess reserves of these banks; the dealers wanted money to fund their positions; the NYC banks, to fund various assets, including dealer loans. At this time, NYC banks lent to dealers at the collateral loan rate, a rate always some spread over the funds rate.

In September 1956, the Comptroller of the Currency (chief regulator of national banks) questioned, in a letter from the National Bank Examiner's office, whether repos should be viewed as bank loans secured by direct obligations of the United States or as investment securities. If repos were officially viewed as the former, the amount a nationally-chartered bank could have lent to one repo borrower would have been limited to 25% of its capital and surplus. Neither dealers nor banks wanted this limitation imposed on bank repo lending. In the end the Comptroller's office compromised. It ruled in July 1957 that repos were to be treated as collateralized loans; however, the amount of repos a bank could do with another bank or a dealer was raised to 100% of the lending bank's capital and surplus, provided that the collateral was U.S. Treasuries maturing within 18 months. Later, this percentage limitation was removed for such collateral. (See Appendixes A–H to this chapter for the relevant letters.)

At this time, lending banks tended to view repos as a secured sale of Fed funds. Moreover, in choosing whether to sell Fed funds or to do repos, lending banks showed little interest in whether they got collateral in exchange for dollars they lent. To them, the major attraction of repo was not lessened credit risk due to the presence of collateral, but rather the large size in which they could do a single repo.

In a 1969 amendment to Regs D and Q, the Fed specified that repos done by bank borrowers were *exempt from reserve requirements and interest rate ceilings.* This indicated that the Fed viewed repos done by banks as liabilities of the borrowing bank and, specifically, as collateralized loans.

This was in keeping with the way banks came to keep their books. In their call reports prior to 1956, banks reported repo transactions as securities owned and often referred to them as "sales contracts" or "delayed delivery contracts." After the Comptroller classified repos as loans, banks reported repos as loans. Dealers were less consistent. Some accounted for repos as sales of securities, while others treated repos as loans and the underlying collateral as part of their position.[1] Presumably because the Fed would do repos with dealers for no longer than 15 days, some dealers took the view that repos for less than 15 days

---

[1] See Peters, "The Repurchase Agreement: Its Position in Today's Money Market" (Thesis, Stonier Graduate School of Banking, 1962), p. 29.

were loans whereas those for longer periods were investments. This distinction makes *no* economic sense. A change in the maturity of a repo has no impact whatsoever on its fundamental characteristics. Also, most bank loans are, with the exception of sales of Fed funds and repos, done for periods far in excess of 15 days.

The money market banks

Money market banks, always hungry for yet more funding, noted, as they watched the growth of repos by dealers, that they too owned government collateral. Specifically, they held governments in their investment portfolios and still more governments in their dealer positions. Soon money market banks too were repoing their holdings of governments; doing so gave money market banks access to a new, cheap, dependable source of funds.

Prior to the end of World War II, when money market banks were deposit rich, they viewed their government portfolios as a liquid investment in securities that they could sell when they needed extra funds, for example, to fund a spurt in commercial and industrial loans. Governments viewed thusly have a name, "secondary reserves."

Once money market banks became deposit poor and had to buy large amounts of the money they lent and invested, it made no economic sense for them to hold governments as secondary reserves. Big banks recognized this and came to hold governments only as an arbitrage, in which they sought to profit by borrowing at a low rate in the repo market funds they invested at a higher rate in the government market. In bankers' parlance, banks sought to earn *positive carry* on their portfolios.

Banks also held governments as a position play—hoping that a correct view on interest rates would lead them to stock up on long governments whenever interest rates were poised for a sharp drop and the bond market for a sharp rally. Whatever the purpose for which they held governments, money market banks learned to repo them to the last dollar.

Municipal investors

Once the repo market was recognized as a legitimate market in which to borrow and lend funds, more and more participants entered this market. In particular, state and local government bodies became, for easily understood reasons, big investors in repo. Muni bodies are frequently required by law to hold their excess cash in bank deposits or to invest it in governments and agencies. Also, muni bodies are typically not permitted to take a capital loss on their investments, which means in effect that they cannot invest in a security unless they are sure they will be able to hold that security until it matures. Thus, repos collateralized by governments and agencies offer muni bodies—who are permitted by their investment parameters to do such repos—an attractive way to invest an amount of their choosing to a date of their choosing. Over time, the volume of money going into the repo market from state and local governments has risen from meager beginnings to huge sums. Today, if New York State sells $3 billion of bonds, all that money is immediately invested in repo and stays there until it is needed.

THE BEGINNING: REVERSE REPURCHASE AGREEMENTS

Here's a second, perhaps apocryphal, story of how *the first reverse repo* was done. Inevitably, there came the day when GM asked Discount to do a term repo at a time when Discount expected market rates to rise and was therefore bearish. To Discount, future *tails*, even if created at a locked-in, positive carry, seemed a bad bet. But there was GM wanting to invest. What to do? The answer required creative thinking.

At the time, tax laws gave banks an incentive to bunch capital gains on securities sales into one year, capital losses into another. This being the case, Discount realized that there must be out there, somewhere in the big universe of banks, one bank that needed funds but wasn't willing to sell securities to get them because to do so would entail its taking a capital loss in what it had determined would be for it a "gain year." Would not such a bank be willing to repo out the securities it was unwilling to sell in order to meet its needs for additional funds? Discount posed the question to Manufacturers Hanover Trust, which was in precisely the position described; Manny liked the idea.

To get in Manny's securities, Discount did a *reverse repurchase agreement* with Manny; this transaction was identical to the repurchase agreements Discount had been doing with GM except that, in the current deal, Discount was lending, not borrowing, funds, and it was taking in, not putting out, securities. (A key point: *One man's repo is always another man's reverse, and vice versa.*)

Discount had no money to finance holding Manny's securities, but it had a customer on the other side who did, GM. To complete the deal, Discount repoed out Manny's securities to GM taking out for itself "the middle," a spread between the rate at which it lent to Manny and the rate at which it borrowed from GM. This transaction was historic in two ways; it was the first *reverse* done, *and* it was the modest start of something that later grew big, the running of matched books by dealers. More on the latter in Chapter 16.

OPTIONS AND FLEXIBILITY

In conclusion, we should note that, over time, a hallmark of the repo and reverse markets has been the creativity that both borrowers and lenders of money have applied to their use of repo and reverse trades. In the next chapter, we discuss two trades that became popular: reverses to maturity and the creation of tails. Here, we indicate how investors learned to use repo to obtain added options and flexibility in their investments.

The repo market gives an investor who's willing to base his investments on market judgments flexibility with respect to where along the yield curve he chooses to commit his funds. If the answer is at the very base of the yield curve, he can roll overnight repo indefinitely; and at times, doing so can be very attractive. A historical example: in early 1982, when yields were high and looking as if they might go higher, Fed funds and repo traded in the range of 14–15% while short bills were yielding only 12–13%. Thus at that time a portfolio manager who owned short bills could have picked up 200–300 basis points in yield by selling his bills and investing in the same instrument under repo. Later in1982, as it became clear that rates had started to decline, it was more attractive for the portfolio manager to own securities outright because doing so offered an opportunity for capital appreciation.

Many investors, including municipalities and some financial institutions, cannot take a capital loss because of legal or self-imposed restrictions, but they can take an interest loss. Suppose such an investor has money that he thinks he will have available for six months but that he might need sooner. He can't invest in 6-month bills because, if he did, he might incur an *accounting loss* if he sold them. He can, however, take in 6-month bills on a 6-month reverse, that is, invest in 6-month term repo. If three months later the investor finds that he needs his money and that the bill market is in the "chutes" (prices are down), he can repo out the collateral he has taken in. In doing so, he may incur a *loss of interest—* negative carry on his offsetting repo positions (this will occur if the repo rate at which he borrows exceeds the repo rate at which he has invested); however, he won't, in this situation, incur a capital loss. Often, municipalities can repo out securities that they have obtained on a reverse but not securities they own outright. Consequently, a number of municipalities invest in term repo to get the protection and flexibility described in the example above.

THE NEXT CHAPTER

Repos are no longer just a financing tool. Today, they are routinely used as one leg of various money market arbitrages. In the next chapter, we describe two such arbitrages that are routinely done by traders. We also talk more about repo-market practices.

Appendixes to Chapter 9
Early regulatory rulings

APPENDIX A
Letter of the Comptroller of the Currency re repurchase agreements

September 27, 1956

**TO ALL EXAMINERS AND ASSISTANT EXAMINERS
IN THE FOURTH FEDERAL RESERVE DISTRICT**

Re: Purchase and sale of U. S. Government
securities under repurchase agreement

The following is a copy of a self-explanatory letter dated September 20, 1956 addressed to the office by the Comptroller of the Currency:

"We have had occasion to consider whether under certain circumstances R.S. 5200 or R.S. 5136 is applicable in a transaction between two banks involving the purchase and sale of United States Government securities under an agreement whereby the selling bank agrees to repurchase the securities.

"The details incident to one such transaction and conclusion reached by us as set out in the enclosed copy of a letter to the bank concerned are self-explanatory.

"You will please be guided accordingly in the treatment in future reports of examination of transactions of the character described in the letter."

C. B. REDMAN
Chief National Bank Examiner

Attachment

APPENDIX B

September 14, 1956

_____, President,
Y National Bank,

_____

Dear Mr. _____:

   This refers to report of examination of your bank completed ———— —, 1956.

   On page — of the report the examiner scheduled as exceeding the legal lending limit of your bank under R.S. 5200 the obligation of X National Bank arising out of its agreement to repurchase $———— in par value of United States Treasury Notes 1⅝ due 5-15-57. The securities were purchased by your bank on ———— —, 1956 at par flat and repurchased by the X National Bank on ———— —, 1956 at par plus interest at the rate of 2½% annually for the period of one day the funds were employed by the X National Bank.

   On ———— —, 1956 we advised the District Chief National Bank Examiner that we had under study the applicability of R.S. 5200 or R.S. 5136 to such a transaction, and our conclusion was that when assets purchased subject to a repurchase agreement are eligible investment securities, no limitation based on R.S. 5200 would be imposed because of the existence of a repurchase agreement. The District Chief National Bank Examiner was, therefore, asked to inform you that the transaction referred to on page — of the current report of examination did not involve a violation of R.S. 5200.

   In the course of our further studies we have concluded that if the actual purpose and character of the transaction is that of a loan, the provisions of R.S. 5200 are applicable. In the instant case, your bank purchased the United States Government securities at par and they were repurchased by the selling bank at par the following day. The circumstances surrounding the transaction, the purchase and sale under agreement to repurchase without regard to the quoted value of the securities or the accrued interest thereon and the payment of interest for the period the funds were employed by the X National Bank, clearly reveal that the transaction was a loan by your bank to the X National Bank, not unlike a sale of Federal Funds for a one-day period with the advance collateraled by the pledge of a like amount of par value of securities.

   Under such conditions, the transaction falls within the purview of R.S. 5200 and R.S. 5202, and not R.S. 5136, and since the obligation of the borrowing (selling) bank exceeded 25% of the capital and surplus of your bank, as the lending institution, it was a violation of the provisions of R.S. 5200. Also, funds advanced by the lending institution should be included in "Loans and Discounts," and so reported in Call Reports of Condition.

   It will be necessary that you be governed accordingly in future transactions of this character.

                                        Very truly yours,

                                        (signed) L. A. Jennings
                                        Deputy Comptroller of the Currency

APPENDIX C
Recommendation of the Comptroller of the Currency, 1956

An excerpt from:

RECOMMENDATION OF THE COMPTROLLER OF THE CURRENCY

Letter of Transmittal

To SENATOR A. WILLIS ROBERTSON

By the SECRETARY OF THE TREASURY

on October 1, 1956

LOANS SECURED BY OBLIGATIONS OF THE UNITED STATES

Existing Law

Title 12, U.S.C., sec. 84 (U.S.R.S., sec. 5200).—The total obligations to any national banking association of any person, copartnership, association, or corporation shall at no time exceed 10 per centum of the amount of the capital stock of such association actually paid in and unimpaired and 10 per centum of its unimpaired surplus fund. The term "obligations" shall mean the direct liability of the maker or acceptor of paper discounted with or sold to such association and the liability of the endorser, drawer, or guarantor who obtains a loan from or discounts paper with or sells paper under his guaranty to such association and shall include in the case of obligations of a copartnership or association the obligations of the several members thereof and shall include in the case of obligations of a corporation all obligations of all subsidiaries thereof in which such corporation owns or controls a majority interest. Such limitation of 10 per centum shall be subject to the following exceptions:

● ● ● ● ●

(8) Obligations of any person, copartnership, association, or corporation in the form of notes secured by not less than a like amount of bonds or notes of the United States issued since April 24, 1917, or certificates of indebtedness of the United States, Treasury bills of the United States, or obligations fully guaranteed both as to principal and interest by the United States, shall (except to the extent permitted by rules and regulations prescribed by the Comptroller of the Currency, with the approval of the Secretary of the Treasury) be subject under this section to a limitation of 15 per centum of such capital and surplus in addition to such 10 per centum of such capital and surplus.

Recommendation

It is recommended that exception eighth of section 5200 of the Revised Statutes be amended so as to eliminate the words "in the form of notes."

Reasons

Frequently the obligations referred to in exception 8 are not in the form of promissory notes but are repurchase or some other form of binding obligations. These agreements are considered to be of equal stature with a promissory note and therefore should be treated as an obligation as defined in the first paragraph of section 84.

It is believed that the requirement that the obligation in the case of such loans must be "in the form of a note" is too restrictive and that such loans should be permitted when the obligation held by the lending bank meets the definition of the term "obligations."

APPENDIX D
Letter confining lending regulation applicability to repurchase between
banks only

February 1, 1957

TO ALL EXAMINERS AND ASSISTANT EXAMINERS
TENTH FEDERAL RESERVE DISTRICT

In Re: Purchase and sale of U. S. Government
Securities under an agreement.

Please refer to bulletin No. 99, dated September 25, 1956, wherein is quoted a letter received from Deputy Comptroller L. A. Jennings dated September 20, 1956, referring to the matter under caption.

There is quoted below, for your guidance, a supplemental letter from Mr. Jennings which is self-explanatory.

"Referring to our letter of September 20, 1956 pertaining to certain circumstances where R.S. 5200 or R.S. 5136 is applicable in a transaction between two banks involving the purchase and sale of United States Government securities under an agreement whereby the selling bank agrees to repurchase the securities, you are advised that this position should be limited strictly to transactions between two banks and not to repurchase or resale agreements between a bank and a Government Securities dealer or broker. Please advise all of your examiners of this position as we have been informed that some examiners have taken the position that transactions between banks and dealers. are subject to the same restrictions as those between two banks".

R. S. Beatty
Chief National Bank Examiner
Tenth Federal Reserve District

APPENDIX E
Letter from Comptroller raising lending limitation on government collateral to 100%

TREASURY DEPARTMENT
COMPTROLLER OF THE CURRENCY
WASHINGTON 25

ADDRESS REPLY TO
"COMPTROLLER OF THE CURRENCY"

July 23, 1957

TO ALL NATIONAL BANKS:

We are enclosing for your information copies of (1) the Investment Securities Regulation, as amended, and (2) a new regulation covering Loans Made by National Banks Secured by Direct Obligations of the United States. The two regulations were published in the Federal Register on July 17, 1957, and will become effective August 16, 1957.

The Investment Securities Regulation is issued by the Comptroller of the Currency under the authority contained in paragraph Seventh of section 5136 of the Revised Statutes (12 U.S.C. 24) and the purpose of this regulation is to prescribe the limitations and restrictions under which national banks, as well as State member banks of the Federal Reserve System, may purchase investment securities for their own account and to define the term "investment securities."

Under the existing regulation there has been doubt as to the eligibility of certain small issues of special revenue obligations because of the present distribution requirements set forth in paragraphs (a) and (b) of section 1. The new regulation clarifies the position that has been taken by the Comptroller with respect to the eligibility of small issues of special revenue obligations. While the distribution standards as stated in paragraphs (a) and (b) of section 1 of the present regulation and paragraphs (1) and (2) of section 2 of the new regulation may not be met by some small special revenue issues, it is recognized that many of such issues possess a high degree of credit soundness which assures marketability to the point contemplated by section 5136 of the Revised Statutes.

The restrictions in the present regulation governing the purchase or sale of securities by banks under repurchase or resale agreements are no longer considered desirable because of the basic nature of such transactions and are deleted from the new regulation. Experience has shown that repurchase or resale transactions in securities are used for the lending and borrowing of money. They will henceforth be treated as loan or borrowing transactions governed by sections 5200 and 5202 of the Revised Statutes (12 U.S.C. 84, 82) and not by section 5136 of the Revised Statutes (12 U.S.C. 24). This means that a bank selling securities under an agreement to repurchase them at a future date will be borrowing funds from the purchasing bank and section 5202 provides that national banks may not borrow an amount in excess of their capital stock except from a Federal Reserve Bank or as permitted under other exceptions to section 5202. The purchasing bank will be lending funds to the selling bank and, if direct obligations of the United States are involved, national banks, under the provisions of a new regulation discussed below, may lend up to 100% of their capital and surplus accounts on the basis of such security provided the amount of the loan in excess of 25% of capital and surplus is secured by direct obligations of the United States having maturities not exceeding 18 months.

The restrictions in the present regulation governing the amortization of premiums paid on investment securities are being amended in the new regulation to permit amortization to the maturity date rather than the call date of the issue, if Federal Internal Revenue Laws and regulations issued thereunder, disallow amortization deductions from gross income when computed to the nearest call date. Also amendments are being provided in the new regulation to clarify the section

APPENDIX E (*concluded*)

pertaining to securities convertible into stock. It has also been deemed advisable to incorporate into the new regulation a provision carrying out the present administrative practice which requires that investment securities owned by a bank be supported by adequate information in the files of the bank as to their investment quality.

The new regulation, "Loans Made by National Banks Secured by Direct Obligations of the United States", issued by the Comptroller, with the approval of the Secretary of the Treasury, under the authority contained in paragraph (8) of section 5200 of the Revised Statutes, as amended, prescribes conditions under which national banks may make loans to one borrower in excess of 25% of capital and surplus, and up to 100% of capital and surplus when such loans made in excess of 25% of capital and surplus are secured by direct obligations of the United States which will mature in not exceeding 18 months.

Under the terms of paragraph (8) of section 5200 of the Revised Statutes, national banks may lend to a single borrower an additional 15% of capital and surplus (in addition to the customary 10% limitation) on obligations secured by not less than a like amount of bonds or notes of the United States, certificates of indebtedness of the United States, Treasury Bills of the United States, or obligations fully guaranteed both as to principal and interest by the United States. Because of the amendments being made in the Investment Securities Regulation which will place resale and repurchase transactions in bonds under sections 5200 and 5202 of the Revised Statutes (12 U.S.C. 84, 82) rather than section 5136 of the Revised Statutes (12 U.S.C. 24), the present 25% limitation embodied in section 5200 is believed to be too restrictive with respect to loans to one borrower which are secured by not less than a like amount of direct obligations of the United States. Under the provisions of section 5136, repurchase and resale transactions involving United States Bonds have not been subject to any limitation measured by capital and surplus. The issuance of this regulation is necessary to implement the making of such loans above 25% and up to 100% of the bank's capital and surplus, provided they are secured by direct obligations of the United States which will mature within 18 months.

As stated above, the two regulations become effective August 16, 1957. It was not possible to include the regulations in the 1957 Supplement to the Digest of Opinions which has now been distributed to national banks. We will issue an investment securities Supplement to the Digest in approximately 30 days, which will include the new regulations and appropriate comments relating thereto in the paragraphs of the Digest dealing with the subject matter of the regulations.

Very truly yours,

R. M. GIDNEY
Comptroller of the Currency.

Enclosures

APPENDIX F
Investment regulation

TREASURY DEPARTMENT
COMPTROLLER OF THE CURRENCY
WASHINGTON 25

INVESTMENT SECURITIES REGULATION

SECTION 1 — SCOPE AND APPLICATION.

(a) This regulation is issued by the Comptroller of the Currency under authority of paragraph Seventh of Section 5136 of the Revised Statutes, as amended (12 U.S.C. 24);

(b) This regulation applies to the purchase for its own account of investment securities by a national bank or a State member bank of the Federal Reserve System.

SECTION 2 — DEFINITION OF THE TERM "INVESTMENT SECURITIES".

(a) An obligation of indebtedness which may be purchased for its own account by a national bank or State member bank of the Federal Reserve System in order to constitute an "investment security" within the meaning of paragraph Seventh of Section 5136 of the Revised Statutes, must be a marketable obligation, i.e., it must be salable under ordinary circumstances with reasonable promptness at a fair value; and except as provided in (b) and (c) below, there must be present one or both of the following characteristics:

(1) A public distribution of the securities must have been provided for or made in a manner to protect or insure the marketability of the issue; or,

(2) Other existing securities of the obligor must have such a public distribution as to protect or insure the marketability of the issue under consideration.

(b) In the case of investment securities for which a public distribution as set forth in (1) or (2) above cannot be so provided, or so made, and which are issued by established commercial or industrial businesses or enterprises, that can demonstrate the ability to service such securities, the debt evidenced thereby must mature not later than ten years after the date of issuance of the security and must be of such sound value or so secured as reasonably to assure its payment; and such securities must, by their terms, provide for the amortization of the debt evidenced thereby so that at least 75% of the principal will be extinguished by the maturity date by substantial periodic payments: Provided, that no amortization need be required for the period of the first year after the date of issuance of such securities.

(c) Special revenue obligations of States or local governments or of duly constituted public Authorities thereof which possess a high degree of credit soundness, so as to assure sale under ordinary circumstances with reasonable promptness at a fair value, but which do not meet the distribution standards of (a) (1) or (a) (2) above, may be considered to constitute "investment securities."

(d) Where the security is issued under a trust agreement, the agreement must provide for a trustee independent of the obligor, and such trustee must be a bank or trust company.

(e) All purchases of investment securities by national and State member banks for their own account must be securities "in the form of bonds, notes, and/or debentures, commonly known as investment securities"; and every transaction which is in fact such a purchase must, regardless of its form, comply with this regulation.

APPENDIX F (*concluded*)

SECTION 3 — LIMITATIONS AND RESTRICTIONS ON PURCHASE OF INVESTMENT SECURITIES FOR BANK'S OWN ACCOUNT.

(a) Although the bank is permitted to purchase "investment securities" for its own account for purposes of investment under the provisions of R. S. 5136 and this regulation, the bank is not permitted otherwise to participate as a principal in the marketing of securities.

(b) The statutory limitation on the amount of the "investment securities" of any one obligor or maker which may be held by the bank is to be determined on the basis of the par or face value of the securities, and not on their market value.

(c) The purchase of "investment securities" in which the investment characteristics are distinctly or predominantly speculative, or the purchase of securities which are in default, whether as to principal or interest, is prohibited.

(d) Purchase of an investment security at a price exceeding par or face value is prohibited, unless the bank shall:

(1) Provide for the regular amortization of the premium paid so that the premium shall be entirely extinguished at or before the maturity of the security, and the security (including premium) shall at no intervening date be carried at an amount in excess of that at which the obligator may legally redeem such security, unless the amortization which would be necessary to meet the latter requirement would not be allowable as a deduction from gross income under applicable Federal Internal Revenue laws and regulations issued thereunder, in which case the rate of amortization shall be sufficient to extinguish the premium by maturity; or

(2) Set up a reserve account to amortize the premium, said account to be credited periodically with an amount not less than the amount required for amortization under (1) above.

(e) Purchase of securities convertible into stock at the option of the issuer is prohibited.

(f) Purchase of securities convertible into stock at the option of the holder or with stock purchase warrants attached is prohibited if the price paid for such security is in excess of the investment value of the security itself, considered independently of the stock purchase warrants or conversion feature. If it is apparent that the price paid for an otherwise eligible security reflects the investment value of the security and does not include any speculative value based upon the presence of a stock purchase warrant or conversion option, the purchase of such security is not prohibited. If the price paid for a convertible security provides a yield reasonably similar to that of non-convertible securities of similar quality and maturity, a speculative value will not be deemed to exist.

(g) All investment securities shall be supported by adequate information in the files of the bank as to their investment quality.

SECTION 4 — EXCEPTION TO LIMITATIONS AND RESTRICTIONS.

The restrictions and limitations of this regulation do not apply to securities acquired through foreclosure on collateral, or acquired in good faith by way of compromise of a doubtful claim or to avert an apprehended loss in connection with a debt previously contracted, or to real estate securities acquired pursuant to Section 24 of the Federal Reserve Act, as amended.

SECTION 5 — EFFECTIVE DATE.

This regulation is effective August 16, 1957.

RAY M. GIDNEY
Comptroller of the Currency

APPENDIX G
Lending regulation, August 16, 1957

TREASURY DEPARTMENT
COMPTROLLER OF THE CURRENCY
WASHINGTON 25

REGULATION REGARDING NATIONAL BANK LOANS SECURED BY DIRECT OBLIGATIONS OF THE UNITED STATES

Section 5200 U.S.R.S. (12 U.S.C. 84) provides as follows:

"Sec. 5200. The total obligations to any national banking association of any person, copartnership, association, or corporation shall at no time exceed 10 per centum of the amount of the capital stock of such association actually paid in and unimpaired and 10 per centum of its unimpaired surplus fund. The term 'obligations' shall mean the direct liability of the maker or acceptor of paper discounted with or sold to such association and the liability of the indorser, drawer, or guarantor who obtains a loan from or discounts paper with or sells paper under his guaranty to such association and shall include in the case of obligations of a copartnership or association the obligations of the several members thereof and shall include in the case of obligations of a corporation all obligations of all subsidiaries thereof in which such corporation owns or controls a majority interest. Such limitation of 10 per centum shall be subject to the following exceptions:

*   *   *   *

"(8) Obligations of any person, copartnership, association, or corporation in the form of notes secured by not less than a like amount of bonds or notes of the United States issued since April 24, 1917, or certificates of indebtedness of the United States, Treasury bills of the United States, or obligations fully guaranteed both as to principal and interest by the United States, shall (except to the extent permitted by rules and regulations prescribed by the Comptroller of the Currency, with the approval of the Secretary of the Treasury) be subject under this section to a limitation of 15 per centum of such capital and surplus in addition to such 10 per centum of such capital and surplus."

SECTION 1 — SCOPE AND APPLICATION.

(a) This regulation is issued by the Comptroller of the Currency with the approval of the Secretary of the Treasury under authority of paragraph (8) of section 5200 of the Revised Statutes, as amended (12 U.S.C. 84), and section 321 (b) of the Act of August 23, 1935 (49 Stat. 713);

(b) This regulation applies to loans made by national banks secured by direct obligations of the United States which will mature in not exceeding 18 months.

SECTION 2 — GENERAL AUTHORIZATION.

The obligations to any national banking association in the form of notes of any person, copartnership, association, or corporation, secured by not less than a like amount of direct obligations of the United States which will mature in not exceeding eighteen months from the date such obligations to such national banking association are entered into shall be limited to 75 per centum of the capital and surplus of such association in addition to the 10 per centum of such capital and surplus prescribed in the opening paragraph of said section 5200 and the 15 per centum limitation referred to in paragraph (8) of section 5200.

SECTION 3 — EFFECTIVE DATE.

This regulation is effective August 16, 1957.

RAY M. GIDNEY
Comptroller of the Currency

Approved:
GEORGE M. HUMPHREY
Secretary of the Treasury

APPENDIX H
Lending regulation, April 18, 1958

TREASURY DEPARTMENT
COMPTROLLER OF THE CURRENCY
WASHINGTON 25
REGULATION REGARDING NATIONAL BANK LOANS SECURED BY DIRECT OBLIGATIONS OF THE UNITED STATES

Section 5200 U.S.R.S. (12 U.S.C. 84) provides as follows:

"Sec. 5200. The total obligations to any national banking association of any person, copartnership, association, or corporation shall at no time exceed 10 per centum of the amount of the capital stock of such association actually paid in and unimpaired and 10 per centum of its unimpaired surplus fund. The term 'obligations' shall mean the direct liability of the maker or acceptor of paper discounted with or sold to such association and the liability of the indorser, drawer, or guarantor who obtains a loan from or discounts paper with or sells paper under his guaranty to such association and shall include in the case of obligations of a copartnership or association the obligations of the several members thereof and shall include in the case of obligations of a corporation all obligations of all subsidiaries thereof in which such corporation owns or controls a majority interest. Such limitation of 10 per centum shall be subject to the following exceptions:

* * * *

"(8) Obligations of any person, copartnership, association, or corporation in the form of notes secured by not less than a like amount of bonds or notes of the United States issued since April 24, 1917, or certificates of indebtedness of the United States, Treasury bills of the United States, or obligations fully guaranteed both as to principal and interest by the United States, shall (except to the extent permitted by rules and regulations prescribed by the Comptroller of the Currency, with the approval of the Secretary of the Treasury) be subject under this section to a limitation of 15 per centum of such capital and surplus in addition to such 10 per centum of such capital and surplus."

SECTION 1 — SCOPE AND APPLICATION.

(a) This regulation is issued by the Comptroller of the Currency with the approval of the Secretary of the Treasury under authority of paragraph (8) of section 5200 of the Revised Statutes, as amended (12 U.S.C. 84), and section 321 (b) of the Act of August 23, 1935 (49 Stat. 713);

(b) This regulation applies to loans made by national banks secured by direct obligations of the United States which will mature in not exceeding 18 months.

SECTION 2 — GENERAL AUTHORIZATION.

The obligations to any national banking association in the form of notes of any person, copartnership, association, or corporation, secured by not less than a like amount of direct obligations of the United States which will mature in not exceeding eighteen months from the date such obligations to such national banking association are entered into shall not be subject to any limitation based upon the capital and surplus of the association.

SECTION 3 — EFFECTIVE DATE.

This regulation is effective April 18, 1958

RAY M. GIDNEY
Comptroller of the Currency

Approved:
ROBERT B. ANDERSON
Secretary of the Treasury

Chapter 10

Two repo-market arbitrages and more on market practices

WHILE REPOS STARTED AS FINANCING TRANSACTIONS, such trades and reverses soon became an accepted part of various money market arbitrages. In this chapter, we describe two arbitrages, one that uses a repo, another that uses a reverse. We also talk some more about repo market practices.

TWO REPO-MARKET ARBITRAGES

Strictly speaking, a money market trader, dealer, or investor is said to do an *arbitrage (arb)* whenever he *simultaneously* buys and sells securities or borrows and lends money—basically, does several legs of a multilegged trade—at rates or prices such that he locks in a profit. Most money market arbs are in truth bets placed by a trader in situations where some *uncertainty* exists with respect to the outcome of the trade. When a money market trader speaks of putting on a "risk" arb (an expression that a pure economist might argue is a contradiction in terms), he's describing the putting on of a multilegged trade that will, with a high degree of probability, earn him a positive return. He's talking about taking a gamble, the odds on which are, in his estimate, in his favor; in the argot of probability theorists, such a gamble is known as a "favorable bet."

Tails

When dealers first began to borrow from corporations by doing repos, they typically used such funds to finance the inventory they would normally hold as market makers. Later, they got a notion of how to use repo money more profitably. When a corporation came to a dealer saying, "We have money to go for 60 days," the dealer it approached did a quick calculation: "XYZ wants to give me money for 30 days. If, to satisfy his demand for collateral, I buy 90-day bills in the auction and then finance those bills with him for 30 days, I'll have a 60-day 'tail' [60-day future security] coming back at me 30 days hence. My carry is positive, and currently the 60-day bill rate is below the 90-day bill rate. Unless rates go up, look at the money I'll make selling the tail!" In this instance, the dealer is betting on the future market value of collateral (bills) he purchased specifically to cover the repo contract desired by the corporation. The profit potential in such trades (i.e., creating tails) caused dealers to seek out financing for longer periods, to look to do *term repos*.

Creating a tail is a form of risk arb that money market traders frequently do. If a trader, simultaneous to creating a tail, sells in effect that tail by shorting a futures contract, he may be able to eliminate all risk in his trade; whether he does so depends on how closely the futures short and the cash-market tail he creates match.[1]

Reverses to maturity

As the repo market matured, clever traders found all sorts of profitable trades to do with repos and reverses. Here's one trade that was created for the "I-can't-take-a-loss" portfolio manager.

In a world where interest rates go both up and down, some portfolio managers will inevitably end up holding at times securities having a current *market value* that is less than their current *book value,* that is, securities in which the investor has a *paper* (unrealized) *loss;* in Street-speak, such securities are described suggestively as being "underwater." Banks, savings and loan associations (S&Ls), savings banks, and credit unions may all carry securities on their books at market value or at book value, whichever is greater. Frequently, this option creates the following choice for such institutions: (1) sell underwater securities, book a loss, and reinvest the proceeds at a higher yield, one that, because it raises the yield on the portfolio, more than covers the loss booked plus the yield forgone on the securities sold; or (2) hang onto the underwater securities until they mature, avoid booking a loss, and earn a

---

[1] See the appendix to this chapter, for two numerical examples of trades involving tails. This appendix also introduces the concept of the *implied repo rate* on a cash-and-carry trade using futures.

lower yield on the portfolio than the first choice would produce. Faced with these options, institutions frequently opt for the second choice.

In periods when rates have risen, this decision locks many institutions into holding securities at yields below those they could get on alternative investments of comparable maturity. Clever dealers have custom designed a special trade for portfolio managers holding an underwater bond, typically one that is in its last coupon period (six months or less from maturity).

A dealer, noticing on the quote sheet an old, low-coupon bond (or note) that is in its last coupon period and that is selling below par, will ask two questions: (1) If I were to reverse in that security for a period equal to its *current maturity* (time left to maturity) and if I were then to immediately sell that security in the market, what's my break-even (zero-profit-to-the-dealer) reverse rate on the loan that I'd have to make to the security owner? (2) Is there some other investment—term Fed funds maybe—of equal maturity on which the security owner could get a rate at least 50 points above my break-even reverse rate? If so, I will set my lending rate, on a reverse to maturity of that security, 50 basis points below the best rate at which the security owner could invest, for the life of the reverse, the funds I lend him.

The dealer, who sets his reverse rate this way, offers the security owner the opportunity to do a profitable arbitrage. The dealer describes the arb as follows: "Borrow from me at rate X, for a period equal to the current maturity of your securities, a sum approximately equal to the market value of those securities. Invest the funds you borrow in term Fed funds at X plus 50 basis points. By doing so, you will pick up 50 basis points of yield above what you would have earned if you held your underwater bonds to maturity and did no reverse." Fifty basis points is the golden number because it seems to be the yield pick up that is both necessary and sufficient to move a hold-until-maturity portfolio manager to reverse out securities and do an arbitrage.

Reverses to maturity (RTMs, as some are wont to call them) are important because they are common and much understood. Regulators are wont to view reverses to maturity as risky. In fact, they are about the only reverse transaction in which both the lender and the borrower lock in a profit and incur *no* market risk of any sort. At maturity, the dealer offsets the amount he has lent to the investor plus accrued interest on the reverse against the face value of the security he has reversed in, plus its final coupon payment; settlement is made via a difference check; consequently, credit risk on the transaction is also small to negligible for both parties.

Another interesting characteristic of a reverse to maturity is that it is the one repo-market transaction where the lender of funds always sells out the collateral he gets immediately and never buys it back for redelivery to the supplier of collateral. The supplier of collateral typically assumes that the dealer holds the collateral he receives until it matures and is redeemed by the Treasury for face value. The supplier of collateral is surprised to learn, if he ever does, that the dealer in fact sold his collateral at the time the reverse was put on.

Reverses to maturity are the one instance in which a repo-type trade comes closest to resembling a securities sale. This is ironic for two reasons. First, in such a trade, the supplier of collateral has done what amounts to a security sale without knowing it and without booking it as such (dealers book reverses to maturity as securities trades, not loans). Second, in a reverse to maturity, the supplier of collateral is doing a trade that he could have done without help from the dealer and without giving the dealer a slice—sometimes the lion's share—of the profit inherent in the trade. The sole reason the security owner needs and uses the dealer is that he is unwilling to book the loss he would incur if he did an outright, undisguised sale of his underwater security.

A dealer's break-even rate on a reverse to maturity.   In a discussion of reverses to maturity, a natural question to ask is the following: How can one calculate a dealer's break-even rate on a reverse to maturity? This calculation is one that any dealer doing reverses to maturity must make and one that investors doing the trade should also make—the latter to check out the fairness of the terms they are getting from their dealer.

Calculating a dealer's break-even rate on a reverse to maturity turns out to be simple. It involves two steps. Step one is to calculate the *true* yield to maturity of a particular short government or agency; that yield may differ significantly from the figure on a quote sheet for the security's yield to maturity because the accepted industry formula for calculating yield to maturity on short coupons is incorrect on several counts. Step two in the break-even calculation is to convert the security's true yield to maturity to the basis (360-day) on which the reverse rate is quoted.[2]

CUSTOMER ARBS

When a dealer shows a customer an attractive opportunity to do a reverse to maturity and invest the proceeds, the customer likely ends up doing an arb. Customers also do similar arbs in which the reverse is not a reverse to maturity. A customer might, for example, reverse out for 30

---

[2] For a precise description of these calculations, see Marcia Stigum and John Mann, *Money Market Calculations: Yields, Break-Evens, and Arbitrage* (Homewood, Ill.: Dow Jones-Irwin, 1981), chap. 8, pp. 93–95.

days securities in his bond portfolio and then invest the proceeds in some 30-day instrument whose yield exceeds the 30-day reverse rate. An institution doing such an arb suffers an apparent loss of liquidity because, once securities are put out on a term reverse, the reverse agreement cannot be broken, and thus, the underlying securities cannot be sold. For this reason, one might argue, as some have, that banks and S&Ls that put securities in their *liquidity portfolios* out on term repo are impinging on their liquidity. In all probability, however, they are not. Most of the time they are reversing out securities that they would in almost no circumstance consider selling. Also, if worst comes to worst, they can raise cash by selling or repoing the asset they have acquired as the other leg of the arbitrage.

Real risk in the arb game occurs when an unsophisticated portfolio manager buys, say, long bonds or Ginnies and promptly reverses them out, often to the selling dealer, at a short-term reverse rate that is low relative to the long-term yield on the securities purchased. The objective of the investor is to garner, without putting much money (margin) down, the spread between the reverse rate and the yield on the securities he purchases. His risk—a *big* one—is that rates will rise and thereby cause to occur two particulars: (1) his arb spread narrows, even turns negative, and (2) the price of the securities he is long plummets. Arbs of this genre, which are supposed merely to sweeten current earnings a bit, have bankrupted more than one credit union and S&L. Concerning such arbs, a dealer's comment, made circa 1978, is as apropos today as it was then: "Buying the 8s of 86 at a book yield of 10.05½ and repoing them at 7½ can look attractive to a small investor when the idea is presented to him. But should interest rates rise, he may get burned on this strategy, because he loses more money selling these bonds than he has earned arbitraging against them."

MORE ON REPO-MARKET PRACTICES

In the remainder of this chapter, we talk about practices that evolved in the repo market, principally those designed to deal with the credit risk inherent in repo-market trades.

Credit risk

While many of the trappings of a securities transaction have been given to repos—they start with a sale of securities and end with a purchase of securities—repos remain in their gut (in their true economic significance) collateralized loans. As such, a repo always creates credit risk for the lender of money.

As the repo market was reborn, dealers sought to structure repos so as to minimize credit risk to investors in repo and to increase, thereby, the willingness of investors to place money in repo. Early repos were, as noted, done on a *delivery* basis—the dealer delivered to the investor whatever collateral he was financing in exchange for the money the investor lent to him. The notion was that if the dealer were to go belly-up and thus be unable to repay at maturity the investor's loan to him, the latter could always make himself whole by selling off the collateral the dealer had placed in his possession. The investor had, moreover, the right, in the event of the dealer's bankruptcy, to sell the latter's collateral pronto; that was important because the value of any collateral the investor might hold was subject to market risk—in particular to the risk that a sharp upswing in interest rates might cut the market price and thus the value of that collateral.

Pricing of collateral.   For the giving of collateral to fully protect the lender of money against credit risk, it was crucial that the collateral be properly priced. On repos, the proper price was taken to be current market value—except that, as time passed, accrued interest on interest-bearing securities was not, as it would be in a cash-market trade, included in the calculation of market value. Recall from Chapter 4 that the market value (full price) that a cash buyer of a government bond or note must pay for that security is its current market price *plus* any interest accrued from the last coupon date.

Margin.   Due to market risk, the value of securities collateral is subject to unpredictable changes. To cover this risk, the practice grew up that, in a repo, the borrower of money would give the lender of money *margin;* for example, a dealer financing a government bond that was trading at 102 might ask for a loan of only 100; in doing so, the borrower of money was giving the lender of money a 2-point margin as protection against market risk. In Street-speak, the giving of margin is often referred to as a *haircut.*

The margins given by borrowers in the repo market vary over time with market conditions. However, it is always the case that most lenders want more margin the less liquid a security is and the more volatile its price is. Consistent with this practice, repo lenders typically take less margin if the collateral repoed is Treasury bills with short current maturities than if the collateral repoed is long Treasury bonds or GNMAs.

Margin calls.   On longer repos *(term repos),* there is always the possibility that adverse price movements may swamp any margin given. To protect against this eventuality, the practice became that, on term repo agreements, the investor had the right to make a *margin call* on the borrower of money in the event that the market value of the collateral given initially to him fell appreciably. A margin call required that the collateral be repriced at its then current market value and that an adjustment be made to bring the amount of money lent into line with the current value, properly haircut, of that collateral. When the value of collateral given by the borrower of money fell, he could make this adjustment either by providing additional collateral or by repaying some of the money he had borrowed.

Treatment of coupon interest.   In repos and reverses, it used to be standard practice to ignore accrued coupon interest in pricing collateral. It's easy to guess how this practice arose. When the repo market was first revived after World War II, interest rates were low; and the interest accrued on, say, a government long bond during a six-month coupon period did not amount to the big bucks that it did in the late 1970s, early 1980s, when long-term interest rates soared to the high teens. Another reason for ignoring accrued interest in pricing repo collateral was surely that the calculation is a nuisance. Also, repo market participants could reason, "What the heck, repo is structured so that the lender of money gets margin; by ignoring accrued interest in pricing repo collateral, we're just making margin a little richer on repos collateralized by interest-bearing securities."

The practice of excluding repo interest from the calculation of the market value of repo collateral was discontinued after the failure of Drysdale. At that time, the market changed to what's called *full accrual pricing* (Chapters 13 and 14).

Interest due on notes and bonds is paid on semiannual coupon dates (Chapter 4). Whenever a coupon payment is made on a security that serves as collateral in a delivery repo, the interest due is paid to the lender of money, since it is he who is holding the collateral. It is market practice, however, that any and all coupon interest paid on securities that serve as repo collateral is the property of the ultimate owner of those securities. Thus, if during the term of a repo, the lender of money receives a coupon payment on collateral delivered to him, he is expected to transfer that payment to the repo borrower who is the ultimate owner of the collateral.

Credit risk to the reverse party.   While the margin mechanism was set up to protect the lender of money against credit risk, credit risk in a repo is in fact a *two-way* street. The giver of collateral must ask, "What happens if the lender of money goes belly-up and I do not get my collateral back?" Because of the margin mechanism, a dealer or other party reversing out securities *always* faces credit risk: in the event of bankruptcy by the investor, he risks losing the margin he has given the latter, and until recently (until after Drysdale's default), he also risked losing any accrued interest on his securities if the latter were interest bearing.

Because credit risk is a two-way street, margin calls can be made in *two* directions. A borrower of money might, if the market value of his collateral rose, want to ask the lender of money either for more money or for a return of some of his collateral.

From the start of the repo market, the mechanism—market practices—were in place to give a wary lender of money full protection against credit risk and to give a wary giver of collateral reasonable protection against credit risk. The key elements of this protection were delivery, proper pricing, and the maintenance over the life of the repo of margin at a reasonable level. Over time, as the repo market grew and as more and more participants became investors and borrowers in this market, slippage occurred in the adherence of many repo participants to these market practices. That slippage set the stage for the sizable losses that various participants in the repo market experienced due to the many dealer bankruptcies that occurred in the late 1970s and early 1980s. More about that in Chapters 13 and 14.

Everyone's market

The all-private repo market began its post–World War II revival as a strictly wholesale market in which substantial, well-known, creditworthy institutions were present on both the lending and borrowing sides. Over time, more and more participants entered this market as repos became familiar to an increasing number of money market folk. Also, every uptick of interest rates drew yet more participants into the market by raising perceptibly the opportunity cost incurred by a holder of idle funds.

The entry of so many participants into the repo market, many of whom do small deals, has created a situation in which there are many different repo markets: the national repo market centered in and brokered in New York and a host of smaller regional and local repo markets. In the latter, regional dealers all over the country do repos with their retail customers at rates that reflect, but may be a spread off, rates in the national market. Below the regional markets are local markets in which, for example, the local school district may do repos with a local bank. Deals done by a true country bank with a local municipal body are often small. Many municipal bodies are required by law to do their repos with a bank that is chartered to do business in their state. Where municipalities have big deals to do in repos, these are sometimes booked by a local bank that lays off the money taken in with a New York dealer who supplies collateral for the trade.

The last group to enter the repo market was consumers, a group for whom repo investments were neither designed nor intended. Consumers were drawn into the repo market by the rise to historic highs of interest rates during the late 1970s and early 1980s. Consumers who invested in repo did so mostly with local depository institutions, and the sums they invested were small; such consumers thought that investing in repo was akin to investing in a money market mutual fund. A few such consumers ended up doing repos with institutions—including at least one secondary dealer—that eventually went belly-up; those consumers got a rude awaking and an education, sometimes expensive, about the way that credit risk can creep insidiously into a seemingly safe, simple, straightforward transaction.

THE NEXT CHAPTERS

In the next two chapters, we turn first to the clearing of money market trades, and then to the clearing of repo and reverse trades—subjects of considerable interest to the many lawyers who have become involved in the various repo cases that have in recent years wended their way through the courts. These chapters set the stage for Chapter 13 in which we talk about the use by investors, for holding both repo collateral and other securities, of dealer safekeeping and of custody banks.

Appendix to chapter 10
Two examples of "tails"

Tails can be confusing. The easiest way to explain what is involved is with examples. In this appendix, we first present a classic cash-market trade. We then work through a cash-and-carry trade involving futures; trades of the latter sort became possible and popular after the introduction in 1976 of trading in T bill futures.

TAILS: A CASH-MARKET TRADE

Assume a dealer is operating in an environment in which the 90-day bill is trading at a rate one-eighth below the Fed funds rate. Assume also that Fed funds are trading at 8.075, the 90-day bill at 7.95, and 30-day term repo at 7.50.

If in this environment the dealer were to buy 90-day bills and finance them with 30-day term repo, he would earn over the 30-day holding period a positive carry equal to

$$7.95 - 7.50$$

or a profit equal to 45 basis points over 30 days. He would also have created *future* 60-day bills, namely, the unfinanced *tail* of the 90-day bills purchased.

If he thought, as dealers do, of the carry profit over the initial holding period as raising the yield at which he in effect buys the future security, then by purchasing the 90-day bill at 7.95 and repoing it for 30 days at 7.50, he would have acquired future 60-day bills at a yield of 8.05.[3] The 45-basis-point carry, which is earned for 30 days, adds only 10 basis points to the yield at which the future security is effectively purchased because the latter has a maturity of 60 days, which is twice as long as the period over which positive carry is earned.

Faced with this opportunity, the dealer would ask himself: How attractive is it to contract to buy a 60-day bill at 8.05 for delivery 30 days hence? Note the dealer would precisely break even, clearing costs ignored, if he were able to sell that future bill at a rate of 8.05. Thus, contracting to buy the future bill would be attractive if he believed he could sell the future bill at a rate below 8.05.

The dealer's answer to the question he has posed might run as

---

[3] Note that the *higher* the yield at which a discount security is purchased, the *lower* the purchase price. So buying the future security at 8.05 is, from the dealer's point of view, better than buying it at 7.95.

follows: Currently, the yield curve is such that 60-day bills are trading 15 basis points below the rate on 90-day bills. Therefore, if the 60-day bill were to trade at 8.05 one month hence and if yield spreads did not change, that would imply that the 90-day bill would be trading at 8.175 and Fed funds at 8.30, that is, at levels approximately ¼ above the present rates. I do not believe that the Fed will tighten or that yield spreads will change unfavorably; therefore, I will do the trade.

If the dealer were correct and the Fed did not tighten and yield spreads did not change, he would be able to sell 30 days hence the future 60-day bill he had created at 7.80, which is the rate that would be the prevailing rate at that time on the 60-day bill, if his predictions with respect to yield and yields spread were correct.[4] In doing so, he would make a profit equal to ¼ (the purchase rate 8.05 minus the sale rate 7.80) on a 60-day security.

Of course, the dealer's predictions might prove to be favorable. Note, however, he has some built-in margin of protection. Specifically, if he were able to sell his future bills at any rate above 7.80 but still below 8.05, he would make some profit, albeit less than he would if he sold at 7.80. On the other hand, if rates or rate spreads moved so unfavorably that he ended up selling his future 60-day bills at a rate above 8.05, he would lose money.

For the benefit of those who like to look at dollar numbers rather than yields, we have reworked the example presented in dollars in Table 10–1. Recall the 60-day bill was assumed to be trading at a rate 15 basis points below the rate on the 90-day bill, at 7.95 − .15, or 7.80.

In deciding whether to buy securities and finance them for some period, dealers invariably "figure the tail," that is, determine the effective yield at which they are buying the future security created. Whether the security financed is a discount security or an interest-bearing one, this yield can be figured approximately as follows.[5]

$$
\begin{pmatrix} \text{Effective yield} \\ \text{at which future} \\ \text{security is} \\ \text{purchased} \end{pmatrix} = \begin{pmatrix} \text{Yield at} \\ \text{which cash} \\ \text{security is} \\ \text{purchased} \end{pmatrix} \times \begin{pmatrix} \text{Rate of} \\ \text{profit} \times \text{Days} \\ \dfrac{\text{on carry} \quad \text{carried}}{\text{Days left to maturity}} \\ \text{at end of carry period} \end{pmatrix}
$$

Applying this formula to our example, we get:

$$
7.95 + \frac{.20 \times 30}{60} = 7.95 + .10 = 8.05
$$

---

[4] Recall the 60-day bill was assumed to be trading at a rate 15 basis points below the rate on the 90-day bill, at 7.95 − .15 = 7.80.

[5] There is bias in this approximation. For a formula giving the precise yield calculation on a tail, see Stigum and Mann, *Money Market Calculations,* pp. 41–45.

TABLE 10–1
Figuring the tail: An example*

Step 1: The dealer buys $1 million of 90-day bills at a 7.95% rate of discount

$$\text{Discount at which bills are purchased} = \frac{d \times t}{360} \times F = \frac{0.795 \times 90}{360} \times \$1,000,000$$

$$= \$19,875$$

$$\text{Price at which bills are purchased} = F - D = 1,000,000 - 19,875$$
$$= \$980,125$$

The dealer finances the bills purchased for 30 days at 7¾% repo rate.

$$\text{Financing cost†} = \frac{.0775 \times 30}{360} \times \$1,000,000$$

$$= \$6,458$$

Step 2: At the end of 30 days, the dealer owns the bills at a net cost figure. Determine what yield this cost figure implies on the future 60-day bills created

$$\text{Net cost of future 60-day bills} = \text{Purchase price} + \text{Financing cost}$$
$$= \$980,125 + \$6,458$$
$$= \$986,583$$

$$\text{Net discount at which 60-day bills are owned} = F - \text{Net cost}$$
$$= \$1,000,000 - \$986,583$$
$$= \$13,417$$

$$\text{Rate at which future 60-day bills are purchased‡} = \frac{360 \times D}{t \times F} = \frac{360 \times \$13,417}{60 \times \$1,000,000}$$

$$= .0805$$
$$= 8.05\%$$

Step 3: Future 60-day bills created are sold at 7.80% discount rate. Calculate dollar profit

$$\text{Discount at which bills are sold} = \frac{d \times t}{360} \times F$$

$$= \frac{0.0780 \times 60}{360} \times \$1,000,000$$

$$= \$13,000$$

$$\text{Profit} = \text{Net purchase discount} - \text{Discount sale}$$
$$= \$13,417 - \$13,000$$
$$= \$417$$

Step 4: Figure the annualized yield on a discount basis that $417 represents on a 60-day security

$$d = \frac{360 \times D}{t \times F} = \frac{360 \times \$417}{60 \times \$1,000,000}$$

$$= .0025$$
$$= ¼\%$$

* For explanation of formulas used, see Chapter 3.
† Actually, less than $1 million has to be borrowed, which is one reason why the dealer's approach to figuring the tail is only an approximation. A second reason is that the bill rate is a discount rate, the repo rate is an add-on rate.
‡ Solving the equation

$$D = F(dt/360)$$

for d, gives us

$$d = 360D/tF$$

Risk

A dealer who engages in the sort of transaction we have just described incurs a rate risk. He might end up with a loss or a smaller profit than anticipated because the Fed tightened unexpectedly, because bill rates rose relative to the Fed funds rate due to, say, heavy bill sales by the Treasury; or because a shift in the yield curve narrowed the spread between 60- and 90-day bills. Thus, whether a dealer who thinks such a transaction would be profitable decides to take the position and the size in which he takes it will depend both on the confidence he has in his rate and spread predictions and the amount of risk to which he thinks it would expose him.

The same sort of transaction could also be done in other securities: BAs, commercial paper, or CDs. In each case, the yield spreads that would have to be estimated would differ from those estimated in our bill example. If the instrument purchased and financed were CDs, the risk would be perceptibly greater than if the instrument were bills because supply is more difficult to predict in the CD market than in the bill market, and CDs back up faster than bills.

TAILS: A CASH-AND-CARRY TRADE USING FUTURES

After the introduction of trading in bill futures, it became possible for traders to lock in the price at which a tail they created would later be sold, that is, to *hedge* tails they created. We preface our example of such a trade with a brief description of the bill futures contract.

Bill futures[6]

In January 1976, the International Monetary Market (IMM), now part of the Chicago Mercantile Exchange (CME), opened trading in futures contracts for 3-month Treasury bills. The trading of futures contracts for financial instruments was not new. In October 1975 the Chicago Board of Trade opened trading in futures contracts for Ginnie Mae pass-throughs, and prior to that the IMM had introduced trading in futures contracts for major foreign currencies. Still, introduction of the bill futures contract was an important innovation for the money market because trading in Ginnie Mae pass-throughs and foreign exchange lies at the fringe of what could strictly be called money market activities. In contrast, the bill

---

[6] For a description of the operations of a futures exchange and of the mechanics of hedging, see Marcia Stigum, *The Money Market* (Homewood, Ill.: Dow Jones-Irwin, 1983), chap. 14.

market is a key sector of the money market, and as part of their normal investing or borrowing activities, every money market participant could find potential uses for sales or purchases of bill futures contracts.

The basic bill contract traded on the IMM is for $1 million of 90-day Treasury bills. Currently, a contract matures once each quarter—in those weeks of March, June, September, and December when the newly auctioned 3-month bill is a reopening of an old year bill. Thus, at any time, there are eight contracts outstanding; and when a new contract starts to trade, the furthest delivery date stretches 24 months into the future.

Bills trade and are quoted in the cash market on a yield basis; consequently, the bid always exceeds the offer. Also, when yield rises, price falls, and vice versa. This seems reasonable to a person accustomed to trading money market instruments, but it confuses a person who is accustomed to trading commodities or stocks. The IMM therefore decided not to quote bill contracts directly in terms of yield. Instead, it developed an index system in which a bill is quoted at a "price equal to 100.0 minus yield"; a bill yield of 8.50 would thus be quoted on the IMM at 91.50. Note that in this system, when yield falls, the index price rises; and the trader with a long position in futures profits. This conforms to the relationship that prevails in other commodity futures markets, where long positions profit when prices rise and short positions profit when prices fall.

Price fluctuations on bill futures are in multiples of an 01 (one basis point). Because the contract is for delivery of 90-day bills, each 01 is worth $25.

A cash-and-carry trade

A trade that is done in bill futures in huge volume when rates are right and that tends to link rates on cash and futures bills is one that has been dubbed the cash-and-carry trade. This trade could be done by many investors, but it is most commonly done by professional speculators and large dealers; today every dealer shop has someone who watches the relationship between cash, futures, and term repo rates and puts on this trade in size whenever that relationship makes the trade profitable.

For a leveraged investor, an attractive tactic is to buy a cash bill, finance it with term repo, and cover the rate risk on the resulting tail by selling that tail in the futures market. Whether doing so will be profitable depends on the relationship between the term repo rate, the rate on the long cash bill, and the futures rate. There must be some term repo rate at which a dealer who does the above transaction will just break even; this break-even rate has been dubbed the *implied repo rate*. Whenever the prevailing repo rate is less than the implied repo rate, putting on a cash-and-carry trade yields a profit.

To illustrate this trade, we use rates that prevailed in the market in the fall of 1982, as good a date as any. On October 28, 1982, the 3/24/83 bill, which was the deliverable bill for the December 1982 bill futures contract, was trading at 8.26. On the same day, the December bill contract, which expired 56 days hence, was trading at 8.28.

The repo rate is an add-on, 360-day rate. Thus, to calculate the implied repo rate on a cash-and-carry trade based on the above cash and futures rates, one must calculate the holding period yield (HPY) on a 360-day basis that an investor could have earned if he had bought the 3/24/83 bill at 8.26 and simultaneously sold that bill at 8.28 for delivery 56 days hence in the futures market.

That calculation, worked out in Table 10–2, shows that holding period yield—the implied or break-even repo rate—was 8.51.

Had the actual term repo rate for a 56-day repo been 8.25 on October 28, 1982, then by buying the 3/24/83 bill, financing it for 56 days at 8.25, and selling the resulting tail in the futures market at 8.28, a trader could have picked up $3,908.03 per $10 million of the trade he put on (Table 10–3).

Comparing the 8.25 term repo rate with the 8.51 implied repo rate suggests that this trade offers a locked-in profit of 26 basis points on the amount invested for 56 days. In fact, there are a few slips twixt the cup

TABLE 10–2
Calculating the implied repo rate which equals holding period yield earned on a 360-day basis on the bill*

Step 1 On 10/28/82 purchase $1 million of the 3/24/83 bill at 8.26%.

$$\text{Purchase price} = (\$1,000,000)(.0826)\left(\frac{147}{360}\right)$$
$$= \$966,271.67$$

Step 2 On 10/28/82 simultaneously sell the December 1982 bill futures contract at 91.72, which corresponds to a yield of 8.28%.

$$\text{Sale price} = (\$1,000,000)(.0828)\left(\frac{91}{360}\right)$$
$$= \$979,070.00$$

Step 3 Calculate holding period yield (HPY), which equals the implied repo rate.

$$\text{HPY} = \text{Implied repo rate} = \left(\frac{\text{Sale price} - \text{Purchase price}}{\text{Purchase price}}\right)\left(\frac{\text{Annualization}}{\text{factor}}\right)$$

$$= \left(\frac{\$979,070.00 - \$966,271.67}{\$966,271.67}\right)\left(\frac{360}{56}\right)$$

$$= .0851 = 8.51\%$$

* For a simple formula for calculating the implied repo rate on a bill trade, see Marcia Stigum and John Mann, *Money Market Calculations: Yields, Break-Evens, and Arbitrage* (Homewood, Ill.: Dow Jones-Irwin, 1981), pp. 161–66.

TABLE 10–3
Calculating the profit on a $10 million cash-and-carry trade if rates were those in Table 10–2 and the term repo rate was 8.25%

A: Formula

Profit = (HPY − term repo rate)(Amount invested)(Fraction of year invested)

B: Profit calculation

$$\text{Profit} = (.0851 - .0825)(\$9,662,716.70)\left(\frac{56}{360}\right)$$
$$= \$3,908.03$$

and the lip: a few things that might or will happen to alter the spread earned on the trade. First commissions—what commission a trader must pay on his futures trade—will depend on who he is and the size in which he deals. In the worst case our trader is an investor who pays a $72 commission on his futures trade, far more than a big spec account would pay; that $72 commission would knock down his profit spread by approximately 5 basis points, from 26 to 21 basis points.

A second factor that will affect the outcome of the trade is variation margin.[7] If bill rates rise sharply over the holding period, variation margin in the form of investable dollars will be paid into the trader's margin account, which—assuming he invests these dollars—will raise his return on the trade. Our trader's 26-basis-point profit spread would conversely be threatened by a rally in bills, which would result in margin calls that he would have to meet in cash. How much of a threat do potential margin calls pose to our trader? Relatively little. Even in the unlikely event that bills rallied 100 basis points on the day the trade was settled (10/28/82), the extra margin he would have to put up over 56 days would, assuming a 8.25 financing rate, cost him only 2¼ basis points of his profit spread.

A third factor that might marginally affect the profit earned by our trader is the price at which the 3/24/83 bills and the December bill futures contract *converge* at expiration of the futures contract. The bill futures contract is for $1 million of 90-day bills on which a basis point is worth $25. The deliverable bill is in fact a 91-day bill on which a basis point is worth $25.2777 per million. The trade thus calls for selling bills on which a basis point is worth $25 and delivering bills on which a basis

---

[7] Buyers and sellers of futures contracts must put up initial margin. The futures exchange on which they trade marks each trader's position to market daily. If at any point a trader's paper lesses in his futures position exceed his initial margin deposit, the exchange will require him to meet a *variation margin call* equal to his paper lesses minus whatever margin he has already put up. If, alternatively, the investor earns paper profits, the futures exchange will deposit in his account funds equal to his excess margin.

point is worth $25.2777. If the convergence price on the trade is below the price level at which the trade is put on (i.e., if rates rise), the trader will have lost some of his profit because he will have lost on his cash position basis points worth $25.2777 while gaining on his futures position *a like amount* of basis points worth only $25. Much can be made of *convergence-price risk,* but in fact if the cash and futures prices converged 100 basis points above the price level at which the trade was put on, the trader would lose only 2 of his 26-basis-point profit margin on the trade. Alternatively, if cash and futures converged at a price level well below that at which the trade was put on, the trader would add a couple of basis points to his profit margin on the trade.

A final factor affecting profit on the trade will be transactions costs—back office costs or whatever. Usually these are so small that no one bothers to incorporate them into return calculations.

To sum up, a trader putting on a cash-and-carry trade does not lock in a certain rate of return. However, on a short trade of the sort illustrated, even a 20% rise in bill prices, which is big, would leave most of his profit margin intact.

We have been talking about the signal that the relationship between the implied repo rate and the actual term repo rate gives the leveraged trader. The strictly cash investor who is investing money into December also gets a signal from the relationship between these rates. If the implied repo rate exceeds the term repo rate, then the cash investor will earn more by investing in the long bill and selling December futures than he would by investing in term repo, and probably more than he would by investing in the bill maturing at expiration of the futures contract. If, alternatively, the reverse is true and the leveraged cash-and-carry trade (Tables 10–2 and 10–3) is unprofitable, the short-bill trade offering the cash investor the highest return would probably be to buy the 56-day December bill and mature it.

Chapter 11

The clearing of money market trades: Some basics

THIS CHAPTER MIGHT WELL BE TITLED CLEARING 101. In it, we describe briefly the book-entry system, the Fed wire, and how money market trades are cleared. We also touch on several related topics: pairoffs, fails, reverses to cover shorts, and the right of substitution.

THE BOOK-ENTRY SYSTEM AND FEDWIRE

A discussion of the clearing of repos and reverse must be prefaced with at least a brief description of the book-entry system and of Fedwire. This section presents that preface.[1]

Registered, bearer, and book-entry securities

Prior to the introduction of what's called the *book-entry system,* all securities were issued in *physical form* and were evidenced by a *certifi-*

---

[1] We have included in this chapter far more about clearing than might seem strictly necessary. One reason is that there has been much litigation about repos, and in such litigation, questions about how repos are cleared keep arising. This chapter, which the reader may skim without loss in continuity, also provides background for our discussion in Chapter 14 of dealer safekeeping and bank custody arrangements.

For an in-depth description of all aspects of the clearing of money market trades, see Marcia Stigum, *After the Trade: Dealer and Clearing Bank Operations* (Homewood, Ill.: Dow Jones-Irwin, 1987).

cate. In the case of notes and bonds, this certificate has always been an elaborate engraved affair. In the case of BAs and CDs, in contrast, the certificate is a not-so-impressive slip of paper.

Physical securities come in *two* forms, registered and bearer. In the case of *registered* securities, the issuer (more likely, his *agent*) maintains a list of the holders of record of its issue; and it transmits, automatically to those holders, any payments due them. A *bearer* security does not have the name of its owner inscribed on it. A bearer security is assumed to be owned by he who bears it. Bearer notes and bonds (except for *zero-coupon* bonds, which are non–interest-bearing bonds) always have attached to them dated *coupons,* which look like oversize postage stamps. When a coupon date arrives, the owner of the bond clips the appropriate coupon and presents it, often via a commercial bank, for payment of interest due him. Registered notes and bonds have no attached coupons, since the issuer or his agent always maintains a record of who owns such securities and to whom periodic payments of coupon interest are therefore due. While the payment of coupon interest to the holder of a registered security is automatic, the owner of such a security must, when his security matures, present his certificate to receive payment of principal. All physical securities have certificate numbers.

Today, all Treasury securities, most federal agency securities, many municipal notes, and some other securities as well are no longer issued in physical form. Instead, they have been converted to book-entry form.

Two brief definitions

The book-entry system is a scheme whereby, first, the Treasury and, later, federal credit agencies substituted, for physical securities (bearer and registered), computerized records of ownership and other interests in securities held in the system. Book-entry records are maintained by the Federal Reserve, by commercial banks, and by other parties who figure in the tiered structure of the book-entry system (Figure 11–1, pp. 151–53).

Fedwire is a communications network and means of settlement that links Federal Reserve Banks to any bank or other depository institution that wants and is willing to pay fees to link up to it. Fedwire is used, by institutions linked to it, to direct the Fed, usually via a computer-to-computer message, to transfer money (Fed funds), book-entry securities, or both.

The Monetary Control Act of 1980

As background for a discussion of the book-entry system and, later, of the Fed wire, a few words must be said about reserve requirements, Fed services, and the Monetary Control Act of 1980. Anyone whose study of economics predates 1980 will surely recall, from the discussion of monetary policy, that in textbook discussions banks used to appear in *two* flavors. Some banks—the group comprised all nationally chartered banks and a number of big, state-chartered banks—were *member banks,* that is, members of the Federal Reserve System (FRS). Many other small-to-medium-size, state-chartered banks were *nonmember banks.* All member banks were required to hold at the Fed reserves equal to a percentage—the percentage varied with the type of deposit—of the total deposits, by type, made with them. Nonmember banks were not subject to reserve requirements.

Reserve requirements. The Fed used to offer member banks various services, such as check clearing, *free of charge.* Also, only member banks had direct access to the Fed wire for money and securities transfers. These were the pluses a member of the Fed enjoyed—the big minus was that club dues were high: a member bank was required to hold reserves in a non–interest-bearing account at the Fed.

Congress legislated reserve requirements because its members observed that in the past runs on banks had often led banks that had exhausted their liquidity to shut their doors. Requiring banks to hold reserves, Congress reasoned, would contribute to bank liquidity and, thereby, decrease bank closings. That made as much sense as Congress writing a hunger-prevention statute that stated: henceforth, every citizen is required to keep a $100 minimum balance in his checking account so that he will always have enough money on hand to buy groceries. The fallacy of such a law is that, once a citizen got down to his last $100, he would have, if he wanted to abide by the law, one choice: to starve. Required reserves do not and never did contribute to bank liquidity.

In the minds of many, required reserves are also supposed to serve a second useful function: to make it possible for the Fed to carry out monetary policy by raising or lowering the supply of reserves available to banks relative to the amount of reserves that banks are required to hold. This notion, too, is incorrect. The Fed, it's easy to show, could tighten or ease credit through open market operations just as well whether required reserves were 0% (no required reserves) or 10%.

The above facts are understood, vaguely at least, by the powers that be in Washington; but required reserves, like the poor, are still with us—and probably always will be. In practice, requiring banks to hold non–interest-bearing reserves at the Fed has turned out to be something its originators never envisioned: a *hidden tax* on banking, the proceeds of which go to the Treasury. The mechanics of this tax are simple. The Fed enforces reserve requirements and invests all the free funds banks give it in interest-bearing Treasuries and agencies. By doing so, the Fed has acquired a $211 billion portfolio of securities. In 1986, the Fed earned on this portfolio over $17 billion; it spent $1 billion on operating costs and transmitted the balance to the Treasury under the euphemistic and misleading entry, "Interest on Federal Reserve Notes."

Small banks have always understood that meeting reserve requirements costs them money. With respect to Fed membership, they made a simple calculation: reserve requirements cost us X; the free services we get from the Fed are worth Y; X exceeds Y; therefore, we will opt out of the Fed; and any services, such as check clearing and access to the Fed wire, that we need we will buy from a correspondent bank who is a Fed member.

Changes under MCA. During the 1970s, more and more banks left the Fed System, a trend that worried the Fed. It argued that the exit of these banks from the system was impairing its ability to implement monetary policy. At the same time, big money center banks complained that the U.S. branches of foreign banks were subjecting them to unfair competition: foreign bank branches and agencies were not required to hold reserves against deposits they received. Consequently, domestic bankers argued, such banks had a lower cost of funds than did domestic banks.

These perceived problems, plus the obvious need to get rid of the last vestiges of pernicious Regulation Q[2] (before it destroyed what was left of the banking and S&L industries) led to the passage in 1980 of the *Monetary Control Act* (MCA).[3]

To keep the Fed and domestic money market banks happy, the MCA also had something to say about reserve requirements. Over an eight-year phase-in period, the Fed was to impose reserve requirements on all nonmember banks and on all other DIs as well. This change was not all that expensive for S&Ls and other thrifts, because during the phase-in period, reserve requirements on savings and time deposits held by individuals were eliminated.

---

[2] Reg Q, promulgated by the Fed, barred member banks from paying market (i.e., competitive) rates of interest on deposits made with them. The FDIC and regulators of nonbank DIs established similar regulations that together clamped lids on the rates that all but a handful of other uninsured DIs could pay. As interest rates soared in the late 1970s, Reg Q and its cousins spawned the $200 billion-plus money fund industry. These regs also made many individuals active investors in Treasury bills and other money market paper; to them, 10% T bills sounded like a far better deal than a 5% or 5¼% savings account at a bank or other DI.

[3] MCA provided for the gradual phasing out, now complete, of all regulatory ceilings on rates paid by all *depository institutions (DIs)*, which comprise banks, savings and loans *(S&Ls)*, trust companies, credit unions, savings banks, and foreign bank branches. Little DIs, in particular, small banks and small S&Ls, did not like this aspect of MCA, but they had two choices: try to live with it or die for sure. They opted for choice one.

The MCA made all DIs pay the Fed dues that only member banks previously had to pay; so, logically, the law mandated that, henceforth, *all* DIs, foreign bank branches included, would have access to *all* services provided by the Fed and to loans at the discount window as well. After the MCA was passed, the terms *member bank* and *nonmember bank* nearly became obsolete—many Fed regulations now apply to DIs, and Fed statistics that once described member banks now describe DIs.

Not all DIs are created equal. Fed descriptions of the book-entry system, like the one quoted below, now refer, not to member banks, but to DIs. It is true that the MCA further blurred the line of demarcation between commercial banks and thrifts, but money market banks, small banks, and thrifts remain different animals. Of the 20,000 DIs in this land, only 5,500 have book-entry accounts at the Fed; of these, only 1,000 have on-line book-entry accounts. Presumably, the 14,500 DIs without book-entry accounts at the Fed figured that having such accounts would cost them more than it was worth. DIs that lack Fed book-entry accounts, use banks that have such accounts as custodians for any book-entry securities they own or hold for customers.

Book-entry securities

In brief, the book-entry system was designed to replace physical securities, which are issued by the Treasury and others, with book-entry accounting entries.

Registered and bearer Treasury securities. Until the late 1960s, the Treasury issued its securities in *definitive* form: all Treasury bills, notes, and bonds were issued as either bearer or registered securities. For registered Treasuries, of which there are still some outstanding, the Treasury maintains in Washington a record of who owns such securities and to whom periodic payments of coupon interest are therefore due.

The switch to book-entry. Physical securities are expensive to clear and to store; also, in an environment lacking tight security, they invite theft. To reduce the costs and problems associated with the trading and holding of physical securities, the Treasury and the Fed devised, beginning in 1968, a book-entry system for Treasuries. The intent was to eliminate *physical* Treasury securities by providing an alternative means for the issuance, maintenance, and transfer of such securities.

Under the book-entry system, entries are made in the accounts of Federal Reserve Banks, of commercial banks, and of other DIs to record both *ownership* of and other *"interests"* (custodial, trust, and pledges, for example) in Treasury securities. Most, if not all, book-entry records are computerized; and most, but not all, transfers of book-entry securities are made using the Fed wire. "Fedwire," as the Fed calls its wire, is a computerized communications network that links each Federal Reserve Bank with other Federal Reserve Banks and with local institutions that maintain book-entry accounts with it.

Today, not only Treasury securities, but securities issued by most federal credit agencies (including many mortgage-backed issues) either can or can only be held in book-entry form. Both the dollar face amount and number of securities originally issued in, or convertible to, book-entry are constantly growing. The present book-entry system was not devised and implemented overnight; it evolved in a number of steps that spanned over a decade. The evolution of the book-entry system continues today. In 1983, the Fed completed a major upgrading of its computer facilities; that upgrading permitted the Fed to handle and process more messages and to track "interests" in a vastly greater number of book-entry issues.

Current structure of the book-entry system[4]

Each of the 12 district Federal Reserve Banks and each of their 25 branches establishes and maintains book-entry accounts for depository institutions located within its district or area. Only depository institutions are eligible to maintain book-entry accounts at Reserve Banks, but any individual or entity may maintain a book-entry account at a depository institution.

The Federal Reserve book-entry system is, thus, a *tiered* system of accounts. *Interests* of a depository institution are recorded on the books of a Reserve Bank; *interests* of others are recorded on the books of a depository institution. If a customer of a depository institution is another bank or a securities dealer, that bank or securities dealer may also maintain book-entry accounts for its customers; securities in such accounts will be reflected in the book-entry account maintained, at the depository institution, by that bank or securities dealer. (Figure 11–1, added by the author, portrays the tiered book-entry system of accounts.)

---

[4] Material under this heading is excerpted, with numerous editorial changes including the deletion of technical footnotes and the addition of Figure 11–1, from Mary Sue Sullivan, "The Treasury Book-Entry System," a Federal Reserve paper reprinted in *Government Securities: Counselling and Regulation* (New York/Washington, D.C.: Law & Business Inc./ Harcourt Brace Jovanovich, 1985), pp. 354–62. Ms. Sullivan is Assistant Counsel of the FRBNY. Her piece may be obtained in its entirety by writing the FRBNY, 33 Liberty Street, New York, NY 10045.

All the rules and regulations under which the book-entry system currently operates are described in the following Treasury "Operating Circulars": OC No. 21 (revised December 12, 1977), Appendices A–E to OC No. 21, OC No. 21A, and First Supplement to it, Appendices A and B to OC No. 21A, and Exhibit to OC No. 21A. These circulars, too, may be obtained from the FRBNY.

FIGURE 11–1
The Federal book-entry system*

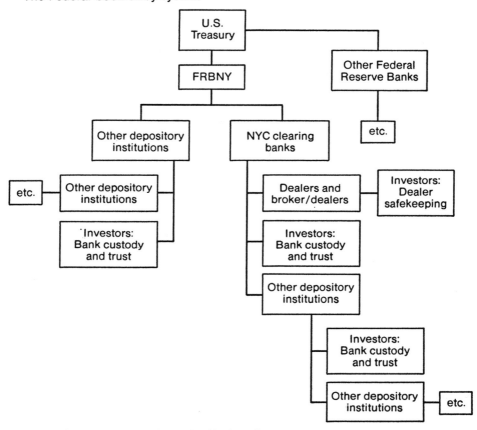

* See explanatory material; figure added by the author.

Explanation of Figure 11–1

Book-entry is a tiered system for recording *interests, only some of which reflect owner-ship,* in securities maintained in the system. Figure 11–1 depicts the relationships among different tiers of the book-entry system that, *given current market practices,* are most common.

Figure 11–1 shows, at the top tier of accounts and recordkeeping, an issuer of book-entry securities, the U.S. Treasury. The Treasury's records show, for each of its issues, what total amount is outstanding and what amounts of the issue are held by different Federal Reserve Banks.

All money market instruments used to be, and many still are, in physical form. Clearing a trade of money market instruments in physical form requires, more often than not, that securities be moved from one place to another: from one clearing bank to another or from a clearing bank to a custodial bank. Because it is *cheaper* and *quicker* to have a messenger walk two or three blocks carrying securities than it is to send securities, no matter how it is done, on cross-country jaunts, most clearing of money market trades is done in one city, New York. West Coast dealers use, as their clearing agent, a NYC bank, not the B of A. Security Pacific, the one West Coast bank that has moved into clearing in a big way, has done so through a NYC subsidiary.

Investors in money market instruments are scattered about the country. An out-of-town, hold-to-maturity investor, who buys long-lived instruments, such as GNMAs, may want his GNMAs delivered either to his local bank for custody or to himself if he has a vault, as a bank or S&L would. However, *out-of-town (outside NYC)* delivery of physical securities (as opposed to book-entry securities) is expensive and makes little sense for short-term paper such as CDs, BAs, and commercial paper; this is so even if the investor plans to hold such securities to maturity. Out-of-town delivery of physical securities makes absolutely no sense for an active portfolio manager who trades often and must, to prevent expensive fails, have his trades cleared on the day he makes them or on the following business day. A big hidden cost for a dealer on delivering paper out of town, say to Chicago, is that he must pay for the paper in NYC the day he accepts delivery of it, but he will receive payment for that paper only the next day when he delivers it in Chicago; on such a delivery, the dealer thus incurs a one-day financing cost.

All large portfolio managers—pension funds, insurance companies, nonfinancial corporations, and others—use the services of a custodial bank. This bank, acting as agent for the investor, accepts delivery of securities the investor buys against payment, safekeeps securities he buys, delivers securities he sells against payment, collects coupon interest, collects principal at maturity, and prepares periodic statements of account activity as well as any other reports the investor wants. In the case of book-entry securities, clearing of both the investor trades and the collecting of interest and principal payments could be done by a local bank anywhere in the country. However, since many money market instruments are in physical form and since most physical securities never, for reasons explained above, leave New York City, the bulk of bank custodial work for money market investors continues to be done, as it was done before book-entry, by NYC banks. This explains why 60% of all book-entry securities held by DIs are held in the accounts of NYC banks at the FRBNY (see Table 11–1).

Lots of John Does leave any securities, from stocks to T bills, that they buy from a broker/dealer with that broker/dealer for safekeeping. Also, many smaller institutional investors, following the John Doe pattern, safekeep any money market securities or governments, physical or book-entry, that they buy with the dealer or broker/dealer from whom they bought them.

Bearing the above in mind, look again at Figure 11–1. Federal Reserve Banks, which maintain book-entry accounts in which depository institutions hold securities in which they have interests, form tier two of the book-entry system. We have put the FRBNY in the center of tier two of Figure 11–1 because of New York City's position as the center of the national money market.

Currently, about 5,500 out of the 20,000 eligible DIs have opened book-entry accounts at a Reserve Bank. The costs associated with having such an account are such that institutions doing only a few securities trades find it cheaper to use another DI to clear their trades in governments and to safekeep securities for them than to have their own book-entry account. Depository institutions that maintain accounts at the FRBNY fall into *two* categories. *Some are clearing banks* which clear each day tens of thousands of trades for client dealers and broker/dealers; a clearing bank maintains, for each of its dealer clients, a clearing account in which the dealer deposits money and both book-entry and physical securities. Clearing banks hold securities not only for dealers, but for investors and other depository institutions that do not have accounts at the Fed.

Most NYC banks are not in the clearing business. Such institutions do not hold securities for dealers, but they do hold securities for other depository institutions and for investors. (See tier three of Figure 11–1 under FRBNY.) This pattern is repeated by depository institutions that have accounts with Federal Reserve Banks other than the FRBNY (Figure 11–1, far left branch).

An investor, wherever he may be located, may hold book-entry securities in a custody account at either a NYC bank or an out-of-town bank, or he may hold such securities in a

TABLE 11-1
Marketable U.S. Treasury securities and portion in book-entry form
1968-81, Federal Reserve Bank of New York (April 1982)*

End of period	Marketables† (billions)	Book-entry holdings‡			Definitive§ outstanding (billions)
		System total (billions)	%	New York (billions)	
1968	$236.8	$ 36.5	15.4	$ 21.0	$200.3
1969	235.9	38.2	16.2	21.2	197.7
1970	247.7	121.3	48.9	96.6	126.4
1971	262.0	152.6	58.2	124.6	109.4
1972	269.5	160.2	59.4	129.2	109.3
1973	270.2	176.6	65.4	135.6	93.6
1974	281.3	201.4	71.6	151.5	79.9
1975	363.2	285.1	78.5	194.5	78.1
1976	421.3	354.1	84.0	232.4	67.2
1977	459.9	428.2	93.1	284.5	31.7
1978	487.5	457.4	93.8	307.4	30.1
1979	530.7	497.8	93.8	317.4	32.9
1980	623.1	585.2	93.9	378.4	37.9
1981	720.2	686.0	95.2	426.8	34.2

Marketable government agency securities and portion in book-entry form

1974	71.9‖	23.2	32.2	8.4	48.7
1975	74.4	40.5	54.4	16.1	33.9
1976	78.9	64.2	81.4	29.3	14.7
1977	84.2	77.9	92.5	38.0	6.3
1978	99.6	96.3	96.6	44.6	3.3
1979	114.1	111.8	98.0	51.0	2.3
1980	127.7	127.2	99.6	58.2	0.5
1981	147.9	147.8	99.9	65.1	0.1

* Marketable debt excludes debt issued to foreign central banks and to trust funds, such as the fund for social security, the Railroad retirement fund, etc. Unfortunately, the Fed no longer updates this table, but the table does show important past trends.
† Source: Monthly Statement of the Public Debt; excludes Federal Financing Bank for July 1974 et. seq.
‡ Source: Treasury Department and FRBNY.
§ Includes both bearer and registered securities.
‖ Dealer quotation sheets, PD and agencies estimates.

dealer safekeeping account maintained by a dealer in governments (lower tiers of Figure 11-1).

All entities at each tier of the book-entry system always maintain records that show both what securities, if any, they own and what securities they are holding, in any capacity, for entities at a lower tier of the system.

Each depository institution may establish up to seven standard book-entry accounts at its Federal Reserve Bank. These accounts are denominated "General," "Investment," "Trust," "Dealer," "Special," "Select," and "Clearance." In addition to these, a qualified DI may set up two international accounts. Although the account titles are suggestive, they exist solely for the convenience of the depository institution's own book-keeping, and a depository institution may elect to hold all of its book-entry securities in a single account. The Fed does not monitor the character of transactions processed in each type of account. Rather, a depository institution's entire book-entry securities portfolio is "subject to the sole order of the [depository institution] depositor." In turn, the depository institutions are expected to maintain appropriate records in regard to their customers, covering such matters as transfer of the securities, pledge interests in the securities, and redemption of the securities and payment of interest thereon.

Current operation of the book-entry system

The book-entry system is designed to handle the issuance, maintenance, and transfer of all issues put into the system.

New issues. On original issue date, the 12 Reserve Banks electronically issue book-entry debt through entries in the accounts of depository institutions. Each entry takes the form of a single dollar amount representing the portion of the aggregate principal amount of the issue designated for delivery to that depository institution. The Reserve Bank makes a simultaneous debit to the reserve account of the depository institution in the amount of the purchase price and credits that dollar amount to the Treasury's cash account. Based on delivery instructions submitted by its customers, the depository institution makes entries on its own books that identify its customers' interests in the securities issued to it by the Reserve Bank.

Payment of principal and interest. The Treasury uses a similar method to pay interest and principal. On payment date, the Fed debits the Treasury's cash account and credits the reserve account of the depository institution whose book-entry accounts contain the issue for which an interest or maturity payment is due. These payments are made at the opening of business on payment date. Thus, entitlement to payments is based on the Fed's records as of the close of business on the preceding day.

Secondary-market trades. Trades in Treasuries that occur after their original issue, that is, *secondary-market transactions,* are also completed through the book-entry system. If securities are transferred "free," the Fed debits the securities account of the sending depository institution and credits the securities account of the receiving depository institution by the principal amount specified in the transfer instruction. If the securities are transferred against payment, the Fed also credits the reserve account of the sending depository institution and debits the reserve account of the receiving depository institution by the dollar amount specified in the instruction. Transactions between depository institutions that are not located in the same Reserve district or branch territory require entries on the books of two Reserve Banks or branches.

The vast majority of book-entry transfers occur on a direct computer access (on-line) basis. In an on-line transaction, the depository institution sending securities controls the transfer by entering a command in the book-entry system that causes the debits and credits described above to occur automatically. As a result of the high level of automation in the market, Fedwire processes on average 30,000 transactions per day for securities valued at $225 billion.[5] In contrast, transactions that require manual processing by Fed personnel (off-line) average 420 transactions per day.

Financing of wire transfers of Treasury securities. After it receives securities transferred against payment for the account of a customer, the receiving DI can either accept the transaction or reverse it. If it accepts the transaction and the customer has insufficient funds to cover the payment, the depository institution must extend daylight credit (overdraft). If the customer's failure to pay persists, that daylight credit becomes an outright or term loan. DIs that process transactions for dealer customers extend daylight credit in an aggregate amount of billions of dollars per day. Overnight credit reaches a more modest $2.6 billion on average each week.

Growth of book-entry. Once the book-entry system was introduced, it was rapidly accepted by investors. Since 1977, over 90% of all governments have existed in book-entry form; today, the figure is near 100%. The book-entry system was also expanded to cover an ever-increasing number of issues sold by various federal credit agencies. Today, almost 100% of all eligible agencies are in book-entry form.

Fedwire

Fedwire is basically a communications network and settlement system that links Fed banks and offices to any insured DI that wants to link up to the Fed. Institutions linked to the Fed use Fedwire both to transfer money (Fed funds) and to transfer book-entry securities to accounts at other DIs.

---

[5] Note: since one dealer's buy is another dealer's sell, the number implies that dealers together instruct on an average day their clearing banks to clear 60,000 trades.

Securities may be transferred over the Fed wire "free," but most often, they are transferred DVP *(delivery versus payment).* For example, a *free delivery* would occur if an investor, who switched from dealer A to dealer B, asked dealer A to transfer securities, which dealer A had been safe-keeping for it, to dealer B for safekeeping. Purchases and sales of book-entry securities result almost always in DVP transfers of securities.

Figure 11–2 shows a wire transfer used to settle a DVP trade in Treasury notes. Since parts of the message look as if they were constructed by a cryptographer, we have also included Figure 11–3, which decodes the more mysterious entries on the wire.

While many transfers of funds over Fedwire are generated by securities deliveries, many more are generated by other types of transactions. A *reverse to maturity* may be settled by a *difference check,* that is, a check for the difference between what X owes Y and what Y owes X. A repo may require a wire of accrued interest on a coupon day. Also, a call for margin on a repo may be met by a wire of funds rather than securities.

Besides securities-related transfers of funds, a vast number of funds transfers occur as a result of nonfinancial business transactions, Firm A wires funds to Firm B or some other party.

A key feature of Fedwire, whatever the use to which it is put, is that it is a means of settlement in which balances due are paid *transaction by transaction.* CHIPS and several private clearing systems, which are used to clear trades of certain types of securities (corporate stocks and bonds and muni bonds, to name a few), do not work this way. Instead, they call

FIGURE 11–2
A Fedwire message indicating to a clearing bank, Manny, that $4,630,000 of the 10⅞ of 2/15/87 are being delivered by Ninth CHGO/CUST PVD to ABC Title & Trust. The amount of the payment due is $5,012,166.67.

			MANUFACTURERS HANOVER TRUST COMPANY	**1**
			BROKERS AND DEALERS CLEARANCE DEPT.	INCOMING
DUE TO	TYPE		NEW YORK, NEW YORK 10015	TRANSFER OF
0210003062C				SECURITIES

DUE FROM: 070000000   00   REF 0005   AMOUNT $5,012,166.67

ORDERING BANK AND RELATED DATA
NINTH CHGO/CUST

MFRS NYC/DEALER A

ABC TITLE & TRUST

SECURITY IDENTIFICATION AND PAR AMOUNT
NOTE 02/15/87 10.875 (9128270L9) $4,630,000.00 –1239*

MESSAGE ACKNOWLEDGEMENT
02181239 GA503 0005 *GENEAA*02181239 BBA01 0208

AUTHORIZED SIGNATURE

Note: See Figure 11–3 for further explanation of entries and codes.
Source: Manufacturers Hanover Trust.

FIGURE 11–3
Wire of incoming securities versus money—explanation of entries
and codes

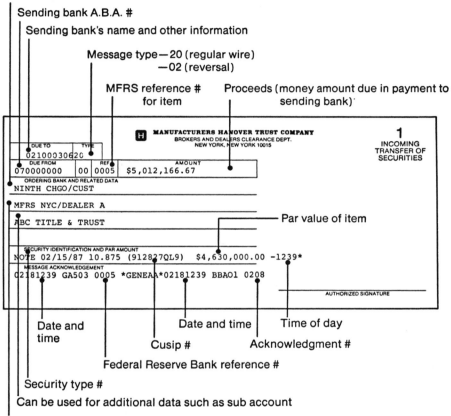

Receiving bank A.B.A. #

Sending bank A.B.A. #

Sending bank's name and other information

Message type—20 (regular wire)
—02 (reversal)

MFRS reference #   Proceeds (money amount due in payment to
for item   sending bank)

MANUFACTURERS HANOVER TRUST COMPANY
BROKERS AND DEALERS CLEARANCE DEPT.
NEW YORK, NEW YORK 10015

1
INCOMING
TRANSFER OF
SECURITIES

DUE TO	TYPE
0210003062C	

DUE FROM		REF	AMOUNT
070000000	00	0005	$5,012,166.67

ORDERING BANK AND RELATED DATA
NINTH CHGO/CUST

MFRS NYC/DEALER A

ABC TITLE & TRUST   Par value of item

SECURITY IDENTIFICATION AND PAR AMOUNT
NOTE 02/15/87 10.875 (912827QL9) $4,630,000.00 -1239*

MESSAGE ACKNOWLEDGEMENT
02181239 GA503 0005 *GENEAA*02181239 BBAO1 0208

AUTHORIZED SIGNATURE

Date and   Date and time   Time of day
time
                Cusip #   Acknowledgment #

Federal Reserve Bank reference #

Security type #
Can be used for additional data such as sub account

Receiving bank's name and other data

A.B.A. is an acronym for American Bankers Association.
The time/date on the lower left of the wire message states when the message was entered by the sender into its computer; it is called the *input message sequence number* (*IMSN* in Fed jargon).
The time/date on the lower right of the wire message states when the message arrived at the receiving institution; it is the *output message sequence number* (*OMSN* in Fed jargon).
The two times will differ if the sending bank holds the message in pending mode waiting for inventory to come in.
Source: Manufacturers Hanover Trust.

for a *net* settlement at day's end, where the settlement is based on everything that has gone, during the day, both *into* and *out of* a participant's pot or pots (account or accounts with it). For example, Chase is a member of CHIPS. At the end of each business day, CHIPS zips Chase a message: "We settled today this long list of transactions for you. Total transactions resulting in a debit to your account summed to X; total transactions resulting in a credit to your account summed to Y. X exceeds Y by Z; wire us Z dollars." Or, alternately, the message might end: "Y exceeds X by Z; we will wire you, at settlement, Z dollars."

How Fedwire works.   Most, but not quite all, messages sent over the Fed wire are sent by a computer over a leased line and received by a computer at the other end of that line.

Goodbye throttle and choke.   In the early 1980s, the Fed wire was taxed to its limit with the result that it was subject daily to "throttle," and it tended to "choke." *Throttle* occurred when traffic on Fedwire was so heavy that the wire, instead of taking messages from banks at its normal rate, three to six per minute, took them at a lower speed. From the user's point of view, throttle at the Fed was like being put on hold for some time every time one called a message into the Fed. Throttling meant that the Fed had to extend daily the hours Fedwire was open just to handle the volume of messages put into the system.

In the early 1980s, Fedwire was also overtaxed in a second way: the automated system then used by the Fed tended to *choke* when it was asked to handle more than 700 issues.

In August of 1983, the Fed finally made a change, one long awaited by the Street, in the automated system it uses to support Fedwire. The Fed replaced its computer hardware and totally redesigned its system to maximize *"throughput," the number of transactions the system can handle per unit of time.*

The Fed's new automated system has a throughput of 10 to 15 transactions per minute. Currently, this system has the capacity to handle 38,000 issues; and by making some adjustments in peripheral equipment, the Fed could expand the system's capacity to 100,000 issues, the number of issues that the system was modeled to carry.

Book entry and Fedwire today.   Since the Fed introduced its new automated system, the number of issues on book-entry and the volume of messages passing through the system daily have grown explosively. Today, Fedwire handles within the NY district 23,000 messages on an average day and as many as 58,000 messages on peak days.

With choking a thing of the past, the Fed's computer currently tracks the interests of banks and other DIs in about 28,000 different issues. The aggregate face value of these issues exceeds a trillion dollars; this number comprises $80 billion of book-entry Treasuries, $80 billion of long-term agencies, $20 billion of agency discount paper, $150 billion of mortgage backs, and securities issued by three international agencies: the World Bank, the Inter-American Development Bank, and the International Bank for Reconstruction and Development.

THE ESSENCE OF CLEARING

In essence, the clearing of securities trades is a simple operation. A dealer buys and sells securities over the phone. To effect a buy, the dealer must accept delivery of the securities and pay out money; to effect a sell, the dealer must deliver out securities and accept money. A dealer could do these things for himself, and some dealers do self-clear, partially or totally, certain of their trades. However, many dealers do not want to get involved in making and receiving what are likely to amount, over a month, to many thousands of deliveries and receipts of money and securities. Instead, they hire a clearing bank to do all this receiving and delivering of money and securities for them. Also, in the case of wireable securities, a dealer could not self-clear his trades even if he wanted to because a dealer can neither get direct access to the Fed wire nor have a book-entry account at the Fed as may a bank. Even a dealer who self-clears physical securities must rely on his clearing bank to make and receive payments over the Fed wire for him. Thus, one of the major functions of a dealer's back office is to give to the dealer's clearing bank—each time the dealer does a trade to be cleared, wholly or partially, by that bank—accurate instructions as to what money and securities the clearing bank must receive or deliver on the dealer's behalf to clear that trade.

On a buy by the dealer, the clearing bank is responsible for collecting the securities bought and for paying for these securities. On a sell by the dealer, the clearing bank is responsible for delivering the securities sold and collecting payment for them. For each trade a dealer does, the clearing bank either makes a payment out of or receives a payment into a *money account* that it maintains for the dealer. Simultaneously, it either accepts a delivery into or makes a delivery out of a *securities account* that it also maintains for the dealer. A dealer's money and securities accounts at its clearing bank together comprise that dealer's *clearing account.* Securities in a dealer's clearing account are referred to as its *box position;* this term dates from the days when all securities were in physical form, and a clearing bank literally stored a dealer's securities in a box. *That's clearing in a nutshell.*

In the course of a day, a major clearing bank clears 10,000, 15,000, or maybe more trades in different securities, the aggregate value of which may amount to $75 billion to $100 billion. For the bank to do all this accurately and on a timely basis (not next week), both it and the dealer's operations area must follow many detailed procedures. Running a clearing bank operation resembles staging a Wagnerian opera. For the performance to be a success, a host of people have to be in the right place, at the right time, doing the right thing.

The clearing banks

In terms of volume of securities cleared, the biggest clearing banks are Manufacturers Hanover Trust, the Bank of New York, Irving Trust, and a relative new comer to the business, Security Pacific, a West Coast bank. All of the above institutions are *banks* (a bank subsidiary in the case of Sec Pac). This fact is unsurprising; to act as a clearing agent, an institution must have access to the Fed wire for money and securities transfers. Until recently, the only institutions that had such access were banks.

All major clearing banks are New York banks or, in the case of Security Pacific, a New York subsidiary of an out-of-town bank. As noted earlier in this chapter, the reason for this is grounded in history. It used to be that all securities, including governments, came in physical form. Thus, it made sense to center the bulk of the nation's clearing activity in a single geographic location. That location turned out to be New York City, which was and is the nation's major financial center.

Above, we were speaking of banks that regard clearing as an important profit center and actively solicit clearing business. Many other banks also clear trades for customers who hold securities in custody with them, for correspondent banks, for their dealer operation if they have one, and so on. Thus, for example, every big New York bank does a lot of clearing even though it may not be a major clearing bank as we have used the term.

CLEARING TRADES IN BOOK-ENTRY SECURITIES

The biggest, single job that clearing banks do for dealers is to clear their trades in book-entry securities. The Fed says that, on an average day, it transfers $140 billion of securities over the wire. The clearing banks together clear a much larger volume of securities; well over 10% of all trades cleared by a major clearing bank are between two of its clients. No wire transfer of securities is required to clear such a trade. One clearing banker estimates that the top three NYC clearing banks clear, on average, close to $300 billion of securities a day. That number sounds reasonable, since every $1 billion of securities that moves over the Fed wire requires banks to clear $2 billion of buys and sells.

Clearing a dealer-to-dealer trade

The easiest way to describe what's involved in clearing a trade in a book-entry security, is to walk, step-by-step, through the clearing procedure. We illustrate with a dealer-to-dealer trade.

Doing the trade. Suppose that Treasury-note traders at Sali and Merrill agree over the phone to do a $5 million trade in the 2-year note, Merrill sells to Sali.[6] Merrill's trader will write a *trade ticket* saying, "We, Merrill, sold to you, Sali, $5 million of 2-year, U.S. Treasury notes maturing on such and such a date and carrying such and such a coupon. The dollar price on the trade is 99–26 ($99 plus $26/32$ per $100 of face value). The trade date is . . . (today's date), the settlement date is . . . (usually date of the next business day)." Sali's trader will also write a ticket containing precisely the same information, only the Sali ticket will begin "We, Sali, bought from you, Merrill, ..."

Clearing procedures: Dealer operations. Once the traders at Merrill and Sali have completed their trade tickets describing Merrill's sale to Sali, each will give his ticket to someone in his *operations area*—also dubbed "cage" or "back office." A dealer's operations people have several responsibilities. First, operations must *clean up* the information on the trader's ticket, check that the information the trader has scribbled in haste is accurate, and add any other information its clearing bank will need to clear the trade. Second, operations must send to the counterparty a written *confirmation slip (confirm)* that states the details of the trade agreed to orally. Third, operations must send to the dealer's clearing bank accurate instructions as to how to clear the trade. Finally, operations must, once the trade is cleared, prove the trade: check that the clearing bank's record of what it did jibes with the dealer's record of what it was supposed to do.

To clear a trade in the 2-year note, the first thing operations people at Sali and Merrill do is an *extension:* calculate how many dollars and cents $5 million of the 2-year note is worth at 99–26 when accrued interest is added to principal.

Once a shop has figured the money on a trade, this number is written on the trade ticket. To execute the trade, a clerk in operations first cleans up, if necessary, the information on the trade ticket. (Has the trader written, for the face amount of the trade, just 5 instead of 5MM? The letter, M, is the Street's shorthand for thousand.) Next, the clerk types into a computer all the information on the trade ticket. He also inputs to the computer any other information that the dealer or its clearing bank will need to execute the trade: the CUSIP number of the security traded and the counterparty's proper name, address, and in-house ID number, if it

---

[6] Actually, two primary dealers are more likely to trade through a broker than direct. In that case, each of *two* dealer/broker trades is cleared following the same procedures described in our Sali/Merrill example.

has one.[7] On a sell, in which the securities bought by the investor are not to be safekept by the dealer or its clearing bank, the file on the trade must also include the counterparty's standing *delivery instructions,* where it wants its securities delivered—to account X at bank Y in city Z (usually NYC). Once the dealer's clerk has input into the dealer's computer all this information, he directs the latter to produce a confirm for the customer, duplicate of that confirm for the dealer, and clearing instructions for the dealer's clearing bank.

Suppose that Merrill clears through Manufacturers Hanover Trust, Sali through the Bank of New York. Merrill's clearing instructions will tell Manny to clear its trade with Sali. Meanwhile, Sali's clearing instructions will tell BONY to clear its trade with Merrill.

Clearing procedures: The clearing banks. Different dealers transmit instructions to their clearing banks in different ways. Some big New York dealers have a computer-to-computer link with their clearing banks. Small Newport Beach, California, dealers use the phone to call in instructions for clearing cash trades and Express Mail to send confirms for trades that settle the next day. Dealers falling in between in size and volume of trades may use a dedicated Telex machine to get messages to their clearing bank. However a dealer communicates with his clearing bank, the information communicated is always the same: This is what I bought or sold; I did the trade with X; the money was Y; and so on.

Back to Merrill and Manny. Manny's computer reads Merrill's message (clearing instructions) and says, "Ah ha, Merrill has sold 2-year notes to Sali. We must get ready to deliver those securities and to receive payment for them." To do this, Manny's computer creates what is called a *pending mode;* it commits to memory Merrill's instructions; then it spits out a ticket describing Merrill's note trade with Sali and tickets describing all of Merrill's other trades as well; and it's set for action.[8]

The tickets, produced by Manny's computer, are sorted by issue and then go to Merrill's account manager at Manny. He notes what trades Merrill has done and checks on a CRT whether Merrill has in its *box position* (clearing account at Manny) the various securities it has sold, including the notes it has sold to Sali. Suppose Merrill does not have any 2-year notes to deliver to Sali. No problem. The Merrill account manager sets the Merrill ticket aside and waits for some 2-year notes to be delivered into Merrill's account.

---

[7] *CUSIP* is an acronym for the *Committee on Uniform Securities Identification Procedures.* Treasury securities, most federal credit agency securities (including mortgage backs), municipal bonds, corporate stocks, and corporate bonds all have identifying CUSIP numbers. These numbers are assigned, for a fee, by Standard & Poor's.

[8] The march of technology: for big accounts, tickets created by a clearing bank's computer are being replaced at some clearing banks by information displayed on CRTS.

Merrill, having sold 2-year notes to Sali, must get these securities into its account either by buying them or, if Merrill has shorted the 2-year note, by reversing them in. Otherwise Merrill will *fail* on its promised delivery to Sali. A fail to deliver would cost Merrill money: the 2-year note keeps accruing interest; consequently, the amount of accrued interest Merrill would have to pay to buy these notes goes up each day the fail continues; meanwhile, the amount of accrued interest Sali has agreed to pay Merrill stays constant.

Back to our example. Time passes, and $29 million of 2-year notes come into Merrill's account at Manny. The Merrill account manager checks to see whether he can now make Merrill's delivery to Sali. He can't. Merrill, after it sold $5 million of 2-year notes to Sali, sold another $25 million of this issue to Goldman.

Like most dealers, Merrill does not want its sell tickets cleared on a first-in, first-out basis. It wants its biggest sells in an issue delivered first, its smallest sells delivered last. There's a good reason. Suppose Manny delivered first the $5 million of 2-year notes Merrill has sold to Sali. This would leave $24 million of the 2-year notes in Merrill's box position, $1 million too few for Merrill to make delivery to Goldman. If nothing else happened in Merrill's account during the day, say, due to the failure by some customer to deliver $1 million of 2-year notes to Merrill, Merrill would be stuck with $24 million of undelivered 2-year notes. When it became inevitable that Merrill would fail to Goldman, Merrill would have to finance these notes overnight at Manny's dealer loan rate. Fails that have to be financed by a dealer's clearing bank are expensive, since the dealer ends up in effect being *double financed;* so dealers try mightily to avoid such fails.

Suppose that Merrill gets enough 2-year notes in the box to make its $25 million delivery to Goldman and to cover any other large sells it has in this issue. It may now say to its account manager at Manny, "We've got $8 million of 2-year notes in the box, our big deliveries are done, so shoot those $5 million of the 2-year note that we owe Sali over to them."

The Fed wire and book-entry settlement. When he gets Merrill's message to make delivery, Merrill's account manager at Manny types a message into a terminal to tell Manny's computer to send $5 million of 2-year notes taken out of Merrill's box position to the account of Sali at BONY. Manny's still-in-the-pending-mode computer gets the message it has been waiting for, and zips a true KISS (keep it short and simple) message to the Fed's computer. The reason: Just as dealers have two accounts at their clearing bank, Manny and all other large banks have two sorts of accounts at the Fed, a money (reserve) account and at least one account in which they hold book-entry securities.

Manny's message to the Fed goes, "This is Manny calling. Transfer,

DVP [delivery versus payment], from our account, X, with you, $5 million of securities with CUSIP number, Y, to Sali care of BONY account, Z." The last part of this message is referred to as the receiving bank's *format*.[9] A deliver message will fly on the wire only if the delivery instructions, included by the dealer's operations area in its instructions to its clearing bank, were correct, or if they were not, have been put in correct form by the clearing bank.

All the Fed's computer wants to know is who (spelled correctly) is sending what (amount and proper CUSIP number) to whom (also spelled correctly, please). Knowing who, what—$5 million of securities with CUSIP number X worth Y dollars—and to whom allows the Fed's computer to get into action to clear Merrill's sell to Sali. The Fed's computer debits Manny's appropriate account for the amount of the issue to be transferred and credits those securities to the appropriate account at BONY. Simultaneously, since this is a delivery-versus-payment transfer, the Fed's computer debits, without asking if it's OK, BONY's reserve account with it for Y dollars and credits Manny's reserve account for the same amount.

BONY has not been sleeping while Manny and Merrill were preparing, by getting Manny's computer into a pending mode, to shower it with securities and to whisk away precious reserve dollars. Sali's back office, like Merrill's, has also sent instructions to its clearing bank saying, "We, Sali, bought from Merrill securities X for Y dollars. Please take them in against payment." That instruction got BONY's computer into its equivalent of a pending mode, so it was not surprised when the Fed's computer summarily credited one of its accounts for $5 million of securities for the account of Sali and debited its reserve account for Y dollars. It recognized the delivery as something it was supposed to receive.

In many cases, a clearing bank's computer is programmed either to kick back ("DK" for don't know) any Fedwire that it gets but does not anticipate, or at least to signal to someone at the bank to call the receiving dealer and to ask whether it should accept an unanticipated trade or a trade on which the money is off. If BONY, for some reason, were to DK the delivery from Manny, then the Fed's computer would credit to BONY's reserve account the dollars it has just debited this account, thus putting the account back where it started; the Fed would get the money to do this by debiting Manny's reserve account for a like amount. Simultaneously, the Fed would transfer the $5 million of securities that it had transferred from a Manny account to a BONY account back from the BONY account to the Manny account. For obvious reasons, this procedure is called a *reversal*. BONY might DK a delivery from Merrill to Sali if some piece of information in the transfer wire—CUSIP number, money,

---

[9] Recall Figures 11–2 and 11–3.

or whatever—did not agree with the information on the trade transmitted to it by Sali.

Crediting and debiting money and securities. Once BONY takes in securities for Sali, BONY's computer will automatically credit Sali's clearing account for the $5 million of securities received and debit Sali's money account for the Y dollars paid out for these securities. At the same time, Manny's computer would debit Merrill's clearing account with it for the $5 million in 2-year notes delivered to Sali and credit Merrill's account with it for the Y dollars received in payment for those securities.

All of the above credits and debits to various securities and money accounts are easy to follow because the money and securities sides of the transaction always lead, for each party, to a pair or to several pairs of offsetting debits and credits. For example, Sali's clearing account at BONY will show two offsetting changes in assets: *minus Y dollars in its money account and plus $5 million of 2-year notes worth Y dollars in its security account. Meanwhile, BONY's accounts at the Fed will undergo the same offsetting changes that occurred in Sali's accounts at BONY. At the same time, BONY will experience two offsetting changes in its liabilities: plus $5 million of 2-year notes worth Y dollars in Sali's securities account with it and minus Y dollars in Sali's money account with it.*

No Fedwire. Actually, Sali clears 2-year notes through Manny, not BONY. That changes the clearing story, but just two steps of it, one near the beginning and one at the end. Assume again that Merrill sells $5 million of 2-year notes to Sali. That trade sets in motion precisely the same clearing procedures described above. Only this time Sali, like Merrill, sends its instructions to clear the trade to Manny. When Merrill's account manager at Manny decides he can finally deliver securities to Sali, he will recognize that Sali is a customer of Manny and that the trade can therefore be cleared *without using the Fed wire,* which he in fact could not use, even if he wanted to, because the securities are not, from the Fed's vantage point, going anywhere; to clear the trade, Merrill's and Sali's account managers at Manny simply direct Manny's computer, which is in its usual pending mode, to make appropriate changes that it was waiting to make in both Sali's and Merrill's money and securities accounts at Manny. Manny's reserve and securities accounts at the Fed undergo *no* change. Trades cleared without use of the Fed wire are referred to as *pairoffs* or *internals.*

Lawyers and prosecutors are wont to describe trades that they want to discredit for one reason or another as *paper trades. Real trades,* which are always understood to be fine and upstanding, have various characteristics *(indicia)* not shared by paper trades; of these—the list is not always the same—the most commonly mentioned is that real trades are trades that clear over the Fed wire. By this definition of "real," well over 10% of the trades made between primary dealers, operating under the Fed's ever-watchful eye, are unreal.

Pairoff by difference check

Pairoffs at the clearing bank level are not the only pairoffs that occur in clearing. Frequently, two dealers, or a dealer and a broker, or even a dealer and a customer, will in the course of active trading end up both buying a particular issue from and selling that same issue to a particular counterparty, both trades for settlement on the same day. For example, during a given trading day, Merrill might sell Sali $5 million of issue X for next-day settlement and later buy $5 million of that same issue from Sali, also for next-day settlement.

Such offsetting trades by a dealer can always be cleared one at a time by the dealer's clearing bank, but this procedure would cost the clearing bank effort and time, and it would cost the dealer fees. To minimize the latter, every dealer tries to spot offsetting trades and to settle these, if its counterparty is willing, via a pairoff and a *difference check*. To illustrate, if Merrill sold 5MM of issue X to Sali for Y dollars and then bought back from Sali the same amount of that issue for Y + 1,000 dollars, and if both trades were to settle on the same day, the two trades could be cleared on a *net* basis simply by Merrill sending (wiring) $1,000 to Sali. Dealers do such pairoffs routinely.

Whenever two parties clear two or more trades via a pairoff, they must *kill* any instructions they previously sent to their respective clearing banks directing the latter to clear the trades to be paired off on a one-by-one basis.

A dealer-to-customer trade:
No dealer safekeeping

We have described how a dealer-to-dealer trade is cleared. A dealer-to-customer trade is cleared in much the same way, except that a large institutional investor typically uses as agent the custodial area of a bank, often a NYC bank.

To illustrate, suppose that Merrill sells $10 million of 3-month bills to the Ford portfolio. Ford cannot hold book-entry securities itself; it must have some financial institution hold them for it. It could have a selling dealer safekeep for it securities it bought from that dealer, but suppose that, like many big accounts, it does not want to expose itself to the credit risk it feels it would incur if it left securities with a dealer for safekeeping.[10]

To avoid incurring this perceived credit risk, large portfolio managers typically have a bank hold for them all securities they own; they also have that bank clear for them whatever buys and sells they do, both of book-entry and physical securities. Accounts in which a bank holds securities for a customer are called custodial, safekeeping, or segregated accounts. There is no consistency in jargon. We will use the term *custodial account* to indicate an investor's account at a bank.

A custodial bank may perform various levels of service for a customer. The minimum it will do is hold a customer's securities, clear its buys and sells, and collect any interest payments and dividends due to the customer. For additional fees—custody is a big fee area for banks—a custodial bank may do bookkeeping for the customer and prepare various reports analyzing the customer's portfolio.

The clearing banks at work. For a clearing bank, the first step in clearing a securities trade is the same whether the securities are book-entry or physical. The instructions as to what the bank must do must be input to its computer so that the latter gets into a pending or equivalent mode. On digesting its instructions from Merrill, the computer at Merrill's clearing bank (assume again it is Manny) will say, "Ah ha, Merrill has done a trade and, to clear it, I must do X, Y, and Z."

Manny's computer will spit out an instruction that goes to the Merrill desk at Manny. Meanwhile, Sali will instruct its clearing bank, say it's Irving Trust, to prepare to deliver, against payment, $10 million of Chase CDs to Merrill at Manny. Assume that the trade is made for next-day settlement and that Sali has the Chase CDs, to be delivered to Merrill, in its box position. Then, on receipt of Sali's instructions, Irving will instruct its vault personnel to *pull* $10 million of the correct Chase CDs (right coupon and right maturity date) out of the vault in which it stores physical securities for Sali; an Irving clerk will carefully count and verify—Is everything OK?—the securities pulled from the vault to check that no mistake has been made and that the securities pulled are in good order.

Irving will then send, via messenger, to Manny the CDs that Sali has

---

[10] Big investors are wont to ask, "Where would I stand if a dealer with whom I had left millions of dollars of my valuable securities for safekeeping went bankrupt?" Banks that make money on custody accounts naturally encourage an investor to think that his securities are safer if he leaves them in custody with a bank than if he safekeeps them with a dealer or does in-house repo with a dealer. Some top-of-the-pile dealers resent this attitude. Such a dealer reasons, "We've got as much or more capital than some custody banks, and we haven't got loans to LDCs. So how can someone say that an institution that is a bank is necessarily a better credit than us just because that institution is a bank?"

instructed it to deliver there for the account of Merrill. These securities will come in "over the window" at 40 Wall Street. The clerical worker at Manny, who takes the securities in, will give Irving's messenger a stamped receipt saying that Manny has accepted the securities on behalf of Merrill. The stamped receipt Manny gives the Irving messenger is actually a stamped copy of a *delivery bill* that the Irving messenger presents to the Manny clerk when he delivers the securities. A delivery bill is precisely what its name indicates, a bill that accompanies a delivery.

Manny retains a copy, time-stamped by it, of the delivery bill that Irving's messenger gave it. The delivery bill tells Manny what securities have been delivered to it, for whose account those securities were delivered, and the amount that Manny will be expected to pay out, in this case, to Irving for the account of Sali.

On the Street, deliveries of physical securities are always accepted *subject to count and examination.* The receiver of the securities promises to pay, by writing Fed funds, for the securities received as soon as it has examined these securities to verify that they are in good order: that the correct securities have been delivered in the correct amount, that the securities are properly signed, if necessary, and so on.

Back to our example: The CDs that Manny had taken in over the window from Sali would go to Merrill's desk at Manny. There, an account manager would check the delivery against instructions received by Manny from Merrill: Have the correct securities been delivered? Are they in good order? Is the money correct? If the securities delivered were *not* in good order—the size was wrong or the coupon or maturity date was incorrect—Manny would notify Irving to pick up these securities along with a form showing Manny's reason for rejecting the delivery; naturally, Manny would make *no* payment to Irving for the rejected delivery. In the more likely event that the securities delivered were in good order, Manny would instruct its money transfer department to wire the appropriate money to Irving for the account of Sali.

Once the Chase CDs delivered to Merrill by Sali were on the Merrill desk at Manny, Merrill's account manager would check Merrill's pending instructions to see whether any of these securities had been sold by Merrill and should be delivered out by Manny on behalf of Merrill.

Getting back to our example, we assume that Ford uses Morgan, New York, for custody. Most, but not all, managers of large portfolios choose a NYC custody agent because a bank with direct access to the New York Fed can provide more rapid and efficient clearing services than can a regional bank. Also, clearing of *physical* securities is expensive and difficult for out-of-town banks to do.

The first steps that occur in a dealer-to-customer trade resemble closely those that occur in a dealer-to-dealer trade. To continue our example, Ford's and Merrill's traders strike their deal on the phone—Ford's trader agrees to buy $10 million of 3-month bills at a discount of 7.95. Each trader writes a trade ticket detailing the essentials of the trade.

The Merrill trader will send its ticket to its back office, as it would for a trade with Sali, and its back office will go through the same procedures described above: clean up the information that the trader has given it and add any further information needed to clear the trade. The latter would include the CUSIP number of the bill issue and Ford's standing delivery instructions to Merrill. Once Merrill has prepared a file in its computer containing all relevant information on the trade, it will prepare a computer-generated confirm for Fed as well as instructions to its clearing bank (Manny) directing it to clear the trade.

Ford, meanwhile, will also have an operations person preparing a complete record of all details of its trade with Merrill; using that information, its operations people will prepare instructions for its custodial bank (Morgan) to clear its trade with Merrill. Ford's instructions to Morgan would say, "We have bought from Merrill $10 million of bills, CUSIP number Y, maturing in X days. Please accept delivery of these securities, and pay out, versus delivery, the money due, which is Z dollars. Settlement is today."

Once Morgan receives Ford's instructions, it will feed this information into its computer and it will be on the lookout for Merrill's delivery to Ford. Poised on the opposite side of the street, Manny's computer will, when it receives Merrill's delivery instructions, go into a pending mode and shoot out a ticket of instructions to the manager of the Merrill account. From there on in, delivery will proceed as in our earlier example of a Merrill-to-Sali delivery.

CLEARING TRADES IN PHYSICAL SECURITIES

A number of important money market instruments have not yet been converted to book-entry. The principal reason is that such securities are too heterogeneous with respect to the name of the issuer, the dates of issue and maturity, the face amount, and the coupon or discount rate paid to be converted with ease to book-entry. Money market securities still in physical form include CDs, BAs, commercial paper, muni notes, and certain types of mortgage-backed securities.

Clearing a dealer-to-dealer trade

Clearing a trade in physical securities, bearer or registered, requires some movement of certificates or other paper from one bank's vault to another's or, at least, from one place in a given bank's vault to another. To illustrate what is involved in clearing such a trade, we will walk, step by step, through the clearing of a dealer-to-dealer trade in CDs.

Assume that Merrill's CD trader buys $10 million of Chase CDs from Sali's trader, and assume that both dealers use clearing banks to clear their CD trades. Each trader will write a trade ticket. From these tickets, operations people at both shops will produce confirms. Sali's confirm to Merrill will say, "Dear Merrill: We sold you today, for settlement tomorrow, $10 million of Chase CDs maturing on day X and carrying a coupon of Y; the yield on the CDs is 8.15%; the dollar value of the principal plus accrued interest is Z dollars." Merrill will produce a "We bought . . ." confirm for Sali containing the same information.

Once this is done, Sali will send an instruction to its clearing bank telling the latter to deliver the securities in question to Merrill against payment. At the same time, Merrill will instruct its clearing bank to take in the securities to be delivered to it by Sali against payment of funds.

Clearing a customer-to-dealer trade

Clearing goes pretty much the same way on a dealer-to-dealer customer trade of physical securities. For example, Merrill might well have sold $2 million of the Chase CDs to the GE portfolio, whose custodial agent is, we'll assume, Citibank. If so, Manny would send, by messenger to Citi for the account of GE, $2 million of the Chase CDs that Sali has delivered into the Merrill account.

When Manny delivered its Chase CDs for Merrill to Citi, the stamped delivery bill it received would state that the securities had been accepted subject to counting and examination and that, if all were in order, payment for these securities would be made later in the business day.

CLEARING FEES

Thanks to the efficiency of operation made possible by the book-entry system, clearing banks are able to clear a trade in book-entry securities with one-third to one-half the labor they need to clear a trade in physical securities. Clearing bank fees reflect this differential. Currently, clearing banks charge around $6 a trade for clearing trades in book-entry securities. To this basic fee, they add $2.25 to cover the fee they must pay the Fed for each Fedwire message they send. Clearing fees on physical securities are much higher than those on book-entry securities. To clear a trade in physical securities, clearing banks charge from $15 to $25, depending on the security cleared.

Not all dealers are charged precisely the same fee by their clearing bank. A dealer who has a highly automated, high-volume system that puts out "clean" instructions pays the basic fee. In contrast, a dealer who sends in instructions that the clearing bank must "clean up" (i.e., correct) pays a higher fee. Lower clearing fees are a secondary, but significant, payoff that accrues to dealers who maintain an efficient back office.

Consistent with their philosophy—the more work, the higher the fee— clearing banks charge, for transfers of securities between a dealer's clearing and safekeeping accounts, a fee that is about two-thirds the fee they charge to clear a straight trade in book-entry securities.

Clearing bank fees cover several different services that a clearing bank provides its customers. These services are: execution, the assumption of risk of loss due to errors in execution, the provision of access to daylight overdraft to dealer clients, and the assumption of some credit risk vis-à-vis each such client.

THE NEXT CHAPTER

In this chapter, we touched briefly on the highlights of how trades in governments and money market securities are cleared. In the next chapter, we describe step-by-step how repo and reverse trades are cleared. We also focus on some related topics, such as pairoffs and fails.

Chapter 12

The clearing of repo
and reverse trades

IN THIS CHAPTER, we work step-by-step through first how a repo and then how a reverse trade are cleared. In particular, we show trade tickets, confirms, clearing bank tickets, and Fedwire messages. At the end of the chapter, we turn to some related topics, such as fails and pairoffs.

CLEARING REPOS AND REVERSES

A substantial portion of the securities trades cleared each day by clearing banks are one leg, front or back, of either repo or a reverse. When a dealer does a repo he writes *two* tickets, a *sell* ticket that initiates the transaction and a *buy* ticket that ends the transaction (or just one ticket if he's so automated that his system will produce the second ticket from the first). The sell side of the transaction typically settles on the trade date or on the following business day; the buy side settles a day or more later. When a dealer does a reverse, there are also two sides to the transaction, but, in this case, the buy side settles before the sell side. Repos and reverses are done in both book-entry and physical securities.

Whenever a dealer does a repo or a reverse with a customer or with another dealer, its operations area makes up and sends out (1) instructions to its clearing bank to clear the trade and (2) appropriate confirms to its counterparty.

A buy or a sell confirm that describes the terms of one leg of either a repo or a reverse may, but need not, contain *trailer information,* that is, information indicating some or all of the following: that the trade being confirmed is a repo or a reverse; that the term of the transaction is X days; that the trade is being done at rate Y; and that the collateral, if the trade is a repo, is to be safekept by the dealer.

So far as a dealer's clearing bank is concerned, buys and sells generated by repos and reverses differ in no significant way from outright buys and sells; both are cleared in precisely the same way.[1] To a dealer's clearing bank, all trailer information that may appear on either a repo or a reverse confirm or other clearing instruction, including identification of the trade as either a repo or a reverse, is information to be ignored because it is *irrelevant* with respect to anything the clearing bank must or must not do.

In particular, if a dealer indicates on a sell confirm, which is leg one of a repo, that he will safekeep the securities for the customer, this indication is not taken by the clearing bank as an instruction to move securities from the dealer's clearing account to his safekeeping account, if he has one. A dealer who desires that such a transfer be made must issue a separate instruction to its clearing bank directing the latter to effect, for a fee, the desired transfer of securities from the dealer's clearing account to some other account maintained by the dealer.

The exception that proves the rule: there is one situation in which a clearing bank really cares whether a given transaction is a repo because in that case the clearing bank has extra responsibilities to assume, namely, acting as custodian of the repo collateral. This unique case involves *tri-party* repos, which are discussed in Chapter 13.

CLEARING A REPO AND A REVERSE: EXAMPLES

In the beginning of this chapter, we sketched out how repos and reverses are cleared. Here, we walk step-by-step through two examples: first, the clearing of a 118-million, overnight repo; second, the clearing of a 25-million reverse. Our examples are liberally sprinkled with bits of paper: trade tickets, confirms, clearing instructions, wire transfers. Actually, the clearing of a repo or a reverse needn't call for the production of every one of these bits of paper. Today, dealers and their clearing banks are trying, with some success, to automate away such bits of paper to reduce both their costs and their opportunities for error.

---

[1] Exception: an entity that repoed registered, physical securities would not want the "buyer" (lender of money) to register those securities in his name.

Clearing an overnight repo

Well before the usual (at most offices) 9 A.M. start of the business day, traders who man the repo desks of dealers will be busy contacting major investors and striking deals with them. Suppose, to get our example going, that a trader on the Merrill repo desk does a big overnight repo with a large money fund. Specifically, assume that this trader repoes notes having a par value of 100 million with an investment officer at The Trust for U.S. Treasury Obligations, a big ($5.5 billion net asset value), governments-only, money fund in Federated Securities' family of mutual funds.

The trade ticket. Merrill's trader will immediately write a trade ticket (Figure 12–1). This ticket shows that the trade is a repo (as opposed to a reverse), that the trade runs from 12/9 to 12/10; that the collateral is 100 million (par value) of U.S. Treasury notes, the 13¾s of 5/92; that these securities are priced at a premium, 118; and that the rate on the repo is 6¾.

FIGURE 12–1
Merrill trade ticket: Repo of T notes with Federated

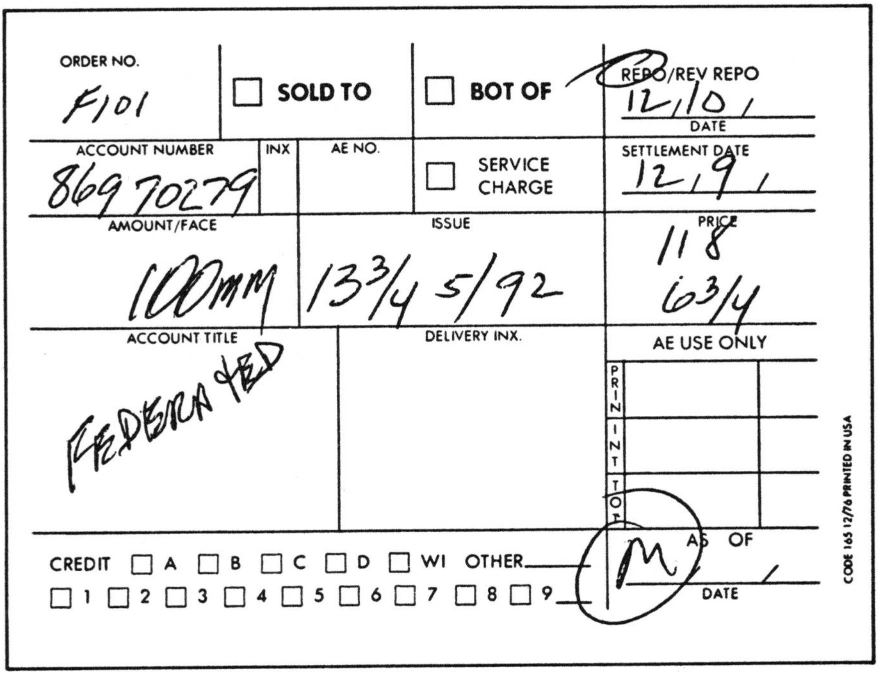
ORDER NO. F101
SOLD TO
BOT OF
REPO/REV REPO 12/10/
DATE
ACCOUNT NUMBER 86970279
INX
AE NO.
SERVICE CHARGE
SETTLEMENT DATE 12/9/
AMOUNT/FACE 100MM
ISSUE 13¾ 5/92
PRICE 118 6¾
ACCOUNT TITLE FEDERATED
DELIVERY INX.
AE USE ONLY
PRINT IN TOT
M
AS OF
DATE
CREDIT A B C D WI OTHER
1 2 3 4 5 6 7 8 9
CODE 165 12/76 PRINTED IN USA

The confirmation. Working from this trade ticket, Merrill's operations area will produce two confirmation slips to be sent to Federated. The first confirm says, "You, Federated, have done a repo with us for 100 million (par amount) of the 13¾s of 5/15/92; these securities are priced flat at 118; both the trade and the settlement dates for leg one of the repo [Merrill delivers securities to Federated against money] are 12/09/87." (See Figure 12–2.)

Note, not every dealer uses the same format for a repo confirmation. See, for example, the Morgan repo and reverse confirms in Chapter 18, the latter more typical repo confirms state explicitly: "We sold . . . ," and "We bought. . . ."

Clearing instructions. At the same time that it is producing a confirm for Federated, Merrill's operations area will also instruct its clearing

FIGURE 12–2
Merrill confirmation to Federated of a repo: *Leg one,* the *sale* of T notes to a Federated mutual fund

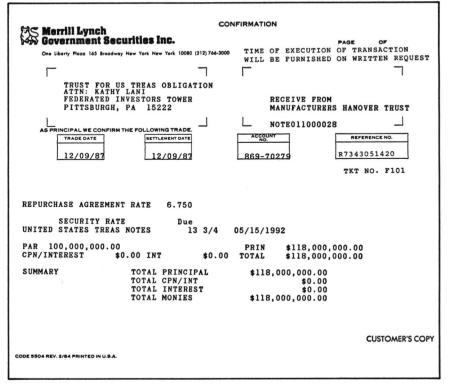

Receive from Manufacturers Hanover Trust tells Federated what bank will be delivering securities to it.

bank, Manufacturers Hanover Trust, to deliver out of its clearing account against payment the securities it has repoed to Federated's Trust of U.S. Treasury Obligations. When Manny receives Merrill's instruction, its computer will produce a ticket that instructs the Manny account manager on the Merrill desk to clear Merrill's repo trade with the Federated fund (Figure 12–3).

FIGURE 12–3
Ticket instructing manager of Merrill desk at Manny to clear Merrill's *repo (sale)* of T notes to a Federated fund, trust for U.S. Treasury Obligations

MERRILL LYNCH GOVERNMENT SECURITIES INC	Cleared By **MANUFACTURERS HANOVER TRUST COMPANY** H
	BROKERS & DEALERS CLEARANCE DEPT. 40 WALL STREET, 3RD FLR., NEW YORK, N.Y. 10015

REFERENCE NUMBER	TRADE TYPE	TRADE DATE	SETTLE DATE	DELIVERY DATE
R7343051420	SALE	12/09/87	12/09/87	

ACCOUNT NAME	SPECIAL INSTRUCTIONS

STATE STREET BOSTON TRUST
FOR US TREAS OBLIGATION

CUSTOMER NO.

ABA NO.

QUANTITY	CUSIP NUMBER	SECURITY DESCRIPTION
100,000,000.00		T NOTES 13 3/4% DUE 5/15/92

PRICE	NET AMOUNT
	118,000,000.00

PRINCIPAL

INTEREST

FEE

TAPE SEQ. NO.   TRAN NO.

TICKET SEQ. NO.   TIME

20913F

3/86

Upon delivery of the securities described hereon, which are attached hereto, to the purchaser or his designee, the purchaser shall acquire all rights in such securities which we had or had actual authority to convey, and the risk of loss shall pass to the purchaser, provided however, that if full payment for such securities has not been received at or by the time of delivery thereof; it is agreed that a purchase money security interest in favor of the above mentioned Broker/Dealer shall attach to such securities, which interest shall not terminate until such time as full payment therefor has been received by us.

FIGURE 12–4
Wire transfer of securities against money: Manny sending securities for
Merrill to the Federated fund's account at the State Street Bank, Boston

```
PRT026 65 BE3 09-DEC-1987       11:22:11.93 [TTP48:0]  TRAN# 11008
                            [H] MANUFACTURERS HANOVER TRUST COMPANY                              1
     DUE TO         TYPE          BROKERS AND DEALERS CLEARANCE DEPT.
                                      NEW YORK, NEW YORK 10015              OUTGOING   INCOMING
  02100030620|                                                                        TRANSFER OF
     DUE FROM          REF            AMOUNT                                           SECURITIES
  011000028        |0136|  $118,000,000.00
   ORDERING BANK AND RELATED DATA
  MFRS NYC/MERRILL

  STATE ST BOS/SPEC



   SECURITY IDENTIFICATION AND PAR AMOUNT
  13 3/4% NOTE B 92 (912827NE8) $100,000,000.00-1055
   MESSAGE ACKNOWLEDGEMENT
  12091055 AL139 0136*GENEAA*12091055 BSB20 1021

                                                              AUTHORIZED SIGNATURE
```

Wire transfer. To do so, Manny will wire transfer against payment the 100 million (face amount) of securities Merrill has repoed to the account of the Trust for U.S. Treasury Obligations, at the latter's custody account at the State Street Bank. (This Boston bank is used by many mutual funds as a clearing and custodial agent.) Manny's wire (Figure 12–4) shows that Manny is wiring for Merrill to the State Street Bank $100 million (face amount) of 13¾s T notes against money of $118 million.

Leg two of the repo. The trade we have been describing is an overnight repo, leg one of which was done for same-day settlement on 12/9/87. On the next day, 12/10/87, *leg two* of the repo occurs: Merrill receives back from the Federated fund the securities it repoed out to them on the 9th against payment on the 9th of $118 million. When the securities are returned to Merrill on the 10th, Merrill pays the Federated fund $118,022,125.00; this sum represents $118 million of repo-loan principal plus $22,125.00 of repo interest. Note repo interest on the one-day trade equals the $118 million lent to Merrill times the 6¾ repo rate times 1/360 (recall that, in calculating repo interest, a 360-day year is assumed); thus, the repo-interest calculation is:

$$(\$118 \text{ million})(0.0675)(\tfrac{1}{360}) = \$22,125.00$$

Once one has checked that $22,125.00 is indeed the right sum for repo interest, Figures 12–5 through 12–7 are self-explanatory. Figure 12–5 shows Merrill's confirmation to the Trust for U.S. Treasury Obligations for leg two of the repo. Figure 12–6 shows the ticket prepared by Manny's computer telling the manager of the Merrill desk at Manny to

FIGURE 12–5
Merrill confirmation to Federated of a repo: *Leg two,* the *repurchase* of T notes from a Federated mutual fund

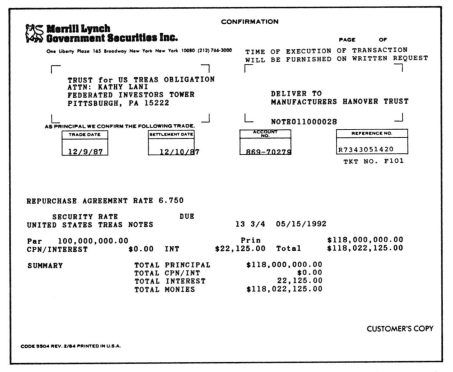

Deliver to Manufacturers Hanover Trust tells Federated to which bank it must send Merrill's securities.

anticipate receiving 100 million of T notes (the 13¾s of 5/15/92) against payment out of Merrill's account of $118,022,125.00. Figure 12–7 shows wire transfer message received by Manny confirming delivery of these securities over the Fed wire.

Clearing an overnight reverse

To illustrate the clearing of a reverse, we assume that Merrill reverses in from Sali 25 million of T bonds, the 8⅞s of 8/15/17. As the trade ticket (Figure 12–8) shows, the trade begins on 12/7 and ends on 12/8. The reverse rate on the trade is 6½.

Once the trade is done, Merrill sends a confirm to Sali (Figure 12–9) and clearing instructions to Manny. Manny's computer, on receipt of these instructions, produces the ticket shown in Figure 12–10 alerting

FIGURE 12–6
Ticket instructing manager of Merrill desk at Manny to clear Merrill's
repurchase (buy) of T notes from a Federated fund, trust for U.S.
Treasury Obligations

| MERRILL LYNCH GOVERNMENT SECURITIES INC | Cleared By **MANUFACTURERS HANOVER TRUST COMPANY** BROKERS & DEALERS CLEARANCE DEPT. 40 WALL STREET, 3RD FLR., NEW YORK, N.Y. 10015 | H |

REFERENCE NUMBER	TRADE TYPE	TRADE DATE	SETTLE DATE	DELIVERY DATE
R7343051420	BUY	12/9/87	12/10/87	

ACCOUNT NAME	SPECIAL INSTRUCTIONS
STATE BOSTON TRUST FOR US TREA OBLIGATION	

CUSTOMER NO.

ABA NO.

QUANTITY	CUSIP NUMBER	SECURITY DESCRIPTION
100,000,000.00		T NOTES 13 3/4% DUE 5/15/92

PRICE	NET AMOUNT
	118,022,125.00

209 13F

PRINCIPAL

INTEREST

FEE

3/86

TAPE SEQ. NO.   TRAN NO.

TICKET SEQ. NO.   TIME

FIGURE 12–7
Wire transfer of securities against money: State Street Bank sending
securities for a Federated fund to the account of Merrill at Manny

```
PRTO26 70 BE3 10-DEC 1987 15:33:32.92 [TTP31:0]    TRAN #10988
                          MANUFACTURERS HANOVER TRUST COMPANY
                          BROKERS AND DEALERS CLEARANCE DEPT.
                          NEW YORK, NEW YORK 10015
  DUE TO        TYPE
01100002820
  DUE FROM          REF        AMOUNT
021000306      00  0200   $118,022,125.00
ORDERING BANK AND RELATED DATA
STATE ST BOS/SPEC

MFRS NYC/MERRILL



 SECURITY IDENTIFICATION AND PAR AMOUNT
13 3/4 NOTE B 92 (912827NE8) $100,000,000.00
  MESSAGE ACKNOWLEDGEMENT
12101535 AL139 013*GENEAA*12101535  BSB20 0000
```

1
INCOMING
TRANSFER OF
SECURITIES

AUTHORIZED SIGNATURE

FIGURE 12–8
Merrill trade ticket: Reverse of T bonds with Salomon Brothers

FIGURE 12–9
Merrill confirmation to Sali of a reverse: *Leg one,* the *purchase* of T bonds from Sali

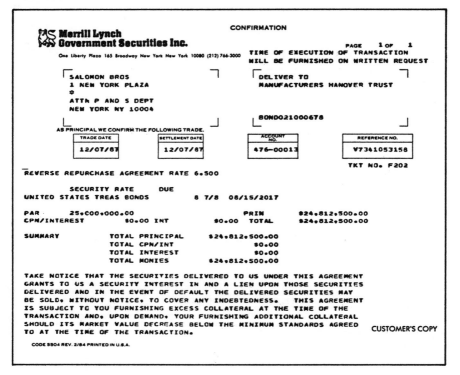

the manager of the Merrill desk at Manny that a delivery of 25 million of bonds is being made by Sali to Merrill. Next day, the trade is unwound (Figures 12–11 and 12–12).

No Fedwires are shown in our example of a reverse. The reason is that we are assuming that Sali, like Merrill, uses Manny to clear its trades in Treasury bonds. Thus, Manny can clear each leg of Merrill's reverse of securities from Sali by doing an *internal* (i.e., a *pairoff* at the clearing bank level). Fedwires would be inappropriate, since from the Fed's vantage point, the bonds traded do not move.

PAIROFFS AGAIN

Pairoffs also occur in connection with repos and reverses done between dealers and their customers. Routinely, investors will do the following trade: purchase a security and simultaneously ask the selling dealer to finance that purchase. For example, an S&L might buy a mort-

FIGURE 12–10

Ticket instructing manager of Merrill account at Manny to clear Merrill's
buy from (*leg one of a reverse* with) Sali

	Cleared By
MERRILL LYNCH GOVERNMENT SECURITIES INC	**MANUFACTURERS HANOVER TRUST COMPANY** [H] BROKERS & DEALERS CLEARANCE DEPT. 40 WALL STREET, 3RD FLR., NEW YORK, N.Y. 10015

REFERENCE NUMBER	TRADE TYPE	TRADE DATE	SETTLE DATE	DELIVERY DATE
V7341053158	BUY	12/07/87	12/07/87	

ACCOUNT NAME	SPECIAL INSTRUCTIONS

SALOMON BROS

CUSTOMER NO.

ABA NO.

QUANTITY	CUSIP NUMBER	SECURITY DESCRIPTION
25,000,000.00		T BONDS 8 7/8% DUE 8/15/17

PRICE	NET AMOUNT
	24,812,500.00

PRINCIPAL

INTEREST

FEE

TAPE SEQ. NO.   TRAN NO.

TICKET SEQ. NO.   TIME

20913F

3/86

Upon delivery of the securities described hereon, which are attached hereto, to the purchaser or his designee, the purchaser shall acquire all rights in such securities which we had or had actual authority to convey, and the risk of loss shall pass to the purchaser, provided however, that if full payment for such securities has not been received at or by the time of delivery thereof; it is agreed that a purchase money security interest in favor of the above mentioned Broker/Dealer shall attach to such securities, which interest shall not terminate until such time as full payment therefor has been received by us.

gage-backed pass-through, such as a GNMA, from a dealer and immediately reverse that security back to the selling dealer. In that case, it
would make no sense for the dealer to deliver out the securities purchased by the investor and then to require the investor to send back
those securities as collateral for the reverse. Instead, such paired buy

FIGURE 12–11

Merrill confirmation to Sali of a reverse: *Leg two,* the *purchase* of T bonds from Sali

```
                                                    CONFIRMATION
  Merrill Lynch
  Government Securities Inc.
                                                              PAGE    1 OF    1
     One Liberty Plaza 165 Broadway New York New York 10080 (212) 766-3000   TIME OF EXECUTION OF TRANSACTION
                                                    WILL BE FURNISHED ON WRITTEN REQUEST
  ┌                              ┐    ┌                              ┐
   SALOMON BROS                         RECEIVE FROM
   1 NEW YORK PLAZA                     MANUFACTURERS HANOVER TRUST
   *
   ATTN P AND S DEPT
   NEW YORK NY 10004
  └                              ┘      BOND021000678
                                                                              ┘
  AS PRINCIPAL WE CONFIRM THE FOLLOWING TRADE.
        TRADE DATE       SETTLEMENT DATE        ACCOUNT NO.         REFERENCE NO.
        12/07/87           12/08/87            476-00013          V7341053158

                                                            TKT NO. F202

  REVERSE REPURCHASE AGREEMENT RATE 6.500

        SECURITY RATE       DUE
  UNITED STATES TREAS BONDS       8 7/8  08/15/2017

  PAR     25,000,000.00               PRIN      $24,812,500.00
  CPN/INTEREST        $0.00 INT    $4,480.03 TOTAL   $24,816,980.03

  SUMMARY             TOTAL PRINCIPAL      $24,812,500.00
                      TOTAL CPN/INT              $0.00
                      TOTAL INTEREST          $4,480.03
                      TOTAL MONIES        $24,816,980.03

  TAKE NOTICE THAT THE SECURITIES DELIVERED TO US UNDER THIS AGREEMENT
  GRANTS TO US A SECURITY INTEREST IN AND A LIEN UPON THOSE SECURITIES
  DELIVERED AND IN THE EVENT OF DEFAULT THE DELIVERED SECURITIES MAY
  BE SOLD, WITHOUT NOTICE, TO COVER ANY INDEBTEDNESS.  THIS AGREEMENT
  IS SUBJECT TO YOU FURNISHING EXCESS COLLATERAL AT THE TIME OF THE
  TRANSACTION AND, UPON DEMAND, YOUR FURNISHING ADDITIONAL COLLATERAL
  SHOULD ITS MARKET VALUE DECREASE BELOW THE MINIMUM STANDARDS AGREED
  TO AT THE TIME OF THE TRANSACTION.                         CUSTOMER'S COPY

  CODE 5504 REV. 2/84 PRINTED IN U.S.A.
```

and financing transactions are settled by a pairoff: money in the form of margin passes hands, but the securities purchased stay put.

FAILS TO DELIVER

Whenever a seller of securities does not deliver to the buyer, on a timely basis, the precise amount of the precise security traded, the seller is said to have *failed* on the delivery.

Fails occur routinely in the clearing of securities trades. For example, a dealer might fail to deliver out Y million of issue X because a customer (seller) had failed to deliver those securities to him, because his delivery got caught in the before-close rush of traffic on the Fed wire, because his back office made a mistake (e.g., sent the wrong issue, sent the wrong amount of the right issue, used the wrong delivery instructions), and so on.

Every dealer and investor loves to be "failed to," provided that the fail

FIGURE 12–12
Ticket instructing manager of Merrill desk at Manny to clear leg two of
Merrill's *reverse* of T bonds from Sali (a *sell* by Merrill)

Cleared By
MANUFACTURERS HANOVER
TRUST COMPANY
BROKERS & DEALERS CLEARANCE DEPT.
40 WALL STREET, 3RD FLR., NEW YORK, N.Y. **10015**

MERRILL LYNCH GOVERNMENT
SECURITIES INC

REFERENCE NUMBER	TRADE TYPE	TRADE DATE	SETTLE DATE	DELIVERY DATE
V7341053158	SALE	12/07/87	12/08/87	

ACCOUNT NAME	SPECIAL INSTRUCTIONS
SALOMON BROS	

CUSTOMER NO.

ABA NO.

QUANTITY	CUSIP NUMBER	SECURITY DESCRIPTION
25,000,000.00		T BOND 8 7/8% DUE 8/15/17

PRICE	NET AMOUNT
	24,816,980.03

PRINCIPAL

INTEREST

FEE

TAPE SEQ. NO. TRAN NO.

TICKET SEQ. NO. TIME

20913F

3/86

Upon delivery of the securities described hereon, which are attached hereto, to the purchaser or his designee, the purchaser shall acquire all rights in such securities which we had or had actual authority to convey, and the risk of loss shall pass to the purchaser, provided however, that if full payment for such securities has not been received at or by the time of delivery thereof; it is agreed that a purchase money security interest in favor of the above mentioned Broker/Dealer shall attach to such securities, which interest shall not terminate until such time as full payment therefor has been received by us.

does *not* cause him to fail on the other side. If a seller of securities fails to deliver the securities he has sold on the agreed settlement date, *the party failed to* (i.e., the buyer) *earns accrued interest as if he owned the securities, but he need put up no money until the securities are actually delivered.* This is *important* because an investor who is failed to is given, in effect, the opportunity to be *double invested,* that is, to own $2 of assets for every $1 he was supposed to pay but did not have to pay for the securities he failed to receive. Being doubled invested is such an attractive state that investors sometimes exercise various ploys to achieve it. For example, one astute Wall Streeter is said to have always bought lots of 13 Treasury bonds for his family trust. His reason was not faith that the number 13 was lucky; rather, experience had taught him that the bank that sold bonds to the trust would always fail for days on a delivery of 13 off-the-run bonds.

Every dealer makes some person responsible for seeing to it that the dealer earns rather than loses money on fails. Every dealer knows that he will experience some fails on deliveries to him. Playing the *fails game* calls for the dealer to ensure that he makes no unnecessary fails and that, if he is forced into a fail by, say, a late delivery or a fail to deliver to him, he makes the smallest possible fail on the opposite side: Perhaps by reducing his box position, he can match a $5 million fail to deliver to him with just a $1 million fail to deliver on his part.

When a dealer is threatened with a fail because he has been failed to on the other side, he will sometimes use a *reverse* to prevent that fail. For example, a dealer who has sold 50 million of an issue, received in only 40 million of that issue, and is thus 10 million short of the issue, might, to save himself from a costly fail, reverse in 10 million of the issue; he would then deliver out 50 million of the issue; the 10 million he has reversed in plus the 40 million he has in the box. The use by dealers of reverses to cover shorts, both advertent and inadvertent, raises an important aspect of repos and reverses, control over collateral.

CONTROL OVER COLLATERAL

We said in Chapter 1 that repos resemble in many aspects a collateralized loan and that the economic essence of a repo is, typically, that of a collateralized loan. There is, however, one important aspect in which a repo differs from a standard collateralized loan; that aspect concerns *control over collateral.* Most times, at least on a large repo of book-entry securities, the borrower of money actually delivers out to the lender of money whatever securities he uses to collateralize his repo loan. In this case, both parties to the repo acknowledge—recall that leg one of a repo is a sale of securities—that, during the term (life) of the repo, the holder of collateral has *absolute* control of that collateral. In particular, the holder of collateral (lender of money) may sell his collateral, hypothecate it, lend it out, or whatever. His sole obligation to the borrower of money is to return, at the expiration of the repo, precisely the same collateral given to him at the start of the repo.[2] In a typical collateralized loan, say a home mortgage, the lender of money has only the right to hold the collateral he receives—unless, of course, the borrower of money defaults on his loan. Consumer Smith would be shocked to find that his bank, while he was making prompt mortgage payments, had sold his home; not so the repo borrower.

While the right of the receiver of collateral in a repo to do as he pleases with his collateral is absolute, that right is circumscribed by certain practical considerations. To illustrate, consider a dealer who is short the *current (most recently auctioned)* 2-year note; there is no reason why such a dealer should hesitate to reverse in that issue (to lend money against that specific issue), and then to use that collateral to cover his short. Dealers use reverses to cover shorts all the time—shorts created by customers who fail to make timely deliveries to them, shorts they create as a market play, shorts they create to hedge their position in other securities, and so on. The reason that dealers can short and cover with reverse current, *on-the-run* (i.e., *on the broker's run*) Treasuries is that such issues are easily available and actively traded in the market; consequently, a dealer who takes in the current 2-year note and who then uses it to cover a short, normally need not be concerned whether he will be able to repurchase that security. Many securities—bank CDs, BAs, commercial paper, and muni notes—are, unlike Treasuries, highly *heterogeneous:* each such security has its own issuer, maturity date, and coupon. No trader will short heterogeneous paper, such as bank CDs, because he knows that if he did so, it would probably prove impossible for him to buy back paper identical to the paper he had shorted; and if he couldn't do that, he would be unable to cover his short. Many investors are tuck-away-until-maturity investors, so the fact that paper exists is no guarantee that it can be bought in the market at any time. This being the case, if a trader were, for example, to short a Morgan CD, then—even if Morgan had sold many CDs with the coupon and maturity date of the paper shorted—chances are that a trader hunting that specific paper would be unable to find it.

We have said that most times there is enough of a Treasury issue in the market, at least of a new issue, that buying the issue is no problem. Actually, there are occasional squeezes even in new Treasury issues. In 1980, Arab investors laden with oil money bought from U.S. dealers $3 billion of a new, $2 billion Treasury issue, the 12s of 87; that left the dealers with a $1 billion short in the issue, and there was no way they

---

[2] Reverses to maturity are an exception. In that case, the dealer sells out his collateral immediately upon receiving it; he settles leg two of the reverse with a difference check (see Chapter 9).

could cover this short unless the Arabs swapped out of some of their holdings of the issue. Finally, the Fed induced Arab investors to do just that. In May 1985, it was the turn of Japanese investors to create a squeeze in Treasuries. By not swapping out of the 9¼s of 2/15/16—as big U.S. dealers anticipated they would—when a new, similar Treasury issue, the 7¼s of 5/15/16, came to market, the Japanese created a squeeze in this issue, one that cost U.S. dealers millions of dollars.

The right of substitution. Not surprisingly, receivers of collateral can be divided into two classes. First, there are traders and dealers who seek a specific issue to cover a short. Second, there are investors who don't much care what securities they get as collateral. Such an investor may well say, " I want as collateral short-governments because the long bond bounces around too much in price." If he does, what he means is not that he wants as collateral a specific issue, say the current 3-month bill, but rather that he wants to reduce his perceived credit risk by holding the most liquid collateral possible and by thus being well positioned to sell that collateral if his dealer should perchance default on the repo. It is common for a repo investor to set limits on the classes of collateral he will accept; since every investor would prefer to have the most liquid collateral possible, dealers normally must pay up slightly to repo, as they do, less liquid paper, such as mortgage-backed pass-throughs.

Often, a dealer who borrows money from an investor who isn't concerned about what specific issue he gets as collateral will ask the investor for *the right of substitution,* that is, the right to substitute during the term of the repo one issue to serve as collateral for another. A dealer might want the right of substitution for one of several reasons: he is using term repo to finance inventory from which he might make a sale at any time; he is running a matched book, and an issue that he has financed with repo might turn into a *special (much-in-demand)* issue against which he could borrow at a rate below, perhaps far below, the going repo rate on *stock* (plain vanilla) collateral. (An issue turns into a special when many traders on the Street have shorted it and must, to make delivery, either borrow or reverse in the issue; see Chapter 13.)

It is common today, though less common than it used to be, for investors in repo to grant the giver of collateral the right of substitution. On a delivery repo, a problem for both the giver and receiver of collateral is that whenever the giver of collateral exercises his right of substitution, he incurs clearing fees and bookkeeping costs and so too does the receiver of collateral. This being the case, dealers who receive the right of substitution on a repo are cautious about exercising that right. No dealer wants to annoy a good term-repo customer by constantly exercising his right of substitution. At some point, such a customer, faced with a continuing stream of substitutions, might well object, saying, "Hey, this is costing me time, money, and aggravation. I am going to give my money to some other dealer who, hopefully, will be able to make up his mind about what collateral he wants to give me." One advantage of tri-party repos (see Chapter 13) is that the transaction costs associated with a substitution of collateral are much less under such an arrangement than they are on a straight delivery repo.

Note the presence of the right of substitution on some repos is indicative of the fact that the true essence of a repo is not that it is a securities transaction but rather that it is a collateralized loan. An investor who was making a true purchase of securities, say IBM stock, would surely be most troubled if his Merrill registered rep called up to say, "Hey, for that money you sent us, we are giving you not the IBM stock you thought you bought, but rather some GM stock; that works better for us." In contrast, the lender of money in a repo will, if he has given his dealer the right of substitution, face with equanimity a substitution of one security he has "bought" for another.

THE NEXT CHAPTER

In Chapter 13, we turn to several important topics: dealer safekeeping, tri-party repos, and bank custody. This chapter sets the stage for Chapter 14 in which we discuss dealer failures and the tidying up of repo-market practices.

Chapter 13

Dealer safekeeping and bank custody of investor securities

IN THIS CHAPTER, WE DISCUSS DEALER SAFEKEEPING OF REPO collateral, tri-party repos, and bank custody of repo collateral. We then turn in Chapter 14 to a number of related topics: investor losses in the repo and reverse markets, the tidying up of repo-market practices—including the writing of repo agreements, and the Government Securities Act of 1986.

DEALER SAFEKEEPING OF REPO COLLATERAL

While delivery of collateral to the lender of money was common in the early repos done between big dealers and big investors, some customers, instead of taking delivery of repo collateral or even of securities purchased outright, have long left such securities with their dealer for safekeeping.

Reasons for dealer safekeeping

Some, but not all, dealers offer to safekeep securities for customers at no charge. One reason a dealer may do this is to nurture customer relationships by providing to his customers, at no cost to them, a service that they would otherwise have to buy. A second reason some dealers prefer, on overnight repos, to safekeep customer securities, especially physical securities, is that delivery would, relative to the interest paid on the repo, be costly to both parties. A third reason some dealers prefer to safekeep customer securities is risk of a subsequent fail. Dealers reason, "If I deliver out, as collateral for an overnight repo, $10 million of bills to XYZ Corp., I must worry about whether XYZ will return my collateral tomorrow in time for me to redeliver it to another repo customer or to an outright buyer. If, alternatively, I safekeep, overnight, for XYZ his collateral, I know that, tomorrow when my repo with XYZ comes off, I'll have my bills in time to make good delivery of them to another customer." Still a fourth reason why dealers like dealer safekeeping is that, under this arrangement, it is the dealer, not the customer, who will profit if the dealer is *failed to* on a delivery of securities that he [the dealer] has promised to safekeep for the customer. In this case, the dealer will honor his promise to safekeep his customer's securities only when those securities finally come in, which may be a day, or many days, after his trade with the customer settles.

Exempt versus regulated securities

In discussing dealer safekeeping, it is important to distinguish between regulated and exempt securities. The SEC legislation passed in the 1930s brought under federal regulation trading in corporate stocks and bonds, but not trading in most money market instruments. Today's roster of exempt securities comprises government and federal agency securities, BAs, CDs, commercial paper with an original maturity of 270 days or less, and municipal securities. Regulation of municipal securities, introduced in 1975, is carried out by the Municipal Securities Rulemaking Board (MSRB), not the SEC. Regulation of government securities, introduced in 1986 to 1987 with the passage of the Government Securities Act (GSA) of 1986, is now carried out by the SEC, the Treasury, and bank regulators.

Regulated securities. Any broker/dealer who deals in regulated securities is required by Rules 15c2-1 and 15c3-3 of the Securities Exchange Act of 1934 and by Article III Section 19(d) of the Rules of Fair Practice of NASD to hold all fully paid-for securities that he safekeeps for a customer in a denominated, segregated account in which the customer is afforded significant protection. In particular, a broker/dealer holding securities in such an account may neither hypothecate nor negotiate such securities unless he is specifically instructed by the customer to do so. Also, a customer who holds fully paid-for securities with a regulated broker/dealer for safekeeping may, at any time, demand immediate delivery of those securities. Normally, a dealer will maintain a safekeeping account for customer securities at his clearing bank, either in the clearance area or in the custody area. A dealer who does so must, to ensure that he can meet a customer's demands for securities, create, for each security not in his actual custody, records that indicate both where the security is located and how it may be identified as belonging to a specific customer. Also, a dealer must ensure that his records match customers with their securities and that his clearing bank employs a system that permits retrieval of each security upon a customer's request.

Margined securities held by a regulated broker/dealer for a customer are afforded less protection. A broker/dealer may hold such securities in his clearance account and he may hypothecate them; this makes sense, since the principal way broker/dealers get the cash necessary to finance their customers' margin accounts is by borrowing against the securities that their customers buy on margin.

Exempt securities.   Prior to passage of the Government Securities Act (GSA) of 1986, firms that dealt solely in exempt securities, including the *Government Securities, Inc. (GSI)* subsidiaries that some broker/dealers created to deal in exempt securities, did not have to register with the SEC or with any regulatory body for that matter. Also, most SEC rules arising out of the 1934 act, with the exception of the antifraud provisions of this act, did not apply to such firms; in particular, SEC rules with respect to the safekeeping of customer securities applied only to firms dealing in regulated securities. With the passage of GSA in 1986, various rules and regulations, both new and existing, were applied to dealers in governments.

Operation of dealer safekeeping

Dealers who dealt solely in exempt securities and who offered dealer safekeeping could and did use various arrangements for holding customer securities. Some such firms, mainly smaller ones, simply held customer securities in their clearing account. Doing so saved a dealer money, because a clearing bank charges a fee each time a dealer moves securities from his clearing account to his safekeeping account, or vice versa. (The fee for such a transfer is approximately two-thirds of the normal clearing fee for wireables, much less than two-thirds of the normal clearing fee for physicals.)

Despite the fees that a dealer incurs when he opens a safekeeping account for customer securities, most unregulated dealers who were, prior to 1986, safekeeping securities for customers did have a safekeeping account at their clearing bank. Under the most typical arrangement, the dealer was and still is free to move securities into and out of this account at will. The clearing bank had and still has *no* information about which customers' securities are in the dealer's safekeeping account; the clearing bank knows the account solely as one of several accounts the dealer maintains and over which he exercises *sole* control.

Dealer safekeeping of this ilk is referred to as *trust-me* safekeeping; to give customers a greater level of comfort, some dealers in exempt securities have set up customer safekeeping accounts that contain various safeguards akin to those associated with safekeeping accounts maintained by broker/dealers who deal in regulated securities. If there is one generalization that holds about the safekeeping practices followed by dealers in exempt securities, it is that these practices *did lack and still do lack uniformity.*

Responsibilities of the clearing bank

We said above that, when a dealer in exempt securities sets up at his clearing bank a safekeeping account, that account is under the dealer's sole control—the fact that the account bears the title "for the sole benefit of customers" notwithstanding. Moreover, the dealer's bank has *no responsibility under securities law* to police movements of securities into and out of that account. Since the latter point has been the subject of several suits and a source of misunderstanding to many investors, the point is worth restating with emphasis.

With respect to a clearing bank's responsibilities, a Washington securities lawyer, formerly with the SEC, noted, "We've done work in connection with a major dealer bankruptcy and have gotten into this. Independent of any regulation, the government securities dealer, through contractual relationships with the clearing entity, works out some kind of arrangement to safekeep securities. From that standpoint, some obligations [on the part of the clearing bank] may be created by contract law, but *I have come across nothing, in what I've read or seen, where those obligations were required by securities laws.*"

A respected clearing banker seconded this opinion by describing, with the following example, what he thinks are his responsibilities: "Suppose that the first transaction a dealer ever does with us occurs when $1 million of bonds comes into his account and $1 million of cash goes out. We've got a $1 million cash overdraft, but we've got $1 million of collateral in the dealer's account. The dealer then tells us that he sold those very same securities to a customer and would we be good enough to move them from his dealer account to that customer's account. We would do it only when and if he funded that $1 million shortfall in cash. Now, assume that he did, that he took the $1 million the customer paid him and paid us. We would cover his overdraft with the cash, and, thereafter, we'd view his security as excess collateral; we'd put it anywhere he told us to put it. If he told us to put it into a safekeeping account held exclusively for the benefit of his customers, but not specifically for the account of customer XYZ, we'd be happy to do that. If, on the next day, he [the dealer] gave us instructions to take $500,000 of those securities from the customer [safekeeping] account and put it back into his dealer account, we would absolutely do it without question.

"In the clearing environment, we operate on a value-for-value basis. We would hesitate moving a security from a dealer's account to a safekeeping account if, in fact, we had a lien on those securities. That's the only way we would object."

Meaning to a customer of dealer safekeeping: Exempt securities

In discussing the meaning of dealer safekeeping to a customer, it's important to distinguish between what a customer thinks he is getting and what he is actually getting—the two often differ totally. Many customers who utilize the safekeeping facilities offered by dealers in exempt securities are small and unsophisticated.

The customer's view.   The small money market investor who leaves securities with his dealer for safekeeping typically underestimates the resulting credit risk. He often thinks that dealer safekeeping means that his securities are tucked off somewhere safe for him and that they will, under *all* circumstances, always be there whenever he wants them.

Many small investors also have—their depositions in dealer bankruptcy cases so indicate—the notion that dealer safekeeping must generate some paper trail outside the dealership. In particular, such investors, if they deal in book-entry securities, often think that the Fed must have a record of what securities have been delivered on their behalf over the Fed wire. Such investors also often think that the dealer's clearing bank must have a record of what securities the dealer is holding at that bank in safekeeping for them.

The truth: Trust me.   In truth, dealer safekeeping is a *trust-me* arrangement. It generates no customer-specific records outside the dealership. Consequently, regardless of what a dealer does with a customer's securities—place them in a safekeeping account, place them in his clearing account, hypothecate them, or sell them—his act is, from the customer's point of view, an *unverifiable* event.

Should the customer who believes otherwise go to the Fed, he will find that the Fed has *no* record of its having moved securities from bank X to bank Y to be placed in a dealer safekeeping account for the customer's benefit. As noted, the only information in a securities wire with which the Fed concerns itself is (1) what securities are to move, (2) from what bank to what bank they are to move, and (3) what money, if any, is to move.

If the customer asks the dealer's clearing bank for information concerning securities being held by his dealer in safekeeping for him, he will probably receive, as have a number of investors, a letter telling him to direct his request for information to his dealer. Generally, this is all a clearing bank can do, since it has *no* information as to which of a dealer's customers hold which of the securities that the dealer may have in its safekeeping account at the bank.

Since neither the Fed nor the clearing bank maintain any paper trail that would indicate where the customer's securities are, the only way the customer can find this out is to ask the dealer. If the dealer says the customer's securities are at the dealer's clearing bank, the customer is back where he started—with a trust-me arrangement with his dealer.

Since dealer safekeeping is an unverifiable arrangement, any investor who leaves securities with a dealer has made the risk equivalent of an unsecured loan to that dealer.

Fraud associated with dealer safekeeping

In recent years, a string of dealer bankruptcies has shaken the government market.[1] The list of firms no longer with us includes the following somewhat familiar names: Drysdale Government Securities, Lombard-Wall, Lion Capital Group, Comark, RTD Securities, E.S.M. Government Securities, and the Bevill Bresler and Schulman Group. While not all of these firms used precisely the same techniques for getting their fingers into other people's pockets, a number of them discovered that unverifiable dealer safekeeping combined with the trusting nature of many of their smaller customers provided them with an easy means of generating, via various frauds, hundreds of millions of dollars to enhance their capital and to cover, sooner or later, their cumulative trading losses— losses that each firm had and that each firm earnestly prayed would vanish, if not today, then tomorrow.

It has been suggested that a few sharp souls migrated to the government market to become dealers primarily because the opportunity to combine doing repos against governments with unverifiable safekeeping of customer securities provided them an irresistible opportunity to steal. However, it is more likely that no dealer in government securities ever set up shop specifically to make a living from defrauding his customers. Probably in every or almost every case, a dealer who eventually engaged in fraud started out intending to make money running an honest business; then, due to his incompetence and/or to a few unfortunate bets he made on the market, he lost money and ended up broke or worse. At that point, he succumbed to the temptation to reason, "I'm bankrupt at

[1] See pp. 209–211.

the moment, *but,* if I just borrow from customers for a little while, I can recoup my losses." And, thus, started the fraud, the creative accounting, and the deceit. Noted one dealer, "Covering up widespread fraud is such a time-consuming and troublesome chore that it's hard to believe that any dealer would, in a market where it's possible to make money honestly, choose, except under duress, to be dishonest."

Perfection of interest:
Who owns that collateral?

We said above that an investor who leaves securities, securities bought outright or repo collateral, with his dealer for safekeeping has made the risk equivalent of an unsecured loan to that dealer. The investor has no way to verify, other than taking the dealer's word for it, what has been done with his securities; he can only hope that, should his dealer go bankrupt, his securities will be found to be at the dealer's clearing bank either in the dealer's clearing account or in the dealer's safekeeping account, if one exists.

Actually, an investor who has left securities for safekeeping with a dealer who goes bankrupt may, to his great shock, find that thanks to dealer safekeeping he faces not one, but two sequential problems: Are his securities there, and, if so, does he in fact own those securities in the eyes of the law?

Under a state's *Uniform Commercial Code (UCC),* which state-to-state is anything but uniform, a good case can be made that an investor who leaves securities in safekeeping with a dealer instead of requiring that his dealer deliver those securities to him, has failed to *perfect his interest* in the securities. In plain English, the code seems to say that, if an investor does not bother to take possession of securities he bought, either via a purchase or via a repo, he will not be recognized in bankruptcy court as owning those securities. This, for example, is true regardless of whether the bankrupt dealer's records show that a specific security in its possession at the time of its bankruptcy was being held by it in safekeeping for a specific customer. In particular, even if a bankrupt dealer's records show that a specific security in its safekeeping or clearing account, for example, a specific GNMA with a specific pool number and a specific certificate number, was being held by it for a specific customer, that customer might still have difficulty taking possession of his security. He might have to engage in a costly, outcome-uncertain legal battle to obtain the latter.

Any investor who, to obtain securities he thinks are due him, gets into a dispute in bankruptcy court (1) over whether his interest in certain securities is perfected (i.e., over whether he is a secured or general creditor of his bankrupt dealer) or (2) over whether repo is a securities transaction or a collateralized loan will soon recognize that he has fallen into a slough of legal complexities. There are, moreover, few broad precedents to indicate whether he will win in his struggle to emerge, securities in hand, from this slough. The only sure thing is that he, the investor, will rack up legal bills that he'll not soon forget.

LETTER REPO

Despite the fact that investors have lost, as a result of dealer bankruptcies, hundreds of millions of dollars, often because of their use of dealer safekeeping, nondelivery repos remain common and are often done between major dealers and major investors.

Nondelivery repo goes under a lot of names. Some dealer shops call it *letter repo,* others call it a *due bill,* and still others refer to it as *hold-in-custody (HIC) repo.* Whatever it is called, the reasons for and characteristics of such repos tend to be pretty much the same at major dealers.

Dealer reasons for doing letter repo

The principal reason that dealers use letter repo is to achieve operational efficiencies.

An operations person at one major dealer—a Cadillac credit—described how his firm got into letter repo, "Ten years ago, when we did repo it was always DVP, and delivery on a repo was just like delivery on an outright sale. Typically, at the end of the day, we have very large money amounts of securities in small pieces. We used to dump that stuff into a bank loan at the end of the day, which was expensive. Then one of our guys said, 'Why can't we repo this stuff without having to do all of this paper work?' So we devised a way to generate, via a computer, a confirm to a customer, but without writing a trade report—it was a different system.

"Today, the way our system works is that we enter into our computer all day the dollar values of the letter repos customers want to do with us; the computer knows what classes of securities each customer will accept. At 3:30 or 4 P.M., we press a button and say, 'OK computer, allocate.' The computer spits out confirms to customers and instructions to our clearing bank. The bank then takes the collateral we have assigned to letter repo and moves it out of our clearing account into a customer safekeeping account.

"We know that our bank knows that the collateral is pledged to a customer as part of a letter repo. We next make up a letter of confirmation to each [letter] repo customer, slap onto it a listing of paper collateralizing his repo, and then send that confirm off in the mail to the customer. When the customer gets his paper confirm, he reads that, on Monday, he lent us $100 million and that this was the collateral. The customer can use that document to go back to the bank and ask if that collateral was really in our customer safekeeping account. Occasionally, customers send in an audit guy to do just that.

"The paper work on the sales desk is quite similar for delivery and for nondelivery repo, but there's a big difference in the back-office work associated with the two. The collateral behind a letter repo may be in our own vault rather than at our clearing bank. So we have customers' auditors waltzing, now and then, into our vault as well as into our bank."

The incentive for dealers to use letter repo is greatest when the collateral that the dealer wants to finance could be delivered out only with a lot of bother and cost both to the dealer and to the investor. For this reason, dealers have traditionally done letter repos to finance their holdings of various physical securities and their holdings of odd-lots of wireable securities as well. Firms that deal in commercial paper have, in particular, used letter repo to finance overnight odds and ends of unsold paper they have taken into position. Letter repo is also commonly used by dealers to finance physical pass-throughs, such as GNMAs, which are troublesome and expensive to deliver.

Investor reasons for buying letter repo

We've said that a repo investor who leaves his collateral in safekeeping with this dealer is doing the risk equivalent of extending an unsecured loan to that dealer. Doing so is not necessarily a bad thing. Whether it is or is not depends largely on who is lending to whom.

Many big, sophisticated investors routinely buy commercial paper, which is the equivalent of their making short-term, *unsecured* loans to corporations, financial and nonfinancial. Rarely have investors in commercial paper lost money. The reasons why lie in the way the commercial paper market operates. First, commercial paper is sold by dealers to investors and direct by issuers to investors on the basis of its being exactly what it is—a short-term, *unsecured* note; thus, the first thing that an investor in commercial paper considers is *credit risk*. Second, all commercial paper sold in the national market is rated by a major rating agency: Moody's, Standard & Poor's, or Fitch; investors, precisely because they understand that commercial paper is unsecured, pay careful attention to the ratings the agencies give to the paper of different issuers (few are the investors who will buy commercial paper that does not have a top—A-1 or P-1—rating from one of the major rating agencies); finally, and this is important, the agencies who rate commercial paper are so conservative that they manage, given the importance that investors in commercial paper attach to ratings, to keep the riffraff—marginal borrowers—out of the commercial paper market.

Our remarks above together with the track record of who lost what in the repo market suggest that the making of unsecured loans by investors to borrowers is not per se bad. What is bad and what has occurred all too often in the repo market is that unsophisticated investors in repo have made unsecured loans to dealers without realizing that they were doing so; consequently, these investors have failed to take adequate precautions against credit risk.

Today, many large, sophisticated investors are still, despite the losses that have occurred in the repo market, willing to do letter repo with top-credit dealers. The attractions of such repo to investors are several. First, letter repo is operationally efficient not only for the dealer but for his customers as well. Second, the investor in letter repo can get and wants the extra basis points that his dealer willingly pays to do letter repo as opposed to repo with delivery of wireable collateral. Third, the investor believes that he is smart enough and is big enough (has resources enough) to do a searching evaluation of the borrowing dealer's creditworthiness.

TRI-PARTY REPOS

While some large investors are willing to do letter repo, others are not. To do a variant of hold-in-custody repos with such customers, certain big dealers and their clearing banks invented *tri-party repos.*

It is becoming increasingly common for large investors to negotiate with their dealer and with their dealer's clearing bank tri-party repo agreements in which the clearing bank not only knows both sides of a repo transaction, but holds the repo collateral put up by the dealer in custody for the investor for the life of the repo. Such an agreement has several advantages. It obviates the need for delivery of collateral, while protecting the interests of the investor whose credit risk becomes that of a major bank rather than that of the dealer. A tri-party repo also reduces the clearing costs associated with a large repo and makes substitution of collateral on such a repo cheaper and simpler for both the dealer and the investor.

On a tri-party repo, the dealer pays the clearing bank a fee, but the investor does not. Typically, tri-party repos are done for large sums; such repos may amount to hundreds of millions when the investor is a money fund.

Big investors, who do tri-party repos, may and sometimes do send their auditors around to check whether the clearing bank has in fact segregated their collateral. On such a repo, the dealer's collateral does not come back to him until he repays his loan from the investor.

Operations people at dealers that make use of tri-party repos tend to be very happy with the arrangement. Said one, "Merrill makes a lot of use of the tri-party repo agreement that Manny offers. We think Manny's approach is terrific. It cuts the amount of securities that have to be shipped. In such a repo, Manny always knows who the customer is, since all three parties must sign the same agreement and thus must know who their counterparties are. When such a deal is done, first there are negotiations, perhaps for several months among the lawyers. Once the paper is signed, trades can occur.

"For Merrill to do a tri-party repo with Portfolio XYZ, both Merrill and XYZ would have to open an account with Manny. Manny is fully responsible for the operation of the agreement, and they are responsible that repos done under the agreement are fully collateralized—they are pretty strict about that too.

"If we do an overnight repo, Manny will, at the end of the day, move say $200 million of collateral over to XYZ's account with them and whatever collateral is needed to cover the haircut. At the same time, they will move $200 million of cash from XYZ's account to Merrill's account. The first thing they do the next day at 9 A.M., is to move back the collateral and the money to the accounts from which they were taken. Tri-party repo is very clean and very simple. There are no big deliveries involved.

"From the client's point of view, the good points are that they get a slightly higher rate and they are not subject to collateral changes that might otherwise occur during the day. On a straight repo for $200 million, Merrill might give the client 10 different issues; and, if sometime during the day, 1 of these issues were sold by one of Merrill's traders, Merrill would have to substitute. When a dealer who assigns collateral in the morning must make deliveries, substitutions become a real possibility. That is a nuisance. With a tri-party agreement, neither party has to worry about this so long as they trust Manny. The savings we realized on wires are reflected in the rate that the client gets. Also, the arrangement is much cleaner for the client. He does not have to be on the phone all morning getting lists of collateral because he knows that Manny will send him a nice clean list the following morning telling him what securities collateralized his repo. The whole arrangement is clean, simple, and safe."

The importance of tri-party repos to major dealers is indicated by the comment of one such dealer, "Yesterday we cleared, exclusive of pairoffs, $14 billion of securities over the wire versus payment, and we did another $4 billion–$5 billion of tri-party financing."

THIRD-PARTY CUSTODY

While many small portfolio managers rely pretty much on their dealer to clear their securities trades and to safekeep their securities, major investors, including those who do some letter repos and tri-party repos, almost always hire a *custodial agent bank* both to clear their securities trades and to hold certain or all their securities for them. Recall our example (Chapter 11) in which Ford used Morgan to hold its securities in custody and to clear its trades. The custody-bank approach, which totally eliminates the portfolio manager's credit risk vis-à-vis the dealer, costs money; it also involves, relative to dealer safekeeping, extra steps for both the portfolio manager and the dealer.

The agreement and the mechanics

Institutional investors that aren't depository institutions cannot hold book-entry securities themselves, and most of them don't, for various reasons, want to hold physical securities themselves. Thus large, sophisticated investors, financial (e.g., life insurance companies and money funds) and nonfinancial, use an agent bank or banks to clear their securities trades, to hold securities for them, and to collect and credit to their accounts monies due them when the securities they own pay interest or dividends or, in the case of fixed-income securities, when they mature.

An investor wanting to use an agent bank begins by negotiating and signing a lengthy and complex agreement with a major bank (or several such banks); in this agreement, the investor and the bank stipulate that the bank shall act as the investor's clearing and custodial agent for various securities and that, in doing so, the bank shall assume various responsibilities. As part of the agreement, the bank also stipulates that it will indemnify the investor should it lose the customer's securities, should a bank employee steal the customer's securities, or whatever. Banks that do custody business carry *bankers' blanket bond insurance* to cover any losses they might incur due to this commitment. The amount of such insurance carried by a big money center bank is probably several hundred million dollars. Currently, bankers' blanket bond insurance is difficult to get, and some banks have to take high deductibles to obtain it.

Speed of execution

With respect to bank custody, it is important to note that an agent bank is not a clearing bank with a guaranteed two-minute turnaround time. A custody officer at a New York bank commented, "Sometimes Canadian dealers will try to use custody accounts with us like clearance accounts. We miss several times and they get very irate. We tell them that, if securities get into their accounts before noon, we will deliver out those securities before 2:30 P.M., but only on a best efforts basis. Our bank opens *custody accounts* for customers. If a bank opens a *clearing ac-*

count for a customer, that bank is on the hook; it must meet its performance guarantee [with respect to speed of execution] or eat the fail."

Cost of custody

Custodial fees vary from bank to bank. At one New York money center bank, fees are approximately as follows: $1,500 a year to open an account, go through the legal documentation, and obtain an account number; $30 a year per issue to hold wireable securities at the Fed or at the Depository Trust Company (DTC); $75 a year to hold a physical item; $20 to wire in or deliver out a wireable security; and $45 to receive or deliver a physical security. The $1,500 fee covers a report that the bank prepares for the customer's portfolio showing interest income, dividend income, capital gains and losses on securities transactions—everything an accountant would need for financial reporting purposes. For a further fee, the bank would do other analyses of the customer's portfolio that the customer desired.

It is hard to say what total amount of customer fees a portfolio will incur because that depends on what bank it uses (some banks have lower fee schedules than the one cited above), on how big the portfolio is and on how many issues it holds, on how actively the portfolio is traded, and so on.

An important point to make is that the fees we have just cited are fees that a major portfolio that used as its custodial agent a money center bank would pay. A smaller regional account would be better off using as its custodial agent a regional bank. *For a smaller account, the big difference that results from the choice of a local rather than a New York custody agent is the difference in service, not the difference in cost.*

Safety of bank custody

An overriding concern of all large, sophisticated portfolio managers who open bank custodial accounts is safety for their valued securities, and such safety is precisely what they think bank custody affords them. With third-party custody, as opposed to dealer safekeeping, the investor gets a separate custodial account and clear identification of the securities in that account as his. A dealer safekeeping account, in contrast, is typically of an omnibus-type nature. Moreover, the clearing bank's contractual relationships on a dealer safekeeping account run solely to the dealer, so the clearing bank is, in effect, circumscribed in what duties it presumably owes to the ultimate owners of the securities in that account.

The manager of a major U.S. corporate portfolio, who's a most conservative fellow, explains what he believes are the safeguards of bank custody: "When I enter into a custodial-agency agreement with say

Chase or Citi, that bank acts, under that agreement, as a fiduciary for me. They examine the authenticity of the securities upon advice from me, confirmed in writing; they also will act only on my specific instructions. If I tell them that I expect $100 million in government repo coming in from dealer X, they will not pay out until that occurs. The principle reason I like to have an agency bank is that it will be fully responsible for the validity of the securities and, also, will disburse funds, in accordance with our agreement, only after the securities have been examined, found to be in good form, and identified as being in fact what we described. They [the bank] look at the securities and then pay out funds on the basis of delivery.

"I have never left securities with a dealer for three reasons: (1) I don't know whether the dealer actually has the securities or not; (2) if the dealer is trading these securities actively, my account may never be credited with these securities; and (3) I have found that, due to the frequency of fails in repo, dealers often don't have securities to deliver to customers because they've been failed to themselves. When a dealer fails on a repo with us, we have the use of the funds *and* the dealer is required to pay us interest; we end up being double invested because the dealer pays me and we still have the funds."

Who can afford custody?

Some smaller investors (banks, S&Ls, and municipal bodies) have the notion—so indicate their depositions in dealer bankruptcy proceedings—that they cannot afford bank custody for their securities and that they therefore have no choice but to use dealer safekeeping. For an institution with even so little as $5 million or $10 million of securities, not to speak of $40 million of securities (the amount of securities that the Worthen Bank was safekeeping with Bevill, Bresler and Schulman at the time of the latter's bankruptcy), to say that it cannot afford a few thousand dollars in custody fees makes *no* sense in the same way that it would make *no* sense for a New Yorker with a car and some other assets, which could be taken away from him in a liability suit, to say that car insurance in New York City, which is expensive, is not for him, but only for the Rockefellers and other big-bucks boys.

THE NEXT CHAPTER

In the next chapter, we focus on major problems that have arisen in the repo market in recent years—on the bankruptcies of a number of dealers, each of whom was deep into the repo and reverse markets, and on consequent losses to investors. Specifically, we talk about the sloppiness that crept into repo-market practices, the opportunities that such sloppiness created for certain dealers to create massive, high-risk positions, to incur huge trading losses, and in some cases, to engage in fraud. Finally, at the end of the chapter, we talk about various actions that have been taken in recent years to tidy up repo-market practices and to prevent, one hopes, future reruns of the splashy-dealer-failure-cum-big-losses-to-investors scenario that has been played out so often on the Street in recent years.

Chapter 14

Dealer failures and the tidying up of repo-market practices

IN THIS CHAPTER, WE FOCUS ON THE IMPRECISION that crept over time into some repo-market practices, on dealers that got it wrong—and went bankrupt—and on the tidying up of repo-market practices that has occurred in recent years.

MARGIN AND THE PRICING OF COLLATERAL

Back when Discount and GM, and other dealers and investors as well, first started doing repos after World War II, they priced collateral precisely; that is, they priced discount securities at market value and coupon securities at market value (price) plus accrued interest. Also, in calculating the amount to be loaned, they normally haircut by some small percentage the value of the collateral that was to secure a repo loan. The haircut they took was margin. *Money market people have always viewed the provision of margin in a repo as a market practice that protects the lender of money against a possible decline in the market value of his collateral.*

Evolution away from precise pricing

Precise pricing of collateral was a safe way to do things, but it was also inconvenient because precise pricing led to crazy, odd amounts of money. An investor who had a million to invest did not want a dealer coming back at him with a number like $968,132.23. Many investors were more concerned about getting *all* of their money invested than about getting adequate protection against credit risk. So gradually, dealers got away from precise pricing of collateral. Dealers would borrow 100 against 90-day bills trading at 96 or they would borrow against coupons at "par flat"; that is, they'd price coupons at 100 and ignore accrued interest in their price calculations.[1] Or they would price coupons at some round price flat (e.g., at 98 flat). As one dealer noted, "Market practices deteriorated for the sake of convenience."

Abuses of imprecise pricing

Imprecise pricing of collateral was an invitation to dealers who were short on both capital and integrity to engage in abuses of two sorts. If they were bullish, they were tempted to follow the strategy Eldin Miller made famous: buy bills at 95, repo them for 100, and use the temporary funds thus generated to provide margin for buying more bills.[2] Alternatively, if they were bearish or at least did not anticipate a market rally, they were tempted to follow Miller's strategy two: reverse in high-coupon securities nearing a coupon date and then sell them securities for full market value. A dealer might, for example, lend out against an issue he reversed in 93 per 100 of face value and then sell the issue for 105, thereby creating $8 of extra funds for every $100 of par value of the trade he did. The dealer might then use those funds to cover any trading losses he had incurred, to cover current operating expenses and/or to finance additional speculations.

Neither of the above strategies is illegal or immoral, but both are dangerous. A dealer who uses either risks getting into a situation in which he is so highly levered that the only bets he can afford to make are winning bets. One bad bet—that rates are rising when in fact they are falling—and he's bankrupt. A number of dealers, including Miller, proved this point. They used funds generated in the repo market to stay afloat and to finance more bets. The market went against them, and they ended up, on the courthouse steps, bankrupt.

Here are three war stories.

---

[1] Flat price.

[2] See story of the failure of Financial Corp., pp. 209–11.

DEALERS THAT GOT IT WRONG

In recent and not so recent years, a number of dealers in governments have gone bankrupt with big losses to investors—in particular, to investors in repo and to givers of collateral as well. The early bankruptcy of Financial Corporation should have led to some tidying up of repo-market practices, but it did not. The later bankruptcies of Drysdale, of Lombard-Wall, and of other dealers did produce some changes.

Financial Corporation

In 1975, people on the Street were first made acutely aware of the risks involved in repo and reverse transactions because of the sobering experience to which Eldin Miller, who headed Financial Corporation of Kansas City, treated them.

"Eldin," said a dealer who knew him well, "was a guy who made a fortune in trucking. He came to New York looking like a church deacon. He didn't drink, he didn't smoke, and his personality was such that people tended to trust him."

Eldin rapidly built up a huge (in 1975) portfolio—eventually totaling $1.8 billion—of governments financed almost solely in the repo market. He bought first bills and later coupons. So long as interest rates were falling or flat, there was a profitable arbitrage in this: Eldin borrowed short, invested long, and raked in positive carry. Eventually, however, interest rates moved against him, and carry on his position turned negative. This caused a cash drain, which Eldin met by repoing out at par to unsophisticated investors, including some state and municipal investment officers, T bills selling at 94. He was able to do this because, as one dealer notes, "Eldin ran into some real dummies who said, "OK he has $100 million of bills: The dollar price on them is 94, but we will lend him par because it is too difficult to write funny number tickets."

As interest rates continued to go against him and his cash drain continued, Eldin—who learned Street games fast—started reversing in Treasury bonds and then shorting them. Since it was then normal on a reverse to ignore accrued interest in pricing collateral on a reverse, Eldin was able to generate cash equal to roughly the amount of the accrued interest on a bond every time he reversed in a bond and then sold it.

Even that ploy, however, did not suffice to meet Financial Corp.'s cash needs, and eventually the firm failed. The people who had loaned the firm money against bills had collateral, but the market value of that collateral was often less than the amount of the loan. Meanwhile, the people who had borrowed money from the firm against collateral in the form of coupons found that the amount of money they had was often smaller than the market value (accrued interest included) of the securities they had reversed out to Financial Corp.

Many of those—whom Eldin reminded, by his dealings with them, that the prudent deal only with those they know and trust—were large, respectable, normally astute institutions. That Eldin could fool them made him the object of some admiration among Street traders. Said one, "The guy in Kansas had class. There are people who have embezzled $5 or $10 million. He did $1.8 billion!" Actually that's an exaggeration; when he went belly up, Eldin was estimated to owe a mere $15 million to $24 million to his unpaid creditors.

The failure of Financial Corp. raised crucial questions: Is a repo (or reverse) a true sale-repurchase *or* a collateralized loan? If it is the former and the side owing the money fails to execute the repurchase, does the side holding securities have the right to sell them? If so and there is *overage*—the securities sale produces proceeds that exceed the loan plus accrued repo interest—to whom is the overage due?

It seems startling that people waited until the repo market had become a huge sector of the money market to question the true nature of a repo. In fact, it was a situation the Street slipped into naturally and gradually. Neither Congress nor any other body had ever defined in law what a repo is. That technicality notwithstanding, a repo transaction seemed, first to a few and then to many money participants, a convenient way to do something they wanted to do—be it finance securities, lend securities, or do one leg of an arb; and the repo market grew like Topsy with only a few participants evidencing concern, until Miller came along, over the risk that the transaction might involve.

Miller's failure left in its wake a host of suits in courts around the country, suits that took years to settle. The Street's initial presumption concerning where things stood and probably would stand when the legal dust settled coincided by and large with the opinion expressed in 1977 by one repo dealer, "My position is that, if I have your bonds and you do not pay me back, it is my prerogative to sell those bonds and sue you for any difference. The distinction between repo and a collateralized loan is that in a repo transaction I own those bonds, whereas on a collateralized loan there are release agreements and certain legalities I have to go through before I can handle the underlying collateral as if I owned it."

After some years, the Miller bankruptcy and other dealer bankruptcies that followed it generated rulings on a number of suits. A problem is that these lack consistency and so set no broad precedents. Currently, it is impossible to predict the outcome of a case in any jurisdiction except in the rare instance where a case is exactly like one already tried there.

A few of Miller's customers actually profited from the bankruptcy of Financial Corp. The county of Los Angeles had a contract with Miller which stipulated that it could sell any securities that it might be left holding in the event of default by Miller. When Miller did default, LA County sold out the collateral it held, came out ahead on the deal, and said to Miller, "Sue us if you want the overage."

For most people who had deals with Miller on their books when he went bankrupt, things went less pleasantly. Institutions that had loaned him par against year bills worth 94 had a choice: sell out at a loss or hold the securities to maturity and forget about Miller paying any interest on the reverse. There were also many investors who had reversed at market price to Miller bonds that had three months of accrued interest on them. It was on trades of this sort that the biggest sums were lost in the Miller bankruptcy. People involved in such trades lost both interest accrued on their bonds at the time the reverse transaction occurred and interest accrued during the life of the reverse.

While the rulings on suits arising from Miller's bankruptcy set no overriding precedents, they suggested that the Street had some justification in operating on the working hypothesis that, in the case of default by the borrower of money, the position of the securities holder was: If you've got them, you can sell them.

Drysdale Government Securities

When Financial Corp. went under, people assumed that money market participants had been so chastened by its failure and by the Winters debacle in Ginnie Mae forwards which preceded it that they would henceforth either institute new credit controls or strictly enforce controls already in place. Drysdale Government Securities, a subsidiary of an old-line firm, Drysdale Securities, proved this presumption incorrect.

In its brief—three months—career, Drysdale Government Securities is estimated to have shorted $4 billion of bonds and to have gone long another $2.5 billion on the basis of a mere $20 million in capital. Drysdale's basic game was to reverse in through agent banks—Chase and others—high-coupon securities nearing a coupon date; for collateral, Drysdale put up cash close to the dollar prices at which these securities were trading; it then sold the borrowed securities for principal *plus* accrued interest and in the process garnered for itself significantly more cash than it had paid out.

By the time Drysdale Government Securities started playing Miller's final game, high interest rates had ballooned enormously the sums that could be generated from it. For example, a firm shooting $500 million of a bond carrying a 12% coupon five months into a coupon period could pick up $25 million of cash for a month. Drysdale saw this; its sin, if any, was to abuse the system to its logical conclusion, to say, "Why do this for $500 million? We will do it for $5 billion."

A time-honored Street convention was that, when a firm borrows bonds, it must pass onto the lender of these securities any coupon interest paid on them. When the May coupon date arrived on the bonds Drysdale had borrowed, it was—to the shock of the Street—unable to obtain cash to pay the agent banks through which it had borrowed these securities the coupon interest owed to the ultimate lenders of the bonds.

Then the fun started. Chase said it would not make good on the $160 million of coupon interest owed to investors whose bonds it had loaned to Drysdale on the grounds that it had acted only as agent not principal. Manny, which was hit for a much smaller amount ($29.3 million), and U.S. Trust, which lost a "nonmaterial" amount, paid up right away.

Dealers on the Street reacted with shock to Chase's action fearing not only that they would lose money, but that the Drysdale failure might set in motion a *domino* effect that would bring other dealers on the Street tumbling down with it. Nonreceipt of some portion of the $160 million of missing interest might have been a big hit against the capital of some small firms, especially since at the time a lot of firms were doing poorly anyway because the market was running against them. If some other firms had gone down, their inability to meet their commitments to still other firms might in turn have forced those firms to fail as well. In a worst-case scenario, a scramble by many firms on the Street to raise cash to meet their obligations might have caused a lot of selling of securities, which in turn would have depressed their prices and caused still greater losses for firms with big long positions.

After Chase announced its refusal to pay out the $160 million of interest due from Drysdale for whom it had acted as agent, the New York Fed hastily convened a meeting of Chase and the other dealers. It was widely rumored that at that meeting the Fed did some arm twisting to get Chase to honor what other dealers thought was its obligations and to prevent possible calamity on the Street. Merrill, whose Readi Assets Trust Fund then held $736 million of Chase BAs and CDs, was also reported to have done a little arm twisting on its own.

In the end, Chase agreed to come up with the $160 million of interest due and to take responsibility for that portion of Drysdale's position assumed through trades on which it had acted as agent. Chase also reserved the right to pursue future legal actions against third parties.

Chase's decision caused sighs of relief on the Street. At the same time, it left important questions unanswered: What was Chase's real role and responsibility in the Drysdale debacle, and how did it get itself into such a mess? How did the supposedly savvy Street firms with all their controls on credit exposure allow themselves to get caught in such a snafu? How did Drysdale lose so much money so fast? It cost Chase $285 million pretax to meet Drysdale's interest payments and unwind its positions.

The story runs—as best as can be determined—like this: Drysdale wanted to short a lot of high-coupon bonds carrying big sums of accrued interest for two reasons—to generate cash and because it thought rates would move higher permitting it to profit on the shorts it intended to establish. It got some lower-level officers in Chase's securities lending department to provide it with securities that Chase obtained from Buttonwood and C&W, firms that specialize in finding and borrowing stocks and bonds for a fee.

In taking in these securities, Chase had the delivery tickets made out Chase NY/Cust/Special loan account, as opposed to, say, Chase/Inv, which would have indicated that the securities were destined for Chase's portfolio (inventory), or Chase/dealer, which would have indicated that the securities were destined for its dealer operation.

The way the tickets were made out should have immediately alerted securities lenders to the fact that a third party other than Chase was involved in the deal. Shops that saw this warning signal reacted in several ways. Some refused outright to deal with Chase on those terms unless it revealed the name of the third party involved, which it would not. Others asked Chase for a letter assuring them that Chase was acting as principal; Chase refused to give this letter, which caused these firms to refuse to deal with Chase. Still other firms seeing the Chase ticket took the view that, by not disclosing the third party for whom it was acting, Chase was assuming de facto—and *de jure* should the case ever come to court—the role of principal and that, this being the case, they willingly dealt with Chase. Finally, there were other investors, probably the majority, who paid no attention to what was on the ticket and simply did the trade assuming that Chase was the principal.

The prevailing legal opinion after the dust started to settle on the Drysdale case was that Chase, by acting as agent for an undisclosed third party, had assumed 99.9%, if not all, of the responsibilities of principal. Therefore if it had continued its initial refusal to pay out the $160 million of interest due to bond lenders, the courts would eventually have forced it to do so.

This observation raises the question of how Chase, a top bank, allowed itself to get into the position where it had a credit exposure of over a quarter of a billion dollars to a small, new dealer with $20 million in capital. The answer seems to be that the people in Chase's securities lending department who were doing the business were in over their heads; they thought Chase was acting as agent not principal; and consequently they did not realize the credit risk to which their actions exposed Chase. What they did perceive was that their activities were generating some nice fee income that would add to Chase's return on assets and presumably lead to their earning some recognition in terms of remuneration or stature within the bank. Also, it was widely reported that at least some people at Chase were being paid under the table by Buttonwood and C&W for taking in and funneling securities to Drysdale.

How Drysdale managed to lose as much money as it did playing around for all of three months with $20 million of capital remains something of a mystery. As one astute trader noted, "I find it puzzling that Drysdale could lose so much so fast. If you charged me to lose ¼ of a billion, I think it would be hard to do; I would probably end up making money some of the time because I would buy something I thought was going down and it would go up. They must have been extraordinarily good at losing money." In fact, Drysdale did make money on some of its trades. Noted another trader, "Drysdale did a lot of good trades. From what I saw in the market, I know they bought the 2-year note in February and March—a lot of them—great trades on which they have to have made a huge profit no matter when they sold them; they could not have done otherwise."

The upshot of Drysdale was that Chase lost a lot of money and presumably tightened controls; other dealers lost nothing; securities lawyers spent a lot of time delving into the finer points of the distinction between agent and principal; and the Fed was finally stirred into action. In a letter to all recognized dealers, the New York Fed ordered them to begin in October 1982 to include accrued interest in pricing securities used as collateral in repo and reversed transactions. The reactions of dealers to the switch to *full-accrual pricing* and its ramification for the way repo transactions is discussed below.

Lombard-Wall's downfall

The failure in May 1982 of Drysdale cast doubt on the creditworthiness of small dealers in general. In this climate, it was not hard for Lombard-Wall, another small dealer, to add its name to the casualty list, which it did in August 1982. Unlike Financial Corp. and Drysdale, Lombard-Wall did not abuse the repo market to raise cash to finance speculations. It got into trouble by offering flex repos to its customers, a legitimate transaction but one that requires an ability, which Lombard-Wall apparently lacked, to perceive the full market risk in a position and to manage asset and liability maturities accordingly.

A specialty of Lombard-Wall was to do *flex repos* with housing and other authorities. These authorities floated bond issues to pay for construction projects that required cash payouts over several years; they then invested the bond proceeds over the payout period in flex repos. These repos were often done as part of a package in which the dealer agreed to do the bond underwriting provided the borrower promised to do with him a repo lasting several years. Under a flex repo, it was understood that the borrower would draw funds out of the repo, according to some prearranged schedule. A safe way for a dealer to quote a fixed rate on a flex repo lasting several years would be to buy securities with maturities matching the time spans for which varying amounts of cash were to be lodged by the bond issuer with the dealer: to run—in the jargon of asset and liability managers—a *matched book* on which it locked in a small spread. Lombard-Wall did not do this; instead it mismatched its book on the basis of incorrect predictions of interest-rate trends; this eventually caused it to lose substantial amounts of money.

A common problem with flex repos is that the bond issuer, while required to provide a draw-down schedule, need not adhere to it and often does not. The draw-down schedules of some borrowers are quite predictable, those of others less so. Because uncertainty often exists concerning a borrower's draw-down schedule, the only shops that should be doing flex repos are those that understand the risk and can afford to take it. A large shop doing a flex repo—and large shops do do this business because it is big business—will, in quoting a rate on a flex repo, take into consideration not only the shape of the draw-down schedule, but both the predictability of the borrower in sticking to it and any provisions written into the repo contract that limit the flexibility of the timing of draw-downs.[3]

When Lombard-Wall failed, the NYS Dormitory Authority ended up with a $55 million unsecured claim against Lombard. How this arose out of a repo transaction remains unclear. Presumably Lombard gave the Dormitory Authority not collateral but a safekeeping receipt, which, as it lost more and more money, Lombard was unable to back with securities having a market value equal to that indicated by the receipt.

On a flex repo, the dealer normally has unlimited right of substitution with respect to collateral, and safekeeping receipts are not uncommon. A safekeeping receipt amounts to a guarantee by the dealer that securities have been segregated in a bank account for the repo investor. Most investors, who have an ongoing safekeeping-receipt relationship with a dealer, periodically send their auditor to check that the securities that are supposed to be in their account are in fact there. One can only guess that the Dormitory Authority must have failed to do so.

The Dormitory Authority's well-publicized potential losses led some people to argue that flex repos should be banned. However, it was the Dormitory Authority that chose for a few extra basis points to deal with a poorly capitalized firm like Lombard when it could have struck a similar

---

[3] Flex repos are done not only in connection with municipal issues, but for corporations issuing bonds to finance the construction of plant equipment.

deal with a highly capitalized, well-regarded dealer—DLJ, Goldman, or the B of A to name a few—that have been around a long time.[4]

Tidying up market practices

The Drysdale, Lombard-Wall and later dealer bankruptcies finally forced some tidying up of repo-market practices. That this took so long reflects in part opposition to new rules and regulations by the big dealers. These dealers argued, correctly enough, that no customer had ever lost a penny doing repos and reverses with them and that new rules and regs would stifle innovation and impose costs on sectors of the market in which there had never been a problem.

One oft-repeated suggestion was that the dealers doing repos and reverses introduced some form of self-regulation. Several problems effectively barred this approach. First, the history of the dealer community's efforts to adopt any sort of standardized practice is that they have a really hard time agreeing to do anything. This is not surprising: dealers are human; they are competitors; and some of them have sizable egos. Second, at least some of the senior statesmen of the dealer community felt that self-regulation, however nobly begun, would eventually become counterproductive. On this point, one dealer noted: "Self-regulatory groups start out with the best of motives; they intend to make as few rules as possible and just those that are obvious and to which the dealers with integrity would adhere to in any event because such rules make sense. Then, there are the second, third, fourth, and fifth years. As they roll by, the founding fathers revolve off: the five chairman of their respective companies who started off the thing [the self-regulatory body] are no longer very interested in it. In their place, you now have a bunch of young guys who are do-gooders out to make a name for themselves. The next thing, these guys make all sorts of rules and start changing market practices; among them, there is a tendency for self-aggrandisement, which is human nature."

Since at no point did dealers act to standardize and to tidy up repo market practices, a need was created, at least in the eyes of some, for regulatory action. In due course, both the Fed and the Congress acted.

FULL ACCRUAL PRICING

The Drysdale bankruptcy, perhaps because it caused a large loss to a bank, the Chase, finally stirred the Fed into action. The Fed recom-

---

[4] The Dormitory Authority was reported to have entrusted $305 million of idle funds to Lombard-Wall early in 1982 after taking bids from 15 financial institutions offering various interest rates. For an investor to shop for yield without regard to credit risk and the size of its exposure to a single dealer is to invite trouble.

mended, in a letter to the primary dealers, that they henceforth price repo collateral at market price *plus* accrued interest *minus* a reasonable haircut (see Appendix A). Under this method of pricing, known as *full accrual pricing,* any coupon interest received by the holder of collateral is still transferred on the coupon data to the ultimate owner of the securities serving as collateral; for high-coupon securities repoed with a lot of accrued interest, this transfer leads to an offsetting adjustment in the dollar value of the repo loan, one that reflects the fall to zero in accrued interest on the repo collateral.

Today, the primary dealers and those with whom they deal are back to reasonably precise pricing of repo collateral. However, it is quite possible that smaller dealers dealing with smaller customers out in the hinterlands are still pricing repo collateral way off the market. All it takes to create some badly priced repos is for an aggressive or desperate dealer to find some unsophisticated customers with whom he can do repo.

Repricing collateral.   Typically, term and open repos and reverses have included a right to reprice collateral. Some dealers track daily the value of collateral that they have taken in; if such securities fall in value, they want more collateral. Prior to passage of the Government Securities Act of 1986, not all dealers used, however, to bother to reprice collateral regularly. A common attitude used to be this: we don't reprice collateral because to do so would be a lot of trouble; besides we wouldn't want to insult or inconvenience our valued customers.

A dealer's attorney noted, "Because we are a small shop, we have always marked to market. We found out, however, that a lot of people out there did not mark to market with us. We would ask for margin, if appropriate, but we would never send out additional margin unless they asked for it. Lots of times, people would not ask us. Consequently, we were ahead of the game."

Standardizing haircuts

Prior to the spate of dealer bankruptcies that began in earnest in the early 1980s, a lot of people on the Street—dealers, investors, and others—were rather casual about margin. Depending on who the contracting parties were, haircuts could be just about anything: a big positive number, a small positive number, zero; in some cases, margin was even a negative percentage of the money lent (i.e., the money lent exceeded the value of the collateral).

Today, in contrast, there is more standardization in margin practices: margin is likely to run ¼ of a point per month on Treasury bills, notes, or bonds (⅜ of a point on a 45-day repo); the same on agencies; 2% on letter repos of commercial paper and other securities; and much more on mortgage-backed securities—3 points on a 1-month repo, 4 points on a 2-month repo, and 5 points on a 3-month or longer repo. The figures we have cited for margin on Treasuries refer to dealer-to-dealer trades. Today, some customers, recalling Drysdale et al., demand more margin on repos of Treasuries, as much as 2 points on a repo of a long bond.

Repo agreements

As noted, parties doing repos or reverses with each other frequently exchange a letter of agreement that spells out the terms of the trade: the names of both parties; a description of the asset traded; the pricing of the asset; the rate of interest to be paid to the lender of money; the term of the agreement; and, if the collateral is not to be safekept, where it is to be delivered. In Chapter 7, we reproduced a letter of agreement covering a repo between a dealer and the Fed.

Evolution in market practice. Repo agreements were more common at the start of the repo market than later. As time passed, market participants took the view that *all that had to be said by way of a contract was said in the buy and sell confirms.* Strange as it may seem now, people, primary dealers included, were not terribly concerned about perfecting a lien, provisions of the UCC, and so on.

My word is my bond: The lack of concern that money market people displayed about dotting the legal *i*'s and *t*'s with respect to repo reflected not only their notion that repo contracts could be and were established by virtue of *an exchange of confirms,* but also their notion that they were afforded much protection by the standards of the business in which they operated. Money market folk have always felt, at least until recently, that they are in a business in which people say, "My word is my bond," and mean it; a business in which, if someone says something is "done," it is done. Money market folk also felt protected by the knowledge that people on the Street are generally people of integrity; and just in case they are not, every Street person's rule one is "Know thy customer," which translates to: check everything about the counterparty, including first and foremost, his financials.

The Lombard-Wall ruling. Lombard-Wall came tumbling down in August of 1982. It was school districts and other investors, not the big dealers, who lost money due to Lombard-Wall's failure. Consequently, this failure, like that of Financial Corp., might in time have been forgotten by the Street, but this was not to be. A new bankruptcy code had been adopted in 1978, and there was no definitive history as to how a bankruptcy court would characterize a repo transaction.

When Lombard-Wall filed for bankruptcy in early August 1982, it argued that the federal bankruptcy code prohibited its customers from selling securities it had delivered to them as repo collateral. Specifically, Lombard asked the court for and got a stay in bankruptcy; this means that the firm received the protection of the court and that all of its transactions were *stayed*. This ruling set off alarm bells on the Street. If the repo collateral received from a suddenly defunct dealer were perchance long bonds, one wanted, in the interests of minimizing market risk, to be able to sell those bonds immediately: today, not tomorrow.

The *Lombard-Wall* case offered the first opportunity for a court to characterize repo under the new bankruptcy code. Since the new code contained no specific provisions about how to treat repo, the court had to look for some characterization of repo; its choices were a secured borrowing or a purchase and sale. The court ruled that repo was a secured borrowing, not a securities transaction; and once it did, the automatic stay provisions of the bankruptcy code became applicable. This ruling, together with the application of the automatic stay, "scared," noted one dealer's counsel, "the hell out of the industry."

Basically, dealers and banks (the industry) could not care less what repos and reverses are, so long as they can do them in big volume and with *no* problems. For primary dealers with their huge matched books, the Lombard-Wall ruling created a problem. Said one dealer, "What if you were involved with [had the collateral of] an outfit that got into bankruptcy? You were hung out to dry." Suddenly reverses, one half of their big matched books, were seen by dealers as leading to possible market risk; and dealers do *not* want market risk except when it's volitional—when they get to choose the timing and the tune of the market play.

Prior to Lombard-Wall, Wall Street had always operated on the assumption that, if A did a repo with B and if B went broke with A holding B's collateral, A could sell that collateral, and it could do so *mui pronto*. So long as this assumption appeared tenable, dealers viewed the credit risk inherent in reverses as something with which they could live, provided that they paid attention to margin. Noted one dealer, "If I do a reverse with you, my responsibility is to see that this transaction is properly margined, that we are basically at par in terms of the dollars involved, and that the agreed upon financing cost is all that is out there. If you go bankrupt, I want to sell out those securities immediately. I don't worry about the credit of the issuer, but I do worry about market risk; there's a volatile market out there."

Amending the bankruptcy code. Post Lombard-Wall, the industry said, "Let's get the uncertainty—what kind of trade am I doing? What may I do with collateral?—out of this." They lobbied, through the *Public Securities Association* (PSA), a trade association of which they are a division, for an amendment to the bankruptcy code that would permit a holder of repo collateral to immediately sell out that collateral if the other party defaulted. The Fed, sensing the danger that the Lombard-Wall ruling posed to dealers and thus to the operation of the government market, supported the dealers; and it was the Fed's lobbying in the end that caused Congress to pass the 1984 amendment to the bankruptcy code. This amendment, which has some exceptions, was not all the dealers wished for, but it was all the Fed would go to bat for. As is appropriate for a central bank, the Fed moves in mysterious ways. For reasons known only to it, the Fed did not want repos collateralized by commercial paper to be covered by the amendment; they were not.

While the Lombard-Wall ruling certainly touched off a panic among dealers, it is possible that a similar ruling might in subsequent cases go the other way. In the *Lombard-Wall* case, there was a written repo agreement, which, at the time, was in itself quite unusual. Also, the Lombard-Wall agreement, said one lawyer, "was worded so that it sounded like a collateralized loan." This lawyer continued, "In the *Lombard-Wall* case, the judge was looking at one particular repo. Depending on the type of participant and the type of agreement, another judge could choose to characterize repo in another way." The Lombard-Wall repo agreement is reproduced in Appendix B.

One special aspect of the repos Lombard-Wall did is that they were on average of much longer term than repos done by other dealers. This reflected the fact that Lombard-Wall was doing flex repos.

Writing a new agreement. Basically, the dealers viewed the amendment to the bankruptcy code as a form of insurance. If a dealer were to do a reverse repo with (take in collateral from and lend money to) a party that defaulted, *and* if the bankruptcy trustee were to rule that the transaction was a secured loan, dealers would, for most types of collateral, be able to sell that collateral immediately and therefore not be subject for a possibly long period to likely significant and definitely unwanted market risk.

Once dealers got the bankruptcy amendment, they reasoned as follows: maybe we need a written agreement for repos and reverses. Having such an agreement might put us in a better position if we ever end up in court making claims against a defaulting party; so let's write one. Also, so long as we are going to write an agreement, let's write it so that it gives the repo and reverse trades we do all possible *indicia* of a securities trade. Then our first line of defense against a default on a repo or a reverse will be a document stating that we and the other party contracted to do a pair of securities trades. If the judge respects the expressed [in a document] intent of the contracting parties, which we think he will, we are home free; either we have got money or we have got securities that we can sell immediately; and if we margin properly, our losses will be minimal. On the other hand, if the judge rules that a reverse done by a party in default is a collateralized loan, we will have in most cases protection from the bankruptcy code amendment, and again, if we have margined properly, our losses will be minimal.

Enter the lawyers. The above reasoning led the dealers, one by one, to call down to their corporate counsels and say, "Write us a repo agreement that will *protect us* in all eventualities."

Naturally, this created a situation in which every dealer had produced a multipage repo agreement that he wanted other dealers to sign while he himself was unwilling to sign their agreements because the latter were not—so said his counsel—evenhanded. The contest over whose agreement was going to be signed was bound to end in stalemate because, as one lawyer noted, "Some big egos were involved."

The only possible solution, and the one finally adopted, was for the primary dealers to form within the Public Securities Association a committee charged with drafting a standard repo agreement that would, they hoped, be accepted in some revised form by all primary dealers. Finally, after much effort had been expended and much time had passed, the PSA came up with such an agreement (see Appendix C).

Prior to the writing of the PSA agreement, every dealer who had written his own repo agreement wanted every party with whom he did repos or reverses to sign that agreement. However, a wide range of parties would not; the nonsigners ran the gamut from other dealers to customers of various ilk. As might be expected, many institutions with whom a dealer was doing repos and reverses had lawyers of their own who, for one reason or another, found fault with the repo agreement that the dealer's counsel had written.

Once the dealers' committee at the PSA had hammered out an agreement with which the dealers were happy, the dealers naturally wanted their customers to sign this agreement. Most did, but there are still some holdouts. Municipalities and state government bodies often have their own agreements mandated by law, and they are loath to go back to their respective legislatures to ask for any changes. Mutual funds have also resisted signing the PSA agreement; their trade association, the Investment Company Institute (ICI), has written its own repo agreement, and for reasons that are unique to their industry, mutual funds prefer that repo agreement to the PSA agreement.

The Government Securities Act of 1986

After Eldin Miller's Financial Corp., a fledgling government securities dealer, went belly-up in 1975 with estimated losses of $15 million to $25 million to investors, one could hope that some lessons had been learned: know thy counter-party in a repo; ensure that repos and reverses are properly collateralized; and so on. Alas, memories are unfortunately short. A few years later, there were lots of new faces in the money market—*and* they were people who had never heard of Eldin Miller.

From the late 1970s on, when interest rates were often far higher and far more volatile than they had ever been, a number of smaller dealers—some new, some who had been around for awhile—went bankrupt with large losses to investors. It is estimated that the failure of Drysdale Government Securities in 1982 cost banks and investors $270 million to $290 million, that the failure of Lombard-Wall, Inc. in 1982 cost investors $20 million, that the failure of Lion Capital Group in 1984 cost investors $40 million, that the failure of RTD securities in 1984 cost investors $1.7 million, that the failure of E.S.M. Government Securities in 1985 cost investors $300 million, and that the failure of Bevill, Bresler and Schulman in 1985 cost investors yet another $150 million.

These bankruptcies and others followed a variety of patterns. However, a reasonable generalization is that losses to customers typically resulted from one or both of several factors: (1) the failing firm treated securities, including repo collateral, that it was holding in safekeeping for customers loosely to say the least—sometimes such securities were hypothecated more than once, sometimes they were sold; and (2) the failing firm gave inadequate collateral to customers when it repoed securities out to customers and/or it demanded excessive collateral when it reversed in securities from customers.

It's important to note, with respect to the above failures, that no investor ever lost so much as a penny due to credit and other problems at a major dealer. While the big boys may at times have lost a lot of money due to market turbulence, they stayed, to a man, squeaky clean in their dealings with customers. Another point to note is that, with the exception of the losses by Chase and several other NYC banks during the Drysdale bankruptcy (losses due, at least in the case of Chase, to an admitted failure of the bank's internal controls), no major investor or dealer lost a penny because of the bankruptcies we have listed. It was small investors—school districts, S&Ls, and so on—who saw their money vanish as small dealers in governments went down the tubes. The big, sophisticated players had all protected themselves by following old and respected rules of prudence. To the extent that they dealt at all with the second- or third-tier dealers that failed, the big players to a man had said, "We will buy securities from you, sell securities to you, and do repo with you, but only on a strictly DVP basis and on a basis of reasonable margin." It's hard for a market player to lose big bucks because of a dealer bankruptcy if his rules are these: never give a dealer money except against securities due; never give him securities except against money due; and never do repos and reverses with him except when margin is set and maintained at a reasonable level consistent with accepted market practices.

The Fed acts. Naturally, the problems outlined above raised a brouhaha in Washington and elsewhere. Despite the fact that recent bankruptcies of government securities dealers raised only a rather narrow issue—how to protect *smallish* investors from hanky panky by *smallish* dealers in exempt securities—cries went up for imposing new rules and regs on *all* dealers in governments.

The Fed took a crack at solving the perceived problem by coming up with complex "voluntary" guidelines on capital adequacy, which were supposed to apply to all dealers in governments except the primary dealers whose activities the Fed was already overseeing. The Fed's guidelines, which are extremely complex, require that a dealer maintain sufficient capital to cover (1) the credit risk of its receivables and (2) the market risk of its securities inventory where the latter is calculated, for different types of securities, on the basis of the historic volatility of the prices of those types of securities. This sounds reasonable: make a dealer back his holdings of a safe asset with 2% in capital, his holdings of more risky asset with 5% of capital, and so on. There is, however, as a wise banker once noted, a fallacy in this approach: risk can be accurately gauged only *ex post*. A glance at how various money market participants have lost big (to them and to their regulators if they had them) sums of money suggests the truth in this dictum. In the early 1970s, thrifts lost money by selling GNMA puts because neither they nor their regulators appreciated that this means of garnering *fee income* involved placing a risky bet on the direction of interest rates. Wiser firms have lost bundles learning the risks inherent in *new* products and, when markets were volatile and changing, in *old* products as well. If capital requirements alone sufficed to keep financial institutions afloat, a lot of now defunct banks and thrifts would still be around.

Congress acts. While the Fed was experimenting with new capital rules, Congress, in a typical political response, was debating what *it* should do about dealer bankruptcies. Despite the fact that only a narrow group of dealers had caused losses to investors—by lying about their financial strength, by double pledging securities in the repo market, by demanding excessive collateral on reverses, and by playing other games—Congress felt called upon to focus on the "great problems with respect to *unregulated* government securities dealers"—*all* of them.

After much debate and delay, Congress finally passed, in October 1986, the Government Securities Act of 1986. This act ostensibly fixes a lot of things, many of which were not broken in the first place.

The act requires a number of things. First, all government securities brokers and dealers except registered broker/dealers and financial institutions (domestic and foreign banks, and federally insured thrifts) are required to register with the SEC. Primary dealers as a class are not excepted from this registration requirement. Registered broker/dealers and financial institutions that deal in governments are required to file a notice with their appropriate regulatory agencies (ARAs).

Second, the act requires that the Secretary of the Treasury, in consultation with the SEC and the Fed, promulgate rules regarding the activities of brokers and dealers in governments. These rules relate principally to capital adequacy, custody and use of customer securities, the mechanics of repos and reverses, the carrying and use of customer deposits or credit balances, financial reporting, and recordkeeping.

Capital requirements. Under the new regulatory regime, broker/ dealers who deal directly (not through a GSI) in governments will continue to be subject, as they were before, to the capital requirement imposed by the SEC under 15c3-1 of the Securities Exchange Act of 1934; banks that deal in governments will be subject to capital requirements imposed by bank regulators; and other dealers will be subject to new capital requirements fashioned by the Treasury, which used as its model the complex, voluntary capital guidelines created by the Fed for government securities dealers. SEC capital requirements follow a different format than Treasury capital requirements, but one is not clearly more onerous than the other.

Financial reporting. Besides respecting a new net capital rule, dealers who were previously unregulated will now be required to have annual audits of their financial statements, a procedure that will be overseen by the National Association of Securities Dealers (NASD).

Repos, reverses, and safekeeping. Several things were done by the Treasury and the SEC in their regulations to pare the risks associated with repos and reverses. In particular, both the Treasury and the SEC imposed complex capital charges on repos and reverses. One purpose of these requirements was to create incentives to encourage dealers doing repos and reverses to operate as follows: collateral is to be reasonably priced; the amount of money that changes hands is to be a reasonable percentage of the collateral's market value; and, finally, margin calls are to be made if significant changes occur in that market value.

Also, under the new regs, a dealer, before doing repo with a customer, must send to the customer a written agreement that includes a specifically worded disclosure regarding the dealer's right to substitute collateral. A dealer must also send to a customer confirms on all transactions, including repos and reverses. Also, a dealer *must segregate* in a safe-keeping account at his clearing bank and on his books any customer securities, including repo collateral, that he holds for customers. On hold-in-custody repos, a dealer, on his confirms to customers, is supposed to list collateral separately—he can no longer write "various." Also, he is supposed to state the market value of the securities that he is giving to the customer as collateral.

The difficulties that regulatory authorities experienced in setting up new regulations under the Government Securities Act of 1986 suggests that such regulations will be subject to evolution over time.

A dealer's view. When asked his view on how GSA will impact the repo market, one top dealer commented: "In the repo market, abuses of taking excessive haircuts and of not margining properly did occur. Now, under GSA, there will be a price to pay in terms of capital charges for a firm that continues these abuses. I think that this is terribly significant.

"The repo market suffers from too many variables, from too much to negotiate. Repo is a complicated trade with a lot of particulars to settle: a start date, an end date, the choice of collateral, the pricing of that collateral, the amount of initial margin, and so on; those things are a pain in the neck. Salespeople are paid to generate a lot of tickets, and the least attractive business for a salesperson to do with a customer is short-term repo, especially since such business may involve margin calls to the customer. A margin call is the worst call a salesperson can make to a customer, particularly if the customer is highly creditworthy; no salesperson likes to make that call.

"In the past we dealers have used things like margin to ingratiate ourselves with a customer. I might get an edge with a customer by telling him that I am not going to make any margin calls on him. I know a customer is creditworthy, so I say, 'I'll do this reverse with you, and I won't be bothering you with margin calls every two weeks in a down market.' The new regs [under GSA] will not in and of themselves introduce uniformity in margin practices, but they will cause firms, unless they want to incur capital charges, to focus on this issue. I, for one, would like to see more uniformity in this area.

"I think that letter repo is a useful option both for us and for the investor, and I hope that we will never be precluded from doing it. However, if you look back at all of our disasters in the repo market, most of them involved letter repo, delivery bills—some version of nondelivery repo.

"In doing letter repo we [dealers] play this game of charades with the customer: we do not really explain to customers that they do not have in any way, shape, or form a perfected interest in any collateral and that anything we name in this due bill or letter repo is hocus pocus. If we [a dealer] go bankrupt, the customer cannot come in with the letter and say, 'These are my bonds,' because they are not his.

"The GSA regs require us to have a separate segregation account at our clearing bank. I am one of the few dealers that never had a separate seg account because it promotes the idea that the customer can have access to collateral in it, which he may not. The seg account is *my account, not the customer's account.* The customer cannot walk into my clearing bank and ask for his collateral; that bank does not know that he exists. I never went through the expense of segregating collateral for letter repos, and I never told the customer that I was doing so; rather, I told the customer: 'I acknowledge that I have certain bonds, and that *I* have access to that collateral.'

"There are several problems with letter repo. One is that when we do it with a customer, there is always the possibility that the customer's trader may reason on his own, 'Well the credit of a top dealer is good enough for me, so I do not need to perfect my lien on a repo with them.' We do not always know that such a trader has the approval of his organization for doing letter repo with us. Hopefully, requiring a written contract [which GSA does] will ensure in the future that such business is never in conflict with the customer's investment parameters.

"A second problem with letter repo is that, in the past, we did not tell the customer what he was buying. We sell commercial paper, and it is a completely respectable instrument because we outright say to the customer and to his boss that the paper is unsecured. When we sell letter repo, list collateral, and further promote the charade [that letter repo is other than an unsecured lending] by saying that the collateral is in a seg account at our bank, we are—to secure a lower borrowing rate for ourselves—giving the customer the notion that he has some collateral. There is in fact no case that has definitely settled what a seg account does for a customer. It [the charade] is a bad practice and requiring a contract [which GSA does] is a good way of making letter repo more like commercial paper and hence more respectable."

THE NEXT CHAPTER

In the next chapter, we focus on several related topics: repo and reverse rates, the brokering of repos and reverses, and the use—as an alternative to the borrowing of securities—of reverses to cover shorts.

Appendix A

Federal Reserve Bank of New York policy letters of April 21, June 18, and August 27, 1982

FEDERAL RESERVE BANK
OF NEW YORK

April 21, 1982

RETAIL AND WHOLESALE
REPURCHASE AGREEMENTS

To the Chief Executive Officer of Each State Member Bank
in the Second Federal Reserve District:

The usage by banking organizations for funding purposes of
repurchase agreements involving U.S. government or agency securities
has increased dramatically over the past several months. Although to date
there have been few problems associated with this activity, we believe that
it is appropriate to bring to your attention some considerations to rein-
force your awareness of the need to proceed cautiously in offering
these instruments.

With respect to retail repurchase agreements (retail repos), bank
management should bear in mind that in some cases it is dealing with
customers who do not normally engage in large denomination, money market
transactions. In addition, because of the complex nature of retail repos
and the possibility that retail repos may be confused with insured deposits
by the general public, all material facts of a retail repo transaction
should be disclosed to the customer. As you are probably aware, the
Securities and Exchange Commission has taken the position that the antifraud provisions of Federal securities laws apply to the sale of retail
repos, and these instruments may be further subject to various State
securities laws. Banking organizations engaging in or planning to engage
in the sale of retail repos are urged to consult and obtain the opinion
of legal counsel competent in the field of securities laws to determine
what constitutes sufficient disclosure to customers as well as to ensure
compliance with the antifraud and other applicable provisions of Federal
and State securities laws.

-2-

The face of all retail repurchase agreements should state conspicuously and in bold-face type that "the obligation is not a deposit and is not insured by the Federal Deposit Insurance Corporation," and care should be taken to avoid the potential misrepresentation that retail repos are guaranteed by the U.S. government. In addition to ensuring that retail repos are not misconstrued as insured deposits, we believe that, at a minimum, the following information concerning retail repos should be communicated to customers:

1. The nature and terms of retail repos, including interest rates paid, maturities and any prepayment fees.

2. A description of and approximate market value of the underlying security or fractional interest thereof collateralizing the agreements.

3. A statement that the interest paid on a retail repo is not necessarily related to the yield on the underlying collateral.

4. A statement that the bank will pay at maturity a fixed amount, including interest on the purchase price, regardless of any fluctuation in the market value of the underlying collateral.

5. A statement that general banking assets will most likely be used to satisfy the bank's obligation rather than proceeds from the sale of the underlying security.

6. A statement that the market value of the collateral could depreciate before the maturity of the agreement, thus making the investor an unsecured creditor of the bank for the difference between the repurchase price of the retail repo and the market value of the underlying collateral.

7. Information advising the customer whether he or she has a perfected lien on the underlying collateral under state law, and whether it is being held by an independent trustee or custodian. If the customer does not have a perfected security interest, the legal consequences, including the possibility of becoming an unsecured general creditor, should be described.

8. Appropriate information regarding the bank and its financial condition.

If the retail repo agreement itself does not include all material disclosures, the face of the agreement should make specific reference to other documents provided to the customer containing sufficient material disclosures.

Care should also be taken with respect to the advertising and marketing of retail repos. All advertisements, announcements, and

-3-

solicitations for retail repos should state that they are not deposits
of the issuing bank and are not insured by the FDIC. Advertisements and
other documents provided to the customers that refer to the underlying
U.S. Government or agency obligations securing retail repos should disclose sufficient information to avoid the potential misrepresentation
that retail repos are guaranteed by the U.S. government.

As a matter of prudent banking practice and in order to provide
a cushion of protection for individuals who purchase retail repos, the
market value of the underlying security should be equal to or exceed the
purchase price of the retail repo at the time of issuance. In addition,
in order to avoid the potential for conflicts of interest, a bank should
not sell its retail repos to its own trust department or to trust agency
accounts over which it or any affiliate has investment discretion.

Since both retail and large denomination wholesale repurchase
agreements are in many respects equivalent to short-term borrowings at
market rates of interest, banks engaging in repurchase agreements should
carefully evaluate their interest rate risk exposure at various maturity.
levels, formulate policy objectives in light of the institution's entire
assets and liability mix, and adopt procedures to control mismatches
between assets and liabilities. The degree to which a bank borrows
through repurchase agreements also should be analyzed with respect to its
liquidity needs, and contingency plans should provide for alternate
sources of funds in the event of a run-off of repurchase agreement
liabilities.

Bank management also should be aware of certain considerations
and potential risks associated with wholesale repurchase agreements
entered into in large volume with institutional investors and/or brokers.
If the value of the underlying securities exceeds the price at which the
repurchase agreement was sold, the bank could be exposed to the risk of
loss in the event that the buyer is unable to perform and return the
securities. The possibility of this occurring would obviously increase if

-4-

the securities are physically transferred to the institution or broker
with which the bank has entered into the repurchase agreement. Moreover,
if the securities are not returned, the bank could be exposed to the
possibility of a significant write-off to the extent that the book value
of the securities exceeds the price at which the securities were originally
sold under the repurchase agreement. For this reason, banks should
obtain sufficient financial information on and analyze the financial
condition of those institutions and brokers with whom they engage in
repurchase transactions.

Federal Reserve examiners will be asked to review each bank's
internal procedures and practices for consistency with the considerations
discussed above.

ANTHONY M. SOLOMON,
President

FEDERAL RESERVE BANK OF NEW YORK

NEW YORK, N.Y. 10045

AREA CODE 212-791-5000

June 18, 1982

As you are aware, a study committee of the Primary Dealers Association is preparing a report suggesting some changes to market practices on financing transactions. Basically the Association is recommending that "standard operating procedure with regard to <u>all</u> repurchase agreements and related financial transactions, regardless of maturity, will <u>include</u> accrued interest on the underlying collateral...". We fully support this effort by the Association and are participating actively in its progress.

In this regard, we would like to have each dealer supply to us an estimate of the effects of the proposed changes on their own operations and costs. In a broader sense we would be interested in knowing each firm's view of the effect on the market both in the short run and the longer term.

All information about individual firms will be held in the strictest confidence by us, but we would be prepared to submit a report to the Association with a general characterization of the responses.

We would like to have this information by June 30, 1982.

Yours truly,

Peter D. Sternlight
Executive Vice President

FEDERAL RESERVE BANK OF NEW YORK

NEW YORK, N.Y. 10045

AREA CODE 212-791-5483

PETER D. STERNLIGHT
EXECUTIVE VICE PRESIDENT

August 27, 1982

In my letter to reporting Government securities dealers of June 18, 1982, I expressed our strong support for the practice of including accrued interest in valuing Government securities used in repurchase agreements. I believe it represents an improved market practice that will help avoid undesirable differences between the market value of securities and the related payments in repurchase and reverse repurchase transactions. In replying to my June 18 letter, nearly all of the reporting dealer firms endorsed this proposal, as has the Association of Primary Dealers. Adoption of this practice was also encouraged in the July 29, 1982 letter from President Solomon of this Bank to chief executives of all the dealer firms.

As you are aware, in the Federal Reserve's repurchase agreements, for its own or customer accounts, interest is now included in the calculation of the value of the securities. We adopted this practice at the beginning of August in part to encourage other market participants to incorporate this procedure in repurchase agreements with other customers. We have experienced little difficulty in processing our own repurchase agreements with dealers using the new procedure. In fact, while we had been prepared to revert to manual accounting procedures if necessary, our staff was able to accomplish the necessary programming changes in time to retain automated handling.

We have become concerned recently with a bogging down in the momentum toward making this widely endorsed change the general practice in the market. Accordingly, Trading Desk officers have had conversations with each of the dealers in the last couple of days, and suggested that for those who have not made the change already, the new procedure be implemented no later than the beginning of October. Virtually every dealer indicated that this was feasible.

Against that background, we now firmly and confidently expect each of the reporting Government securities dealers to value repurchase agreement securities with accrued interest taken into account, starting no later than Monday, October 4, 1982. This should apply generally to repurchase agreements and reverse repurchase agreements in Government securities with all customers.

We believe that customers will want to cooperate with a change widely endorsed by the responsible dealer community and the Federal Reserve as being consistent with sound market practice. Exceptions, such as where state or local government regulations impede the change, should be rare, and it should be possible to overcome these exceptions--once the underlying rationale for the change is explained to these customers.

We do understand that this changeover may require extra efforts from your staff, perhaps involving temporary substitution of manual for automated processing. But we emphasize that your cooperation is important--not only in achieving this desirable change in a particular market practice, but also in demonstrating that members of the primary reporting dealer community can recognize a need and take appropriate action in the interest of improving the market's integrity.

Sincerely,

Peter D. Sternlight

Appendix B

Public Securities Association standard repo agreement and supplements

Public Securities Association
40 Broad Street, New York, NY 10004-2373
Telephone (212) 809-7000

PSA

MASTER REPURCHASE AGREEMENT

Dated as of _____ _____, _____

Between:

_____

and

_____

1. Applicability

From time to time the parties hereto may enter into transactions in which one party ("Seller") agrees to transfer to the other ("Buyer") securities or financial instruments ("Securities") against the transfer of funds by Buyer, with a simultaneous agreement by Buyer to transfer to Seller such Securities at a date certain or on demand, against the transfer of funds by Seller. Each such transaction shall be referred to herein as a "Transaction" and shall be governed by this Agreement, including any supplemental terms or conditions contained in Annex I hereto, unless otherwise agreed in writing.

2. Definitions

(a) "Act of Insolvency", with respect to any party, (i) the commencement by such party as debtor of any case or proceeding under any bankruptcy, insolvency, reorganization, liquidation, dissolution or similar law, or such party seeking the appointment of a receiver, trustee, custodian or similar official for such party or any substantial part of its property, or (ii) the commencement of any such case or proceeding against such party, or another seeking such an appointment, or the filing against a party of an application for a protective decree under the provisions of the Securities Investor Protection Act of 1970, which (A) is consented to or not timely contested by such party, (B) results in the entry of an order for relief, such an appointment, the issuance of such a protective decree or the entry of an order having a similar effect, or (C) is not dismissed within 15 days, (iii) the making by a party of a general assignment for the benefit of creditors, or (iv) the admission in writing by a party of such party's inability to pay such party's debts as they become due;

(b) "Additional Purchased Securities", Securities provided by Seller to Buyer pursuant to Paragraph 4(a) hereof;

(c) "Buyer's Margin Amount", with respect to any Transaction as of any date, the amount obtained by application of a percentage (which may be equal to the percentage that is agreed to as the Seller's Margin Amount under subparagraph (q) of this Paragraph), agreed to by Buyer and Seller prior to entering into the Transaction, to the Repurchase Price for such Transaction as of such date;

(d) "Confirmation", the meaning specified in Paragraph 3(b) hereof;

(e) "Income", with respect to any Security at any time, any principal thereof then payable and all interest, dividends or other distributions thereon;

(f) "Margin Deficit", the meaning specified in Paragraph 4(a) hereof;

(g) "Margin Excess", the meaning specified in Paragraph 4(b) hereof;

(h) "Market Value", with respect to any Securities as of any date, the price for such Securities on such date obtained from a generally recognized source agreed to by the parties or the most recent closing bid quotation from such a source, plus accrued Income to the extent not included therein (other than any Income credited or transferred to, or applied to the obligations of, Seller pursuant to Paragraph 5 hereof) as of such date (unless contrary to market practice for such Securities);

(i) "Price Differential", with respect to any Transaction hereunder as of any date, the aggregate amount obtained by daily application of the Pricing Rate for such Transaction to the Purchase Price for such Transaction on a 360 day per year basis for the actual number of days during the period commencing on (and including) the Purchase Date for such Transaction and ending on (but excluding) the date of determination (reduced by any amount of such Price Differential previously paid by Seller to Buyer with respect to such Transaction);

8/87

(j) "Pricing Rate", the per annum percentage rate for determination of the Price Differential;

(k) "Prime Rate", the prime rate of U.S. money center commercial banks as published in *The Wall Street Journal*;

(l) "Purchase Date", the date on which Purchased Securities are transferred by Seller to Buyer;

(m) "Purchase Price", (i) on the Purchase Date, the price at which Purchased Securities are transferred by Seller to Buyer, and (ii) thereafter, such price increased by the amount of any cash transferred by Buyer to Seller pursuant to Paragraph 4(b) hereof and decreased by the amount of any cash transferred by Seller to Buyer pursuant to Paragraph 4(a) hereof or applied to reduce Seller's obligations under clause (ii) of Paragraph 5 hereof;

(n) "Purchased Securities", the Securities transferred by Seller to Buyer in a Transaction hereunder, and any Securities substituted therefor in accordance with Paragraph 9 hereof. The term "Purchased Securities" with respect to any Transaction at any time also shall include Additional Purchased Securities delivered pursuant to Paragraph 4(a) and shall exclude Securities returned pursuant to Paragraph 4(b);

(o) "Repurchase Date", the date on which Seller is to repurchase the Purchased Securities from Buyer, including any date determined by application of the provisions of Paragraphs 3(c) or 11 hereof;

(p) "Repurchase Price", the price at which Purchased Securities are to be transferred from Buyer to Seller upon termination of a Transaction, which will be determined in each case (including Transactions terminable upon demand) as the sum of the Purchase Price and the Price Differential as of the date of such determination, increased by any amount determined by the application of the provisions of Paragraph 11 hereof;

(q) "Seller's Margin Amount", with respect to any Transaction as of any date, the amount obtained by application of a percentage (which may be equal to the percentage that is agreed to as the Buyer's Margin Amount under subparagraph (c) of this Paragraph), agreed to by Buyer and Seller prior to entering into the Transaction, to the Repurchase Price for such Transaction as of such date.

3. Initiation; Confirmation; Termination

(a) An agreement to enter into a Transaction may be made orally or in writing at the initiation of either Buyer or Seller. On the Purchase Date for the Transaction, the Purchased Securities shall be transferred to Buyer or its agent against the transfer of the Purchase Price to an account of Seller.

(b) Upon agreeing to enter into a Transaction hereunder, Buyer or Seller (or both), as shall be agreed, shall promptly deliver to the other party a written confirmation of each Transaction (a "Confirmation"). The Confirmation shall describe the Purchased Securities (including CUSIP number, if any), identify Buyer and Seller and set forth (i) the Purchase Date, (ii) the Purchase Price, (iii) the Repurchase Date, unless the Transaction is to be terminable on demand, (iv) the Pricing Rate or Repurchase Price applicable to the Transaction, and (v) any additional terms or conditions of the Transaction not inconsistent with this Agreement. The Confirmation, together with this Agreement, shall constitute conclusive evidence of the terms agreed between Buyer and Seller with respect to the Transaction to which the Confirmation relates, unless with respect to the Confirmation specific objection is made promptly after receipt thereof. In the event of any conflict between the terms of such Confirmation and this Agreement, this Agreement shall prevail.

(c) In the case of Transactions terminable upon demand, such demand shall be made by Buyer or Seller, no later than such time as is customary in accordance with market practice, by telephone or otherwise on or prior to the business day on which such termination will be effective. On the date specified in such demand, or on the date fixed for termination in the case of Transactions having a fixed term, termination of the Transaction will be effected by transfer to Seller or its agent of the Purchased Securities and any Income in respect thereof received by Buyer (and not previously credited or transferred to, or applied to the obligations of, Seller pursuant to Paragraph 5 hereof) against the transfer of the Repurchase Price to an account of Buyer.

4. Margin Maintenance

(a) If at any time the aggregate Market Value of all Purchased Securities subject to all Transactions in which a particular party hereto is acting as Buyer is less than the aggregate Buyer's Margin Amount for all such Transactions (a "Margin Deficit"), then Buyer may by notice to Seller require Seller in such Transactions, at Seller's option, to transfer to Buyer cash or additional Securities reasonably acceptable to Buyer ("Additional Purchased Securities"), so that the cash and aggregate Market Value of the Purchased Securities, including any such Additional Purchased Securities, will thereupon equal or exceed such aggregate Buyer's Margin Amount (decreased by the amount of any Margin Deficit as of such date arising from any Transactions in which such Buyer is acting as Seller).

(b) If at any time the aggregate Market Value of all Purchased Securities subject to all Transactions in which a particular party hereto is acting as Seller exceeds the aggregate Seller's Margin Amount for all such Transactions at such time (a "Margin Excess"), then Seller may by notice to Buyer require Buyer in such Transactions, at Buyer's option, to transfer cash or Purchased Securities to Seller, so that the aggregate Market Value of the Purchased Securities, after deduction of any such cash or any Purchased Securities so transferred, will thereupon not exceed such aggregate Seller's Margin Amount (increased by the amount of any Margin Excess as of such date arising from any Transactions in which such Seller is acting as Buyer).

(c) Any cash transferred pursuant to this Paragraph shall be attributed to such Transactions as shall be agreed upon by Buyer and Seller.

2

(d) Seller and Buyer may agree, with respect to any or all Transactions hereunder, that the respective rights of Buyer or Seller (or both) under subparagraphs (a) and (b) of this Paragraph may be exercised only where a Margin Deficit or Margin Excess exceeds a specified dollar amount or a specified percentage of the Repurchase Prices for such Transactions (which amount or percentage shall be agreed to by Buyer and Seller prior to entering into any such Transactions).

(e) Seller and Buyer may agree, with respect to any or all Transactions hereunder, that the respective rights of Buyer and Seller under subparagraphs (a) and (b) of this Paragraph to require the elimination of a Margin Deficit or a Margin Excess, as the case may be, may be exercised whenever such a Margin Deficit or Margin Excess exists with respect to any single Transaction hereunder (calculated without regard to any other Transaction outstanding under this Agreement).

5. **Income Payments**
Where a particular Transaction's term extends over an Income payment date on the Securities subject to that Transaction, Buyer shall, as the parties may agree with respect to such Transaction (or, in the absence of any agreement, as Buyer shall reasonably determine in its discretion), on the date such Income is payable either (i) transfer to or credit to the account of Seller an amount equal to such Income payment or payments with respect to any Purchased Securities subject to such Transaction or (ii) apply the Income payment or payments to reduce the amount to be transferred to Buyer by Seller upon termination of the Transaction. Buyer shall not be obligated to take any action pursuant to the preceding sentence to the extent that such action would result in the creation of a Margin Deficit, unless prior thereto or simultaneously therewith Seller transfers to Buyer cash or Additional Purchased Securities sufficient to eliminate such Margin Deficit.

6. **Security Interest**
Although the parties intend that all Transactions hereunder be sales and purchases and not loans, in the event any such Transactions are deemed to be loans, Seller shall be deemed to have pledged to Buyer as security for the performance by Seller of its obligations under each such Transaction, and shall be deemed to have granted to Buyer a security interest in, all of the Purchased Securities with respect to all Transactions hereunder and all proceeds thereof.

7. **Payment and Transfer**
Unless otherwise mutually agreed, all transfers of funds hereunder shall be in immediately available funds. All Securities transferred by one party hereto to the other party (i) shall be in suitable form for transfer or shall be accompanied by duly executed instruments of transfer or assignment in blank and such other documentation as the party receiving possession may reasonably request, (ii) shall be transferred on the book-entry system of a Federal Reserve Bank, or (iii) shall be transferred by any other method mutually acceptable to Seller and Buyer. As used herein with respect to Securities, "transfer" is intended to have the same meaning as when used in Section 8-313 of the New York Uniform Commercial Code or, where applicable, in any federal regulation governing transfers of the Securities.

8. **Segregation of Purchased Securities**
To the extent required by applicable law, all Purchased Securities in the possession of Seller shall be segregated from other securities in its possession and shall be identified as subject to this Agreement. Segregation may be accomplished by appropriate identification on the books and records of the holder, including a financial intermediary or a clearing corporation. Title to all Purchased Securities shall pass to Buyer and, unless otherwise agreed by Buyer and Seller, nothing in this Agreement shall preclude Buyer from engaging in repurchase transactions with the Purchased Securities or otherwise pledging or hypothecating the Purchased Securities, but no such transaction shall relieve Buyer of its obligations to transfer Purchased Securities to Seller pursuant to Paragraphs 3, 4 or 11 hereof, or of Buyer's obligation to credit or pay Income to, or apply Income to the obligations of, Seller pursuant to Paragraph 5 hereof.

Required Disclosure for Transactions in Which the Seller Retains Custody of the Purchased Securities

Seller is not permitted to substitute other securities for those subject to this Agreement and therefore must keep Buyer's securities segregated at all times, unless in this Agreement Buyer grants Seller the right to substitute other securities. If Buyer grants the right to substitute, this means that Buyer's securities will likely be commingled with Seller's own securities during the trading day. Buyer is advised that, during any trading day that Buyer's securities are commingled with Seller's securities, they [will]* [may]** be subject to liens granted by Seller to [its clearing bank]* [third parties]** and may be used by Seller for deliveries on other securities transactions. Whenever the securities are commingled, Seller's ability to resegregate substitute securities for Buyer will be subject to Seller's ability to satisfy [the clearing]* [any]** lien or to obtain substitute securities.

---

*Language to be used under 17 C.F.R. §403.4(e) if Seller is a government securities broker or dealer other than a financial institution.
**Language to be used under 17 C.F.R. §403.5(d) if Seller is a financial institution.

9. Substitution

(a) Seller may, subject to agreement with and acceptance by Buyer, substitute other Securities for any Purchased Securities. Such substitution shall be made by transfer to Buyer of such other Securities and transfer to Seller of such Purchased Securities. After substitution, the substituted Securities shall be deemed to be Purchased Securities.

(b) In Transactions in which the Seller retains custody of Purchased Securities, the parties expressly agree that Buyer shall be deemed, for purposes of subparagraph (a) of this Paragraph, to have agreed to and accepted in this Agreement substitution by Seller of other Securities for Purchased Securities; *provided, however,* that such other Securities shall have a Market Value at least equal to the Market Value of the Purchased Securities for which they are substituted.

10. Representations

Each of Buyer and Seller represents and warrants to the other that (i) it is duly authorized to execute and deliver this Agreement, to enter into the Transactions contemplated hereunder and to perform its obligations hereunder and has taken all necessary action to authorize such execution, delivery and performance, (ii) it will engage in such Transactions as principal (or, if agreed in writing in advance of any Transaction by the other party hereto, as agent for a disclosed principal), (iii) the person signing this Agreement on its behalf is duly authorized to do so on its behalf (or on behalf of any such disclosed principal), (iv) it has obtained all authorizations of any governmental body required in connection with this Agreement and the Transactions hereunder and such authorizations are in full force and effect and (v) the execution, delivery and performance of this Agreement and the Transactions hereunder will not violate any law, ordinance, charter, by-law or rule applicable to it or any agreement by which it is bound or by which any of its assets are affected. On the Purchase Date for any Transaction Buyer and Seller shall each be deemed to repeat all the foregoing representations made by it.

11. Events of Default

In the event that (i) Seller fails to repurchase or Buyer fails to transfer Purchased Securities upon the applicable Repurchase Date, (ii) Seller or Buyer fails, after one business day's notice, to comply with Paragraph 4 hereof, (iii) Buyer fails to comply with Paragraph 5 hereof, (iv) an Act of Insolvency occurs with respect to Seller or Buyer, (v) any representation made by Seller or Buyer shall have been incorrect or untrue in any material respect when made or repeated or deemed to have been made or repeated, or (vi) Seller or Buyer shall admit to the other its inability to, or its intention not to, perform any of its obligations hereunder (each an "Event of Default"):

(a) At the option of the nondefaulting party, exercised by written notice to the defaulting party (which option shall be deemed to have been exercised, even if no notice is given, immediately upon the occurrence of an Act of Insolvency), the Repurchase Date for each Transaction hereunder shall be deemed immediately to occur.

(b) In all Transactions in which the defaulting party is acting as Seller, if the nondefaulting party exercises or is deemed to have exercised the option referred to in subparagraph (a) of this Paragraph, (i) the defaulting party's obligations hereunder to repurchase all Purchased Securities in such Transactions shall thereupon become immediately due and payable, (ii) to the extent permitted by applicable law, the Repurchase Price with respect to each such Transaction shall be increased by the aggregate amount obtained by daily application of (x) the greater of the Pricing Rate for such Transaction or the Prime Rate to (y) the Repurchase Price for such Transaction as of the Repurchase Date as determined pursuant to subparagraph (a) of this Paragraph (decreased as of any day by (A) any amounts retained by the nondefaulting party with respect to such Repurchase Price pursuant to clause (iii) of this subparagraph, (B) any proceeds from the sale of Purchased Securities pursuant to subparagraph (d)(i) of this Paragraph, and (C) any amounts credited to the account of the defaulting party pursuant to subparagraph (e) of this Paragraph) on a 360 day per year basis for the actual number of days during the period from and including the date of the Event of Default giving rise to such option to but excluding the date of payment of the Repurchase Price as so increased, (iii) all Income paid after such exercise or deemed exercise shall be retained by the nondefaulting party and applied to the aggregate unpaid Repurchase Prices owed by the defaulting party, and (iv) the defaulting party shall immediately deliver to the nondefaulting party any Purchased Securities subject to such Transactions then in the defaulting party's possession.

(c) In all Transactions in which the defaulting party is acting as Buyer, upon tender by the nondefaulting party of payment of the aggregate Repurchase Prices for all such Transactions, the defaulting party's right, title and interest in all Purchased Securities subject to such Transactions shall be deemed transferred to the nondefaulting party, and the defaulting party shall deliver all such Purchased Securities to the nondefaulting party.

(d) After one business day's notice to the defaulting party (which notice need not be given if an Act of Insolvency shall have occurred, and which may be the notice given under subparagraph (a) of this Paragraph or the notice referred to in clause (ii) of the first sentence of this Paragraph), the nondefaulting party may:

(i) as to Transactions in which the defaulting party is acting as Seller, (A) immediately sell, in a recognized market at such price or prices as the nondefaulting party may reasonably deem satisfactory, any or all Purchased Securities subject to such Transactions and apply the proceeds thereof to the aggregate unpaid Repurchase Prices and any other amounts owing by the defaulting party hereunder

4

or (B) in its sole discretion elect, in lieu of selling all or a portion of such Purchased Securities, to give the defaulting party credit for such Purchased Securities in an amount equal to the price therefor on such date, obtained from a generally recognized source or the most recent closing bid quotation from such a source, against the aggregate unpaid Repurchase Prices and any other amounts owing by the defaulting party hereunder; and

(ii) as to Transactions in which the defaulting party is acting as Buyer, (A) purchase securities ("Replacement Securities") of the same class and amount as any Purchased Securities that are not delivered by the defaulting party to the nondefaulting party as required hereunder or (B) in its sole discretion elect, in lieu of purchasing Replacement Securities, to be deemed to have purchased Replacement Securities at the price therefor on such date, obtained from a generally recognized source or the most recent closing bid quotation from such a source.

(e) As to Transactions in which the defaulting party is acting as Buyer, the defaulting party shall be liable to the nondefaulting party (i) with respect to Purchased Securities (other than Additional Purchased Securities), for any excess of the price paid (or deemed paid) by the nondefaulting party for Replacement Securities therefor over the Repurchase Price for such Purchased Securities and (ii) with respect to Additional Purchased Securities, for the price paid (or deemed paid) by the nondefaulting party for the Replacement Securities therefor. In addition, the defaulting party shall be liable to the nondefaulting party for interest on such remaining liability with respect to each such purchase (or deemed purchase) of Replacement Securities from the date of such purchase (or deemed purchase) until paid in full by Buyer. Such interest shall be at a rate equal to the greater of the Pricing Rate for such Transaction or the Prime Rate.

(f) For purposes of this Paragraph 11, the Repurchase Price for each Transaction hereunder in respect of which the defaulting party is acting as Buyer shall not increase above the amount of such Repurchase Price for such Transaction determined as of the date of the exercise or deemed exercise by the nondefaulting party of its option under subparagraph (a) of this Paragraph.

(g) The defaulting party shall be liable to the nondefaulting party for the amount of all reasonable legal or other expenses incurred by the nondefaulting party in connection with or as a consequence of an Event of Default, together with interest thereon at a rate equal to the greater of the Pricing Rate for the relevant Transaction or the Prime Rate.

(h) The nondefaulting party shall have, in addition to its rights hereunder, any rights otherwise available to it under any other agreement or applicable law.

12. Single Agreement

Buyer and Seller acknowledge that, and have entered hereinto and will enter into each Transaction hereunder in consideration of and in reliance upon the fact that, all Transactions hereunder constitute a single business and contractual relationship and have been made in consideration of each other. Accordingly, each of Buyer and Seller agrees (i) to perform all of its obligations in respect of each Transaction hereunder, and that a default in the performance of any such obligations shall constitute a default by it in respect of all Transactions hereunder, (ii) that each of them shall be entitled to set off claims and apply property held by them in respect of any Transaction against obligations owing to them in respect of any other Transactions hereunder and (iii) that payments, deliveries and other transfers made by either of them in respect of any Transaction shall be deemed to have been made in consideration of payments, deliveries and other transfers in respect of any other Transactions hereunder, and the obligations to make any such payments, deliveries and other transfers may be applied against each other and netted.

13. Notices and Other Communications

Unless another address is specified in writing by the respective party to whom any notice or other communication is to be given hereunder, all such notices or communications shall be in writing or confirmed in writing and delivered at the respective addresses set forth in Annex II attached hereto.

14. Entire Agreement; Severability

This Agreement shall supersede any existing agreements between the parties containing general terms and conditions for repurchase transactions. Each provision and agreement herein shall be treated as separate and independent from any other provision or agreement herein and shall be enforceable notwithstanding the unenforceability of any such other provision or agreement.

15. Non-assignability; Termination

The rights and obligations of the parties under this Agreement and under any Transaction shall not be assigned by either party without the prior written consent of the other party. Subject to the foregoing, this Agreement and any Transactions shall be binding upon and shall inure to the benefit of the parties and their respective successors and assigns. This Agreement may be cancelled by either party upon giving written notice to the other, except that this Agreement shall, notwithstanding such notice, remain applicable to any Transactions then outstanding.

5

16. Governing Law

This Agreement shall be governed by the laws of the State of New York without giving effect to the conflict of law principles thereof.

17. No Waivers, Etc.

No express or implied waiver of any Event of Default by either party shall constitute a waiver of any other Event of Default and no exercise of any remedy hereunder by any party shall constitute a waiver of its right to exercise any other remedy hereunder. No modification or waiver of any provision of this Agreement and no consent by any party to a departure herefrom shall be effective unless and until such shall be in writing and duly executed by both of the parties hereto. Without limitation on any of the foregoing, the failure to give a notice pursuant to subparagraphs 4(a) or 4(b) hereof will not constitute a waiver of any right to do so at a later date.

18. Use of Employee Plan Assets

(a) If assets of an employee benefit plan subject to any provision of the Employee Retirement Income Security Act of 1974 ("ERISA") are intended to be used by either party hereto (the "Plan Party") in a Transaction, the Plan Party shall so notify the other party prior to the Transaction. The Plan Party shall represent in writing to the other party that the Transaction does not constitute a prohibited transaction under ERISA or is otherwise exempt therefrom, and the other party may proceed in reliance thereon but shall not be required so to proceed.

(b) Subject to the last sentence of subparagraph (a) of this Paragraph, any such Transaction shall proceed only if Seller furnishes or has furnished to Buyer its most recent available audited statement of its financial condition and its most recent subsequent unaudited statement of its financial condition.

(c) By entering into a Transaction pursuant to this Paragraph, Seller shall be deemed (i) to represent to Buyer that since the date of Seller's latest such financial statements, there has been no material adverse change in Seller's financial condition which Seller has not disclosed to Buyer, and (ii) to agree to provide Buyer with future audited and unaudited statements of its financial condition as they are issued, so long as it is a Seller in any outstanding Transaction involving a Plan Party.

19. Intent

(a) The parties recognize that each Transaction is a "repurchase agreement" as that term is defined in Section 101 of Title 11 of the United States Code, as amended (except insofar as the type of Securities subject to such Transaction or the term of such Transaction would render such definition inapplicable), and a "securities contract" as that term is defined in Section 741 of Title 11 of the United States Code, as amended.

(b) It is understood that either party's right to liquidate Securities delivered to it in connection with Transactions hereunder or to exercise any other remedies pursuant to Paragraph 11 hereof, is a contractual right to liquidate such Transaction as described in Sections 555 and 559 of Title 11 of the United States Code, as amended.

20. Disclosure Relating to Certain Federal Protections

The parties acknowledge that they have been advised that:

(a) in the case of Transactions in which one of the parties is a broker or dealer registered with the Securities and Exchange Commission ("SEC") under Section 15 of the Securities Exchange Act of 1934 ("1934 Act"), the Securities Investor Protection Corporation has taken the position that the provisions of the Securities Investor Protection Act of 1970 ("SIPA") do not protect the other party with respect to any Transaction hereunder;

(b) in the case of Transactions in which one of the parties is a government securities broker or a government securities dealer registered with the SEC under Section 15C of the 1934 Act, SIPA will not provide protection to the other party with respect to any Transaction hereunder; and

(c) in the case of Transactions in which one of the parties is a financial institution, funds held by the financial institution pursuant to a Transaction hereunder are not a deposit and therefore are not insured by the Federal Deposit Insurance Corporation, the Federal Savings and Loan Insurance Corporation or the National Credit Union Share Insurance Fund, as applicable.

[Name of Party]   [Name of Party]

By _____   By _____

Title _____   Title _____

Date _____   Date _____

6

Public Securities Association
40 Broad Street
New York, NY 10004-2373
(212) 809-7000
Telecopier: (212) 797-3895

August 25, 1987

MEMORANDUM REGARDING REVISIONS TO
PSA MASTER REPURCHASE AGREEMENT

The Public Securities Association ("PSA") is adopting
revisions to the prototype master repurchase agreement (the
"PSA Master Agreement") which it issued in February 1986. The
revisions reflect the new requirements applicable to
hold-in-custody repo agreements with government securities
brokers and dealers under the July 24, 1987 final regulations
of the Department of the Treasury implementing the Government
Securities Act of 1986 (as well as similar requirements
applicable to registered broker-dealers under regulations of
the Securities and Exchange Commission). The revisions are
not intended to make substantive changes to the February 1986
version of the PSA Master Agreement except to the extent
necessary to satisfy applicable regulatory requirements
(including an anticipated change in the Treasury's book-entry
regulations).

The PSA Master Agreement, as revised, is being
reprinted in its entirety (the "Revised Agreement"). In
addition, to facilitate parties' adoption of mandated changes
in their repurchase agreements by the regulatory deadlines,
PSA has also developed:

(i)   a form of amendment, reflecting the
specific changes embodied in the Revised Agreement,
that could be used to modify an existing master
repurchase agreement modelled on the February 1986
PSA Master Agreement (the "Amendment"); and

(ii) a form of supplemental agreement that
could be used to incorporate the substance of these
changes into existing master repurchase agreement
documentation without reference to particular
provisions of such documentation (the "Supplemental
Agreement").

The Amendment would amend specific provisions of the PSA Master Agreement and thus would be appropriate for use only between parties which had previously entered into that agreement. The Supplemental Agreement, on the other hand, could be used by firms which have entered into a variety of forms of master agreements with counterparties (including, of course, agreements in the form of the PSA Master Agreement) since it does not contain any references to specific language in prior master repurchase agreements between the parties.

For simplicity, the discussion below is keyed to specific provisions of the revised form of the PSA Master Agreement.

A. Substitution

Treasury regulations provide that a government securities broker or dealer generally may engage in intra-day commingling of securities retained by it under a hold-in-custody repo agreement only if its customer consents to substitution in writing. Accordingly, a new Paragraph 9 granting the Seller the right to substitution in hold-in-custody repo transactions has been added to the PSA Master Agreement. The right to substitution is conditioned upon the substituted securities having a market value at least equal to the securities for which they are substituted.

B. "Required Disclosure"

The revisions to the PSA Master Agreement also include the "Required Disclosure" language specifically required by Treasury regulation for hold-in-custody repo transactions. As required by Treasury regulation, this language has been placed immediately prior to the new substitution provision. Where the "Required Disclosure" language for financial institutions differs from that for other government securities brokers and dealers, the relevant language has been bracketed and the category of institution for which it is appropriate has been indicated in explanatory footnotes.

C. Disclosures Relating to Certain Federal
     Protections

The revisions to the PSA Master Agreement also include the addition of a new paragraph 20 containing disclosures, required by Treasury regulation, relating to the possible unavailability to hold-in-custody repo counterparties

- 2 -

of protections under the Securities Investor Protection Act of 1970 and the federal deposit insurance laws. As included in the revisions, the mandatory disclosures have been drafted in a form which could be used by any government securities broker or dealer, regardless of whether it is a financial institution or is registered under section 15 or section 15C of the Securities Exchange Act of 1934.

       D.   <u>Transfer</u>

       The revisions also reflect a minor modification to the definition of the term "transfer" in Paragraph 7 of the PSA Master Agreement designed to reflect an anticipated change in the Treasury's book-entry regulations expected to be issued in final form this fall.

       E.   <u>Segregation</u>

       The revisions contain, in addition, a modification to the segregation provisions in Paragraph 8 of the PSA Master Agreement intended to clarify that intra-day commingling of securities retained under hold-in-custody repo transactions may occur to the extent permitted by applicable law (including applicable regulations of the Department of the Treasury and the Securities and Exchange Commission).

Public Securities Association
40 Broad Street, New York, NY 10004-2373
Telephone (212) 809-7000

PSA

SUPPLEMENTAL PROVISIONS TO
MASTER REPURCHASE AGREEMENT

Dated as of _____ ____, _____

Between:

_____

and

_____

The parties hereto agree that, notwithstanding any prior agreements between them, the following terms and conditions shall govern all transactions hereafter entered into between them in which one party ("Seller") agrees to transfer to the other ("Buyer") securities or financial instruments ("Securities") against the transfer of funds by Buyer, with a simultaneous agreement by Buyer to transfer to Seller such Securities at a date certain or on demand, against the transfer of funds by Seller (each such transaction referred to herein as a "Transaction"):

1. **Disclosure Relating to Certain Federal Protections.** The parties acknowledge that they have been advised that:

(a) in the case of Transactions in which one of the parties is a broker or dealer registered with the Securities and Exchange Commission ("SEC") under Section 15 of the Securities Exchange Act of 1934 ("1934 Act"), the Securities Investor Protection Corporation has taken the position that the provisions of the Securities Investor Protection Act of 1970 ("SIPA") do not protect the other party with respect to any Transaction hereunder;

(b) in the case of Transactions in which one of the parties is a government securities broker or a government securities dealer registered with the SEC under Section 15C of the 1934 Act, SIPA will not provide protection to the other party with respect to any Transaction hereunder; and

(c) in the case of Transactions in which one of the parties is a financial institution, funds held by the financial institution pursuant to a Transaction hereunder are not a deposit and therefore are not insured by the Federal Deposit Insurance Corporation, the Federal Savings and Loan Insurance Corporation or the National Credit Union Share Insurance Fund, as applicable.

**Required Disclosure for Transactions in Which the Seller Retains Custody
of the Purchased Securities**

Seller is not permitted to substitute other securities for those subject to this Agreement and therefore must keep Buyer's securities segregated at all times, unless in this Agreement Buyer grants Seller the right to substitute other securities. If Buyer grants the right to substitute, this means that Buyer's securities will likely be commingled with Seller's own securities during the trading day. Buyer is advised that, during any trading day that Buyer's securities are commingled with Seller's securities, they [will]* [may]** be subject to liens granted by Seller to [its clearing bank]* [third parties]** and may be used by Seller for deliveries on other securities transactions. Whenever the securities are commingled, Seller's ability to resegregate substitute securities for Buyer will be subject to Seller's ability to satisfy [the clearing]* [any]** lien or to obtain substitute securities.

---

*Language to be used under 17 C.F.R. §403.4(e) if Seller is a government securities broker or dealer other than a financial institution.
**Language to be used under 17 C.F.R. §403.5(d) if Seller is a financial institution.
8-87

2. Substitution. (a) Seller may, subject to agreement with and acceptance by Buyer, substitute other Securities for any Purchased Securities (as defined below). Such substitution shall be made by transfer to Buyer of such other Securities and transfer to Seller of such Purchased Securities. After substitution, the substituted Securities shall be deemed to be Purchased Securities for purposes of this Agreement or any prior Agreement between the parties with respect to Transactions hereunder.

(b) In Transactions in which the Seller retains custody of Purchased Securities, the parties expressly agree that Buyer shall be deemed, for purposes of subparagraph (a) of this Paragraph, to have agreed to and accepted in this Agreement substitution by Seller of other Securities for Purchased Securities; *provided, however,* that such other Securities shall have a market value (determined as previously agreed between the parties or, in the absence of any such prior agreement, as the parties may hereafter agree) at least equal to the market value (as so determined) of the Purchased Securities for which they are substituted.

(c) As used herein, "Purchased Securities" shall mean the Securities transferred by Seller to Buyer in a Transaction hereunder, and any Securities substituted therefor in accordance with this Paragraph. The term "Purchased Securities" shall also include any other Securities delivered to Buyer pursuant to any margin maintenance or similar agreements between the parties and shall exclude any Securities returned pursuant to any such agreements.

3. Transfer. As used herein, and in any prior agreement between the parties with respect to Transactions hereunder, "transfer" is intended to have the same meaning as when used in Section 8-313 of the New York Uniform Commercial Code or, where applicable, in any federal regulation governing transfer of the Securities.

4. Segregation. Seller shall be required to segregate Purchased Securities in its possession from other securities in its possession and to identify such Purchased Securities as subject to this Agreement (and any prior agreement between the parties with respect to any Transactions hereunder) solely to the extent that such segregation and identification are required by aplicable law or to effect validly a transfer hereunder.

[Name of Party]   [Name of Party]

By _____   By _____

Title _____   Title _____

Date _____   Date _____

8/87

Appendix C

Document relating to the Lombard-Wall bankruptcy in 1982

Copy of the Lombard-Wall Incorporated
Repurchase Agreement

This Repurchase Agreement (the "Agreement") dated on or as of the date set forth in Exhibit A hereto, by and among the party named on the signature page hereof as Trustee (the "Trustee") under the resolution described in Exhibit A hereto (the "Resolution") adopted by the party named on the signature page hereof as the Issuer (the "Issuer"). the Issuer and LOMBARD-WALL INCORPORATED, a Delaware corporation having its principal place of business at 140 Broadway, New York, New York (the "Corporation").

WHEREAS, the Issuer contemplates issuing the Bonds described in Exhibit A hereto (the "Bonds") and using the proceeds thereof pursuant to and as provided in the resolution; and

WHEREAS, the Trustee will act as trustee for the benefit of the holders of the Bonds pursuant to the Resolution; and

WHEREAS, the moneys to be utilized for the purposes provided for in the Resolution are to be held by the Trustee in the fund established under the Resolution (the "Fund") and to be released in accordance with the conditions specified in the Resolution; and

WHEREAS, the Issuer contemplates that from the proceeds of the sale of the Bonds the amount specified in Exhibit A hereto is to be deposited into the Fund and held by the Trustee for the purposes provided in the Resolution; and

WHEREAS, the Issuer desires that moneys in the Fund be invested to yield a specified return for the benefit of the holders of the Bonds pending the utilization of such moneys and has, by resolution duly adopted, authorized the Trustee to enter into this Agreement; and

WHEREAS, the Trustee has delivered to the Corporation true and accurate copies of the Resolution, certified by the Issuer, and any preliminary or final official statement or prospectus or other disclosure document and any indenture of trust or similar instrument to be used in connection with the issuance of the Bonds; and

WHEREAS, THE Corporation is willing, on the terms and conditions set forth below (i) to sell to the Trustee certain Investment Securities (hereinafter defined) to be held in the Trustee's account at the location specified in Exhibit A hereto and (ii) to repurchase such Investment Securities from the Trustee at a price which will guarantee the rate per annum specified in Exhibit A hereto on the moneys used by the Trustee to purchase such Investment Securities.

NOW, THEREFORE, in consideration of the foregoing, the undersigned hereby agree as follows:

1. On the first business day after the Bonds are sold and delivered, the Trustee will utilize the moneys on deposit in the Fund to purchase from the Corporation the Investment Securities specifies on Exhibit B hereto.

2. All Investment Securities are to be held by the Trustee in its account at the location specified in Exhibit A hereto pending their repurchase by, or return to, the Corporation. So long as an Event of Default (as hereinafter defined) shall not have occurred and be continuing, the Trustee shall, not later than the first business day after receipt thereof, pay to the Corporation a sum equal to the interest payments paid with respect to Investment Securities held by the Trustee. Any principal payments on Investment Securities held by the Trustee shall be paid to the Corporation upon the delivery by the Corporation to the Trustee of substitute Investment Securities, as provided in Section 3.

Upon payment of the Repurchase Price (as hereinafter defined) therefor, Investment Securities repurchased by the Corporation will be returned to the Corporation and the interest of the Trustee in such securities shall terminate.

3. At any time that an Event of Default shall not have occurred and be continuing, the Corporation shall have the right to substitute for any Investment Security held by the Trustee, any other Investment Security, the fair market value of which is at least equal to the fair market value, at the time of substitution, of the security for which substitution is made. The Corporation's determination of the fair market value of an investment Security shall, for all purposes of this Agreement, be deemed to be the fair market value of such security.

4. As used in this Agreement, the term "Investment Security" or "Investment Securities" shall mean and include any and all of the securities specified in Exhibit C hereto, and any principal payments received by the Trustee on the payment on redemption of any such securities.

5. The Corporation shall repurchase all of the Investment Securities held by the Trustee upon termination of this Agreement and the Corporation shall repurchase all or any of the Investment Securities held by the Trustee at any time during the term of this Agreement on the dates requested by the Issuer upon two business days prior notice by the Issuer. Any such repurchase shall be for cash in an amount equal to (i) the purchase price of the Investment Security to be repurchased, or any security substituted therefore hereunder, as set forth in Exhibit B hereto ("Repurchase Price") plus (ii) interest ("Repurchase Interest"). As used herein "Repurchase Interest" at the time of any repurchase shall mean interest at the daily rate specified in Exhibit A hereto on the Repurchase Price for the Investment Securities repurchased at the time, computed for the period from the last day of the preceding calendar month for which interest has been paid as provided in Section 6 hereof or, if no such interest has beenpaid, from the date of the payment of the purchase price of such Investment Securitied, to the date of such repurchse. The Issuer and the Trustee agree that they will not reinvest any funds received upon any such repurchase except as provided in or permitted by the Resolution.

6. Until all Investment Securities held by the Trustee hereunder have been repurchased by the Corporation, the Corporation agrees to crdit the account, within two business days after the last day of each interest period, interest at the rate specified

in Exhibit D hereto, calculated on the basis of a 360-day year.
Interest shall be credited semi-annually.

7. At all times suvsequent to the date of this Agreement
and prior to their repurchase by and delivery to the Corporation,
title to the Investment Securities held by the Trustee hereunder
shall be in the Trustee.

8. The following events are Events of Default under this
Agreement: (i) If the Corporation, at any time, fails to repurchase
Investment Securities at the Repurchase Price, together with
Repurchase Interst in accordance with the terms of this Agreement,
and such failure continues for three business days or one business
day after notice thereof by the Trustee to the Corporation; (ii)
If the Corporation fails to make any payment of interest when due
pursuant to the provisions of Section 6 hereof, and such failure continues
for three business days or one business day after notice thereof by
the Trustee to the Corporation; (iii) If the Corporation files a
petition in bankruptcy, is adjudicated an insolvent or bankrupt,
petitions or applies for the appointment of any receiver or trustee
for itself or any substantial part of its property or if the Corporation initiates any proceeding relating to it under any reorganization, arrangement, dissolution or liquidation law or if any such
procedure is initialted against it and if the Corporation indicates
in any manner its consent thereto or if such proceeding is not
dismissed within 30 days, (iv) If any of the representations made
hereunder by the Corporation shall prove to be untrue in any material
respect or if the Corporation fails to prmorm any of its obigations
hereunder (other than those descrived in clauses (i) and (ii)
of this Section 8) and such failure shall continue for five business
days after notice thereof by the Trustee to the Corporation.

Upon the occurrence of any such Event of Default, except insofar
as the Trustee may be precluded from doing so by the Bankruptcy
Code of 1978, the Trustee shall have the right to declare this
Agreement to be in default and to terminate this Agreement on or
after the business day following notice thereof by the Trustee to
the Corporation if such Event of Default is not cured prior to
such termination or the Corporation shall not have tendered to the
Trustee cash in an amount sufficient to immediately repurchase all
Investment Securities as provided in this Agreement. If the Trustee
so terminates this Agreement, the Investment Securities and the Trustee
shall have the right, in addition to any other available remedies, to
dispose of the Investment Securities and the Corporation shall remain
liable for the excess of (x) the Repurchase Price plus Repurchase
Interest accrued to the date of termination of this Agreement over
(y) the amount realized by the Trustee upon dispositon of the Investment Securities; provided, however, that in the event that the Trustee
shall have the right to dispose of any Investment Securities as
provided herein, the Trustee shall take such action within a reasonable period of time after the occurrence of any Event of Default
hereunder.

Upon the occurrence of an Event of Default specified in
clause (i) of this Section 8, the Trustee shall have the option of
either (x) declaring this Agreement to be in default and terminated
or (y) of declaring a limited default to exist with respect to only
those Investment Securities which the Corporation shall have failed

to repurchase in accordance herewith; in the event the Trustee
declares such a limited default to exist, the Trustee may exercise
its rights to the extent necessary to enforce its remedies with
respect to such securities, and the rights and obligaitons of the parties
hereto with respect to the repurchase of other Investment Securities will
remain in full force and effect.

9. The Corporation agrees to determine the fair market value
of each of the Investment Securities held by the Trustee hereunder
as of the end of the first business day of each calendar week
during the term of this Agreement ("Valuation Day") and, on the
next business day following a request therefor by the Trustee, to
provide to the Trustee (by telex or telecopier or similar means if
feasible) an inventory detailing the description, principal amount,
coupon maturity and fair market value of each such Investment Security.
The bid side of the Federal Reserve Composite Quote sheet shall
be the final determinant of fair market value.

In the event that the aggregate of the fair market values
of the Investment Securities held by the Trustee hereunder as of
any Valuation Day is less than the percentage specified in Exhibit
A hereto of the Repurchase Price of such securities ("Repurchase
Price Percentage Requirement"), the Corporation shall deliver to
the Trustee, within three business days after such Valuation Day,
additional Investment Securities having a fair market value sufficient
to cure such deficiency.

In the event that the aggregate of the fair market values
of the Investment Securities held by the Trustee hereunder as
of any Valuation Day exceeds the Repurchase Price Percentage Requirement, the Trustee agrees, if required by notice given by the
Corporation, to transfer to the Corporation and release from the
Trustee's interest hereunder, within three business days of such notice,
Investment Securities having a fair market value sufficient to
eliminate such excess.

10. Unless otherwise mutually agreed in writing, all payments
hereunder shall be by wire transfer, The Corporation shall bear all
costs of effecting such wire transfers charged by the Corporation's
custodian bank. The Issuer shall bear all costs of effecting such
wire transfers charged by the Trustee or its bank.

11. The Corporation represents and warrants that it is duly
authorized toenter into this Agreement and the transactions
contemplated hereunder, that this Agreement is a valid and binding
obligaiton of the Corporation and does not conflict with, violate or
cause a default under any other agreement or instrument to which the
Corporation is a party, that the Investment Securities delivered to
the Trustee hereunder will be delivered to the Trustee free of
all liens, and that the person signing this AGreement on its behalf
is duly authorized to do so.

12. The Trustee and the Issuer, each for itself, represents
and warrants that it is duly authorized to enter into this Agreement
and the transacations contemplatedhereunder, that this Agreement is a
valid and binding obligation of the Trustee and the Issuer and does
not conflict with, violate or cause a default under any other agreement
or insturment to which the Trustee or the Issuer is a party, that
the Investment Securities to be delivered to the Corporation during the
ʹerm of this Agreement, in substitution for other Investment
Securities, upon repurchase by the Corporation or otherwise, will

be delivered to the Corporation free of all liens, and that the person signing this Agreement on its behalf is duly authorized to do so.

13. The Corporation, the Issuer and the Trustee each represents and warrants to the others that neither the execution and delivery of this Agreement nor the performance of their respective obligations hereunder (including the directions given by the Issuer to the Trustee pursuant to the Resolution), will violate any federal or state law or any order, decree, license, permit or the like by which it is bound. In the event this Agreement shall become unenforceable by operation of law, the rights and obligations hereunder shall terminate and the parties hereto agree to mitigate losses and damages to the other parties.

14. This Agreement shall terminate on the date specified in Exhibit A hereto.

15. For the convenience of the parties, this Agreement may be executed in any number of counterparts and each such counterpart executed shall be, and shall be deemed to be, an original insturment and to have the force and effect of an original.

16. This Agreement and all obligations and rights arising hereunder shall be binding upon and inure to the benefit of the parties hereto and their respective successors in interest and assigns.

17. This Agreement shall be governed by the law of the State of New York (regardless of the laws that might be applicable under principles of conflicts of law) as to all matters, including but not limited to matters of validity, construction, effect and performance.

18. All notices pursuant to this Agreement shall be in writing, be effective on receipt thereof and shall either be delivered or mailed by certified or registered mail, return receipt requested, postage prepaid to the attention of the persons listed below and to the party intended as the recipient thereof at the address of such party set forth below, or at such other address or to the attention of such other person as such party shall have designated for such purpose in a written notice:

    The Corporation:

        Lombard-Wall Incorporated
        140 Broadway
        New York, New York 10005
        Attention: Harold W, Kurtz, President

    The Trustee and the Issuer as indicated in Exhibit A hereto.

IN WITNESS WHEREOF, the parties hereto have each caused this Agreement to be executed by their duly authorized officers and their corporate seals to be herunto affixed and attested as of the day and year set forth in Exhibit A hereto as the date of this Agreement.

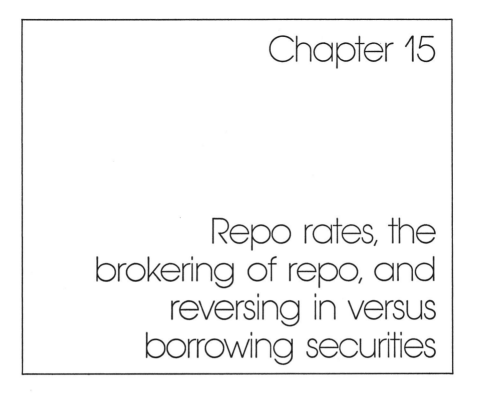

Chapter 15

Repo rates, the brokering of repo, and reversing in versus borrowing securities

THERE IS NO FREE LUNCH; likewise, there is no free repo. In this chapter, we talk about repo and reverse rates and the forces that determine them. We also talk about two other important repo-market particulars: (1) the operation of brokers of repo and reverse, and (2) the considerations that come into play when a dealer decides whether to cover a given short with a reverse or with a borrowing of securities.

REPO RATES

On any day, repos are done not at a single rate, but at several different rates: the overnight rate, the rate on open repos, the 30-day rate, the 60-day rate, and so on. See, for example, the money market rates in Table 15–1. As the numbers in this table suggest, for any period considered the rates on repos of varying maturities are always closely tied to money market rates for top-grade investments of the same maturity. In particular, the overnight repo rate hovers, most days, at a spread *below* the overnight Fed funds rate (Figure 15–1), while the 30-day repo rate hovers at a spread below the 30-day term Fed funds rate and not far from the 30-day bill rate.

The reason lies in the behavior of both lenders and borrowers in the repo market. Lenders have no special attachment to doing repos. They

TABLE 15–1
Money market rates (percent) April 4, 1988

	Overnight	Open	One month	Three months	Six months
Fed funds (domestic)	6¹¹⁄₁₆–6¾	*	6¹³⁄₁₆–6¹⁵⁄₁₆	6¹⁵⁄₁₆–6⁷⁄₁₆	7⅛–7¼
Repos†	6.53–6.55	6.55	6.55–6.50	6.70–6.55	6.80–6.70
CDs (domestic)	*	*	6.65	6¾	7.05
BAs (domestic)‡	*	*	6.62	6.68	6.78
T bills‡	*	*	5.66	5.85	6.40
Muni notes	*	*	4¾	4	4
Euro time deposits	6⁷⁄₁₆	*	6¾	6⅞	7
Discount rate	6	*	*	*	*

* Not applicable.
† Against Treasury collateral.
‡ Money market (360-day) basis; CD equivalent yield.
Source: J. P. Morgan Securities.

will do a repo only if the repo appears, in terms of rate, liquidity, and return offered (i.e., in terms of what money market folk call *relative value*), attractive compared with alternative investments they might make. This means, for example, that the 30-day repo rate, although it may diverge from, can never fall far below other 30-day money market rates. If it did, no investors would do 30-day repos.

The behavior of repo borrowers, on the other hand, prevents repo rates from *rising* to levels out of line with other money market rates. In financing their inventory and trading positions, dealers will always look at the dealer loan rate, which keys off the Fed funds rate, before they decide how much repo to do. Also, if repo rates are low compared to other money market rates, dealers will be offered an opportunity to earn a spread, "positive carry," on positions they finance with repo, and this will encourage them to take on bigger positions and to do more repos. Conversely, if repo rates are high compared to other money market rates, dealers will incur "negative carry" on positions they finance with repo, and this will discourage them from taking on bigger positions, and it will encourage them to do fewer repos.

Banks, also big borrowers in the repo market, can borrow by selling any one of several liabilities (CDs, BAs they have accepted, Euro time deposits) and by buying Fed funds. Thus, in deciding how much repo money to buy, banks ask not only whether carry would be positive if they financed their securities holdings with repos, but whether repo rates compare favorably with rates in other markets in which they can also buy funds.

To use economists' jargon, the supply of funds available in the repo market from investors will be greater the higher repo rates are relative to other money market rates, whereas the demand for funds in the repo market from dealers and banks will be smaller the higher repo rates are relative to other money market rates. Consequently, in equilibrium repo rates should not be far from other money market rates on instruments of equivalent maturity, and in practice they rarely are.

The overnight repo rate

The overnight repo rate (see Figure 15–1) normally lies slightly below the Fed funds rate for two reasons. First, a repo transaction is in essence

FIGURE 15–1
The overnight repo rate tracks the (effective) overnight Fed funds rate closely

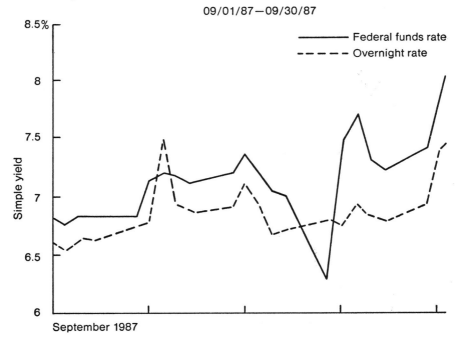

09/01/87–09/30/87

——— Federal funds rate
– – – – Overnight rate

Simple yield

September 1987

a secured loan, whereas the sale of Fed funds is an unsecured loan. Second, many investors—corporations, state and local governments, and others—who can invest in repo cannot sell Fed funds.[1]

---

[1] Such institutions can't sell Fed funds because banks are not permitted under Reg Q to pay interest on overnight money they take domestically from nonbank sources.

An institution that can't sell Fed funds could invest short term by buying securities due to mature in a few months or even a few days. Doing so, however, is usually unattractive. The yield on the 3-month bill typically hovers around the repo rate, and on still shorter bills, yield goes through (below) the repo rate. One reason is that many investors, including some state and local government bodies, can't invest in repo; they have to own the securities outright. A second reason for the thin supply of short bills is that they are often used by dealers as collateral for short positions (holding short bills for collateral exposes a dealer to no significant price risk). A third reason short bills are in thin supply is that many of them are held by investors who intend to roll them at maturity and who never consider the alternative of selling out early to pick up additional basis points. Finally, there are the money funds who tend to sop up any short paper, including bills, that they can find to keep the average maturity of the securities in their portfolio short. "There are," as one portfolio manager noted, "a lot of distortions in market rates because of the severe legal or self-imposed restrictions under which many portfolios are run."

The spread between the Fed funds rate and the repo rate can be anything from a full several points to just a few basis points. How wide it is depends partly on the supply of collateral available. At times, when the Fed is doing a lot of adding—for example, to offset a shift in Treasury balances—the supply of collateral on the Street will dry up, and the spread between the repo rate and the funds rate will widen. At other times, when the Treasury has just sold a large amount of new debt that has yet to be fully distributed, dealers will have a lot of collateral, and the spread between the funds rate and the repo rate will narrow.

The effective Fed funds rate.   Our words—reasonings—on what the relationship ought to be between the Fed funds rate and the overnight repo rate do not seem to jibe fully with what Figure 15–1 shows. There's an explanation. Most dealers do their repos early: they are done latest 10 A.M. Fed funds, in contrast, are traded throughout the day, a period long enough to permit the funds rate to bounce around a bit. The Fed funds rate plotted in Figure 15–1 is an *effective* funds rate for the day; in plain English, it is a weighted average of the funds rates that prevailed during the day where the weights are the amounts of funds traded at different rates. It is conceivable and occasionally happens that the funds rate will trend downward after the repo market has essentially closed for the day. Whenever this occurs, the effective Fed funds rate for the day may well end being below the rate at which overnight repo traded in the early morning.

Non–government collateral.   Most of the borrowing done in the repo market is collateralized by governments and agencies. Dealers, however, also repo CDs, BAs, and commercial paper, and mortgage-backed securities. The spread between the repo rate on governments and that on other securities can be negligible if there is a shortage of collateral on the Street, but normally this spread is 5 to 10 basis points, and it can widen to 15 basis points.

No forward market exists in either overnight repo or term repo. However, a dealer or a bank will occasionally negotiate a forward repo deal with, for example, a government body that knows that money will be coming in on a tax date.

The rate on open repo

Under an *open* repo or *continuing contract,* a lender agrees to give a dealer funds for an indefinite period. The agreement can, however, be terminated by either side at any time. Also, the dealer typically reserves the *right of substitution;* that is, he can take back securities he needs—because he has sold or wants to sell them—and give the lender other collateral.

The rate paid on an open repo, which often varies from day to day, is normally set slightly above the overnight repo rate. On an open repo, a dealer incurs smaller clearing costs than when he does a series of overnight repos; he is thus willing to pay up for money obtained on an open repo.

Rates on term repo

Dealers enter into term repo agreements to speculate—to create, for example, future securities they view as attractive.[2] Dealers and others also do huge amounts of term repo, when the structure of interest rates is such that cash-and-carry trades are profitable.[3] Some large banks use term repo to finance the longer governments in their portfolios to keep their book from being too short. Other large banks, however, rely strictly on overnight repo to finance their portfolios. Said one banker typical of the latter group, "We do mostly overnight repo and feel comfortable with that because the demand placed on us for collateral far exceeds the supply we have. We could repo our government portfolio two or three times over every day."

In the repo market, as in other markets, the yield curve normally slopes upward, but at the very short end of the market, the curve frequently inverts; in particular, the overnight rate is often a few basis points higher than the rate on 1- or 2-week repo. The reason is that short-period

---

[2] See Chapter 10, p. 128, and Appendix.
[3] See Chapter 10 Appendix.

repo competes with commercial paper for investors' dollars, while the overnight repo rate relates to the frequently higher dealer-loan rate that in turn keys off the Fed funds rate. Precisely what relationships exist among repo rates of differing maturities depends on the availability of financing to dealers and on the amount of collateral they have to finance.

In recent years, there has been an extraordinary increase in the amount of funding to dates—tax dates, oil payment dates, and the like— that corporations do, and corporations as a result have become big lenders in the term repo market. The oil companies in particular have to accumulate huge dollar sums to pay the OPEC nations; these funds have to be stockpiled somewhere, and a lot of them are put into term repo. Public bodies are another big source of money in the term repo market. For the investor wanting to fund to a specific date, a big attraction of term repo is that it can usually be done in size to any date he chooses; term repo thus eliminates the investor's need to scour the world for BAs or CDs maturing on his chosen date.

Right of substitution. In situations where they want it, dealers are normally willing to pay up a couple of basis points to obtain the right of substitution on a term repo. "Instead of 6.60, we might," noted one big dealer, "pay 6.62 to get the right of substitution. Some accounts will give us that right, others will not."

Figuring repo interest

The calculation of interest due on a repo at maturity is easy, since the repo rate is a *simple* interest rate quoted on the basis of a *360-day year.* To illustrate, look at the repo confirms, start and end, in Figure 15–2. The rate quoted on this repo is 6.25; the amount loaned is 49.8 million; and the transaction is outstanding one day. To obtain repo interest due, we simply multiply the repo rate (as a decimal) times the amount borrowed times an annualizing factor (the fraction of a 360-day year that the transaction is outstanding). This simple calculation,

$$\begin{pmatrix} \text{Repo interest} \\ \text{due} \end{pmatrix} = (0.0625)(\$49,800,000.00)\left(\frac{1}{360}\right)$$

$$= \$8,645.83$$

gives us a figure of $8,645.83 for interest due at maturity of the repo, a number that jibes with the number given in Figure 15–2B for repo interest due.

FIGURE 15–2
Confirms on an overnight repo: Sale and buy back
A. Repo leg one: Dealer sells bills

```
                    J.P. Morgan Securities Inc.
                       GOVERNMENT BOND DEPARTMENT
                       23 WALL STREET. NEW YORK. N Y 10015
                            TELEPHONE (212) 483-5271

                                              DATE PREPARED  TRADE DATE  TRANSACTION NO
  AS PRINCIPAL WE CONFIRM OUR SALE TO YOU     11/30/87 -  11/30/87   500345
QUANTITY        RATE    MATURITY DATE   PRICE      YIELD  BASIS            SETTLEMENT DATE
  50,000,000.00  6.25   12/01/1987   99.60                6.25            11/30/87
  REPURCHASE AGREEMENT                              PRINCIPAL       49,800,000.00

  USA TREASURY BILL

  DUE 12/31/1987
  CUSIP 912794NU4
  1 DAYS a  6.25000 %
              SECURITY NUMBER  SALESMAN CUSTOMER NO. ACCOUNT NUMBER
              95 RSA5C0345   130   648901        NET              49,800,000.00
              99 A19871231                        PAYMENT AND DELIVERY INSTRUCTIONS
         NORGES BANK
         P.O. BOX 1179 SENTRUM                    A.WIRE VS. FED FUNDS
         OSLO 1 NORWAY

  CONFIRMATION
                                                  151540 1 C CC0000000        0
```

B. Repo leg two: Dealer buys back bills

```
                    J.P. Morgan Securities Inc.
                       GOVERNMENT BOND DEPARTMENT
                       23 WALL STREET. NEW YORK. N Y 10015
                            TELEPHONE (212) 483-5271

                                              DATE PREPARED  TRADE DATE  TRANSACTION NO
  AS PRINCIPAL WE CONFIRM OUR PURCHASE FROM YOU   11/30/87   11/30/87   500345
QUANTITY        RATE    MATURITY DATE   PRICE      YIELD  BASIS            SETTLEMENT DATE
  50,000,000.00  6.25   12/01/1987   99.60                6.25            12/01/87
  REPURCHASE AGREEMENT                              PRINCIPAL       49,800,000.00

  USA TREASURY BILL

  DUE 12/31/1987
  CUSIP 912794NU4 INTEREST FROM 11/30/87 TO 12/01/87
  1 DAYS a  6.25000 %                             INTEREST AMOUNT       8,645.83
              SECURITY NUMBER  SALESMAN CUSTOMER NO. ACCOUNT NUMBER
              95 RSA50C345   130   648901        NET              49,808,645.83
              99 A19871231                        PAYMENT AND DELIVERY INSTRUCTIONS
         NORGES BANK
         70 PINE STREET                           A. WIRE VS. FED FUNDS
         NEW YORK, NEW YORK  10270

  CONFIRMATION
     DUPLICATE CONFIRMATION - INFORMATION ONLY    151540 1 C CC0000000        0
```

Maturity of repos

Whenever a dealer speaks of *the* repo rate, he's certain to be referring to the overnight repo rate. The majority—maybe 70%—of the repo a dealer does is overnight. About 20% has a week's maturity, the other 10% a longer maturity. Just what the maturity distribution of repo is depends a lot on investors' expectations with respect to the trend in interest rates. When rates seem to be falling off, investors in repo are more likely to want to extend, to do 2- and 3-month repos. Conversely, when rates appear to be rising, customers are likely to want to stay *short*—close to their cash.

REVERSE RATES

In talking about the rates at which reverses are done, we must distinguish between reverses of stock collateral and reverses of specials. Reverses of *stock collateral* are reverses in which the investor of money is interested only in receiving collateral that meets his general requirements (e.g., "I'd like short governments only, please."); in a reverse that is dubbed a *special,* the investor is interested in gaining control over a fixed amount of some *specific* issue—the current 2-year note or whatever.

Stock collateral

On reverses of stock collateral, whatever the maturity, prevailing rates are going to be pretty much identical to rates on repos of the same maturity; recall that one man's repo is another man's reverse. To this, we add that a big dealer who does both a lot of repos and a lot of reverses (see Chapter 16 on matched book) will, because his name is known well in the national repo market, be able to do repos of a given maturity at a rate some basis points below the rate he charges on reverses of that same maturity; in other words, he'll be able to *borrow* money at a rate slightly lower than the rate at which he *lends* it—and thereby, to earn a spread.

The specific issues market

Dealers go short for various reasons: as a speculation, to hedge a long position in a similar security, or to reduce their position so that they can make a big bid in a coming Treasury auction. The theory behind going into an auction short is that the new issue will, until it is distributed, yield more than outstanding issues; that, however, doesn't always occur when the Treasury is paying down its debt as it sometimes does, particularly on a seasonal basis. Whatever his motivation may be, a dealer who shorts a given issue has to obtain those securities somehow to make delivery. Often, the way he does so is by reversing them in rather than borrowing them.[4] Some widely placed issues are easy to find. Others he must hunt up on his own or with the help of a firm that brokers reverses.

The borrowers of collateral. The market for reverses to cover shorts is often referred to as the *specific or special issues* market because dealers shop in it for specific issues. Typically, a dealer won't find another dealer who has the particular issue he needs and who also wants to finance it for some period. So dealers are only a minor supplier of collateral to the specific issues market. There is also a second reason for this. Said one dealer, "I deal in specific issues only for myself. I will give them to some of my dealer friends but only because they will do the same for me. I try not to support the market for specific issues because I know that, if I give a guy $50 million year bills, he is shorting them and that is going to drive the market down. So all I am doing is hurting myself. If I can get an issue that is likely to be shorted in the future, I will hold it for myself."

The suppliers of collateral. The major suppliers of securities to (borrowers of money in) the specific issues and the general reverse markets are banks. This accounts for the fact that the top banks in the country, and in particular the top New York and Chicago banks, all borrow substantial sums from the dealers. Because banks reverse out so many securities to dealers, their net loans to dealers are much smaller than their total dealer loans.

S&Ls and certain other financial institutions are also large suppliers of collateral in the specific issues market. So too are a few municipalities and a few corporate portfolios. Reverses are, as noted, not well understood except by those who do them, so it is not surprising that one corporate portfolio manager commented, "I reverse out securities to dealers, but I never refer to it around the company as 'lending out' our valuable securities."

Reverses in the specific issues market usually have a term ranging from a week to a month. Some such reverses are, however, done on an open basis. If a customer of a dealer, perhaps another dealer, borrows securities from that dealer on an open basis, he has the right to send back those securities to the lending dealer any business day before 10 A.M. Also, if the lending dealer is trying to sell the securities, he can call up the borrower of the securities before 10 A.M. and say that he needs his securities back to make a delivery—that the repo is no longer open. Typically, the rate on an open reverse may vary from day to day.

---

[4] See final section of this chapter.

With respect to the clearing of an open reverse, note that a dealer's trader must put some maturity date on the ticket that opens the trade in order to get that ticket through the dealer's computer. One approach is to start the trade with an overnight maturity. In that case, each day that the trade is extended, a new close ticket must be written and the old close ticket killed. A simpler approach is for the dealer first to write the close date as infinity and then to issue a new close ticket, just one, when the end date of the open reverse is known. One dealer who does basically this begins by dating the maturity of any open reverse he does with six 9s, a number that his computer knows as infinity.

Activity in the specific issues market is greatest during a bear market because dealers increase their shorts during a declining market.

Commenting on this, one dealer noted: "At any time, carry is all over hell's half acre. It so happens that the 90-day bill is always at positive carry, but carry on it is nowhere near where you'd expect based on the Fed funds rate. There are squeezes and there are shortages. A reverse rate can look ridiculous but be real. Recently, I thought a particular bill issue looked as if it were becoming short in supply. I bought hundreds of millions of that issue, and next day, I financed all those bills at 1%. That seemed an absurd rate, but at the time, everyone wanted to borrow those bills; consequently, they could not be borrowed at a rate cheaper than 1%."

The reverse rate on specific issues. When a dealer lends out money as part of a transaction in which he is reversing in securities to

TABLE 15–2
Selected repo and reverse rates on January 22, 1987
(at that time, the year bill—the January 19, 1989,
bill—and the 10-year note—the 8⅞s of
11/15/97—were, as indicated by the rates quoted,
specials)*

Term	Type of transaction	Rate (%)
Open (day-to-day)	Repo of general collateral	6¼
	Reverse of general collateral	6⅜
	Reverse of the year bill	4
	Reverse of the 10-year note	5⅞
25 days (to auction of a new 10-year note)	Repo of general collateral	6½
	Reverse of general collateral	6.65
	Reverse of the year bill	5⅜
	Reverse of the 10-year note	4¼

* Often, for a given term of trade, the discrepancy between the reverse rate on a special issue and the reverse rate on general collateral is much greater than it was on the day these quotes were obtained.

cover a short, the rate he gets on his money is often significantly lower than the going rate for financing general collateral in the repo market. "The rate on a reverse depends," as one dealer noted, "on the availability of the securities taken in. In today's market, the repo rate available to an investor willing to take in any type of collateral is 8¼. If I reversed in the year bill to cover a short, I might get only 7.60 on my money. If, alternatively, I shorted something in more plentiful supply, I might get 8%. There are no standard relationships. It is entirely a question of demand and supply."

When supply of a specific issue becomes extremely tight, the reverse rate paid to someone reversing in that security may be full points—sometimes many points—below the prevailing repo rate (see Table 15–2).

THE BROKERING OF REPO

It used to be that little brokering of stock repo was done, that is, the repo normally done by dealers and banks to finance their positions and portfolios. Banks and dealers have a customer base with which they can do such transactions directly and efficiently. Also, they view repo as part of their customer line—one more thing they can show customers.

This has changed a great deal over the last decade. Today, dealers are using repo much more actively, not just as a financing tool, but as a trading tool. Half of the multibillion-dollar matched books that most dealers run are necessarily repo transactions. Dealers can do that volume of trading efficiently only by relying on brokers for a lot of the trading.

Noting the change in the way repo is used by dealers today, one broker, whose volume has multiplied rapidly noted: "The repo traders at many dealerships now view the repo market just like any other market. They will give you bids against securities and rates at which they will offer securities based on their expectation of rates. Today, our market is as actively traded as the CD or BA market."

Several major firms—Garvin GuyButler, Eurobrokers, MKI, Prebon, and Tullett Riley—dominate the brokering of repo and reverses, but a number of smaller shops are also in the business.

A broker's run

Repo brokers used to quote rates by giving runs over the phone. Then, like brokers of cash governments, they switched to putting their quotes on proprietary *screens (CRTs)*. Table 15–3 reproduces quotes from the Garvin GuyButler screen for August 19, 1987. Note that the top line on the screen quotes the time of day and the Fed funds rate: bid, asked, and

TABLE 15–3
Repo quotes, Garvin Guybutler screen, August 19, 1987

```
.REPO                              08:51 FF  6 5/8    6 11/16:@ 6 5/8
     O/N BILLS   6.53 (100) 6.45 (100) 1YR:BILL.9/03      ( )       ( )
     O/N (2YR    6.55 ( 50) 6.45 (OLD) 2YR:     8/31      ( )       ( )
     O/N (5YR    ( )        ( )        3YR:     1 WK      ( )    5.50(50)
     O/N (10YR   6.55 (100) ( )        4YR:     1 WK      ( )    5.875(OLD)
     O/N BONUS   ( )        ( )        5YR:     1 WK  6.25 (25)     ( )
     O/N AGENC   6.65 (15)  ( )        5YR:     1 MO      ( )       ( )
                 ( )        ( )        5YR:     2 MO      ( )       ( )
     3MO BILL.   ( )        ( )        5YR:     9/03  6.25 (25)5.75 (25)
     6MO BILL.   1.50 ( 25) ( )        7YR:     1 MO  5.875(25)     ( )
     1YR BILL.   6.25 ( 25) 6.00 ( 25) 7YR:     9/21  5.875(25)     ( )
     2YR         ( )        ( )        7YR:     0/05‡ 5.80 (25)5.00 (25)
     3YR         6.50 (OLD) 6.40 (OLD) 7YR:     D/30§     ( )       ( )
     4YR         6.125( 25) 5.875( 25) 10YR:    1 WK      ( )       ( )
     OLD5YR      ( )        6.25 ( 25) 10YR:    2 WK  6.45 (25)     ( )
     5YR         6.40 ( 25) 6.25 ( 25) 10YR:    1 MO      ( )       ( )
     7YR         3.50 ( 25) 3.00 ( 25) 10YR:    2 MO      ( )       ( )
     OLD 10YR    ( )        ( )        10YR:    3 MO      ( )       ( )
     10YR        ( )        6.375( 25) 10YR:    N/16  5.50 (OLD)5.20(OLD)
     OLD. LB.†   6.45 ( 25) 6.375( 25) LB.      1 MO      ( )       ( )
     LB          ( )        6.375(100) LB.      2 MO      ( )       ( )
                                       LB       4 MO  6.00 (25)     ( )
                                       LB       N/16‖ 5.45 (25)5.30 (25)

  Bid or reverse level    Offer or repo level
```

* Bid or offer goes "old" after 10 minutes in open market, 20 minutes in term market.
† Long bond.
‡ 10/5.
§ December 30.
‖ November 16.

last. The first six lines of the left-hand side of the body of the table quote *overnight (O/N)* rates (bid and asked) for different classes of collateral—Treasuries of different maturities and agencies. The amounts inside the parentheses give the amount in millions that are bid or offered at the quoted rate. A bid or offer goes "old"—is no longer good unless reconfirmed—after 10 minutes in the open market, after 20 minutes in the term market.

The quotes on the lower left-hand side of Table 15–3 give bids and offers for particular issues. Observe that the rate on *the* 7-year note on the date in question was 3.50 (bid on a reverse)—3.00 (asked), well below the 6%-plus rate on stock collateral. Obviously, the current 7-year note was at the time a special.

The quotes on the right-hand side of Table 15–3 show the rates bid and asked on *term* repos to be done at various maturities against various collateral.

Give-up-name versus principal brokers

Except for Garvin, brokers of repo and reverse all act on a give-up-name basis: they cross a trade; they then tell each of the two parties to the trade who their counterparty is; and they leave it to these two parties to clear this trade. Note this modus operandi is akin to what goes on in the brokering of Fed funds and Euro time deposits.

Garvin, the exception, acts, often though not always, as a principal when it brokers repo and reverse: it takes in, against money, securities from the giver of collateral and then delivers out those securities, again against money, to the party who is the ultimate lender of money. Repo brokers other than Garvin have preferred not to act as principal for several reasons. First, they reason that, to act as principal, they would have to set up a big organization just to clear trades on which they usually earn at most a modest fee. Also, acting as principal would expose them to *delivery risk;* a broker who takes in, as principal, either securities serving as repo collateral or special issues must redeliver those securities on a timely basis—make "good delivery"—or he will be stuck financing those securities overnight. If a broker gets stuck this way on a big trade, there may go his week's earnings. "We have," said a man on the repo desk of a major dealer, "done that to Garvin several times without meaning to. We get in securities at the last second and deliver them out to Garvin, who gets them too late to turn them around and ends up having to finance them. If Garvin gets stuck with 100 million over the weekend, that will wipe out a whole week's profits." Garvin also incurs some credit risk by dealing as principal: What if one counterparty in a trade it brokers does not or cannot hold up its end of the deal struck?

An interesting question is: What is the position of a principal broker—is he acting as agent or truly principal? Dealers are wont to say, "He's acting as principal, and he's on the hook if a trade he has brokered does not go through." Such a broker argues, on the other hand, that he is merely an agent in bringing two parties together, and that whether the trade goes through on the agreed-upon terms is the responsibility of these parties.

One reason a dealer may prefer to use Garvin rather than a give-up-name broker of repo is because it wants anonymity. "If," said one big dealer, "we have 100 million of an issue and do not want anyone to know who owns the issue, we will use Garvin to fund [repo] that position."

Brokering fees

A broker collects a fee of 5 basis points (an 05) on overnight repos of stock collateral and also on specials in which he works on a give-up-name basis; usually, the broker collects this fee from both sides of the trade. On term trades, say 2- or 3-week repos, the broker collects around an 02; we say "around" because brokerage on a term repo is not fixed. While the brokerage rate is lower on a term trade than on an overnight trade, brokering a term trade is likely to prove richer for the broker than brokering an overnight trade because of the term trade's longer maturity.

To illustrate, suppose that a broker arranges a 10 million repo of the 14s of 11, which are priced—we assume to keep the numbers round—precisely at 150. His fee will be figured on a 15 million trade. If that trade is overnight, his fee will be an 05 from both sides, for one day; in dollars this works out to:

$$(.0005 + .0005)(\$15 \text{ million}) \left(\frac{1}{360}\right) = \$41.67$$

If, alternatively, the repo broker arranges the same exchange of collateral for money at an 02 on a 1-week term trade, his fee on the trade will be 2 basis points from each side on $15 million for seven days. In dollars this amounts to:

$$(.0002 + .0002)(\$15 \text{ million}) \left(\frac{7}{360}\right) = \$116.67$$

Contribution of the brokers

Repo brokers, just like brokers of other money market instruments, provide for a fee an information—communications—service. Because there are so many players in the repo-reverse market, it is clear that brokers, by providing such a service, are giving to their clients information on rates and on the availability of and demand for collateral that is more accurate and timely than would be the information that these clients could obtain by acting on their own. One trader, echoing this conclusion, observed: "With the brokers, you can see the market on a screen. If you are looking for an issue, instead of calling five dealers, you can just go to the screen and find where the issue is being offered or, if it is not, you can put a bid on the screen. Brokers make the repo market more efficient; this market now trades, at times, almost like the bill market with the bid and offer rates separated only by an 01."

Increased market efficiency notwithstanding, brokers of repo are unpopular with some dealers. In the cash market, brokers, with the exception of Cantor, give access to their screens to only the primary and aspiring (to be primary) dealers, a universe of 50-plus firms. Dealers like this arrangement because it gives them their own *inside market* from which their retail customers are excluded. Brokers of repo have, like Cantor in the cash market, gone national: they give access to their screens to regional banks, who have traditionally been retail customers of big dealers. It used to be that a regional bank that had 100 million of an issue that it wanted to put out for a week had to go through one of the dealers. Now, a regional bank can do this trade direct. Consequently, big dealers have lost some retail business that, in their view, rightly ought to remain theirs.

THE BROKERING OF REVERSES

Dealers who want to reverse in a specific issue will often turn to a broker of repo and reverses. Such brokers make it their business to know where various special issues are and at what rates they can be reversed in. The brokers are efficient in this area and can often get bonds for a dealer at as good a rate as he would if he could find the bonds. A repo-reverse broker acts in effect as a commission salesman for the dealers; if he finds bonds, he earns a commission or a spread; if he does not, he is paid nothing for his trouble.

The brokers try not to take bonds from one dealer and give them to another. The dealers talk to each other and could arrange trades of this sort themselves. As a rule, the brokers will try to pull specific issues out of regional banks, S&Ls, and other smaller portfolios. In doing so, they are using their own special knowledge and thus providing a real service to the dealers.

When a broker acts on a give-up-name basis in a reverse transaction, he gets the fees described above. When he acts as a principal in a reverse transaction, he works for whatever spread he can get; normally it ranges from an 01 to ⅛, with the average being 1/16. If, however, the broker finds a firm that wants to repo stock collateral and another that wants to borrow the same collateral as a special, he might be able to earn ¼.

In covering a short, a dealer won't go first to the brokers' market. Typically, he will first try in-house accounts: see if he can get the securities he needs from one of his retail accounts—an insurance company, a credit union, or a pension fund. If not, he will often talk directly to other dealers such as Sali. If he still can't find the issue, he will then go through a broker, maybe put a bid on a broker's screen. In this respect, it's worth noting that a dealer does not necessarily try to cover every inadvertent short. "The way we work," said one dealer, "is that, if we bought 100 million and then sold it and the 100 million did not come in, we would not try to cover our resulting fail: if the 100 doesn't come in, the 100 doesn't go out; and we end up with offsetting fails. If, however, we bought 4 by 25, sold 2 by 50, and only 75 came in, we might borrow 25 as a hedge to ensure that we'd be able to deliver out all of the 75 that did come in. In covering such shorts, it would be rare that we did not show our needs to another dealer."

Many of a dealer's shorts are created by traders as a speculation, as part of an arbitrage, or as a hedge. For example, some of a dealer's shorts are shorts he creates in Treasuries to hedge his positions in other types of security. In particular, a dealer's trades of mortgage-backed securities often short the 10-year note to hedge—albeit imperfectly— their positions; similarly, traders of muni notes and corporate bonds commonly hedge their positions by shorting a Treasury issue or issues. A dealer's retail business with customers in Treasuries may also lead a dealer to short Treasuries. For example, a customer might come in and sell a dealer an off-the-run, 2-year note. If he did, the dealer might cover his resulting long position in that off-the-run note by shorting the current 2-year note; by doing so, the dealer would end up net, net flat, and consequently, he'd have negligible market risk.

Most of the shorts that a dealer creates to hedge as well as the shorts that its arbitrage desk creates turn out to be in *active* or *current* (i.e., most recently auctioned) issues. There is a reason: traders like to be in the *fast lane*: to establish shorts in active issues, like the current 10-year and current 2-year notes. The advantage of shorting active issues is that such issues are the easiest issues to buy back, and every short must, one day, be covered.

The brokering of reverses to portfolio managers

When a portfolio manager does a reverse, it's often because some broker has presented that trade to him as part of an arbitrage. Typically, a broker who does this brokers a range of money market instruments; he is thus in a good position both to point out attractive arbitrage opportunities to an investor and to provide that investor with "one-stop shopping." A broker of such reverses must be a salesman as opposed to someone who is just fast on the phone: he must convince the customer to take in money and simultaneously to put it out elsewhere.

"We do not," commented one such broker, "just go in and say: 'Hi. 30, 60, 90 days at 30, 45, and 55. Do you want to add $25 million?' We have to show people a reason to do a reverse. To be a good reverse broker, you have to know as many alternative uses as possible for money, to have a working knowledge of and a feel for more areas than in any other money market job.

"You do not just walk in and do a trade with a guy, and you do not take no for an answer. There is some rate at which a trade will go. To put together a trade on which you make money takes time and work. You have to know what your customer can do in terms of investments and what the lender is going to demand in terms of margin. Every trade that is agreed upon with respect to amount and rate is done subject to *pricing*.[5] Different accounts demand different amounts of margin. Sometimes we can't get a trade off because the two sides are half a point away on the pricing. If we get in a bind on pricing, we just start all over again."

In the brokers' market for repo and in the market in general, trades are agreed upon for round-lot sums, for example, $10 million. Then the precise amount of the loan is calculated, taking into account pricing and the way the agreement is set up. Thus, on a $10 million trade, the dollars lent might be more or less than $10 million.

Brokers' screens

Brokers' screens for a given instrument, such as reverses, usually do not show precisely the same information for several reasons. First, each dealer probably uses at most several brokers, so the bid and offers any one broker shows reflect in part what his particular client base is or is not doing. Second, in the case of reverses, the trade involves so many variables—What is the term? What is the collateral? Is the issue a special?—that it would be odd indeed if two brokers of reverses came up with identical formats for their screens. In Tables 15–4 and 15–5, we give the screens of two more brokers of reverse, MKI and RMJ Securities.

In comparing the rates in Tables 15–4 and 15–5 (all for the same day), note that while rates quoted by different brokers for identical or nearly identical trades are not always precisely the same, these rates must, due to competition and comparative shopping, be extremely close to each other.

BORROWING VERSUS REVERSING IN SECURITIES

Earlier, we said that a dealer, who for one reason or another is short securities that he needs in order to make deliveries, can, in governments at least, usually avoid a fail to deliver either by reversing in or borrowing securities. In this section, we describe briefly the mechanics of each procedure, its pros, and its cons.

Throughout this discussion, it will help the reader to bear in mind that the difference between a reverse and a borrowing of securities is simply this: *In securities lending, the investor swaps collateral for collateral; in a reverse, he swaps collateral for money.*

---

[5] *Pricing* refers here to the value that will be assigned to the securities reversed out. Margin is created for the lender in a reverse transaction by pricing the securities below market value plus accrued interest.

TABLE 15–4
Reverse quotes, MKI Securities, August 19, 1987

PREBON*		PREBONFF	6 5/8 6 11/16 6 5/8		
TERM			**TERM SPECIALS**		
ON	6.50 -6.45	100 +x100	1YR9-3§	-5.125	x25
ON	-6.40	x100TB†	02YR1WK	6.35-6.125	100x40
1WK	6.60 -6.50	25(5‡x25(5	2YR1WK	-5.00	x25
2WK	6.60 -6.45	25(5 x25(5	2YR8-31	5.90 -5.70	25x25
3WK	6.60 -6.45	25(5 x25(5	2YR9-1	5.90 -5.75	25x25
1MO	6.58 -6.50	25(2 x25(5	3YR11-16	6.10 -	100x
2MO	6.625-6.50	25(5 x25(5	4YR1WK	6.20 -5.65	25x25
3MO	6.63 -6.60	50(5 x50(5	4YR2WK	-	x
6MO	-	x	4YR1MO	-5.65	x25
OPEN SPECIALS			5YR9-3	6.25 -	25x
3MO	-	x	7YR1WK	-4.50	x*25
6MO	-	x	7YR2WK	6.25 -5.125	25x25
1YR	-6.00	x25	7YR9-21	5.75 -5.30	25x25
2YR	5.50 -5.00	50 x25	7YR10-5	5.65 -5.20	25x50
3YR	-6.40	x25	7YR12-30	-	x
4YR	6.125-5.875	35 x*25	10YR1MO	-	x
5YR	6.375-6.25	25 x25	10YR2MO	5.875-	25x
7YR	3.875-3.125	50 x25	10YR11-16	5.55 -	25x
10YR	-6.40	x50	LB‖1WK	-	x
LB	-	x	LB1MO	-	x
07YR	-	x	LB2MO	-	x
0LB	-6.375	x25	LB11-16	5.45 -5.30	25x25
TB7-7	-	x	LB4MO	5.90 -5.35	25x25
				09:27:3090	

* Prebon quotes, Fed funds.
† TB—Treasury bills.
‡ 25[25 million in five 5 million pieces.
§ Old 2-year note, 7⅜s 6/89.
‖ LB—long bond.

Reversing in securities

One man's repo is always another man's reverse: the two transactions really amount to the same thing. When a dealer does a repo he is looking to borrow money; when he does a reverse, he is looking to borrow securities. The quid pro quo that a dealer seeking to borrow securities, via a reverse, offers to the lender of the securities is a loan of money. If this seems confusing, recall that the economic substance of either a repo or a reverse is always that the transaction, whatever it is called, is a *collateralized loan.* Also, whether a transaction is called a repo or a reverse, it is always the lender of money who gets margin.

Generally, a dealer will reverse in securities on an *open* basis, which means that the transaction can be terminated at the request of either party; and, if the party wanting to terminate the transaction calls before 10 A.M., the securities become returnable the same day. Most securities

TABLE 15–5
Reverse quotes, RMJ Securities, August 19, 1987

8/19/87				9:26:35
GOVERNMENT SPECIALS		TERM SPECIALS		
3MO		O/N BILLS 6.55	(100)-6.45(OLD)Bills	
6MO	1.00 (25)	1 YR 8-25		
YEAR	6.25 (25)-6.00(25)	1 YR 8-27	6.00 (50)-5.00 (50)	
2 YR	5.45 (60)-5.15 50	1 YR 9-3	-5.00 (25)	
3 YR	6.50 (50)-6.30 50	2 YR 5DY	5.75 (25)	
4 YR		2 YR 6DY	-5.375(25)	
6 5/8 5-92 .		2 YR 1WK	-5.25 (50)	
5 YR	6.35 (25)-6.25(25)	2 YR 8-31	5.875(25)-5.65 (25)	
7% 4-94		2 YR 1MO		
7 YR	3.875(OLD)	3 YR 1WK	-6.30 (25)	
8 1/2 5-97	6.375(20)-6.20(25)	4 YR 1WK	6.125(25)-5.75 (25)	
10 YR		4 YR 1MO	-5.40 (25)	
8 3/4 5-17	-6.40(36)	5 YR 1WK	6.25(OLD)-5.625(25)	
BOND	6.50 (25)-6.25 25	5 YR 9-3	-5.875(25)	
OFF THE RUN		5 YR 1MO	6.45(OLD)-6.125(25)	
12 5/8 11-87	6.45 (31)-5.75(25)	5 YR 2MO	6.50(OLD)-6.20 (25)	
12 3/8 1-88		7 HR 1WK		
12-31	6.50 (10)	7 YR 2WK	5.80 (25)-4.60 (25)	
7 7/8 5-90	6.50 (35)-6.375(30)	7 YR 9-21	5.65 (25)-5.35 (OLD)	
12 8-13	6.125(15)-5.90 15	7 YR 10-5	5.65 (25)-5.25 (25)	
9-8	6.25 (25)-5.50 (25)	10 YR 1MO		
12 1/2 6-14	-5.00(OLD)	BOND 2MO		
11-05		BOND 11-16		

lending programs operate this way, but some have requirements for next-day termination.

Sometimes, a dealer will do a *term* reverse: take an issue that he thinks—hopes—will become hot and tie it up on term for at least a week. Often, the trader who does this is speculating that the issue will become hot, be shorted by traders, and therefore become *tight* in supply; if this occurs, the issue becomes what is known as a *special:* an issue that is in such demand that it can be reversed out (used to borrow money) at a rate below—perhaps full points below—the repo rate. The trader who wins on such a speculation ends up lending money, when he reverses in securities, at a rate well above the rate at which he borrows money when he subsequently reverses out those same securities. In other words, he ends up earning a positive spread on a two-legged arbitrage.

Borrowing securities

When a dealer borrows securities, it is often from a very conservative portfolio that wants full protection from risk. The standard arrangement is that the dealer borrowing, say, $10 million of Treasuries gives the lender of securities $10.2 million of other securities as collateral for his borrowing. He also pays the lender of securities a fee of 50 basis points.

A special aspect of a borrowing of securities is that the margin resembles that on a repo, but it goes to the lender not of money, but of securities. The reason that the borrower of securities ends up becoming the giver of margin is that the transaction is driven by his need to borrow securities. A dealer, if he wants to have a viable program for borrowing to cover shorts, must be able to go to an institution holding securities and say, "Look, if you will lend me your bonds, I will make that an extremely safe and attractive transaction for you. I will pay you a fee of 50 basis points so that you don't have to worry about arbitrage, market conditions, reinvestment, timing, moving monies, and so forth. Also, I will give you protection in the form of collateral equal to 102% of the value of the bonds you lend me; and I will maintain that 102% level of collateralization over the life of the transaction."

Historically, banks have been the biggest and best-organized lenders of securities. They provide institutional custody, and to make their fees palatable to their customers, they offer a securities-lending service. This is a natural for such banks. They have easy access to the securities and records of what securities are in whose portfolios. Custody banks are not so good at investing the proceeds of a repo, so they would just as soon, if they are lending securities to a dealer, lend for collateral and a borrowing fee of 50 basis points. That fee is split between the bank and the bank's customer.

While custody banks have taken the lead in securities lending, they have preferred to do that business as *agent for an undisclosed third party* rather than to disclose to the dealer what portfolio is on the other side of the transaction. One motive a bank has for doing this is that it does not want a dealer, who has borrowed securities from one of its custody customers, to go directly to that customer should the dealer need those same securities a second time. A bank could achieve the same objective by acting as principal in the transaction, but a number of banks have been unwilling to accept the full responsibility for the risks to them that would be inherent in their securities-lending business if they acted as a principal. This situation has made some dealers—post the Drysdale failure, which involved big borrowings of securities and big losses—cautious about which banks they will deal with when they either lend or borrow securities.

Coupon interest and full accrual pricing

Whenever securities pass temporarily, via either a reverse or a borrowing, from one party to another, the current market practice is to price those securities at market plus accrued interest: to use what is called *full accrual pricing* in setting the terms on which particular securities are exchanged either for money or for other securities. If it happens that during the holding period, a coupon date occurs, the coupon interest is paid to the temporary holder of the securities, who is obligated to pass on that interest to the true owner of the securities. Normally, after a coupon payment, the transaction is repriced so that the originally agreed upon haircut is maintained. These arrangements are designed to minimize credit risk.

Which to do and why

Some years ago, the market swung in favor of reverse repos over borrowing securities. The primary advantage of a reverse repo over a borrowing of securities is that a reverse is operationally simpler: A reverse requires only *one* delivery of securities, whereas a borrowing requires *two* deliveries. Just the same, both types of transactions commonly occur depending on the particular circumstances under which a deal is struck.

Normally, an investor dealing directly with a dealer won't want to go to the bother and cost of doing a reverse unless he can pick up at least 50 basis points on the deal. Often, an investor holding securities has an arbitrage lined up where he expects to get at least a 50-basis-point spread between the rate at which he borrows money from the dealer and the rate at which he can invest that money. Such an investor will want to reverse out, rather than lend, securities to a dealer. In the other cases, the investor says, "Give me collateral, not money, and I'll take my 50 basis points as a fee." Some investors won't do reverses because they lack reinvestment capabilities and don't, therefore, want cash.

Some investors are set up both to reverse out and to lend securities. They will go the reverse route if the spread on the arb is more than 50 basis points. If it is not, they will go the securities-lending route.

A dealer wanting to cover his shorts must be prepared to go both ways, to reverse in securities or to borrow them. How a given deal is struck involves both an investor, who holds securities, and a dealer, who wants securities, responding to relative rates and to availability in deciding what they want to do.

Since a lot of borrowing of securities by dealers is done to prevent "fails to receive" from creating "fails to deliver," a lot of dealers borrow securities from other dealers 10 minutes before the close of the Fed wire or during the *reversal period* (at the end of the day, banks are given a half-hour period to DK any incorrect deliveries that may have been made to them).

THE NEXT CHAPTER

In the next chapter, we turn to one of the most interesting phenomena that the rebirth post–World War II of the repo market hath wrought, namely the creation by major dealers of multibillion-dollar matched books in repo and reverse. In operating such a book, a dealer becomes in part a financial intermediary—a mini (maybe "medium-size" would be a better choice of words) bank of sorts.

Chapter 16

Matched book: Operation

MATCHED BOOK IS AN INCIDENTAL, but important, side effect of the invention of repo. Once the repo trade was designed and done by traders, it was inevitable that the flip side of this trade, reverses, would also be done by them and that the world of matched book would be with us.

In this chapter, we talk about a dealer's matched book and several topics to which such a discussion naturally leads: liquidity, interest rate exposure, the financing of dealer positions, and profit maximization by dealers.

MATCHED BOOK

The term *matched book* describes offsetting positions in repos and reverses that a dealer creates by reversing in securities and simultaneously "hanging them out" on the other side: by matching his *reverses-in* of securities with *repos-out* of the identical securities. Part of the impetus for the development by big dealers of huge matched books came from the failure of Financial Corp.; this failure made investors wary of engaging in a repo transaction with a firm whose name and credit were not well known to them.[1] Firms that subsequently experienced

---

[1] For a discussion of the failure of Financial Corp., see pp. 209–11.

some difficulty in borrowing directly from retail in their own name began to borrow from big dealers.

Fed statistics on dealers repos and reverses

Today, the running of matched books has become a big business, one that accounts for many billions of the assets and liabilities on the books of every major dealer. While no statistics are collected on matched book per se—a feat that would be difficult, since different dealers tot up different things in measuring their matched books—Fed statistics on dealer repos and reverses are revealing (Figure 16–1). These statistics

FIGURE 16–1
Average daily repos and reverses by U.S. government securities dealers ($ billions)

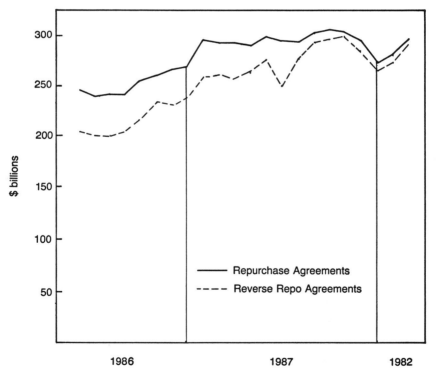

show that the reporting dealers were, on an average day in the fall of 1987, borrowing in the repo market $300 billion, while at the same time, they were lending in the reverse market almost as much—$295 billion.

Those are big numbers. To put them in perspective, we note that, in October 1987, a mere 5 billion of the total 300 billion that reporting dealers were raising in the repo market failed to be matched by reverses on the other side. This 5 billion, a mere 1.7% of the 300 billion dealers were sourcing in the repo market, represents the net amount dealers were borrowing in this market to finance their positions. Just what those positions were is interesting. In October 1987, reporting dealers were net *short* 15.4 billion of Treasury securities; their long positions were all in agency securities (34.0 billion), in CDs (7.5 billion), in BAs (2.9 billion), and in commercial paper (7.4 billion). As Table 16–1 shows, the numbers we have cited vary widely from one reporting period to another; this is natural because what amounts of what securities dealers want to be long or short depends largely on two constantly changing variables—dealers' perceptions of *current* market conditions and dealers' expectations with respect to *future* market conditions.

While the numbers in Table 16–1 vary widely from period to period, they display constancy in several key respects: first, dealer participation in the repo and reverse markets is predominately matched-book trading; second, the volume of such trading has expanded over the last several years at a torrid pace.

Source to dealers of collateral

Today, minor dealers supply some collateral to the dealers who run books in repo. Banks are another big source. Said one dealer: "The banks who supply the collateral are not the New York City banks. It is the superliquid regional banks like the Wilmington Trust, Seattle First, the U.S. National Bank of Oregon. Such banks have large portfolios for their size. They do not trade these portfolios actively; instead they make long-term investments which seem to suit at the time they make them. If the securities later go under or above water, it does not really matter to them because they are running a standard, old-fashioned government portfolio; and they are going to hold onto these securities forever. If they have some 8s of 94, they will have them until 1994 with 90 degree probability. If the liability manager at such a bank sees an opportunity to sell 90-day Euros at 8.25%, he will come into the market and ask a dealer, 'What will you lend me against $29 million 8s of 94?' Frequently such banks are able to borrow locally at below-market rates but only in small amounts. When they want big money they have to come to the Street. I might offer a lend to him at 7.75. If he took the money, he would probably also use the offices of my firm to sell his Euros."

Aggressive corporate portfolio managers, S&L managers, and others also supply collateral to the dealers. The collateral offered here is stock collateral that the dealer takes in, not because he wants to short particular issues, but because he can refinance that collateral at a profitable spread.

TABLE 16–1
U.S. Government securities dealers Positions and Financing (averages of daily figures, in billions of dollars)[1]

Item	1984	1985	1986	1987						
				Apr.	May	June	July	Aug.	Sept.	Oct.
				Positions						
Net immediate[2]										
1 U.S. Treasury securities	5.4	7.4	13.1	−7.0	−13.5	−8.0	−8.9	−10.9	−23.3	−15.4
2 Bills	5.5	10.0	12.7	−.8	−5.9	2.3	5.0	5.6	2.40	7.3
3 Other within 1 year	.06	1.0	3.7	3.1	3.5	2.1	1.3	.5	−.76	−.6
4 1–5 years	2.2	5.1	9.3	2.5	1.1	.4	−2.3	−6.0	−10.1	−4.9
5 5–10 years	−1.1	−6.2	−9.5	−5.9	−7.6	−7.5	−7.0	−5.7	−8.1	−8.7
6 Over 10 years	−1.2	−2.7	−3.2	−5.8	−4.5	−5.2	−5.8	−5.0	−6.7	−8.4
7 Federal agency securities	15.3	22.9	33.1	32.9	32.8	31.9	33.2	33.3	33.7	34.0
8 Certificates of deposit	7.4	9.2	10.6	8.5	9.0	8.6	7.4	7.9	8.0	7.5
9 Bankers' acceptances	3.9	4.6	5.5	3.7	3.7	3.8	3.2	3.4	3.0	2.9
10 Commercial paper	3.8	5.6	8.1	6.3	6.6	7.2	6.5	5.8	6.4	7.4
Futures positions										
11 Treasury bills	−4.5	−7.3	−18.1	−5.0	1.8	−.6	.9	−2.0	−.2	2.5
12 Treasury coupons	1.8	4.5	3.5	3.9	2.6	3.2	6.2	6.3	7.3	8.8
13 Federal agency securities	.2	−.7	−.2	−.095	−.098	−.1	−.1	−.95	−.09	−.1

Forward positions										
14 U.S. Treasury securities	-1.6	-.9	-2.3	-2.4	-4.3	-.9	-1.8	-1.9	-.19	.2
15 Federal agency securities	-9.2	-9.4	-11.9	-15.8	-20.3	-19.2	-20.2	-22.4	-21.8	-22.8
Financing[3]										
Reverse repurchase agreements[4]										
16 Overnight and continuing	44.1	68.0	99.0	129.4	122.1	100.7	124.9	128.1	139.8	131.2
17 Term agreements	68.3	80.5	108.7	133.8	151.1	149.7	150.3	160.7	164.7	164.4
Repurchase agreements[5]										
18 Overnight and continuing	75.7	101.4	141.7	176.3	165.7	172.5	168.9	174.2	182.5	177.0
19 Term	57.0	70.0	102.6	108.8	124.6	121.8	120.2	127.4	125.7	123.4

1. Data for dealer positions and sources of financing are obtained from reports submitted to the Federal Reserve Bank of New York by the U.S. Treasury securities dealers on its published list of primary dealers. Data for positions are averages of daily figures, in terms of par value, based on the number of trading days in the period. Positions are net amounts and are shown on a commitment basis. Data for financing are in terms of actual amounts borrowed or lent and are based on Wednesday figures.

2. Immediate positions are net amounts (in terms of par values) of securities owned by nonbank dealer firms and dealer departments of commercial banks on a commitment, that is, trade-date basis, including any such securities that have been sold under agreements to repurchase (RPs). The maturities of some repurchase agreements are sufficiently long, however, to suggest that the securities involved are not available for trading purposes. Immediate positions include reverses to maturity, which are securities that were sold after having been obtained under reverse repurchase agreements that mature on the same day as the securities. Data for immediate positions do not include forward positions.

3. Figures cover financing involving U.S. Treasury and federal agency securities, negotiable CDs, bankers' acceptances, and commercial paper.

4. Includes all reverse repurchase agreements, including those that have been arranged to make delivery on short sales and those for which the securities obtained have been used as collateral on borrowings, that is, matched agreements.

5. Includes both repurchase agreements undertaken to finance positions and "matched-book" repurchase agreements.

NOTE. Data on positions for the period May 1 to September 30, 1986, are partially estimated.
Source: *Federal Reserve Bulletin.*

Functions of matched book

Strictly speaking, matched book refers to a dealer's lending and borrowing against identical securities. In practice, however, dealers tend to regard a wider range of transactions as part of their matched book. Also, dealers have learned to *mismatch* their *matched* books: to mismatch asset and liability maturities in their books in order to turn those books into a play or bet on the direction of interest rates. The upshot of the above is that a dealer's repo desk may regard its "matched-book" responsibilities as comprising as many as five distinct things.

FINANCING THE DEALER'S POSITION

Typically, a dealer's repo desk is first responsible for financing as much of the dealer's long position, normal inventory plus trading positions, as possible. For dealers, repo is the cheapest money around; the overnight repo rate on government collateral is normally a spread *below* the Fed funds rate, whereas the dealer loan rate at New York clearing banks is a spread *above* the funds rate (recall Figure 15–1). Most big dealers work the repo market hard, financing there every bit of inventory they can. A good dealer will finance at his clearing bank at its posted dealer loan rate only odds and ends that cannot, often because of transaction costs, be economically repoed.

Sometimes a trader will borrow (or reverse in) securities not because he is short those securities, but because he thinks he might want to short those securities in the future as the market breaks; if he does this, he will cover his cost of borrowing (recoup the money he has lent) by relending (repoing) the securities he has taken in until he decides to short them. Running a matched book gives a dealer tremendous flexibility.

From the above comments, it is obvious that a dealer who, to cover a short, borrows or reverses in securities for a fixed period is not constrained to wait until the end of that period to buy the issue he has shorted as he eventually must. He can liquidate, without penalty, his short before his borrowing or reverse terminates simply by doing an offsetting trade for the remaining term of his borrowing or reverse. For example, if a dealer who has shorted an issue and covered that short by doing a reverse for some number of days decides to liquidate his short by buying the issue, he simply repos the securities he is purchasing until the end of the reverse and then delivers those securities to the party with whom he did the reverse. With a matched book, many things become not only possible, but simple to do.

Here's another example: a matched-book trader who anticipates that the Street will short an issue and force that issue to become a special in the reverse market can bet on this happening by reversing in the issue while it is still in plentiful supply. Said one practitioner of this art: "I think of a reverse book as reversing in what you think you will become scarce and then lending it out and collecting a nice spread, maybe five points on a good day." (Recall Table 15–2, p. 262.)

COVERING SHORTS

A second responsibility of a dealer's repo or matched-book desk is to cover the dealer's shorts by reversing in securities that the dealer then uses to make good delivery of securities that he has sold, but does not own. When a dealer does a reverse to cover a short, his obvious objective is to obtain control over a specific amount of specific collateral.

A reverse to cover a short contrasts sharply with most repos. Normally, control over collateral is not a key element in a repo trade; the lender of money demands collateral only to limit his credit risk, and any concern he has over which collateral he gets, bills or 30-year bonds, exists only because of a credit-risk concern: If his counterparty in the trade were to go bankrupt, would his collateral—which, in that event, he would immediately sell—be liquid, and to what market risk might holding that collateral, even briefly, expose him?

ACTING AS A FINANCIAL INTERMEDIARY

When dealers moved from using repos simply to finance their positions to using repos to run matched books, they took a giant step: they diversified in a big way into a new-to-them business, financial intermediation. A *financial intermediary* is an institution that (1) solicits funds from funds-surplus units in exchange for claims against itself and (2) passes on those funds to funds-deficit units in exchange for claims against the latter. Banks, S&Ls, credit unions, life insurance companies, mutual funds, and other financial institutions are all financial intermediaries; so too is a dealer to the extent that he does matched book.

The matched part of matched book is taking in collateral (any old collateral will do), hanging out that collateral on the other side, and "taking the middle." Borrowing funds at one rate and relending them at a *higher* rate to earn a spread—that's what dealers running matched books do—is pure and simple, for-profit financial intermediation.

Primary dealers include among their ranks firms such as Discount, Sali, Goldman, and Merrill, who can borrow with ease many billions of dollars apiece in the national repo market. The big lenders in the repo market know the names and the credits of these dealers, and they are happy to deal with and make secured loans to them. The same is not true for many other would-be borrowers in the repo market: small dealers, small banks, and S&Ls.

Most money market investors have no interest in and little appetite for assuming credit risk. They see themselves as stewards of funds earmarked for other purposes down the road; they seek to earn a high return on these funds, but they correctly perceive that it would be inappropriate for them to assume, in their search for return, credit risk of any sort. The aversion to credit risk on the part of short-term portfolio managers is clearly reflected in the assets they acquire: governments (no credit risk), federal agency securities (*de jure* or de facto guarantee by the federal government), liabilities of top U.S. banks (de facto guarantee of the central bank), muni notes (mostly general obligation securities of top-rated issuers), top-rated commercial paper, preferably of firms whose bonds have a triple A rating.

The aversion of short-term portfolio managers to credit risk combined with the desire of many smaller institutions to borrow in the repo market created the opportunity for major dealers to become, as part of their matched-book operations, credit intermediaries. The manager of a big corporate liquidity portfolio does not want to worry about the creditworthiness of small dealer X or of small bank Y of whom he has never heard. However, a major dealer with its credit department is willing to evaluate and assume the risk of dealing with these credits in order to earn the spread it gets between the reverse rate it charges smaller borrowers and the repo rate at which it can borrow from large investors.

Actually, large dealers assume little credit risk in lending, in part, to smaller borrowers. These dealers are protected not only by their credit departments, but, more important, by the collateral they require borrowers to deliver to them and by their practice of taking and monitoring margin.

Capturing the middle is not the only benefit a big dealer gets from providing repo money (via reverses) to smaller institutions. Large dealers get additional business, trading and retail, from the smaller dealers and financial institutions to whom they provide credit.

Fattening the spread

The spread at which a dealer puts on a matched-book trade is not necessarily fixed in stone. Suppose, for example, that our dealer takes in collateral for a month and simultaneously repos, with the right of substitution, that collateral for a month. Later, our dealer gets a call from a bank or another dealer saying that it needs the specific issue our dealer has out on repo for a month.

Whenever a party asks for *specific* collateral, he will have to pay a price—to lend money cheaply—to get that collateral. Let's consider an example drawn from market rates that prevailed one day early in 1988: the rate on 1-month repo was 6.60; our dealer was paying 6.62 to repo issue X with the right of substitution; and issue X, for which demand was high, had become a *special*—commanded a reverse rate of 6.25 or less. Had a party asked our dealer to reverse out issue X to him, our dealer would have exercised his right of sub, gotten issue X back from the investor with whom he was financing it at 6.60, and refinanced it at the more advantageous rate of 6.25.

By doing the above, our dealer would have increased his *spread* on his initial matched-book trade in issue X (presumably, the dealer reversed in issue X from someone) by 37 basis points: 6.62 minus 6.25. A part of the game that a good matched-book trader plays is to try to acquire and to repo *with the right of sub,* issues that he anticipates will become specials.

MATCHED BOOK AS A FACILITATION DEVICE

Over the years, as their matched books made dealers in effect a source of credit, one function of their matched books became to facilitate sales of securities by providing credit to would-be buyers of these securities. Here's an example. An S&L wants to bolster its earnings by adding to them some positive carry. So it buys high-yield Ginnies, reverses them back to the selling dealer, and earns the difference between the yield on the Ginnies and the reverse rate. As noted elsewhere, this is dangerous for the S&L, because it is assuming a lot of price risk to earn just a little carry.

We talk more about matched book as a facilitation device in Chapter 17.

GENERATING BORROWED FUNDS

It used to be that dealers running a matched book regularly did trades in which they borrowed on the repo side half a point or more than they lent on the reverse side. A well-run matched book could and did generate borrowed funds for the firm that ran it. The circumstance that made this possible was concern over credit risk.

A small institution that borrows funds from (reverses out securities to) a large dealer for whatever purpose—to fund its position, to finance the acquisition of securities that it wants to buy now but cannot pay for until X days hence, or to turn temporarily underwater securities into money without having to sell these securities and book a loss—is in effect using the name of the large dealer from whom it borrows to gain access to funds available in the national repo market. For this reason, it is willing not only to pay a rate slightly above the rate prevailing in that market, but to get a loan slightly smaller against its collateral than the loan the big dealer gets against that same collateral. 'Slightly smaller' might mean half a point, borrowing 99½ as opposed to 100.

The funds dealers generate in their matched book is not free money; it costs the repo rate at which they borrow it. To make money generating borrowed funds in its matched book, a dealer must use those funds in a way such that they will yield him a greater return than the repo rate he is paying. That's easy for dealers to do.

Dealers are professional risk takers who have a wide array of profitable bets they can make: positioning securities, putting on arbs, creating tails, and so on. If a dealer balloons his balance sheet by adding to his capital funds he borrows at the repo rate, he will, so long as he earns a higher rate on these funds than he pays for them, raise both his total profits and his rate of return on capital. That's the *law of leverage*.

How much borrowed money a dealer doing matched book can raise depends a lot on his customer base and on his modus operandi. In the past, the amount of funds a big dealer could raise was a big number. Today, it is much smaller, perhaps *zero*—even *negative*—in some cases. Because of the well-publicized losses that investors in repo have sustained in recent years, big investors in repo often demand today, even when they are dealing with highly creditworthy dealers, more margin than they used to. Also, dealers realize that, in some cases at least, the more margin they give a customer, the lower the repo rate the latter will require.

Profit on a "matched" matched book

If a dealer repos out securities for the same period that he reverses them in (for example, hangs out on repo for 30 days any collateral he reverses in for 30 days), he is running a "matched" matched book: he has no mismatch of maturities. Spreads on matched-maturity repos and reverses are narrow, but a dealer doing such trades can make money by doing a large volume of them. Also, he can live with a small spread because he incurs no interest-rate risk and only minimal credit risk. One trader, commenting on the profitability of a "matched" matched book, observed, "A Fed funds broker gets 50 cents a million per trade but has no clearing costs. A dealer making a book in repo gets more but incurs clearing costs. Still, if he can make a net nickel [5 basis points] on a matched sale book, that amounts to $1.40 per million per day, which is $1,400 per billion per day; and all you need to run such a book is a kid from Queens who can add."[2]

---

[2] This quote exaggerates, as Street folk are wont to do. Trading a book that is mismatched and serves many functions obviously *requires skill*. Needless to say, matched books come, like dealers, in many shapes and sizes.

TRADING COLLATERAL—MISMATCHING THE BOOK

Money market dealers have long used standard, cash-market instruments to establish bets of various sorts. They have gone long money market instruments when they were bullish; used bills, BAs, and CDs to establish tails; put on arbs in the government market; and so on. Matched book gave them yet another game to play, "trading collateral" of different maturities—mismatching their books in bankers' parlance.

To understand what's involved, one must visualize precisely what it means for a dealer to run a book in repo. Part A of Figure 16–2 shows the

FIGURE 16–2
Running a book in repo

A. Reversing in securities and repoing these securities creates a new asset and a new liability on a dealer's book

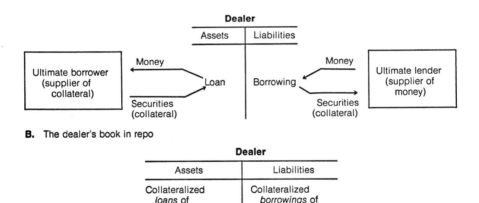

B. The dealer's book in repo

Dealer

Assets	Liabilities
Collateralized *loans* of varying maturities	Collateralized *borrowings* of varying maturities

flows that occur when a dealer reverses in securities on one side and repos them out on the other. As we've said, the essence of a repo transaction is *not* that securities are being sold, but that *secured loans* and *borrowings* are being made. If the securities "sold" are thought of simply as *collateral,* it becomes clear that, when a dealer takes in securities, he is making a *loan* that is an *asset* to him; *and* when he repos these same securities, he is creating a *borrowing* that is a *liability* to him. Thus, a dealer's book in repo and reverse consists of a collection of collateralized loans and borrowings (Figure 16–2B). All of these loans (assets) and borrowings (liabilities) are, moreover, *fixed in term* and *fixed in rate.*

The real money to be made in running a "matched book" comes from mismatching the book with respect to maturity. By adjusting the maturity of the loans and borrowings in his matched book, a dealer can *contrive* bets on future interest rates that expose him to pure *interest rate risk*.

For example, a bullish dealer, anticipating a fall in rates, might reverse in the 2-year note for 60 days and do a 30-day repo against that position. If his interest rate forecast proves correct, the 30-day financing rate will be lower 30 days hence, and he'll make money. The dealer in this instance does not have market risk because he does not own the 2-year note; instead, he has interest rate risk which derives from a possible rise, during the initial 30-day financing period, not in the yield to maturity of the 2-year note, but in the 30-day financing rate. On a matched-book trade, the interest rate risk created is only occasionally, and then only by accident, close to—it's *never* identical with—the market risk associated with holding the underlying collateral.

In this example, the bullish dealer is taking in *long collateral* relative to the repos he puts on. Having long collateral differs from having long securities in several ways. A long position in Treasuries can be sold at any time, whereas a long position in collateral can't. Also, being long Treasuries creates market risk specific to the securities held.

The flip side to having long collateral is to have *short* collateral, reverses that are short in maturity relative to one's repos. For example, a bearish dealer might reverse in securities for 30 days and do a 60-day repo *with a right of sub;* in this case, the dealer's risk is that 30 days from now, when he must again reverse in 30-day collateral to complete his trade (when he must substitute new collateral for "maturing" collateral), he'll find that the 30-day reverse rate, which he's going to earn on the tail of his trade, has fallen, not *risen.*

The position in money market instruments equivalent to having long collateral would be a *forward short* created by a *forward short sale* of securities. Most money market paper, such as CDs and BAs, is heterogeneous; consequently, the only money market instrument a bearish trader can short is bills. An advantage of using a matched book to create bearish bets is that a dealer can create such a bet using any money market instrument as his underlying security in the trade.

Jargon

When a matched-book trader says he is *long collateral,* he means that he is taking a lot of longer-term collateral—lending a lot of longer-term money. If he says he is *short collateral,* he means the opposite. When he says that he has a *mismatch* in his book, he means that there is a significant difference in (average) maturity between his repos and his reverses. If a matched-book trader says to another trader, "How is your mismatch—on the long side or the short side?" and the other trader answers, "It's on the long side," that means that that trader has got collateral and is waiting for rates to fall.

Anyone who studies banking will notice the similarity between a dealer's matched book and *a banker's Eurodollar book.* The latter comprises a bank's Eurodollar time deposits (all fixed in both rate and maturity) and its redeposits of Euro time deposits (also, all fixed in both rate and maturity). A dealer's matched book is simply a collection of assets and liabilities that are fixed with respect to both maturity and rate; and, not surprisingly, the mismatch and trading strategies that a dealer's matched-book trader employs all resemble what traders of bank Euro-books have been doing for a long time. Aside: we cheated a touch in describing a bank's Eurobook as comprising solely fixed-rate, fixed-maturity assets and liabilities; Eurobankers take in *call money* for an uncertain term at a rate that may fluctuate over time; but so too do matched-book traders when they, as they are wont to, open repo.

When a trader of a Eurobook is making a bullish bet, borrowing short and lending long, he says his *book is short.* Conversely, when he is making a bearish bet, he says he is running a *long book.* We mention this because, when it comes to speaking of mismatch, the Eurobook trader's jargon is both clearer and more economical than is that of a matched-book trader; specifically, it's punchier and more direct to speak of a matched-book trader *running a short book* than it is to speak about him *having a mismatch that is short.* We'll use the Eurotrader's jargon later in the next chapter.

A matched-book trader speaks

With the above background in mind, it is interesting to hear a dealer—the quote is old but the technique has not changed—who runs a mismatched book describe how he operates: "Suppose I reverse in the 8s of 86 at par for 90 days at 5⅜. I have assumed a risk. I am now long in 90-day reverse. It is like being long in 90-day bills that you cannot sell—but the yield is higher. I might blow it out [finance the reverse] overnight for a couple of days. Or I might instantly stick it out for 30 to 60 days because I can play the yield curve. Suppose there is a major discrepancy between 90 and 60 days, and I can finance that reverse at 5⅛ for 60 days. Then I have a piece of paper coming back at me in 60 days that I can value. I look at the tail and see I will own 1-month paper [60 days hence] at 5⅞. That seems like a reasonable gamble so, bang, I do it."[3]

Because the pricing of securities repoed depends on their market

---

[3] Recall the discussion in Chapter 10 of tails.

value and thus on interest rates, a firm running a speculative book in reverse incurs not only a rate risk and a liquidity risk but the risk that its position will for some period of time eat up its capital. The same dealer continued, "I have built my tail. If my projection that interest rates are going to fall is correct, I benefit in two ways. First, my 30-day piece of paper comes back at me at 5⅞, and I can bang it out for the last 30 days at 4⅜. Look at the money I have made! Additionally, the 8s of 86 are now worth more money. Consequently, I can borrow [over the last 30 days], say, 103 against them instead of par, which never hurts when you are borrowing at the low end of the yield curve.

"The flip side of that is that there is no more stinko position in a bear market than a reverse position. Say interest rates rise. The 1-month paper I have created comes back at me at 5⅞ but I have to finance it at 6, so I lose money. Moreover, I can now borrow less money, maybe 3 points less. So hundreds of thousands of dollars of my working cash go bye-bye for 30 days. That hurts no matter who you are. You are losing in two directions at the same time. You lose on the trade, and you are out working cash. To run an unmatched book in speculative reverse, you have to be a well-capitalized firm or you will run into massive problems."

Repricing of collateral

To minimize the risk that a position in reverse will eat up capital during a bear market, many dealers running books in repo and reverse reserve the right to *reprice.* Said one such dealer, "In the reverse market there is an informal right to reprice the instrument. If I were to take in $5 million of securities for 6 months and all of a sudden the market dropped 4 points, I would be out $200,000 of my capital. In that case I have the right to call the customer [the borrower] and say it is time to reprice. There is no set time period on repricing. It can be done during any part of the life of the instrument. It is an informal but understood part of the agreement, one that reduces risk for us.

"We ask for the right to reprice because in my opinion we are paid to forecast short-term interest rates, not what a 10-year government is going to be worth 5 or 6 months from now. Maybe I would feel differently if I were a government bond trader, but I am not, and I will not do business with a guy who will not let me reprice. Another reason for repricing is credit risk. Say I am lending a guy 105 on an issue that is worth 101— what if he goes out of business?" While the right to reprice is reserved informally by some dealers, others make it a formal part of a repo agreement.

Note that a dealer reserving the right to reprice does not make a long-term repo borrowing unattractive to the borrower. Suppose a bank borrows 6-month money because it expects interest rates to rise and they do; then, because of repricing, the bank won't get full value for its collateral over the last part of the agreement, *but* it will still be getting cheap money.

Capital requirements, promulgated under GSA, encourage pricing of repo and reverse collateral by penalizing the imprecise repricing, during periods of market volatility, of collateral for term repos and reverses.[4]

Profit in trading a mismatched book

Trading a *mismatched* book in repo and reverse is a trickier game to understand and to play than is trading bills, CDs, or BAs. Also, the matched-book trader has the advantage, which a CD or BA trader does not, of being able to short the market when he is bearish by lending money short term and taking in collateral for a longer term. For both of the above reasons, the profits to be gleaned from running a mismatched book are high when a trader is good at the game. Noted one such trader, "In every place I have worked, I have traded matched book like any other money market security, and my book has always been the most profitable individual item for the firm except for trading Ginnie Maes."

Trading a mismatched book started sometime in the mid-1970s. In recent years it has grown tremendously as more and more dealers have caught onto the idea of using such trades in repo and reverse—as distinct from financing their positions and covering their shorts—as a profit center.

To avoid being misleading, it should be stressed that at some firms running a matched book still means just that—taking in securities for some period and putting them out for precisely or almost precisely the same period for a small spread.

INNOVATION IN MATCHED BOOK

Many people tend to think of matched book as a game in which the collateral is mostly Treasuries. Astute dealers, in contrast, tend to think of any new twist that can be given to matched book as a new product that their matched-book (repo) desk can offer. Such dealers are on the lookout for new products and nurture any that they find; the simple reason: any new product offers new profit opportunities.

In this section, we talk about two new products that have recently wended their way onto some dealers' matched-book desks.

---

[4] See p. 224.

Treasuries

In the last year or two, some dealers have done on their matched-book desks a substantial amount of business with investors—both domestic insurance companies and overseas investors—that want to buy governments for an *extended settlement date*. The motivation of a domestic insurance company that wants to do such trades is typically that it has put in a winning bid on a *Guaranteed Investment Contract* (*GIC*, pronounced *Gik* with the *i* as in *pick*) and thus needs to hedge. GICs began as products that called for the insurance company that wrote them to guarantee an investor a fixed return on a fixed sum invested over a fixed period. Today, some GICs promise that the writer of the GIC will, in exchange for periodic payments from the buyer of the GIC, guarantee that a specified pool of assets will produce a specified pattern of cash throwoffs over some period. Creators of *collateralized mortgage obligations (CMOs),* a derivative of mortgage-backed, pass-through securities, have used GICs of the latter sort to diminish uncertainty with respect to the cash throwoffs that different branches of CMOs, created by them, will produce in the future.

When an insurance company finds that its bid to do a GIC has, in a competitive bidding situation, been hit, it needs to assemble some pretty exotic investments to cover the rate it has promised its new client. In doing so, it faces several difficulties: assembling the exotic investments it wants to make is going to take more than an afternoon; also, it is not going to receive any money from its new client for two to three weeks. These two factors together create a need for the insurance company to put on a hedge, one that ensures that the company will have at least locked in the general level of rates that prevailed at the time it bid on the GIC it has sold. One way an insurance company can hedge is by buying Treasuries *forward* for settlement on the day funds are due it from the buyer of the GIC.

By purchasing forward Treasuries, an insurance company can lock in the level of interest rates that prevailed at the time that it made its GIC bid. An alternative way that it could do the same thing would be by buying futures contracts for Treasuries. Probably, there are some sellers of GICs who do just this, but buying a big position in futures cannot be done without some expenditure of funds (or tying up of assets)—specifically, deposits of initial margin have to be made; and should rates rise, variation margin calls may have to be met.

An insurance company that buys Treasuries forward to hedge the sale of a GIC does not plan to hold those securities indefinitely. Rather, it plans to hold them only until it is able to acquire the exotic investments it planned, from the start, to make to back its contract. When it can, it will sell its Treasuries to buy these investments. The Treasuries hedge the insurance company's risk in the following sense: should the general level of interest rates fall, the insurance company's profit on its forward purchase and later sale of the Treasuries will offset in some degree the higher price that it will probably have to pay for the exotic, interest-bearing instruments in which it planned to invest long term.

We've described why an insurance company selling a GIC might want to buy forward Treasuries. Why, however, should it do such a trade with a dealer's matched-book trader? Conceivably, the company might call the dealer's 2-year-note trader and say, "I want to buy $100 million of 2-year notes for a settlement date that is two weeks into the future." Faced with such a request, the trader would not be able to turn around and buy those notes for future settlement from a trader at some other shop—the forward market in Treasuries is thin at best. Instead, the trader would have to buy the notes desired by the company for cash, regular, or skip-day settlement; then he would have to calculate his profit or loss on *carrying* that item for the ensuing two weeks; and finally, he would have to calculate, on the basis of the cash price *plus* carry, a forward price that was fair to both the dealer and the customer. All that is a bit much for the typical 2-year-note trader. But it's just up the alley of a dealer's matched-book trader. Such a trader deals with financing rates all day long, so it's a snap for him to say: "If I bought for immediate settlement from our trading desk the Treasuries investor X wants and financed them for 14 days, I'd make $50,000. If I put some of that profit back into price, I'd be able to offer that investor those securities for forward settlement at a price Y dollars below the cash price I paid for them and still make some money."

A number of sophisticated investors faced with the problem of wanting to buy forward Treasuries would say, "Hey, I'll buy the securities for immediate settlement and then reverse them back to the dealer." Going that route ought to get the investor roughly the same deal that he would get from the dealer's matched-book desk; many insurance companies choose, however, not to go that route. Maybe they are deterred because they think that going the buy-them-and-reverse-them route would entail explicit margin, possible margin calls, and some extra, perceived-by-them risk or risks; or maybe their pencil is not fast enough to do the requisite math.

Whole loans

A whole loan is a mortgage that has not yet been securitized; it is a loan package with various documents that represent a complete file. A dealer who has a big desk that trades mortgage-backed pass-throughs, such as Ginnie Maes, will also trade whole loans—such loans are, in fact, *actively* traded by dealers. A Ginnie trading desk may acquire whole loans for one of several reasons: the loans may be part of the desk's trading position or the loans are being stockpiled by the dealer to back a CMO that he is assembling and will underwrite. Naturally, the whole loans the dealer buys must be financed; so too must any whole loans reversed in to him by his customers—the latter might include whole loans being stockpiled by, say, an S&L that is putting together in its own name a CMO or whatever, which the dealer will underwrite.

The documents that accompany even 10 million of whole mortgages make up a huge pile. Thus, it would be impractical for a dealer to repo such assets on a delivery basis. Dealers solve this problem by hiring a trustee—Security Pacific is good in this business—to take delivery of, examine, and hold whole-loan documents for them. Dealers then do letter repo with customers to finance the loans represented by these documents.

Many yield-conscious customers will do *letter repo* against whole-mortgage documents held by a trustee, and there is no reason why they should not. If an investor in repo is not going to take delivery of his collateral and if he truly understands the nature of a letter-repo transaction, why should he care whether the collateral the dealer assigns him is T bills or whole mortgage loans? Either way, the investor is making the risk equivalent of an unsecured loan to a dealer whom he (the investor) deems to be highly creditworthy. Most repos of whole loans are done overnight at maybe funds +3/8—the precise spread over funds varying with market conditions. Occasionally, repos of such paper are done for as long as 30 days.

A dealer whose repo desk both finances whole loans and prices and finances forward Treasuries commented: "I tend to think of these different transactions as products because each serves a particular customer need. Doing so helps me focus better than if I just viewed such transactions as additional inventory financing." The repo market which, in the 1950s, began by financing Treasury bills and, now in the 1980s, finances whole mortgage loans, has indeed been indisputably innovative.

THE NEXT CHAPTER

In the next chapter, we turn to some tough-to-answer questions that every astute dealer is asking these days: How big a matched book should he run? What *all-in* contribution does his matched book make to his profits? As preface to this discussion, we talk first about financing and profit maximization by dealers in a world of uncertainty.

Chapter 17

Matched book: Optimal size and profitability

THESE DAYS, EVERY ASTUTE DEALER ends up asking some tough-to-answer questions about how big a matched book he should run and about what *all-in* contribution his matched book makes to his profits. As preface to our discussion of these questions, we pause here to say a few words about dealer financing and profit maximization under uncertainty.

DEALER FINANCING AND PROFIT MAXIMIZATION UNDER UNCERTAINTY

Today, a top dealer is running a matched book well in excess of 10 billion in size—he's borrowing in excess of 10 billion on one side to be able to lend out in excess of 10 billion on the other side; this makes his business, or a part of it, akin to what any bank or S&L is doing. For a dealer who runs a big matched book, the maturation of his role as a financial intermediary has brought into sharp focus certain issues that he always faced even when he was functioning, if he ever did, strictly as a highly leveraged market maker. These issues relate to liquidity risk, interest rate risk, and use and adequacy of capital.

Liquidity and liquidity risk

Thoughtful dealers sound today—when they talk about financing, capital allocation, and the like—rather as thoughtful bankers have long sounded: they are talking about, whatever they may call it, principles of asset and liability management under uncertainty. For any financial institution that operates under uncertainty, liquidity must be a paramount consideration.

Definition. By liquidity we mean *having money when you need it.* More formally, *liquidity is the ability to ensure the availability of funds to meet commitments at a reasonable price at all times.*

Functions of liquidity. Liquidity is not just a nice thing to have. For a financial institution, liquidity serves crucial functions. One is to assure a financial institution's *creditors* that the institution will be able to pay its debts so that these creditors will continue to lend willingly to the institution. A related, but different, function of liquidity is to ensure *the institution itself* that it will always be able to repay its outstanding borrowings, as they come due, without necessarily having to seek to roll them. To illustrate: a dealer who finances overnight reverses with overnight repo has more liquidity than he would if he were financing 1-month reverses with overnight repo. The size and direction of the mismatch, if any, in a dealer's matched book necessarily impinges on his liquidity.

Liquidity also ensures the ability of a financial institution both to meet prior commitments that require funding and to avoid the forced sale of assets. Finally, liquidity precludes an institution's having to pay up in the market to buy funds.

Sources of liquidity. The sources of liquidity to which a financial institution may turn are varied and depend on the precise nature of the institution. These sources include assets maturing in the near term, readily saleable short-term assets, access to purchasable funds, and in some cases last-resort borrowing.

Liquid: To be or not to be? Winston Churchill is reputed to have disposed, during a World War II cabinet meeting, of the topic of domestic agriculture by saying, "Can't we just say that agriculture is a good thing and that we should have more of it?" Whatever the adequacy of Churchill's view on agriculture may have been, it's certain that no responsible manager of a financial institution can dispose of the question of liquidity simply by saying, "Liquidity's a good thing, and we should have more of it."

If the manager of a financial institution that borrows and lends seeks to maximize his profits, what liquidity he will want in a given situation will depend partly on his prediction of interest rates and on his degree of confidence in that prediction. In particular, *if he's convinced that interest rates, however lofty, are about to tumble, that is the moment for him to take a chance: to be as illiquid as he dares.* If he mismatches then, borrows short and lends long, the market will bail him out handsomely as rates fall.

Conversely, *the best time for the manager of a financial institution to choose to be as liquid as possible, even to the point of being overly liquid, is when interest rates have been low and are poised to rise.* If he is right on rates, the market will reward him by permitting him to lend cheap money at progressively higher rates.

Both of these points are telling with respect to the direction and degree of the mismatch that an astute dealer may, at a particular moment, choose to establish in his matched book.

Implications of too much or too little liquidity. When the manager of an institution that borrows and lends decides how much liquidity to buy, it is important that he get it right, because having too much or too little liquidity over a long period will impose a cost on his firm. Liquidity imposes a cost because it must literally be bought. What form the price of liquidity takes depends on market conditions. If the yield curve is *positively sloped,* liquidity costs money because the institution must pay more for long-dated funds than for short-dated funds. Also, with a positively sloped yield curve, the short-run cost of excessive liquidity is, almost surely, negative spreads. If, alternatively, the yield curve is *negatively sloped,* the long-run cost of liquidity—of buying longer-dated funds—is the assumption of interest rate risk: the risk that the yield curve will prove correct and that rates will drop.

Having too little liquidity can also prove costly. A firm that allows its balance sheet to become illiquid may be forced into the market for funds at a time when rates are high and peaking. A firm with too little liquidity forgoes the option of coming to the market when it wants to, whereas a firm with adequate liquidity has the luxury of waiting to buy liquidity until rates come its way.

There is no answer carved in stone to the question of how much liquidity a financial institution should buy. At any point, an institution's decision on this score must reflect not only its view on interest rates, but *its management's propensity to accept the cost of avoiding risk in the form of liquidity exposure.*

Interest rate exposure

Interest rate exposure is the uncertainty introduced into a financial institution's earnings by possible changes in interest rates.

In theory, a financial institution could operate with *no* interest rate exposure. For example, a dealer could opt, as some dealers do, to avoid all interest rate exposure in its matched book by running a matched-maturity matched book. In practice, however, many financial institutions find that they face some *natural* causes of interest rate exposure. For example, simply by playing his role as market maker and unofficial distributor of new Treasury issues, a dealer may at times be forced to assume positions in bills, notes, and bonds that he funds with very short-dated funds; in such situations, hedging is, of course, possible, but it is likely to be imperfect in nature and to impose its own costs.

Natural interest rate exposure aside, it is also true that many financial institutions, when the moment seems propitious, consciously adjust the structure of their balance sheets to increase their interest rate exposure in an attempt to earn profits higher than those that would accrue to them from simple intermediation. In particular, dealers are (recall Chapter 5), inclined to make big position plays when they hold a strong view on interest rates, especially if their view is that rates will fall.

Temptations of the yield curve. Most financial institutions focus on short-run earnings—quarter-to-quarter changes in profits. As a result, the manager of such an institution operates under constant pressure to make money: to increase earnings quarter by quarter, year by year; this pressure, moreover, constantly tempts him to assume interest rate exposure because doing so is one of the principal means he has to increase his firm's earnings. This simple statement is the key to the motivation behind active management—to the extent permitted by customer preferences, market constraints, and so on—of assets and liabilities by many large financial institutions.

A positively-sloped yield curve. The assumption of interest rate exposure involves taking positions in the cash market along the yield curve. If the yield curve is positively sloped, a financial institution is sorely tempted to acquire long-dated, fixed-rate assets and to borrow short to maximize spreads and carry. That tactic enhances short-term profits but increases the institution's interest rate exposure. If the yield curve is correct and rates eventually rise, short rates will change most; the yield curve, as it rises, may flatten or even invert; if so, the institution will end up reaping negative spreads, negative carry, and capital losses—paper or real. This is more likely to occur in the long run than in the short run; so in the short run, the manager finds himself faced with a trade-off between increasing short-run profits and threatening long-run profits. In the long run, concentrating on the maximization of short-run profits will, unless astutely done, almost always rebound adversely on a financial institution, because sooner or later, rates will change in a way that hurts that institution's profits.

A negatively-sloped yield curve. If the yield curve is inverted, things look, at first glance, more attractive to the active asset-and-liability manager. He can increase spreads and short-run profits by buying long-dated funds and lending short; to boot, he increases his liquidity. By doing so, however, he also increases his interest rate exposure—the risk again being that the yield curve will prove correct in the long run, which it almost always is. If rates fall, the institution, instead of making a positive spread on reinvesting its long money, will find itself making a negative spread on long money with which it is stuck; the institution will still have liquidity, but now it will be paying for that liquidity instead of having the market pay for it.

Relationship of liquidity to interest rate exposure

As the above remarks suggest, liquidity and interest rate exposure are, inevitably, inextricably intertwined. When the yield curve is positively sloped, accepting additional interest rate exposure to increase short-run profits also imposes a second cost or risk on a financial institution, namely, a decrease in that institution's liquidity. Alternatively, when the yield curve is negatively sloped, borrowing long and lending short to raise short-term earnings increases a financial institution's liquidity, and that institution is paid by the market for acquiring more liquidity. The liquidity acquired may, however, prove costly in the long run because part of its price is increased interest rate exposure.

No financial institution that is under pressure to increase short-run earnings can escape the temptations of the yield curve. Moreover, the steeper the yield curve, the more alluring it is for such an institution to seek to position its assets and liabilities along the yield curve in a way that promises to increase its short-term earnings, but commits it to accepting additional interest rate exposure.

The essential point is not that a financial institution should never succumb to the temptations of the yield curve; many do so successfully much of the time. Rather, the point is that a financial institution that maximizes *short-run* profits overzealously may in the long run get into deep trouble. The reasons are several: the institution may fail to assess fully the risk it is assuming; the institution may willingly assume more risk than it should; the institution, when it makes a bad gamble, may refuse to cut its losses with dispatch.

OPTIMAL SIZE AND PROFITABILITY OF A MATCHED BOOK

"A key issue," commented an astute dealer, "that the Street must deal with is how profitable the matched book is and how big it should be. I try to draw attention to this point in my own firm."

The Econ-101 answer to how big a dealer's matched book should be is simple: the book earns a spread—a profit—on matched-maturity trades. To maximize profits, the rule should be: balloon the book until this spread falls, at the margin, to zero. A few problems exist with respect to this answer. One is that Econ 101 deals with a world of *certainty,* whereas dealers and all financial institutions necessarily operate in a world of *uncertainty.* In the world of certainty, *equity* capital is irrelevant; firms borrow, at a mythical and solitary *going interest rate,* whatever funds they need to finance the investments they must make to maximize their profits. In the world of uncertainty, some nasty things occur: equity capital assumes importance and is likely to impose binding constraints on growth; liquidity is not infinite—rather, there is liquidity risk; and for a financial institution, interest rate risk lurks everywhere. Below, we talk about these issues as they relate to matched book.

Liquidity risk

Any dealer who manages to stay in business must think a lot about liquidity and liquidity risk. "We must," commented one top dealer, "refinance our business every single day, and to complicate matters, the amount we must finance is changing as we do it."

In funding his operations, a dealer can draw on many sources of funds. He starts with some equity capital. He may be able and choose to issue some medium-term notes; certainly, big banks that deal actively in governments do that. In addition, a nonbank dealer may turn to its clearing bank for limited amounts of secured, overnight funding; and if it's a top credit, to other banks for overnight loans on an unsecured basis: a top dealer can, late in the day, borrow with a simple phone call a half billion unsecured from a foreign bank at funds plus a small spread, and top dealers have contacts with top banks around the globe.

The biggest single source of short-term money to dealers is doing repo. Dealers started out using repo strictly as a financing tool to avoid costly bank loans and, consequently, have developed pronounced strengths in locating cheap sources of repo money. There are still dealers who do not do matched book and who, therefore, always enter the repo market in a borrowing mode. Big dealers all run matched books and are thus both *borrowers* and *lenders* of money in this market. This fact probably increases the access of such dealers to repo financing, since as bankers are wont to observe, the best way to enhance one's ability to borrow in a market (e.g., for a bank to borrow in the Fed funds market or the Euro time deposit market) is to be perceived to be a lender, at least occasionally, in that market.

Doing only delivery repo, period, would set a severe constraint on how much repo financing a dealer could obtain. From an operational point of view, some collateral is just too difficult, too expensive to deliver. Consequently, dealers who are viewed by the market as highly creditworthy do routinely a lot of letter repo.

Yet another source of funds that some dealers, bank and nonbank, may add to the general pool of funds with which they finance their dealer and other operations is the sale of commercial paper by the parent company. An advantage of this source of funds is that the funds a dealer sources in the commercial paper market are likely to be longer-dated than funds he sources in the repo market. While figures vary from firm to firm and from period to period, 70% is probably a good ball-park estimate of the amount of repo funding done that is an overnight deal.

A dealer asking how big a matched book he should run must base his answer partly on the amount of repo funding open to him. That amount is never some simple X billion. A good banker knows that the secret of liability management is to have the person who is giving the bank money think that the bank is doing him a favor by taking it. Similarly, a dealer working the repo market must pay attention to his welcome, as a borrower, there; the last thing he wants to do is to borrow so much in the market that lenders begin to feel "full up on his name" and, worse still, begin to require that he pay up for money—the latter not only costs money, but worse still casts a bad light on the borrower's name.

A second related liquidity question that a dealer, in deciding how big to be, must ask concerns possible worst-case scenarios. A dealer wants to be able to be liquid not just when the sun shines on his fortunes, but in bad times as well: on the day after he takes a big trading loss, on the day after the stock market crashes (at least, if he's a broker/dealer), on the day after the bond market goes down the chutes, on the day after some new rule or reg changes the behavior of some subset of his major creditors, and so on.

To accomplish the above, a dealer must limit his sourcing of funds in different markets so that he is welcome in all of them and has, to boot, some flexibility—the ability to respond to a change, whatever it may be, by shifting a portion of his sourcing of funds from one market to another.

Aside. After these words were written, the stock market crashed on October 19, 1987, with the result that many broker/dealers incurred staggering losses. Worse still, much uncertainty existed, initially at least, as to just how much individual dealers had lost: one reason was that the huge volume of trading had created monumental logjams in dealers' back offices; also, in the markets for some securities, trading became so thin and bid-offered spreads so wide as to throw into question the validity of market prices. In this atmosphere, the reaction of major banks, domestic and foreign, was to begin, suddenly, to view many broker/dealers to whom they routinely extended credit as suspect-at-best credits; this created a potential liquidity problem, the dimensions of which are difficult to gauge because bank lines to dealers and others are undisclosed. It is, however, known that the Fed perceived the potential problem to be serious; the Fed feared that the crash might lead to a liquidity crisis in the dealer community, which in turn would lead to a meltdown in one or more markets for securities and derivative products.

To avert such a crisis, Fed officials acted rapidly. In Washington, the Fed issued a brief statement: "The Federal Reserve, consistent with its responsibilities as the nation's central bank, affirmed today its readiness to serve as a source of liquidity to support the economic and financial system." Simultaneously, the Fed poured reserves into the banking system through open market operations, and it leaned heavily on the big New York banks to meet Wall Street's soaring demands for credit. The Fed's strategy was to ensure that it kept the banks liquid and that the banks in turn kept other major players in the system liquid.

That the Fed was able to act so swiftly, so strongly, and so appropriately was due in part to the foresight of Chairman Greenspan who created, shortly after he took office, a crisis-management team; the responsibility of this team was to examine *in secret* various "flash points" that might cause a financial breakdown and to lay contingency plans for dealing with each such crisis; one flash point was a stock market crash.[1]

The moral of this story is that a dealer needs to be ever vigilant about his liquidity because a threat to his liquidity can occur at any moment not only due to his own actions, but due to unanticipated events beyond his control. For a dealer, liquidity should never be a casual concern.

In evaluating the impact of his matched book on his liquidity, an astute dealer will realize that, if he is running a short book, he has *no* liquidity in that book because he cannot sell the loans he has created by reversing in securities. To illustrate, suppose that a dealer running a short book experiences a change in his view on rates: previously, he thought rates would stay flat or fall; now, he anticipates that rates will rise. To achieve even neutral interest rate exposure, the dealer must *double in size* the currently maturity-mismatched portion of his book. Say he has been financing 45-day reverses with 1-week repo; to close up his book, to get flat, the dealer must now match his 45-day reverses with 45-day repos and his 1-week repos with 1-week reverses. The dealer's liquidity pickle would not surprise a Euro time deposit trader; the latter has long faced an identical dilemma in running his Euro placement book.

What liquidity risk a profitable dealer runs depends not only on how hard he works the credit markets, but on how much capital he has—something we turn to next.

---

[1] See Daniel Hertzberg and James Stewart's "Terrible Tuesday: How the Stock Market Almost Disintegrated a Day after the Crash," *The Wall Street Journal*, November 20, 1987, p. 1; and Allan Murray's "Passing a Test: Fed's New Chairman Wins a Lot of Praise on Handling the Crash," *The Wall Street Journal*, November 25, 1987, p. 1.

Equity capital as a binding constraint

Equity capital is strikingly absent in the certainty model which makes that model deservedly suspect. For a dealer operating under uncertainty, capital is important on a number of counts. Dealers are in the business of making bets, favorable ones they hope. Consequently, every dealer, unless he has God or Jeane Dixon in his pocket, is bound to make a few bad bets. Also, every dealer faces the possibility that one day he'll wake to find that some factor outside his control has cost him a bundle: one of his traders—of futures, mortgage backs, or whatever—has lost some huge sum by taking big positions that were neither authorized nor profitable (dealers put in strong controls to prevent this sort of thing, but it still occurs now and then on the Street and not just in poorly run shops); other exogenous ills may also befall a dealer. Thus, for a dealer, one important function of capital is simply to prevent him from going bankrupt on a bad-luck day—not to speak of on a day on which a poor judgment he has made comes home to roost on his P&L statement.

Put succinctly, *a key function of capital for a dealer is to permit him to assume risk.*

Most dealers have more than enough capital to get by an inevitable bad day, even an October 19, 1987. Still, the events of that day were sufficiently traumatic to call for a second *aside,* especially since they limned the importance of capital to a dealer in governments.

On October 19, while the stock market was making a record plunge, government bonds were rallying. Thus, some broker/dealers found at the end of the day that they had taken a big bath on stocks and various other risk positions but made money on governments. Moreover, the rally in governments, which was fueled both by an investor flight to quality and by the dramatic switch to ease in Fed policy, looked as if it would continue. This being the case, many dealers in governments viewed the time as ripe for increasing substantially their positions. However, some broker/dealers were prevented from doing so by the large losses they had incurred in equities and other areas. These losses had eaten a big chunk of their capital and left them advisedly fearful of taking on other big positions which, if the latter were to go awry, would lead to further losses and thereby to a further diminution of their capital. As trading limits on the government desks of such shops were in fact *cut,* it became all too evident, yet again, to folks on the Street that adequate capital is a sine qua non for assuming risk even when the bet—governments will continue to rally—that a shop wants to make appears enticingly favorable.

A second function of capital at a dealer shop is to keep the regulators happy. Since the passage of GSA, every dealer in governments must have sufficient—in the eyes of his regulator—capital to back his various classes of risk assets and certain off-balance-sheet commitments as well. Capital requirements vary between different classes of dealers;

also, they all have their flaws, the most serious being that the best way to assess the risk associated with any type of asset or commitment is by using *20-20 hindsight,* the faith of regulators in their wisdom, ratios, and omniscience notwithstanding (see the article by Lowell Bryan cited at the end of this chapter). Still, every dealer must meet his regulatory capital requirements to stay legitimately in business.

A third function of capital is that it is the sine qua non of a dealer's liquidity. Every dealer who borrows—and they all do—has a cast of characters who avidly devour his periodic financial statements, his P&L statement, his balance sheet, and his 10-K if he files one. Such numbers-watchers include not just regulators, but the varying entities that lend to him, the firms that rate his commercial paper if he issues any, and the analysts who opine on the value of his common stock if he has any. A sage dealer realizes that to keep out the welcome mat for his firm in various credit markets, he must keep this gaggle of numbers-watchers reasonably happy even if doing so may be difficult and even if it means that he cannot take every step he'd like to to maximize profits.

A bank's Euro time deposit book, something akin to a dealer's matched book, is a low-risk way for a bank to make a small positive spread so long as it controls carefully the mismatch in its book. Econ 101 theorizing suggests that a banker ought to keep expanding his Eurobook until he drives, at the margin, the spread in that book to zero; doing so would, after all, maximize his *return on equity capital* (*ROE*). Bankers, however, do not do this. Surprisingly, they are more concerned with another number, rate of *return on assets* (*ROA*). In the minds of raters of debt, analysts of stock, and lenders of money, not all of whom necessarily have a very good handle on risk in a book, ROA is an important number. Because others look so hard at his ROA, so too must a banker, and because he does, he consciously limits the size of his Eurobook. Dealers, like bankers, face pressure from numbers-watchers to keep up a respectable ROA number.

Amongst numbers-watchers, hand in hand with concern over ROA goes concern over the risks they perceive to be inherent in what they view as high leverage. Unfortunately, raters of commercial paper and other numbers-watchers as well gauge such risk less than astutely. They comprehend well enough that a position in long bonds financed with overnight repo is risky, but they perceive less readily that a well-run, multibillion-dollar matched book may produce, net, little risk of any sort.

Keeping numbers-watchers happy is one constraint that leads big dealers to consciously decide to hold down the size of the matched books they run. At banks, another binding constraint is the rather ungenerous, relative to what nonbank dealers get away with, 25 to 1 capital asset ratio that the Fed imposes informally on bank operations overall. Any dealer or banker who is forced to constrain a spread book he is running to what, in his view, is a suboptimal size naturally responds by trying to maximize the spread he earns on that book.

Capital adequacy is not a new question to Wall Street dealers. Today, however, dealers speak of their business as becoming more and more capital intensive, which is a way of saying that the constraints on their growth that their capital, however large, imposes are becoming progressively more binding. Noted one big dealer, "It is happening at every shop that people are asking more and more, 'Do we have the kind of capital necessary to run all the businesses we are running: dealing, mergers and acquisitions, leveraged buyouts, whatever?' There is a trend toward this becoming an important issue for firms like ours."

Interest rate exposure

Matched book is only one of several or many lines of business in which a dealer engages that subject him to interest rate exposure. A well-run dealer will try to hold his interest rate risk overall to some acceptable level. That's not easy because a dealer can't add apples and oranges—the rate risk that derives from a 1 million position in the long bond and the rate risk that derives from running 1 million of matched book. A good dealer tries to cope with this problem by establishing some sort of formula, however arbitrary, for converting different sorts of risk into some standard unit of measure, for example, the risk inherent in holding a position in 10-year Treasuries, and by then seeking to hold the sum of his risks thus stated within some upper bound, which may in turn be a function, implicit or explicit, of his confidence in his view on rates.

Credit risk

We have said more about interest rate risk than about credit risk. There is credit risk in a dealer's matched book, but this risk is one that a careful dealer can readily control. Evidence of success: the late 1970s, early 1980s spate of dealer bankruptcies that cost investors in repo hundreds of millions of dollars in losses cost primary dealers in governments not one penny of losses. Major dealers who did repo with dealers that failed, and there were those that did, were sufficiently wary of their counterparties to insist on delivery of repo collateral versus payment of repo money when they dealt with these entities.

One big part of credit-risk management on a repo desk is having a credit department that does a good job of carrying out the old Wall Street maxim: *know thy customer.* A second key part is the making of accurate and timely *margin calls.* A good way for a dealer to ensure that proper margin calls are made is to set up firm rules as to what margin calls are to be made and then to give the job of making these calls to operations.

"I think," said one manager of a repo desk, "that it is a conflict of interest for a repo desk to do its own margin calls. It's too easy for a customer to say, 'We do a lot of reverse business with you. Can't you extend our margin call for a couple of days?' We should have a division of labor between us and operations. Still, if a customer goes bust and we have a loss, that loss is my responsibility. So I have a girl who checks that the operations area is making accurate, timely margin calls on at least our weakest customers. If operations gets to a top-credit customer tomorrow, so be it; I'll accept that risk."

MEASURING AND MAXIMIZING MATCHED-BOOK PROFITS

A dealer who runs a matched book is likely to be tempted at some point to ask a couple of questions that sound simple: What profits am I earning on my matched book? What plans should I undertake to maximize these profits? A dealer who tries to answer these questions honestly and thoughtfully will make several discoveries: first, answering question one is anything but simple—measuring profit in a matched book raises complex issues; second, answering question two gets him deep in the area of strategic decision making.

A book on the repo market is not the place for an extended discussion of strategic decision making by dealers. However, it is interesting to look at how questions with respect to the measurement and maximization of matched-book profits lead to wider issues.

A dealer is not a one-product firm; he does not just do matched book or just deal in Treasuries. Reflecting this, the trading floor of a big dealer is broken into a number of areas of responsibility: the government desk, agency desk, repo desk, muni desk, arb desk, and so on. To further complicate matters, big dealers have for years been running foreign offices, which, due to the internationalization of capital markets, have assumed growing importance in the activities and fortunes of such firms.

Presumably, the goal of every dealer creating and selling multiple products through offices around the world is to maximize his total—global—profits subject to the constraints that he assume interest rate risk only on favorable risk-reward terms and that he hold his liquidity risk to an acceptable level. For a dealer, enunciating that goal is easy, albeit doing so requires a mouthful of words; a far harder task is designing strategies that will achieve this goal.

Strategic decision making: Banks

Dealers are hardly the first multiproduct financial institutions with worldwide operations that have struggled with strategic decision making under uncertainty. Anyone familiar with money market banking who listens to a dealer talk, whatever the latter's jargon about asset and liability management may be, is bound to get a feeling of déjà vu. For several decades, big banks have been busily moving up the learning curve with respect to global profit maximization: devising a framework for strategic decision making that will enable them to maximize their global profits.

Dealers and banks, despite certain similarities, are nonetheless quite different sorts of financial institutions. Despite their differences, however, a quick survey of the questions with which bankers have struggled is a useful and thought-provoking preface to even a short discussion of strategic decision making by dealers.

A problem that big U.S. banks faced as they built, beginning in the 1960s, huge Eurobooks was how to control their interest rate exposure globally, not piecemeal as between the domestic book and the Eurobook. The head office of every U.S. bank that started operations in the Euromarket in the early 1960s initially instructed its foreign branches to accept *no* interest rate risk in their Euro operations: managers of Eurobooks were to match fund, period. Then gradually, U.S. banks began to allow their branches to mismatch, which at the time almost always meant running a short book. As the 1970s progressed, head office at many banks became concerned about the risk to which the mismatch limits it imposed on the branches exposed the bank. Often, these limits were couched in percentage terms; and as a bank's Eurobook grew, the absolute amounts represented by these percentages became large. The mismatch risk in a bank's Eurobook, which initially had been minimal, became significant.

At this point, the major banks began to track their branches' mismatch regularly from head office and to set tight mismatch limits based on absolute dollar amounts. Having done that, major banks permitted their foreign branches to operate more or less autonomously. In the late 1970s and early 1980s, a number of banks began to tighten up still further on the freedom they gave their branches, to require that their branches act in conformity with rate views formulated at head office: for the first time, banks were controlling their global book—a new concept—from a central point.

Doing so gave banks obvious advantages. For example, a bank that had a lot of floating-rate loans on its domestic book and wanted to run a neutral position, say out of fear of falling interest rates, might achieve that position by running a short Eurobook, which viewed on a stand-alone basis might appear to be a big source of rate risk.

The lesson of this story is that the risks that a financial institution assumes in different areas of its operation, while they appear to be positions that can be assessed piecemeal, are not necessarily, even probably, additive. A proper analysis of global risk requires an analysis of how risk assumed in one area may offset or perhaps enlarge risk assumed in some other area.

To devise strategies for maximizing their profits on a global book, major banks had to develop a new and proper profit-center analysis. In most major banks, international business had been tacked onto domestic banking activity, almost as an adjunct. So it was natural for a bank to graft its international banking business into its existing profit-center analysis by treating this activity as a separate profit center. Such narrow, profit-center definitions created, however, problems for banks: it prevented them from taking advantage, for example, of opportunities for arbitrage that required the use of domestic funds in the Euromarket or vice versa. How could a bank expect two independent profit centers to agree on a transfer price that made both happy? Banks found that proper profit-center accounting should be based on two broad profit centers: the worldwide lending division and the worldwide treasury division, where the latter encompassed not only funding, but dealing and trading in securities and foreign exchange as well as the acquisition and funding of the bank's portfolio.

Banks that set out to run a global book encountered people problems at two levels. First, they learned that the worst mistake a bank can make is to have its global book run by a group of specialists in the domestic market and a group of specialists in the Euromarket; it will never happen that the two groups agree on an overall strategy that makes sense for the whole bank. Second, banks had to devise ways for giving branch officers some leeway in decision making so that they would continue to have a feeling of autonomy. Finally, there was the question of compensation. The whole concept of a global book, of global profit maximization, is that it does not matter, except for tax purposes, whether profits are booked in New York or London. But with respect to proper compensation of employees, it does matter to what center profits are attributed. Banks found that they needed an internal accounting system to ensure that their employees were compensated in line with their actual, as opposed to their accounting, contribution to profits.

Dealers: Strategic decision making

We have discussed the experience that banks have had with their Eurobooks because this experience is suggestive of issues with which dealers must grapple as they lay plans for maximizing future profits from an array of products, one of which is matched book. For example, as astute dealer might ask: Is there some better way we might measure the apples and oranges of interest rate exposure that result from the firm's positions in different areas, one that would perhaps permit us to regard at times interest rate exposure in the matched book as an offset against risk in a position, long or short, generated in some other area? At least one major dealer always matched maturities in his matched book; perhaps by doing so, he is precluding opportunities to utilize potentially productive strategies for profit maximization.

Matched book as a facilitation device. Because they are multiproduct firms, dealers need to maximize profit not desk by desk—on the government desk, on the mortgage-backs desk, on the repo desk, and so on—but rather globally. This is a point that is particularly apposite to a dealer's repo desk. A reverse that a dealer does with a customer and then books in his matched book frequently facilitates other business: a dealer may be able to sell Ginnies to an S&L because its repo desk is willing to take those securities in on reverses *or* a dealer's money markets desk may be able to sell securities to a customer because its repo desk has reversed in governments from that customer. Because of such possibilities, a dealer who seeks to maximize his global profits clearly must get into some sophisticated analysis of the *all-in* contribution to his total profits that each of his different activities makes.

Once a dealer recognizes that a given reverse may generate profit not only on his repo desk, but on some other desk (maybe his money markets desk), he's naturally tempted to say, "On such a trade, we can shave the profit we take on the reverse because we'll also be earning profit on a second trade that this reverse facilitates." A dealer, who has not analyzed carefully from whence his profits come and who reasons thusly, does so at his own peril: he may, as noted below, end up giving away more than he gets.

ROE on matched book: How high is it? In deciding how big a matched book to run, one variable a dealer ought to be looking at is the *all-in* rate of return on assets that he earns on the book. That number is bound to be bigger than the figure he'd come up with if he looked just at numbers derived from his repo-desk operations.

On a not atypical reverse, a dealer might make a 30-basis-point spread in his matched book. Also, that reverse might enable him to make on the sale of a CD another 10 basis points; some portion of the latter should be attributed back to the repo desk because, without the financing provided by the reverse, the CD would not have been sold. Thus, a dealer's analysis of his matched-book numbers alone might indicate that he was making a 30-basis-point spread on his book, whereas his true return on the book was much higher. In this respect, one dealer noted: "Analysis in our shop shows that the true spread we earn on our matched book is at least double what shows in our books. We have to think of that number in setting a limit on size of the assets in our matched book."

A dealer speaks

Apropos of some of the issues discussed above, a dealer who is responsible, *inter alia,* for his firm's repo desk, noted: "We try to use our matched book as a profit-generating piece of business, one that directly generates profitable spreads and that also facilitates other types of transactions in the firm. When we do a piece of business, we try to understand all that is involved in that transaction. If we are generating some reinvestment in another instrument that we sell, we are willing to be a little more flexible on the profits that we take in the matched book.

"I know that a number of firms on the Street have used matched book as a facilitation vehicle. They have a lot of customers, and when one of these customers comes in to do repo, they do it at a price that the customer will agree to. If the dealer's idea of the market is not good enough for the customer, then the dealer listens to the customer's idea. Like it or not, that has been popularizing.

"It is a good and appropriate use of the matched book—as a facilitating device. It can introduce new relationships; take securities lending— it is marvelous for that purpose. But you don't want to make the mistake of giving away the repo business—do it for 5 basis points which hardly covers operational costs.

"It is also a mistake to use the repo desk as a loss leader because most repo desks are the most efficient profit center that a dealer has. The revenues that it generates flow, to a great extent, more directly to the bottom line than do the revenues generated by some other trading areas.

"Sometimes, a customer will walk in and say, 'I do a lot of money market business with you, and I want you to do repo with me [*on my terms*].' That customer will take $100 of revenue away from me [the repo desk] and try to give it to the money markets desk; but for our firm to stay even, the customer needs to give the money markets desk business having $300 of revenue for every $100 of revenue he takes away from me.

"Each group within a dealership has its own costs associated with generating $100 of revenue. A repo desk is one of the most efficient desks in a dealer's trading room: out of every $100 of revenue we generate, probably $80 flows to the bottom line as profit. The money market or mortgage trading areas, in contrast, require a lot of research and other support personnel; thus, out of every $100 of revenue they generate, they may deliver only $10 or $20 as profit to the bottom line.

"It is going to become increasingly important for a dealer to assess the relationships that he has with customers: to get sophisticated about measuring his profits from a relationship and to then decide which such relationships are most profitable to him. If the *total* return we earn on the business we do with a customer is 20 basis points, that is not enough."

The same dealer went on to talk about matched book and his capital constraint. "It is happening at every shop that people are asking more and more if they have the kind of capital necessary to run all the businesses they are running: mergers and acquisitions, leveraged buyouts, or whatever. There is a trend toward this becoming a fairly important issue for firms like ours.

"The return on equity we earn on our matched book is phenomenal, and I'm sure that this is true of most others' matched books. Naturally, it's hard to estimate ROE for a matched book. Maybe you can't. I use a heuristic approach. I look at what capital regulators require. Then I ask: If my [matched-book] group went comatose, what is the most we could lose? It's not so much, since matched book is a low-risk area. Finally, I add the two [the capital the regulators require plus the most the matched-book group could lose]. As a percentage of this notional and generous measure of the capital we require to back our matched book, our profits on this book run over 100%: notionally, I assign X million of capital to our matched book, and we make X million on it.

"Whenever we do a reverse with a customer, we are renting space to him on our balance sheet; that is a concept that is going to become more popular as our business becomes more capital intensive [as capital becomes an increasingly binding constraint]. In looking at customers who want to rent some space on our balance sheet and in trying to weigh who our good and bad customers are (which customers are most profitable to us), we have to take into account the profitability of all of the business that each of these customers does with us. If a customer gives us business on which volume is insignificant or our profit is low, that does not offset our doing on the repo desk a big volume of business with him for next to nothing."

THE FUTURE

The trend toward innovation in the repo market that has been so pronounced over the last three decades is certain to continue. "The repo market," commented a major dealer in 1987, "is underdeveloped. As we expand our existing lines of business and get into additional lines of business, we dealers find ourselves needing more and more funds. A question I keep asking is: Why, when we can get repo money at funds plus a quarter, should we be borrowing at prime plus two from a bank operating in the domestic market or at even higher rates from a bank operating in Europe? We could repo almost anything: car loans, corporates, whatever. The key is to be innovative and to understand thoroughly both operations and clearance. In this respect, passage of GSA may have helped, rather than hindered us; regulation may well make letter repo more respectable and thereby further expansion of the repo market." [2]

THE NEXT CHAPTER

Our next to last chapter is the lawyers' chapter. In it, we survey the characteristics *(indicia)* of repos and reverses and the answers these indicia suggest, one by one and in toto, to that much-asked question: What is this thing called repo?

SOURCES

For more on asset and liability management, see Marcia Stigum and Rene Branch, *Managing Bank Assets and Liabilities: Strategies for Risk Control and Profit,* (Homewood, Ill.: Dow Jones-Irwin, 1983). A reader of this book who makes proper allowance for the fact that banks and dealers have quite different collections of assets and liabilities will find that many of the principles discussed in the book apply directly to the operations of dealers.

For a thoughtful, well-written, and also damning critique of the imposition of regulatory capital requirements against individual risk assets and off-balance-sheet commitments held by a regulated financial institution, see Lowell L. Bryan, "Capital Guidelines Could Weaken Banks," *The Wall Street Journal,* April 23, 1987. The article cited discusses the proposed imposition by regulators of capital requirements on banks, but it is certainly suggestive of the counterproductive nature of the imposition under GSA of similar capital requirements on nonbank dealers in governments.

---

[2] Recall the discussion of GSA in Chapter 14.

Chapter 18

What is this thing called repo?

AS WE'VE SAID, dealers and investors had, at the time the repo market was revived, good reasons for wanting to keep the nature of repo vague. This they did, and all went well so long as every repo-and-reverse-market participant held up both ends of the bargain he'd struck.

With the failure of Financial Corp., this condition ceased to hold. In fact, starting with the bankruptcy of Financial Corp., a string of dealer bankruptcies raised numerous questions about repo. In particular, lawyers trying to determine who was owed what after different dealer bankruptcies surveyed the various characteristics of repos and reverses and asked, "What is this thing called repo: is it truly a securities transaction or is it truly a collateralized loan?" Lawyers were forced to ask these questions by circumstances: the law specifically addresses the rights and obligations of parties who do a securities trade and of parties who do a collateralized loan; it is, however, silent on the standing of parties who do a repo.

Certainly, one can seek and lawyers, in particular, have sought to answer the question, "What is this thing called repo?" by counting repo-market *indicia* (lawyerese for characteristics) and by saying, "90 percent [or whatever] of the *indicia* of a repo trade are those of a collateralized loan; ergo, repo is a collateralized loan [or should be taken to be so by the courts]."

This answer tampers, however, with reality. Repo is not a collateralized loan, nor is it a securities trade—it is a hybrid. Thus, the position of a lawyer who's forced by his case to ask, "What is repo, truly?" is akin to that of a veterinarian who's asked to opine on whether some farmer's mule is truly a horse or truly an ass. Possession of the wisdom of Solomon would not suffice to permit him to answer this question other than by saying, "Neither." Unfortunately, the answer neither gets a lawyer pleading a repo case precisely nowhere.

MACROECONOMIC SIGNIFICANCE

From the macroeconomic point of view, the repo market is, as noted in the introduction, one vast *credit* market. Any attempt to view this market as something other would require strained reasoning and would lead to conclusions totally unacceptable to any informed observer of the U.S. capital market.

Even *reverses to maturity,* which result in an immediate sale by the lender of money of the "collateral" he receives, are regarded by the borrower of money as strictly a credit transaction—albeit one that he [the receiver of money] undertakes solely to be able to reinvest at a higher rate the funds he is borrowing. *Reverses to cover shorts* appear, perhaps, to be an exception to what we said above, and in a sense, they are; however, in such a transaction, the lender of money is motivated by a desire to *borrow,* not to *buy,* securities, while the borrower of money desires to do precisely what he is doing—to borrow money; moreover, the latter, if it so happens that the issue that changes hands is a special issue, is more than delighted to be able to borrow at a below-market rate of interest.

INVESTORS' PARAMETERS

When dealers first began to seek financing from nonfinancial corporations, they ran into a problem. Most such corporations, whether they were manufacturing autos, transporting freight, or writing insurance, took the position that they were *not* providers of credit. That was a function performed by commercial banks; moreover, it was a function that corporations were often specifically prohibited by their by-laws from performing.

Dealers got around this problem by designing the repurchase agreement with its outright purchase and sale features; doing the other side of a repo with a dealer turned a corporation into a lender without formally labeling it such.

In writing repo agreements, dealers were not in the least rigid. If they encountered an investor with dollars to invest who could do a collateralized loan but not a securities purchase, they structured the repo agreement as a collateralized loan. In effect, dealers opportunistically structured repo agreements so as to get from investors the most money possible at the least cost possible, given the constraint that each portfolio manager with whom they dealt had to stay within his particular investment parameters (guidelines): both those imposed internally and any others imposed by law or regulation.

One dealer commented that, at the beginning of the repo market, there were just a few shops doing it, and repo was what they said it was. "That," he noted, "is the way it should be. We left it purposely *vague* because doing so fit our needs. If a customer said, 'I can't do repo,' we said, 'OK, we will sell you securities and buy them back.' If another customer said he could not buy securities, we said, 'Fine, we will borrow money from you and give you collateral.' It was all very convenient. Now they [the lawyers and judges] have messed it up."

Today, as at the outset of the repo market, a typical repo transaction is arranged so that it consists of two consecutive securities trades, first a buy and then a sell (the reverse for a reverse). This practice keeps a lot of market participants, including the Fed, within investing and borrowing parameters that delimit what they may or may not do. However, this practice has no impact on, and in no way alters, the *economic essence* of the transaction.

THE DEALER AND BANK VIEW OF REPO

The single best word to characterize the view of dealers and of money market banks as to what repo is, is *vague*. As noted in the quote above, dealers and bankers did not want, at least until recently, to define repo more precisely because they feared that, if they did so, they might lose some of their customers and perhaps invite further regulation of repo transactions. There is, however, nothing vague about dealers' and money-market-bankers' understanding of what repo does for them: repo provides these institutions with credit (1) to finance the holding of securities that they own, and (2) to finance, in the case of matched book, their loans to institutions that have reversed securities into them.

To a dealer, the principal substitute for repo financing is bank loans, secured, and in the case of top dealers, unsecured. All dealers regard loans obtained from their clearing banks as expensive, last-resort financing that should be used only to finance that small part of their position that they can not economically repo. If dealers could not get repo money to finance their positions in securities and collateral, they would have to cut those positions to a small fraction of their current levels because the New York clearing banks lack the capital base they would require to meet the total financing needs of the New York dealers. If dealers were to borrow from New York banks an amount equal to their total financing needs, that would destroy the capital to asset ratios of New York clearing banks. This, in turn, would make it impossible for these banks to finance their own operations by buying money in the Fed funds, CD, BA, and Euro time deposit markets.

While New York clearing banks provide some financing to dealers, these banks are, as noted earlier, deposit poor; thus, they and other money market banks regard the repo market as an important source of funding. Banks regard repo money as *bought* money and, more specifically, as a close substitute for the purchase of Fed funds. Because repo money is cheap, big banks repo as much of their portfolios and of their dealing positions (if they have them) as possible. Generally, the overnight repo rate is a spread below the Fed funds rate, so overnight repo is the cheapest financing available to banks. Banks, however, set a limit on the amount of overnight repo money plus Fed funds that they will buy; every bank knows that using a lot of overnight funding would expose it to both a liquidity risk and an interest rate risk. How much overnight funding a bank will think it prudent to use depends partly on its view on interest rates. If a bank feels strongly that interest rates are likely either to stay flat or to fall, it will feel comfortable borrowing large amounts of overnight funds. Conversely, if a bank expects interest rates to rise, it will seek to lengthen, to the extent possible, the average maturity of its total liabilities, of which repos are an important part.

When bankers and dealers think about the risks to which repo might expose them, they at least used to think only of *interest rate risk* and *liquidity risk.* It is a telling point that dealers and bankers became concerned about the *market risk* to which repos and reverses might expose them only after the Lombard-Wall ruling raised for them the specter that one day they might be forced to hang onto, rather than be permitted to sell out, repo collateral taken in from a party in default.

REPO TRADE TICKETS

Repo and reverse repo trade tickets always contain information indicating that the trade is a repo or a reverse, not just a pair of outright buys and sells. Without such information and an indication as well of the rate—unless it's understood—at which the trade is to be done, the dealer's back office could not "figure the money" on leg two of the trade and would thus be unable both to generate a confirm for leg two of the trade and to instruct its clearing bank as to how to clear the trade.

Repo trade tickets strongly indicate that a repo is something other than a straight securities transaction: sell today, buy tomorrow.

REPO CONFIRMATIONS

Banks and dealers doing repos dress up most such transactions as a purchase, followed by a sale, both by the investor, of the underlying collateral. As part of this "dressing up," repo borrowers create and send to the investor (1) a start-date confirmation that typically reads, "We [the dealer] sold . . ." or, "We [the dealer] confirm sale to you . . ."; and (2) an end-date confirmation that reads, "We [the dealer] bought . . ." or, "We [the dealer] confirm purchase from you. . . ." The confirm identifies the specific securities serving as underlying collateral in the trade as well as the price and face amount of these securities. Typically, the confirm also states the repo rate to which the two parties have agreed. However, if the parties agree to do a repo at a rate that varies daily, for example, at the Fed funds rate plus or minus a spread, no repo rate may appear on the confirm.

A repo confirm may contain "trailer information" indicating to the customer that the sell and subsequent purchase are the front and back ends, respectively, of a repo or of a reverse, and if the transaction is not an overnight one, that it has a term of X days.

Figures 18–1 and 18–2 illustrate the features we have just described. In Figure 18–1, we show start- and end-date confirms for a term repo done by J. P. Morgan Securities with a foreign bank. Note the start-date confirm in part A of the figure reads "we confirm our sale to you"; the collateral is U.S. Treasury notes with CUSIP number 912827QN5; the trade and the settlement dates are both 11/30/87; the amount of the repo is 53 million; also, trailer information on the confirm states that the term of the repo is 18 days and that the rate on the repo is 6.45000%.

The end-date confirm in part B of Figure 18–1 reads "we confirm our purchase from you"; the trade date is again 11/30/87, but the settlement date is 12/18/87; the trailer information states that the term of the repo is 18 days. The interest due at the maturity of the repo is $170,925.00, which is figured as follows:

$$(0.645000)(53,000,000) \left(\frac{18}{360}\right) = \$170,925$$

Figure 18–2 presents similar confirms for a reverse repurchase agreement: J. P. Morgan Securities is taking in securities from Norges Bank.

The fact that some dealers send straight buy and sell confirms out when they do repos and reverses could certainly be used as evidence to support the position that such trades are securities transactions, not secured loans. However, the fact that such confirms are sent in no way alters the economic significance of the transaction. Also, repo confirms frequently fail to disclose fully *oral understandings* surrounding the

FIGURE 18–1
Confirms for a term repo
A.   Confirm on start date of the repo

J.P. Morgan Securities Inc.
GOVERNMENT BOND DEPARTMENT
23 WALL STREET, NEW YORK, N.Y. 10015
TELEPHONE: (212) 483-5271

					DATE PREPARED	TRADE DATE	TRANSACTION NO
AS PRINCIPAL WE CONFIRM OUR SALE TO YOU					11/30/87	11/30/87	500342

QUANTITY	RATE	MATURITY DATE	PRICE	YIELD	BASIS	SETTLEMENT DATE
50,000,000.00	6.45	12/18/1987	106.00		6.45	11/30/87

REPURCHASE AGREEMENT   PRINCIPAL   53,000,000.00

U S TREASURY NOTES
SERIES H
11.75000% DUE 05/15/1989
CUSIP 9128270N5
18 DAYS @ 6.45000 %

SECURITY NUMBER	SALESMAN	CUSTOMER NO.	ACCOUNT NUMBER
95 RSA500342	130	648901	
99 C08905834			

NORGES BANK
P.O. BOX 1179 SENTRUM
OSLO 1 NORWAY

NET   53,000,000.00
PAYMENT AND DELIVERY INSTRUCTIONS

A.WIRE VS. FED FUNDS

CONFIRMATION

152019 1 C C00000000   0

B.   Confirm on end date of the repo

J.P. Morgan Securities Inc.
GOVERNMENT BOND DEPARTMENT
23 WALL STREET, NEW YORK, N.Y. 10015
TELEPHONE: (212) 483-5271

					DATE PREPARED	TRADE DATE	TRANSACTION NO
AS PRINCIPAL WE CONFIRM OUR PURCHASE FROM YOU					11/30/87	11/30/87	500342

QUANTITY	RATE	MATURITY DATE	PRICE	YIELD	BASIS	SETTLEMENT DATE
50,000,000.00	6.45	12/18/1987	106.00		6.45	12/18/87

REPURCHASE AGREEMENT   PRINCIPAL   53,000,000.00

U S TREASURY NOTES
SERIES H
11.75000% DUE 05/15/1989
CUSIP 9128270N5 INTEREST FROM 11/30/87 TO 12/18/87
18 DAYS @ 6.45000 %

INTEREST AMOUNT   170,925.00

SECURITY NUMBER	SALESMAN	CUSTOMER NO.	ACCOUNT NUMBER
95 RSA500342	130	648901	
99 C089C5834			

NET   53,170,925.00
PAYMENT AND DELIVERY INSTRUCTIONS

NORGES BANK
70 PINE STREET
NEW YORK, NEW YORK 10270

A. WIRE VS. FED FUNDS

CONFIRMATION

152019 1 C C00000000   0

DUPLICATE CONFIRMATION - INFORMATION ONLY

FIGURE 18–2
Confirms for a term reverse repurchase
A. Confirm for start date of the reverse

B. Confirm for end date of the reverse

trade. For example, a repo confirm may fail to disclose the following: (1) the repo is an open repo on which the rate, maturity, or both are, for the life of the transaction, uncertain; (2) the repo carries the right of substitution; or (3) a transfer of any coupon interest paid during the term of the repo shall be made by the holder of collateral to the owner of that collateral.

REPO RATES

The relationship of repo rates to other money market rates (even on reverses to maturity), supports strongly the argument that repos are collateralized borrowings, not sales of securities. If a repo were a securities sale, the repo rate should relate to the yield to maturity on the underlying collateral. In practice, however, a 30-day repo against, say, a 2-year note, is done at a rate that relates to other 30-day money market rates, not to the yield to maturity on the 2-year note.

The relationship of repo rates to other short-term, money market rates can be explained only by taking into account the behavior of *borrowers* in this market. Note, specifically, (1) that the *total* credit demanded by borrowers in the repo market is a function of the level of repo rates relative to the yields on the securities they would like to position (Is carry positive or negative?); and (2) that the *percentage* of their total credit needs that repo borrowers meet in the repo market is a function of the relationship of repo rates to other short-term rates at which they could borrow. This is an Econ-101 argument, which might be titled "Behavior of Demanders of Funds in a Competitive Capital Market."

So far we have spoken about repo rates as if there were only one rate prevailing at any one time for a repo of a particular term: one overnight rate, one 30-day rate, one 60-day rate, and so on. In fact there are, for any time period, several repo rates; which rate a dealer must pay depends on the type of collateral he wants to finance. For example, if the overnight repo rate on government collateral is X%, then the overnight repo rate on BAs and CDs will be approximately X% plus 15 basis points (a basis point is 1/100th of 1%), and the overnight repo rate on GNMAs will be approximately X% plus 25 basis points. The premiums that it costs to repo different types of collateral can all be rationally explained in terms of the liquidity of the collateral used, the credit risk associated with that collateral, and, in the case of GNMAs, the familiarity of repo investors with the prices at which GNMAs trade. By looking at current quotes on governments, a repo investor can always check how accurately a dealer, with whom he does repos, prices government collateral; however, if the investor does not trade GNMAs, he may feel that he cannot adequately check how accurately a dealer prices GNMA collateral.

The spreads that exist between the rates at which different types of collateral can be repoed make economic sense only if repo is viewed as a secured lending transaction.

PASS-THROUGH OF COUPON INTEREST

Repo agreements are written with the provision that any coupon interest coming due on the securities serving as collateral will be paid out by the "buyer" of the securities serving as collateral to the "seller" of those securities. This arrangement is consistent with the securities buyer (lender of money) making a collateralized loan to the securities seller (borrower of money). It is totally inconsistent with the market practices that prevail when a true sale is made.

When a true sale of a coupon security occurs, that security is always sold at a price per $100 of face value that equals the sum of the security's current market value per $100 of face value *plus* any accrued coupon interest on $100 worth of that security. Example: A security, which carries a 12% coupon and which, three months after its last semi-annual coupon date, is quoted at a dollar price of 99 would cost the investor approximately

$$\$99 + (\tfrac{1}{2})(^{0.12}\!/_2)(\$100) = \$102$$

per $100 of face value.[1]

PRICING OF COLLATERAL

Both the taking of margin on repos and the periodic marking of that collateral to market are inconsistent with the view that a repo is a sale of securities, but these practices are consistent with the view that repo is a collateralized loan, one that exposes the lender of money to a credit risk via-à-vis the borrower of money. Note, if repos were securities sales, the securities sold should be priced at full market value, instead of at market value minus a haircut.

RIGHT OF SUBSTITUTION

It is common in repo agreements for a dealer to have the right—if he sells a security being used as collateral for a repo—to remove that

---

[1] To figure accrued coupon interest to the penny, one must use the *basis* (day count) in the coupon period. See, for example, Marcia Stigum, *After the Trade: Dealer and Clearing Bank Operations in Money Market and Government Securities* (Homewood, Ill.: Dow Jones-Irwin, 1988), pp. 134–36 (especially Table 10–1).

security from the lender's collateral position, provided that he simultaneously substitutes other collateral of equal value and quality for it. So long as repo is viewed as a collateralized loan, the *right of substitution* in a repo agreement makes sense.

Right of substitution makes, however, no economic sense if the front end of a repo trade is viewed as a true buy transaction by the investor. Any buyer of securities ought to care very much what issue he has bought because his choice of issue will determine what coupon interest he gets, how soon the security matures, and what chance he has for earning a capital gain or incurring a capital loss on his investment.

In actual practice, true institutional buyers of bonds engage, before they buy bonds, in a laborious and complex analysis of the potential returns offered by bonds in different sectors and maturity ranges of the bond market. They do so to determine which of the wide range of bonds available offer the greatest *relative value:* mix of risk, liquidity, and return. This being the case, right of substitution on a repo is totally inconsistent with the view that a repo is a sale of securities.

MATURITY OF REPO AND REVERSE TRANSACTIONS

Most repo and reverses are for short periods: overnight, a few days, 30 days, or at most three to six months. The short-term nature of repos and reverses reveals nothing about their true economic nature. The money market is full of traders who do speculative trades as principals for short periods. They buy a security in the morning hoping that by afternoon its price will have risen a small fraction enabling them to close out their intraday position at a profit. Sometimes this occurs, and traders who have gone long on the security make money; other times the reverse occurs, and intraday longs lose money. Either way, there is no doubt that such traders are acting as true buyers and sellers of securities.

Short-maturity transactions make economic sense not only in the world of real buys and sells, but in the dealer-financing world of collateralized loans. A dealer who buys for inventory securities that he hopes to resell shortly (e.g., who buys, during a Treasury refunding, securities to distribute to investors) would logically seek to make short-term collateralized loans to finance his purchases of securities.

SAFEKEEPING OF REPO COLLATERAL

Dealers who borrow in the repo market commonly safekeep collateral for the lender, especially on small transactions. It is also true that broker/dealers commonly safekeep stocks and bonds for small investors who have bought such securities from them. This parallel in market practices provides *no* evidence that a repo is a sale of a security. Dealers began both practices solely out of a desire to provide an attractive service to small investors who did business with them.

Managers of large institutional portfolios rarely avail themselves of the offer dealers make to safekeep customer securities unless they are doing letter repo against securities that are especially difficult and expensive to deliver. Typically, such investors pay custodial banks to safekeep any securities they acquire by doing either outright buys or repos. Also, a number of big dealers who do business mostly with managers of large portfolios do *not* offer to safekeep securities for customers.

Thus, dealer safekeeping practices in the repo market vary, and whatever they are in a given situation, they indicate nothing whatsoever about the true nature of a repo transaction.

ASSIGNMENT OF COLLATERAL

In assigning collateral to particular customers, a dealer's operations area must respect several binding constraints and also seek to be as efficient as possible. In particular, a dealer, in assigning collateral, must respect an investor's repo parameters; he can't give GNMAs to a customer who will take governments only. Also, he must match the term that the customer wants to do with the term he wants to do; he wouldn't want to put out on 30-day repo securities he might sell tomorrow unless he had the right of substitution on the repo. Also, he will want to divvy up collateral between customers so that he has the fewest possible deliveries to make and so that each customer gets the fewest possible issues; it would not make sense, for example, for a dealer to break up a $15 million block of securities into 15 $1 million pieces to deliver to 15 investors, each of whom had done $1 million of repo with him, and then turn around and deliver 15 $1 million pieces, each a different issue, to an investor with whom he had done a $15 million repo.

The way dealers assign repo collateral and investors accept repo collateral is consistent only with repo being a collateralized loan.

CONTROL OF COLLATERAL

The importance of control over collateral to a recipient of collateral in a repo or reverse transaction varies depending on the purpose and nature of the trade.

Many repos are pure financing transactions: for example, DLJ is financing its inventory and position; the Morgan Bank is financing its government portfolio. In such transactions, the lender of money normally wants only to earn interest while incurring the least possible credit risk. Consistent with this desire, the lender may request delivery of repo collateral, but he does so only to ensure that he has a perfected interest in that collateral and can sell out should the borrower go bankrupt or fail for any other reason to repay his loan. In most repos, the customer is totally disinterested in what collateral he gets, provided that it meets whatever broad requirements he may have, for example, that the collateral be short governments, or government and agencies maturing within X months.

Normally, investors who take delivery of collateral on repo transactions of the sort we have just described simply hold that collateral as would a bank that held a customer's stocks or bonds as collateral for a loan. Such an investor would, in particular, never think of selling his collateral, even though he presumably could, because, to go short collateral that he must eventually redeliver would expose him to unwanted market risk.

A dealer who takes in stock collateral as part of his matched-book position is in a slightly different position from an investor such as the Yale endowment fund. The dealer, unlike Yale, has no spare cash to invest. If he takes in stock collateral, he does so to earn a spread by hanging out that collateral on the other side at a slightly lower rate. Such a dealer *must* require delivery of securities he reverses in if he is to have collateral to deliver to the customer to whom he repos those securities. In this case, the dealer is acting only as an intermediary through which funds and securities flow, and his need to take delivery of securities reversed into him indicates nothing about the nature of such trades.

REVERSES TO MATURITY AND THE NATURE OF REPO

There are only two situations in which control of collateral is crucial to the receiver of collateral: reverses to cover shorts and reverses to maturity. On a reverse to maturity, a dealer always calculates the profit there would be in the trade for him on the assumption that he will, immediately upon doing the trade, sell the collateral to be delivered to him; and when a dealer does such a trade, he always does immediately sell the collateral. His doing so indicates nothing about the true nature of repo. The dealer sells the collateral only to lock in, from day one, his profit on the trade; he neither wants to establish, nor does he establish, a short in the security sold. Also, the dealer's sale of the collateral has no impact on the way the trade is unwound. A dealer doing a reverse to maturity with a customer always strikes a deal that ends on the date the security matures; therefore, the only feasible way for him to unwind such a trade is by doing a pairoff and exchanging a difference check.[2] That, however, is

---

[2] Book-entry securities cannot be wired on their maturity date.

precisely what a dealer does when he has sold the securities reversed into him.

REVERSES TO COVER A SHORT AND THE NATURE OF REPO

On a reverse to cover a short, the dealer does care what collateral he gets, and he does deliver that collateral to cover a previously established short; this fact can be cited to support the argument that repos and reverses are securities trades. However, the rate at which a reverse to cover a short is done is totally unrelated to, and often far below, the yield to maturity at which the underlying collateral is trading; this fact fails to support the argument that repos and reverses are securities trades. A reverse that is done to cover a short is closer to a borrowing of securities (a trade commonly used to cover shorts) than to a sale of securities. A dealer who reverses in securities to cover a short goes short the moment he sells those securities, not later when he uses collateral to make delivery.

MATCHED-BOOK TRADES AND THE NATURE OF REPO

Interpreting dealer repo as a securities sale would lead to the absurd conclusion that dealers' huge matched books are a source of *no* risk to them because every security taken in on one side of the book is sold on the other. The conclusion that a matched-book trade entered into by a dealer is always riskless is nonsense, as every dealer monitoring risk in his matched book will say.

Except for reverses to cover shorts, every sort of trade that a matched-book trader does can only be understood when the trade is viewed as creating collateralized loans and borrowings. In particular, the only reason that big dealers are able to earn even a modest spread on running a matched-maturity book is that they are acting as *credit* intermediaries. When a dealer runs a mismatched book, the bets on interest rates that he contrives are bets not on yields of specific securities, but on financing rates for specific periods. This view of risk in a matched book, which is one to which every dealer subscribes, is consistent only with the view that repos and reverses are forms of collateralized borrowing.

The real money to be made in running a "matched book" comes from mismatching the book, taking in securities for 60 days, and financing them for 30 days to create a speculative tail. That sort of transaction is a gamble by the dealer on interest rates and creates *interest rate risk*, as opposed to *market risk*, for him.

One might try to counter this argument by saying that the flip side of viewing repo as a securities sale would be to say that every repo a dealer does is matched by a *forward* purchase of the security repoed and that the latter creates market risk for him. There's a problem with this argument. If a dealer reverses in for 60 days the 2-year note, finances it for 30 days, and thereby creates a 30-day tail, his risk in the trade is not market risk deriving from a possible rise in the yield to maturity of the 2-year note, but interest rate risk deriving from a possible rise in the 30-day financing rate. As noted, on a matched-book trade, the rate risk created is only occasionally, and then only by accident, closely related to—it's *never* identical with—the market risk associated with holding the underlying security.

THE BROKERING OF REPOS AND REVERSES

Repos against stock collateral are brokered with rates being quoted against any acceptable stock collateral. This supports the view that repo is a secured loan. The lender of money strikes a deal on the basis of what rate he gets, not on the basis of the precise collateral he gets.

The brokering of specials is different in that the lender of money does care what securities he is getting, but the borrower of money is induced to borrow because he is offered a loan at a rate that will permit him to do a profitable arbitrage. Repo brokers of specials always show holders of desired securities *two* rates: a *borrowing* (i.e., reverse) rate and some *higher lending* rate at which they could invest any funds they borrowed.

CONCERN OVER CREDIT RISK

A repo or a reverse exposes both parties to the trade to a credit risk. Thus, a key concern of repo market participants, especially lenders of money, is with the creditworthiness of their counterparty in the trade. This concern explains why margin has been part and parcel of prudent lending practices in the repo market since its inception.

It makes good economic sense not only for an institution making a collateralized loan, but for an institution buying a debt security, to be concerned with credit risk. However, the credit risks to which these two types of transactions expose an investor differ totally. An institution extending a collateralized loan should be concerned with the creditworthiness of *the borrower of money,* whereas an institution buying a debt security should be concerned with the creditworthiness of *the issuer of that security*.

Lenders in the repo market are consistently concerned with the creditworthiness of the institutions to which they lend money, and only incidentally concerned with the creditworthiness of the issuers of the securities used to collateralize repo loans. Either repos are collateralized loans or all investors in this market misperceive the nature of the credit risk to which repo exposes them.

A repo trade exposes to credit risk not only the lender of money, but the borrower of money, at least if the latter delivers collateral. Typically, repo collateral is priced at full market value minus a haircut. Also, on term repos, accrued interest will grow over the life of the repo with each day that passes; this growth can amount to a sizable sum on say a $10 million reverse. Because of margin, the growth of accrued interest, and possibly—should interest rates fall—a rise in the market value of the securities repoed, the borrower of money may find, if the lender goes bankrupt with no securities to return to him, that he has incurred a loss; the borrower's loss would equal the difference between the current market value of his lost bonds and his outstanding debt to the lender. So-phisticated managers of large bond portfolios exercise extreme care in determining to whom they will reverse out their *valued* bonds.

FED USES OF REPOS AND REVERSES

Currently, the Fed uses repos and reverses *very* actively in its open market operations, repos to add to bank reserves, reverses to drain reserves. The Fed insists on calling the reverses it initiates *matched sale/purchase agreements* because it is not authorized to do collateral-ized borrowings from bank and nonbank dealers. However, such seman-tics and a few accounting flourishes aside, repos and reverses done by the Fed have the same characteristics that private repos and reverses do and thus boil down to being collateralized loans and borrowings. The Fed does not do either reverses to maturity or reverses to cover shorts—reverses in which control over collateral is essential to the lender of money.

The repos that the Fed regularly arranges for foreign central banks have all the characteristics of an ordinary financing repo, the sort that GM would do with, say, Discount. Foreign central banks that invest through the Fed are looking for short-term investments that pay interest and expose them to *no* market risk, and the repos that these institutions do with U.S. lenders have all the hallmarks of a collateralized loan.

It is interesting that, when the Fed takes off its "I'm-in-compliance-with-the-rules-and-regs-that-state-what-I-may-do" hat and sets about producing either (1) a study of the money market or of banking or (2) a pamphlet that is supposed to be educational, it describes the repos it does as *credit* transactions that add to bank reserves. Clearly, research-ers and officers at the Fed think of repos and reverses as forms of collat-eralized loans. Also, in their analyses of the Fed funds and repo markets, they make precisely the point we did about repo rates—that they are tied to other short-term interest rates in part by the efforts of *borrowers in the repo market* to seek out the lowest-cost financing possible.

Note that the Fed is concerned about credit risk and requires, when it does repo, more margin than many dealers do. If a repo is a securities transaction, then the requiring of margin makes no more sense when the Fed does it than when private parties do it.

When the Fed takes delivery of repo collateral, it just holds it. The Fed has no interest in control over collateral in order to do something with it.

HISTORY OF THE REPO MARKET

It should be clear from what we have said about the history of the repo market that, whatever words people may have used to describe repo and whatever trappings they may have added to repo transactions to stay within investors' parameters, the basic trade was always and remains a collateralized loan: institution X lends money to institution Y, typically against government collateral.

The basic repo trade evolved out of a financing need. So, too, did private reverses and matched book. Basically, matched books are a form of financial intermediation, akin to banking; the dealer accepts secured deposits, demand and time, on one side of his book and extends collateralized loans on the other.

A point worth making is that repos have evolved very little since their revival, post–World War II. If a repo done today is a collateralized loan, then so were all earlier repos, and vice versa. There has occurred since the first all-private, post–World War II repo was done, little, if any, change in the basic characteristics of repo. For example, the pricing of collateral and the margining that are part of a repo trade have always been done in basically the same way, except at times, the pricing—especially as practiced by some fringe dealers—was sloppier than at others. As more people got into the repo market, pricing and margining became a bit sloppy, but once a few investors lost some money, investors and borrowers, at least in the national repo market, started to get back to old pricing and margining practices and to pay more attention to the details of any repo trade into which they entered.

REPOS, REVERSES, AND RISK

A telling characteristic of repos and reverses throughout their history is that one or both parties to the transaction has had as one of its overriding concerns *credit risk.* As noted in our discussion of matched book, dealers' matched-book traders use repos and reverses to create pure *interest rate risk,* but that risk derives not from a repo or reverse transaction itself, but rather from a contrived mismatch in the dealer's book. The only time anyone in the repo market worries about *market risk* in connection with a repo or a reverse is if he thinks he might be forced, during a bankruptcy proceeding, to hold collateral that he would like to sell.

REPOS AS FORWARD TRADES

Government attorneys have argued in certain tax cases that a repo is a forward securities transaction, a cash sale of securities matched with a forward commitment to buy securities.

Forward contracts differ from *futures* contracts. The latter are always traded on an exchange, are standardized, and are strictly margined and marked to market according to rules of the exchange on which they are traded. A forward is an off-exchange contract between two parties (sometimes custom-tailored to meet the needs of one party) to do a trade at an agreed upon price at some future date.

There is plenty of precedent for government dealers and their customers to engage in forward trading. Traders commonly strike forward deals for everything from foreign exchange to Maine onions. In fact, government securities dealers and their customers have for years been striking bona fide forward deals in outstanding government securities. To which it should be added that the forward market in governments is thin, whereas in foreign exchange it is massive.

The forward market for Treasuries

There are several problems with arguing that leg two of a repo is a forward securities transaction. First, there are in the government market bona fide (not to be confused with leg two of a repo) forward transactions. In *The Federal Reserve Bulletin,* the Fed defines such forward transactions as follows:

Forward transactions are agreements arranged in the over-the-counter market in which securities are purchased (sold) for delivery after 5 business days from the date of the transaction for Treasury securities (Treasury bills, notes, and bonds) or after 30 days for mortgage-backed agency issues.[3]

The Fed collects statistics on the average daily amounts of forwards that the primary dealers trade and on their positions in forwards (see Tables 18–1 and 16–1). Look in particular at the Oct. 1987 column in Table 18–1.[4] It shows that, in October of 1987, primary dealers traded on average per day 138.9 billion of governments for immediate delivery,

---

[3] See Table 18–1, note 5.
[4] We cite October 1987 figures because immediately after the October stock market crash, trading dropped to atypically low levels.

TABLE 18–1

U.S. GOVERNMENT SECURITIES DEALERS Transactions[1]

Par value; averages of daily figures, in millions of dollars

Item	1985	1986	1987	1987				1987				
				Oct.	Nov.	Dec.	Nov. 25	Dec. 2	Dec. 9	Dec. 16	Dec. 23	Dec. 30
Immediate delivery[2]												
1 U.S. Treasury securities	75,331	95,445	109,809	138,937	95,689	74,468	86,651	83,095	80,831	82,626	79,999	52,945
By maturity												
2 Bills	32,900	34,247	37,853	41,000	30,259	24,987	29,467	28,953	29,637	24,987	25,355	19,134
3 Other within 1 year	1,811	2,115	3,264	4,405	4,070	2,941	4,199	4,082	3,044	2,941	2,405	3,002
4 1–5 years	18,361	24,667	27,836	41,107	28,364	20,559	25,372	21,649	21,484	20,950	23,682	16,469
5 5–10 years	12,703	20,456	23,941	34,061	19,153	15,699	18,208	17,383	16,395	19,673	17,311	9,094
6 Over 10 years	9,556	13,961	16,915	18,365	13,844	10,283	9,405	11,027	10,272	14,075	11,246	5,247
By type of customer												
7 U.S. government securities dealers	3,336	3,670	2,920	2,750	1,894	2,053	2,308	2,070	1,792	2,052	2,752	1,732
8 U.S. government securities brokers	36,222	49,558	61,459	82,101	55,448	43,045	47,509	47,290	49,031	48,978	45,440	27,557
9 All others[3]	35,773	42,218	45,429	54,085	38,346	29,369	36,834	33,735	30,008	31,595	31,807	23,654
10 Federal agency securities	11,640	16,748	18,872	18,586	17,919	14,276	18,085	15,820	15,952	16,123	12,032	11,426
11 Certificates of deposit	4,016	4,355	4,106	4,927	3,392	3,010	3,329	3,475	3,130	2,945	2,857	2,798
12 Bankers acceptances	3,242	3,272	2,964	3,362	2,727	2,245	2,997	2,409	2,664	2,185	1,935	1,752
13 Commercial paper	12,717	16,660	17,102	19,394	16,007	15,138	15,776	15,373	16,216	16,732	14,594	11,145
Futures contracts[3]												
14 Treasury bills	5,561	3,311	3,224	4,056	2,774	2,335	3,226	3,570	2,652	3,363	1,451	1,670
15 Treasury coupons	6,085	7,175	8,954	11,462	8,489	7,335	7,719	8,427	8,357	9,157	7,459	3,910
16 Federal agency securities	252	16	5	8	2	5	0	0	1	1	*	25
Forward transactions[3]												
17 U.S. Treasury securities	1,283	1,876	2,061	2,653	2,167	1,097	1,450	1,262	934	1,183	1,630	359
18 Federal agency securities	3,857	7,831	9,824	7,676	7,191	5,704	5,885	4,023	6,031	8,136	6,268	3,364

1. Transactions are market purchases and sales of securities as reported to the Federal Reserve Bank of New York by the U.S. government securities dealers on its published list of primary dealers.
Averages for transactions are based on the number of trading days in the period. The figures exclude allotments of, and exchanges for, new U.S. Treasury securities, redemptions of called or matured securities, purchases or sales of securities under repurchase agreement, reverse repurchase (resale), or similar contracts.
2. Data for immediate transactions do not include forward transactions.
3. Includes, among others, all other dealers and brokers in commodities and

securities, nondealer departments of commercial banks, foreign banking agencies, and the Federal Reserve System.
4. Futures contracts are standardized agreements arranged on an organized exchange in which parties commit to purchase or sell securities for delivery at a future date.
5. Forward transactions are agreements arranged in the over-the-counter market in which securities are purchased (sold) for delivery after 5 business days from the date of the transaction for Treasury securities (Treasury bills, notes, and bonds) or after 30 days for mortgage-backed agency issues.

Source: *Federal Reserve Bulletin.*

15.9 billion of futures contracts for Treasuries, and a mere 2.7 billion of Treasuries for forward settlement. Table 16–1 shows that, in the same month, primary dealers were net short 0.2 billion of Treasuries for forward settlement.

Clearly, there is a bona fide forward market in Treasuries, but as the numbers we've cited indicate, that market is minuscule relative to the cash market for Treasuries. In October 1987, primary dealers were doing 300.4 billion of repo and almost as much of reverses. A comparison of these numbers with the Fed's numbers on forward transactions by primary dealers makes it clear that, in the Fed's mind at least, a forward trade of Treasuries is something distinct and different from leg two of a repo or a reverse.

The treatment of margin

The fact that leg two of a repo is not what anyone in the government market or the Fed itself means by a forward trade in governments is not the only problem with viewing leg two of a repo as a forward trade. A second problem concerns margin. For example, if the government argues in a tax case that a financed purchase of bills reduces to a spot purchase of bills, a spot sale of bills, and a forward purchase of bills, the numbers in this trade require the government to incorporate margin some which way into its theory. One tack that the government has taken in tax court is to assert that the payment of margin represents an immediate capital loss: on day one of his trade, the buyer of securities purchases at price X, immediately sells at price X *minus Y dollars of margin,* and thereby incurs a loss of Y *dollars.*

Nobody on the Street—not investors, not dealers, not anyone—keeps their books this way for any purpose, whether it be reporting taxable income, reporting to stockholders, or reporting to regulatory authorities. Moreover, it is probably fair to say that, if margin payments on repo were treated as an immediate capital loss, repo as a borrowing/investment mechanism would vanish from the Street, at least repos on which margin amounted to a significant sum.

Imagine, to take an extreme case, an S&L wanting to buy and finance $10 million of GNMAs in order to earn carry profits; under the theory that a financed purchase of securities reduces to a forward trade, this trade would produce for the S&L an immediate short-term capital loss of 2 points per 100 of face value—about $200,000. Manufactured losses, even if offset by later manufactured gains, are presumably the last thing an S&L wanting to bolster its earnings with carry would want to book.

Yet another problem with viewing leg two of a repo or a reverse as a forward trade is that the numbers—prices—on such trades are all wrong. Because the market for Treasuries is highly competitive, because financing for positions in Treasuries is readily available, and because the spot, forward, and futures markets for Treasuries can be readily arbitraged, there is only *one* rational price for a Treasury security traded in the wholesale market for forward delivery: the price of that security in the spot market *minus (plus)* whatever *positive (negative)* carry could be earned on the security by financing it over the period running from the date of the spot purchase to the date of the forward delivery. Rarely, if ever, will a security be priced on leg two of a repo or a reverse at or reasonably close to its *implied forward price:* the price implied by its spot price, its yield, and the financing rate.

To call leg two of a repo or a reverse a forward contract is to rob the latter term of the meaning that financial folk have traditionally ascribed to it; to do so also renders meaningless the traditional analysis of pricing in forward markets, an analysis that is widely applied not only to forward markets for securities, but to forward markets for gold, for soybeans, for oil—for any commodity routinely traded in large volume for forward delivery.

Does God exist?

A final point. If the government, in repo tax cases, goes on to argue that trades in which the selling dealer shorts securities he sells and then finances that purchase are ipso facto trades in which "no securities exist" (whatever that means), then a new problem arises. What, for example, is the status of the trades that primary dealers did in order to establish a net short position of 23 billion in governments in September 1987 (see Table 16–1)? Was some subset of these trades also trades for which "no securities existed," and are these trades therefore suspect?

It would be tidy if there were some ever-present, foolproof indicia of a real trade. Unfortunately, there are none. Absent a statement by one party to a trade that the trade was a rigged, prices-prearranged fake, trying to prove that a trade is unreal is akin to trying to prove that God does not exist. Neither assertion is *falsifiable:* What evidence could conceivably count against either of them? Therefore, neither assertion is a factually meaningful statement.

The wi market in governments

While it is true that the forward market for outstanding government securities is thin, there are very active, short-lived forward markets for government securities about to be issued. Specifically, Treasury bills, notes, and bonds all trade, for delivery *when issued (wi),* from the time a new issue is announced by the Treasury until it is auctioned and after that until it is settled. The wi trading period is longer for new note and bond issues than it is for new bill issues. A government issue, trading on a when-issued basis, always trades at approximately the yield at which traders and investors believe this issue will trade when it has been auctioned and settled. Prices in the wi market are definitely not funny money prices; quite the contrary, they are easily explained, economically rational prices that relate to the prices of outstanding government issues.

SUMMARY

Factors supporting the view that repo is a secured loan

Most of the factors discussed above support the notion that repos are collateralized loans:

1. Their macroeconomic significance.
2. Their history.
3. The way dealers and banks view them.
4. The way repo trade tickets are written.
5. The structure of repo rates.
6. The way repos are brokered.
7. The right of substitution.
8. The pass-through of coupon interest.
9. The way dealers assign repo collateral.
10. The pricing of collateral.
11. The taking of margin.
12. The marking to market of collateral.
13. Credit risk.
14. The fact that most repo lenders of money do not want control over collateral.
15. The Fed use of repos to finance dealers.
16. The fact that Fed publications consistently describe repos as "credit" transactions.
17. The identification of where risk lies.

Neutral factors

Some of the factors cited above are neutral; they indicate nothing about whether a repo is a secured loan or a securities transaction. Two such factors are the maturity of a repo and the safekeeping of repo collateral.

Factors supporting the view that repo is a securities transaction

A few of the factors discussed above support the view that repos are securities transactions:

1. Many investors would not be permitted by their parameters to do repo if this transaction were defined as a collateralized loan.
2. Over the last several years, repo agreements have begun to be written to indicate that repos are securities transactions (but some parties refuse, for various reasons, to sign such agreements).
3. Some repo (reverse) confirms have no indication that the trade being done is a repo (reverse).
4. The Fed accounts for MSPs as if they were securities trades (but it does not do so for repos).
5. Some parties do reverses to obtain control over collateral.

Repos as a unique trade

We have argued that the economic significance of a repo is almost always that it is a secured lending. One would be hard put to argue the opposite, that repos are securities transactions. One could, however, argue that repos are a unique transaction—a sui generis hybrid. Unfortunately, the latter position, while it may be intellectually sound, is singularly useless as a basis for resolving legal disputes concerning repos and reverses.

THE NEXT CHAPTER

The next chapter, written by Lee Stremba, a partner in the law firm of Parker Chapin Flattau & Klimpl, reviews the highlights of repo litigation that has arisen in the following contexts: federal taxation, federal regulation of securities transactions, and bankruptcy proceedings.

Chapter 19

Highlights of repo litigation[1]

REPO IS A HYBRID TRANSACTION. In *outward appearance,* it is a sale of securities and an agreement to repurchase the same or equivalent securities in the future; in *economic substance,* it is a financing transaction in which the repoed securities are used as collateral for a loan. This duality has made repo an extremely flexible and useful instrument in the money market. Unfortunately, it has also led to substantial legal disputes over the rights and obligations of players in the repo market. These disputes have arisen in diverse and significant contexts: federal taxation, federal regulation of securities transactions, and bankruptcy proceedings. We review here the highlights of legal controversies and decisions in those areas.

Federal taxation of income on repoed securities

Consider a bank that "purchases" *municipal* bonds at par from a bond dealer with a simultaneous agreement by that dealer to "repurchase" those bonds at a later date at par plus the interest accrued on the bonds

---

[1] This chapter was written by Lee W. Stremba. Mr. Stremba, a graduate of New York University School of Law, is a partner in the New York City law firm of Parker Chapin Flattau & Klimpl, where he specializes in securities and accountants' malpractice litigation.

during the term of the repo. Is the bank, as owner of the bonds while they were under repo, entitled to claim the exemption from federal taxes for coupon interest earned on the bonds, or does the tax exemption belong to the dealer who repoed the bonds to the bank? If the transaction is viewed as an actual purchase and resale of securities, then the bank owned the bonds during the life of the repo and it should be entitled to the exemption. If the transaction is viewed as a financing collateralized by a pledge of securities, then the bank did not own the bonds during the repo and it is therefore not entitled to claim the exemption. The tax consequences of repos of municipal bonds to banks have been raised in a number of legal proceedings in which banks sought to obtain tax refunds from the federal government.[2]

Although the decisions in these federal tax cases were not consistent, the government won a majority of them, including all the cases that were reviewed by an appellate court. In the cases that the government won, the courts treated the repos in question as collateralized loans rather than as purchases and sales of securities. The focus of the courts in those cases was on the *economic substance* of the repo transactions. The courts viewed the transactions as a means for a bond dealer to finance his inventory until orders for those bonds were received from customers, at which time the dealer "repurchased" the bonds from the bank and sold them outright to the customers. The outward form of the repos as purchases and sales, and the intention of the repo participants to confer tax benefits on the banks, were not controlling on the issue of tax liability. As the federal Court of Appeals for the Sixth Circuit explained in the case of *Union Planters National Bank of Memphis* v. *United States,* "If the parties' characterization of these transactions is accepted as decisive for federal income tax purposes, they would be able to enjoy the benefit of the double tax advantage which Congress intended to prevent."

Repos under the federal securities laws

Until recently, repo dealers using government securities as collateral have been exempt from federal securities regulation. Nevertheless, victims of unscrupulous repo dealers have typically sought redress under the antifraud provisions of the federal securities laws.[3] Defendants have

---

[2] *First American National Bank of Nashville* v. *United States,* 467 F.2d 1098 (6th Cir. 1972); *Union Planters National Bank of Memphis* v. *United States,* 426 F.2d 115 (6th Cir.), *cert. denied,* 400 U.S. 827 (1970); *American National Bank of Austin* v. *United States,* 421 F.2d 442 (5th Cir.), *cert. denied,* 400 U.S. 819 (1970); *American National Bank of Austin* v. *United States,* 573 F.2d 1201 (U.S. Ct. of Claims 1978).

[3] Most commonly, a plaintiff will seek to allege a claim under Section 10(b) of the Securities Exchange Act of 1934, and the more particular Rule 10b-5 which was promul-

hotly contested the applicability of the securities laws to cases of alleged repo fraud, arguing that the purported fraud was not connected to "a purchase or sale" of securities. The clear trend of decisions indicates that such fraud is so connected.

Following the collapse of Drysdale Government Securities, Inc. in May 1982, the Securities and Exchange Commission instituted proceedings in the federal court in New York alleging securities fraud charges against the following: (1) Drysdale, (2) certain officers of Drysdale, and (3) Warren Essner, who was the Arthur Andersen & Co. partner responsible for the preparation and certification of Drysdale's allegedly false and misleading financial statements. In that action, the SEC accused defendants of, among other things, committing fraud "in connection with the purchase or sale of a security" in violation of Section 10(b) of the Securities Exchange Act of 1934 and Rule 10b-5 promulgated thereunder. The individual defendants other than Essner consented to the entry of permanent injunctions without admitting or denying the SEC charges. Essner, on the other hand, sought to have the SEC's complaint dismissed on the ground that the reach of the federal antifraud provisions did not extend to repo transactions.

In March 1985, Judge Sweet of the New York federal court ruled in Essner's favor, dismissing the SEC's charges.[4] The critical issue before the court was whether the alleged misrepresentations of Essner, which related to the financial condition of Drysdale rather than the value of the government securities involved in Drysdale's repo transactions, were really made "in connection with the purchase or sale of a security," as the securities laws require.

In analyzing the issue, Judge Sweet viewed repos as collateralized loans rather than as purchases and sales of the repoed securities.[5] As such, he was constrained by a prior decision of the Second Circuit Court

---

gated thereunder; both the statute and rule address instances of fraud "in connection with the purchase or sale of a security." The federal securities laws provide procedural benefits including access to the federal court system, which may be a more expeditious and, with respect to commercial matters, more sophisticated forum than the courts of an individual state. These laws also provide the substantive advantage of a standard of culpability that is less stringent than that of outright fraud; this makes the plaintiff's case easier to prove.

[4] *SEC* v. *Drysdale Securities Corp.*, 606 F.Supp. 295 (S.D.N.Y. 1985), *rev'd*, 785 F.2d 38 (2d Cir.), *cert. denied*, 106 S.Ct. 2894 (1986).

[5] In his analysis, Judge Sweet noted that the SEC conceded that repos do not themselves constitute separate securities issued by the repo dealer. If repos were separate securities, then repos would be subject to federal and state securities registration laws, unlike the underlying government securities which are exempt from registration. The prospect of repo registration is so daunting that the SEC has consistently taken the position that repos do not constitute separate securities. See Securities Act Release No. 33-6351, 1 Fed. Sec. L. Rep. (CCH) ¶2024 (September 25, 1981).

of Appeals,[6] which held that misrepresentations concerning the financial condition of a borrower do not qualify as a securities fraud merely because the borrowing is secured by a pledge (a form of purchase or sale for purposes of the securities laws) of stocks owned by the borrower. In the prior case, the fraud, which did not relate to the value of the pledged stock, was not "in connection with" the pledge of stock and was therefore not a securities fraud.

While Essner was fighting the SEC, Arthur Andersen & Co. was defending against civil litigation brought by Manufacturers Hanover Trust Co., one of the two big losers in the Drysdale affair. In an action in the New York federal court, Manufacturers sued Arthur Andersen and others for damages, charging violations of the same securities laws invoked by the SEC. In its defense, Arthur Andersen made the same arguments that Essner had made successfully before Judge Sweet. Judge Owen, who presided over the civil action, nevertheless allowed the case to proceed, and a jury verdict was eventually rendered against Arthur Andersen for $17 million. It was Judge Owen's view that repos are indeed separate securities and that the Drysdale fraud was certainly "in connection with" purchases or sales of those securities.

This dichotomy of opinions was short-lived. The SEC appealed Judge Sweet's decision, and Arthur Andersen appealed the civil judgment. Each of these cases was argued in the Second Circuit Court of Appeals, and in each case the presiding judges ruled that the federal securities laws extend to cases of repo fraud.[7] The SEC's complaint against Essner was therefore reinstated, and the $17 million jury verdict against Arthur Andersen was upheld as well.

In distinguishing its prior decision in *Chemical Bank* v. *Arthur Andersen & Co.,* the Second Circuit reasoned that repos are not typical collateralized loans, the subject of the *Chemical Bank* case, because repo lenders take title to the securities received and can trade, sell, or pledge them during the life of the transaction.[8] The repo lender's promise to return the repoed securities thus forms part of the consideration for the deal, and the repo borrower must rely on the ability of the lender to make good its promise. This difference, according to the court, magnified the importance of the financial condition of Drysdale, the repo lender; and

---

[6] Essner's defense and Judge Sweet's decision were based primarily on another case involving Essner's accounting firm. The case is called *Chemical Bank* v. *Arthur Andersen & Co.,* 726 F.2d 930 (2d Cir.), *cert. denied,* 469 U.S. 884 (1984).

[7] *SEC* v. *Drysdale Securities Corp.,* 785 F.2d 38 (2d Cir.), *cert. denied,* 106 S.Ct. 2894 (1986); *Manufacturers Hanover Trust Co.* v. *Drysdale Securities Corp.,* 801 F.2d 13 (2d Cir.), *cert. denied,* 107 S.Ct. 952 (1987).

[8] In this chapter, the term *repo lender* refers to the repo participant who lends money and receives securities as collateral, and the term *repo borrower* refers to the repo participant who borrows money and gives securities as collateral.

the alleged misrepresentations of Essner were therefore made "in connection with" the transfer of the repoed securities.

In its decisions, the Second Circuit, while expressly avoiding the question of whether a repo is itself a security, ruled firmly that victims of repo frauds, such as those committed in the Drysdale situation, may seek redress under the federal securities laws.[9] This resolution, which serves the interests of the SEC and private plaintiffs alike, reflects a judicial view that, in lawsuits under the federal securities laws, repos are to be given the legal effect of purchases and sales of securities, rather than that of collateralized loans.

Treatment of repos in bankruptcy

In repo litigation, the legal issues having the greatest commercial significance have arisen in the context of the bankruptcy of a repo participant. In this context, the central question is once again whether a repo is to be treated as a purchase and sale of securities or as a collateralized loan.

In the case of *Gilmore* v. *State Board of Administration of Florida,* 382 So.2d 861 (Fla. 1st DCA 1980), a repo borrower declared bankruptcy and defaulted on its obligation to repurchase securities from the repo lender. The lender liquidated the securities, which were in its possession, and kept for itself the proceeds of the liquidation, including certain proceeds in excess of the repurchase price. The trustee for the bankrupt sued for the excess proceeds, arguing that repos are collateralized loans and that, therefore, the bankrupt actually owned the repoes securities and was entitled to any proceeds from the liquidation of those securities over and above the repurchase price that the bankrupt had failed to pay.

Both the trial court and appellate court sided with the repo lender: they ruled that the lender owned the liquidated securities because the repos at issue were actual purchases and sales of those securities. Therefore, the lender was allowed to liquidate the securities and to retain the full proceeds of liquidation when the borrower breached its obligation to repurchase the securities. In reaching this decision, the courts looked primarily to the intentions of the parties and the industry custom and practice to determine the rights of the parties. This approach differs markedly from the analysis of repos by judges in tax cases; the latter

---

[9] Court decisions in the ESM and Bevill, Bresler matters are consistent with the Second Circuit rulings in the Drysdale litigation. See *SEC* v. *Gomez,* CCH Fed.Sec. L.Rep. ¶92,013 (S.D. Fla. 1985); *City of Harrisburg* v. *Bradford Trust Co.,* 621 F.Supp. 463 (M.D.Pa. 1985); *In the Matter of Bevill, Bresler & Schulman Asset Management Corp.,* 67 B.R. 557 (D.N.J. 1986).

considered the intentions of the parties to be secondary to the intent of the federal tax laws.

Two years after the *Gilmore* case, a contrary result was reached by Judge Ryan in the Lombard-Wall bankruptcy.[10] In that case, Judge Ryan held that the repos at issue were to be treated as collateralized loans, and securities received from the bankrupt under repos were therefore still the property of the bankrupt estate. Under this ruling, the automatic stay, which comes into effect upon the filing of a bankruptcy petition and bars anyone from disposing of assets of the bankrupt, had the effect of immediately precluding a repo lender from liquidating repo collateral in its possession.

The Lombard-Wall decision relegated the repo lender to the bankruptcy remedies available to secured creditors. The repo lender might apply to the bankruptcy court for a court order lifting the automatic stay so that the lender's collateral could be liquidated. Alternatively, the repo lender might seek a court order requiring the bankrupt to provide additional or different security to protect the lender's claim. To obtain either relief, however, the lender would bear a heavy burden of proving that the value of his collateral had fallen below the agreed repurchase price, or that the security for his claim was otherwise impaired. In sum, under the Lombard-Wall decision, a repo lender is afforded certain protections in a bankruptcy proceeding, but he is deprived of the liquidity that he expected of his repo.

The Lombard-Wall decision may have been dictated by the unusual nature of the repos at issue in that case: under those agreements, the repoed securities were held by a bank trustee, and the lender was precluded during the term of the repo from dealing with those securities in any way. The decision was, however, of such concern to the securities industry that Congress was prompted to enact Section 559 of the Bankruptcy Code. Under that provision, repos are treated as purchases and sales to the extent that repo lenders are permitted to liquidate, free of the bar of the automatic bankruptcy stay, repo collateral that they hold at the time the repo borrower files for bankruptcy. This treatment gives due weight to the customs and expectations of the repo market. Repos are treated as collateralized loans, however, to the extent that the repo lender is required to refund to the bankrupt any excess proceeds from the liquidation. The Bankruptcy Code thus strikes a balance among the interests of repo participants to counter the imbalance caused by Lombard-Wall. *It provides a hybrid bankruptcy treatment for a hybrid financial instrument.*

---

[10] Judge Ryan's unpublished opinion is cited as *In re Lombard-Wall*, No. 82-B-11556, bench op. (S.D.N.Y. Sept. 16, 1982).

Section 559 of the Bankruptcy Code defined certain rights and duties of persons who hold repoed securities. It did not speak to the rights of participants in nonpossessory repos. That subject has now been reviewed in litigation that arose from the collapse of the Bevill, Bresler entities.[11]

In the Bevill, Bresler litigation, the New Jersey federal court had to determine whether securities held at the clearing bank of the Bevill, Bresler entities were the property of the bankruptcy estates, the reverse repo participants who provided those securities, or the repo participants to whom those same securities were "sold" under nonpossessory repos. To determine the property interests of the various parties, the court had to decide numerous issues, but at the heart of all these issues was the fundamental question which Section 559 of the Code left unanswered, that is, whether repos are loans or purchases and sales of securities.

In its analysis, the court observed that the hybrid nature of repos precluded a rational choice between the loan and sale-purchase characterizations of repos based on a balancing of their economic characteristics. The court concluded, however, that the controlling consideration in determining the property rights of parties in a bankruptcy case is the "intent of the parties viewed in the context of the entire market in which the transactions take place," rather than a balancing of the economic characteristics of the transactions themselves. Based on the language of repo agreements and custom and practice in the market, the court ruled that repos are to be given the legal effect of purchases and sales. The court went on to determine the competing claims of the many parties based on that ruling.

With the addition of the Bevill, Bresler decision to the prior bankruptcy cases dealing with repos, it appears that the characterization of a repo as a purchase and sale has prevailed in bankruptcy courts.

---

[11] The lengthy opinion of Judge Debevoise in this case is cited as *In the Matter of Bevill, Bresler & Schulman Asset Management Corp.*, 67 B.R. 557 (D.N.J. 1986).

Glossary

Common money market and bond market terms

Accretion (of a discount): In portfolio accounting, a straight-line accumulation of capital gains on discount bonds in anticipation of receipt of par at maturity.

Accrued interest: Interest due from issue or from the last coupon date to the present on an interest-bearing security. The buyer of the security pays the quoted dollar price plus accrued interest.

Active: A market in which there is much trading.

Add-on rate: A specific rate of interest to be paid. Stands in contrast to the rate on a discount security, such as a Treasury bill, that pays *no* interest.

After-tax real rate of return: Money after-tax rate of return minus the inflation rate.

Agencies: Federal agency securities. See also **Agency bank.**

Agent: A firm that executes orders for or otherwise acts on behalf of another (the principal) and is subject to its control and authority. The agent may receive a fee or commission.

Agent bank: A commercial bank that does the following for an issuer of, say, commercial paper: prints up notes, delivers them out against money, and redeems them at maturity—all pursuant to the issuer's instructions.

All-in cost: Total costs, explicit and other. Example: The all-in cost to a bank of CD money is the explicit rate of interest it pays on that deposit *plus* the FDIC premium it must pay on the deposit *plus* the hidden cost it incurs because it must hold some portion of that deposit in a non-interest-bearing reserve account at the Fed.

All or none (AON): Requirement that none of an order be executed unless all of it can be executed at the specified price.

Amortize: In portfolio accounting, periodic charges made against interest income on premium bonds in anticipation of receipt of the call price at call or of par value at maturity.

AP (agreement to pledge loan): Loans used by dealers who need to finance physical securities that they self-clear. Such a dealer sends to his bank a list of the collateral he is pledging against his loan from the bank.

Arbitrage: Strictly defined, buying something where it is cheap and selling it where it is dear; e.g., a bank buys 3-month CD money in the U.S. market and sells 3-month money at a higher rate in the Eurodollar market. In the money market, often refers: (1) to a situation in which a trader buys one security and sells a similar security in the expectation that the spread in yields between the two instruments will narrow or widen to his profit, (2) to a swap between two similar issues based on an anticipated change in yield spreads, and (3) to situations where a higher return (or lower cost) can be achieved in the money market for one currency by utilizing another currency and swapping it on a fully hedged basis through the foreign exchange market.

Asked: The price at which securities are offered.

Away: A trade, quote, or market that does not originate with the dealer in question, e.g., "the bid is 98–10 away (from me)."

Back contracts: Futures contracts farthest from expiration.

Back up: (1) When yields rise and prices fall, the market is said to back up. (2) When an investor swaps out of one security into another of shorter current maturity (e.g., out of a 2-year note into an 18-month note), he is said to back up.

Bank discount rate: Yield basis on which short-term, non–interest-bearing money market securities are quoted. A rate quoted on a discount basis understands bond equivalent yield. That must be calculated when comparing return against coupon securities.

Bank line: Line of credit granted by a bank to a customer.

Bankers' acceptance (BA): A draft or bill of exchange accepted by a bank or trust company. The accepting institution guarantees payment of the bill.

BANs: Bond anticipation notes are issued by states and municipalities to obtain interim financing for projects that will eventually be funded long term through the sale of a bond issue.

Basis: (1) Number of days in the coupon period. (2) In *commodities* jargon, basis is the spread between a futures price and some other price. A money market participant would talk about *spread* rather than basis.

Basis point: One-one-hundredth of 1%.

Basis price: Price expressed in terms of yield to maturity or annual rate of return.

Bear market: A declining market or a period of pessimism when declines in the market are anticipated. (A way to remember: "Bear down.")

Bearer security: A security the owner of which is not registered on the books of the issuer. A bearer security is payable to the holder.

Best-efforts basis: Securities dealers do not underwrite a new issue, but sell it on the basis of what can be sold. In the money market, this usually refers to a firm order to buy or sell a given amount of securities or currency at the best price that can be found over a given period of time; it can also refer to a flexible amount (up to a limit) at a given rate.

Bid: The price offered for securities.

Blind broker: A broker does not give up names to either side of a brokered trade. Blind brokering of securities is common, whereas blind brokering of Fed funds and Euro time deposits would be infeasible.

Block: A large amount of securities, normally much more than what constitutes a round lot in the market in question.

Bond power: Assignment form that, when properly executed and attached to a registered security, puts that security into negotiable form (makes it acceptable for good delivery).

Book: A banker, especially a Eurobanker, will refer to his bank's assets and liabilities as its "book." If the average maturity of the liabilities is less than that of the assets, the bank is running a **short** and **open** book.

Book-entry securities: The Treasury and federal agencies are moving to a *book*-entry system in which securities are not represented by engraved pieces of paper but are maintained in computerized records at the Fed in the names of member banks, which, in turn, keep records of the securities they own as well as those they are holding for customers. In the case of other securities for which there is a book-entry system, engraved securities do exist somewhere in quite a few cases. These securities do not move from holder to holder but are usually kept in a central clearinghouse or by another agent.

Book value: The value at which a debt security is shown on the holder's balance sheet. Book value is often acquisition cost ± amortization/accretion, which may differ markedly from market value. It can be further defined as "tax book," "accreted book," or "amortized book" value.

Broker: A broker brings buyers and sellers together for a commission paid by the initiator of the transaction or by both sides; he does not position. In the money market, brokers are active in markets in which banks buy and sell money and in interdealer markets for securities.

Bull market: A period of optimism when increases in market prices are anticipated. (A way to remember: "Bull ahead.")

Buy-back: Another term for a repurchase agreement.

Calendar: List of new bond issues scheduled to come to market soon.

Call: An option that gives the holder the right to buy the underlying security at a specified price during a fixed time period.

Callable bond: A bond that the issuer has the right to redeem prior to maturity by paying some specified call price.

Carry: The interest cost of financing securities held. (See also **Negative and Positive carry.**)

Cash commodity or security: The actual commodity or security as opposed to futures contracts for it.

Cash management bill: Short-maturity bills the Treasury occasionally sells because its cash balances are done and it needs money for a few days.

Cash market: Traditionally, this term has been used to denote the market in which commodities were traded for immediate delivery, against cash. Since the inception of futures markets for T bills and other debt securities, a distinction has been made between the cash markets in which these securities trade for immediate delivery and the futures markets in which they trade for future delivery.

Cash price: Price quotation in the cash market.

Cash settlement: In the money market, a transaction is said to be made for cash settlement if the securities purchased are delivered against payment in Fed funds on the same day the trade is made.

Certificate of deposit (CD): A time deposit with a specific maturity evidenced by a certificate. Large-denomination CDs are typically negotiable.

CHIPS: The New York Clearing House's computerized Clearing House Interbank Payments System. Most Euro transactions are cleared and settled through CHIPS rather than over the Fed wire.

Circle: Underwriters, actual or potential as the case may be, often seek out and "circle" retail interest in a new issue before final pricing. The customer circled has basically made a commitment to purchase the note or bond or to purchase it if it comes at an agreed-upon price. In the latter case, if the price is other than that stipulated, the customer supposedly has first offer at the actual price.

Clear: A trade carried out by the seller delivering securities and the buyer delivering funds in proper form. A trade that does not clear is said to fail.

Clearing account: A cash/securities account maintained by a dealer at its clearing bank.

Commercial paper: An unsecured promissory note with a fixed maturity of no more than 270 days. Commercial paper is normally sold at a discount from face value.

Competitive bid: (1) Bid tendered in a Treasury auction for a specific amount of securities at a specific yield or price. (2) Issuers, municipal and public utilities, often sell new issues by asking for competitive bids from one or more syndicates.

Confirmation: A memorandum to the other side of a trade describing all relevant data.

Convertible bond: A bond containing a provision that permits conversion to the issuer's common stock at some fixed exchange ratio.

Corporate bond equivalent: See **Equivalent bond yield.**

Corporate taxable equivalent: Rate of return required on a par bond to produce the same after-tax yield to maturity that the premium or discount bond quoted would.

Coupon: (1) The annual rate of interest on the bond's face value that a bond's issuer promises to pay the bondholder. (2) A certificate attached to a bond evidencing interest due on a payment date.

Cover: Eliminating a short position by buying the securities shorted.

Covered interest arbitrage: Investing dollars in an instrument denominated in a foreign currency and hedging the resulting foreign exchange risk by selling the proceeds of the investment forward for dollars.

Credit risk: The risk that an issuer of debt securities or a borrower may default on his obligations, or that payment may not be made on sale of a negotiable instrument.

Cross hedge: Hedging a risk in a cash market security by buying or selling a futures contract for a similar but not identical instrument.

CRTs: Abbreviation for the cathode-ray tubes used to display market quotes.

Current coupon: A bond selling at or close to par; that is a bond with a coupon close to the yield currently offered on new bonds of similar maturity and credit risk.

Current issue: In Treasury bills and notes, the most recently auctioned issue. Trading is more active in current issues than in off-the-run issues.

Current maturity: Current time to maturity on an outstanding note, bond, or other money market instrument; for example, a 5-year note one year after issue has a current maturity of four years.

Current yield: Coupon payments on a security as a percentage of the security's market price. In many instances the price should be *gross* of accrued interest, particularly on instruments where no coupon is left to be paid until maturity.

Cushion bonds: High-coupon bonds that sell at only a moderate premium because they are callable at a price below that at which a comparable non-callable bond would sell. Cushion bonds offer considerable downside protection in a falling market.

CUSIP number: *CUSIP* is an acronym for the *Committee on Uniform Identification Procedures*. Treasury securities, most federal credit agency securities (including mortgage backs), municipal bonds, corporate stocks, and corporate bonds all have identifying CUSIP numbers.

Custody bank: A commercial bank that holds securities of any sort in custody for an investor of any ilk.

Day trading: Intraday trading in securities for profit as opposed to investing for profit.

Daylight overdraft: Intraday overdraft that a bank runs with the Fed or that a bank customer runs with a bank. Foreign banks typically run big daylight overdrafts with their U.S. correspondent banks. A daylight overdraft exposes the institution that extends it to a credit risk.

Dealer: A dealer, as opposed to a broker, acts as a principal in all transactions, buying and selling for his own account.

Dealer loan: Overnight, collateralized loan made to a dealer financing his position by borrowing from a money market bank.

Debenture: A bond secured only by the general credit of the issuer.

Debt leverage: The amplification in the return earned on equity funds when an investment is financed partly with borrowed money.

Debt securities: IOUs created through loan-type transactions—commercial paper, bank CDs, bills, bonds, and other instruments.

Default: Failure to make timely payment of interest or principal on a debt security or to otherwise comply with the provisions of a bond indenture.

Delivery bill: A multipart bill that says, in effect, "Pay us 'X' dollars for these 'Y' securities." When a physical security is sold, a delivery bill is delivered along with the security.

Delivery month: A month in which a futures contract expires and delivery may be taken or made.

Demand line of credit: A bank line of credit that enables a customer to borrow on a daily or an on-demand basis.

DI (Depositing Institution): DIs comprise commercial banks, S&Ls, savings banks, credit unions, foreign bank branches in the U.S., etc.

Difference check: The amount of money that changes hands, by check or wire, when two trades are settled by a pairoff.

Direct paper: Commercial paper sold directly by the issuer to investors.

Direct placement: Selling a new issue not by offering it for sale publicly, but by placing it with one or several institutional investors.

Discount basis: See Bank discount rate.

Discount bond: A bond selling below par.

Discount paper: See Discount securities.

Discount rate: The rate of interest charged by the Fed to member banks that borrow at the discount window. The discount rate is an add-on rate.

Discount securities: Non–interest-bearing money market instruments that are issued at a discount and redeemed at maturity for full face value; e.g., U.S. Treasury bills.

Discount window: Facility provided by the Fed enabling member banks to borrow reserves against collateral in the form of governments or other acceptable paper.

Disintermediation: The investing of funds that would normally have been placed with a bank or other financial intermediary directly into debt securities issued by ultimate borrowers (e.g., into bills or bonds).

Distributed: After a Treasury auction, there will be many new issues in dealers' hands. As those securities are sold to retail, the issue is said to be distributed.

Diversification: Dividing investment funds among a variety of securities offering independent returns.

DK: To DK (don't know) a trade is to reject it because it fails to correspond in some way to a purchase that the receiver anticipates getting.

Documented discount notes: Commercial paper backed by normal bank lines plus a letter of credit from a bank stating that it will pay off the paper at maturity if the borrower does not. Such paper is also referred to as **LOC** (letter of credit) **paper.**

Dollar bonds: Municipal revenue bonds for which quotes are given in dollar prices. Not to be confused with "U.S. Dollar" bonds, a common term of reference in the Eurobond market.

Dollar price of a bond: Percentage of face value at which a bond is quoted.

DTC: Depositing Trust Company.

Due bill: An instrument evidencing either the obligation of a seller to deliver securities sold to the buyer or a letter repo agreement (see **Letter Repo**).

Dutch auction: Auction in which the lowest price necessary to sell the entire offering becomes the price at which all securities offered are sold. This technique has been used in Treasury auctions.

DVP: Delivery versus payment, the terms on which most money market trades are cleared.

Edge Act corporation: A subsidiary of a U.S. bank set up to carry out international banking business. Most such "subs" are located within the United States.

Elbow: The elbow in the yield curve is the maturity area considered to provide the most attractive short-term investment; e.g., the maturity range in which to initiate a ride along the yield curve.

Eligible bankers' acceptances: In the BA market, an acceptance may be referred to as eligible because it is acceptable by the Fed as collateral at the discount window and/or because the accepting bank can sell it without incurring a reserve requirement.

Equivalent bond yield: Annual yield on a short-term, non–interest-bearing security calculated so as to be comparable to yields quoted on coupon securities.

Equivalent taxable yield: The yield on a taxable security that would leave the investor with the same after-tax return he would earn by holding a tax-exempt municipal; for example, for an investor taxed at a 50% marginal rate equivalent taxable yield on a muni note issued at 3% would be 6%.

Eurocurrency deposits: Deposits made in a bank or bank branch that is not located in the country in whose currency the deposit is denominated. Dollars deposited in a London bank are Eurodollars; German marks deposited there are Euromarks.

Eurodollars: U.S. dollars deposited in a U.S. bank branch or a foreign bank located outside the United States.

Excess reserves: Balances held by a bank at the Fed in excess of those required.

Exchange rate: The price at which one currency trades for another.

Exempt securities: Instruments exempt from the registration requirements of the Securities Act of 1933 or the margin requirements of the Securities and Exchange Act of 1934. Such securities include governments, agencies, municipal securities, commercial paper, and private placements.

Exercise: To invoke the right to buy or sell granted under terms of a listed options contract.

Exercise price: The price at which an option holder may buy or sell the underlying security. Also called the *striking price*.

Extension swap: Extending maturity through a swap (e.g., selling a 2-year note and buying one with a slightly longer current maturity).

Fail: A trade is said to fail if on settlement date either the seller fails to deliver securities in proper form or the buyer fails to deliver funds in proper form.

Fails game: The strategies dealers use to attain a positive fail ratio and to thereby make money on fails.

Fed funds: See **Federal funds.**

Federal credit agencies: Agencies of the federal government set up to supply credit to various classes of institutions and individuals; e.g., S&Ls, small business firms, students, farmers, farm cooperatives, and exporters.

Federal Deposit Insurance Corporation (FDIC): A federal institution that insures bank deposits, currently up to $100,000 per deposit.

Federal Financing Bank: A federal institution that lends to a wide array of federal credit agencies funds it obtains by borrowing from the U.S. Treasury.

Federal funds: (1) Non–interest-bearing deposits held by member banks at the Federal Reserve. (2) Used to denote "immediately available" funds in the clearing sense.

Federal funds rate: The rate of interest at which Fed funds are traded. This rate is currently pegged by the Federal Reserve through open-market operations.

Federal Home Loan Banks (FHLB): The institutions that regulate and lend to savings and loan associations. The Federal Home Loan Banks play a role analogous to that played by the Federal Reserve Banks vis-à-vis member commercial banks.

Fedwire: A Federal Reserve communications and settlement system that links Fed banks and offices to DI that want to link up to the Fed. Fedwire is used to transfer money and book-entry securities.

Figuring the tail: Calculating the yield at which a future money market instrument (one available some period hence) is purchased when that future security is created by buying an existing instrument and financing the initial portion of life with a term repo.

Firm: Refers to an order to buy or sell that can be executed without confirmation for some fixed period.

Fixed-dollar security: A nonnegotiable debt security that can be redeemed at some fixed price or according to some schedule of fixed values (e.g., bank deposits and government savings bonds).

Fixed-rate loan: A loan on which the rate paid by the borrower is fixed for the life of the loan.

Flat repo: A repo for a variable (usually declining) sum done for some period, often several years.

Flat trades: (1) A bond in default trades flat; that is, the price quoted covers both principal and unpaid, accrued interest. (2) Any security that trades without accrued interest or at a price that includes accrued interest is said to trade flat.

Float: The difference between the credits given by the Fed to banks' reserve accounts on checks being cleared through the Fed and the debits made to banks' reserve accounts on the same checks. Float is always positive, because in the clearing of a check, the credit sometimes precedes the debt. Float adds to the money supply.

Floating-rate note: A note that pays an interest rate tied to current money market rates. The holder may have the right to demand redemption at par on specified dates.

Floating supply: The amount of securities believed to be available for immediate purchase, that is, in the hands of dealers and investors wanting to sell.

Flower bonds: Government bonds that are acceptable at par in payment of federal estate taxes when owned by the decedent at the time of death.

Foreign bond: A bond issued by a nondomestic borrower in the domestic capital market.

Forward Fed funds: Fed funds traded for future delivery.

Forward market: A market in which participants agree to trade some commodity, security, or foreign exchange at a fixed price at some future date.

Forward rate: The rate at which forward transactions in some specific maturity are being made (e.g., the dollar price at which DM can be bought for delivery three months hence).

Free box: Securities that a dealer has in his clearing and that he has not pledged as collateral for a dealer loan or for a repo.

Free delivery: Delivery of securities with no offsetting payment of funds.

Free reserves: Excess reserves minus member bank borrowings at the Fed.

Full-coupon bond: A bond with a coupon equal to the going market rate and consequently selling at or near par.

Futures market: A market in which contracts for future delivery of a commodity or a security are bought and sold.

General obligation bonds: Municipal securities secured by the issuer's pledge of its full faith, credit, and taxing power.

Give up: The loss in yield that occurs when a block of bonds is swapped for another block of lower-coupon bonds. Can also be referred to as "after-tax give up" when the implications of the profit (loss) on taxes are considered.

Glass-Steagall Act: A 1933 act in which Congress forbade commercial banks to own, underwrite, or deal in corporate stock and corporate bonds.

Go-around: When the Fed offers to buy securities, to sell securities, to do repo, or to do reverses, it solicits competitive bids or offers, as the case may be, from all primary dealers. This procedure is known as a go-around.

Good delivery: On *the Street* this term refers to delivery of the *correct* security in an *acceptable* form (e.g., in the case of a registered security, with a properly executed bond power attached).

Good funds: A market expression for immediately available money (i.e., Fed funds).

Good trader: A Treasury coupon issue that can readily be bought and sold in size. If a trader can short $10 million or $20 million of an issue and sleep at night, that issue is said to be a good trader.

Governments: Negotiable U.S. Treasury securities.

Gross spread: The difference between the price the issuer receives for its securities and the price investors pay for them. This spread equals the selling concession plus the management and underwriting fees.

GSCC: Government Securities Clearing Corporation.

GSI (Government Securities, Inc.): Some dealers that deal in both SEC-regulated and exempt securities have formed a GSI subsidiary in which they deal only in exempt securities, primarily governments and agencies.

Haircut: Margin in a repo transaction; that is, the difference between the actual market value measured at the bid side of the market and the value used in a repo agreement.

Handle: The whole-dollar price of a bid or offer is referred to as the *handle*. For example, if a security is quoted 101–10 bid and 101–11 offered, 101 is the handle. Traders are assumed to know the handle, so a trader would quote that market to another by saying he was at 10–11. (The 10 and 11 refer to 32nds.)

Hedge: To reduce risk (1) by taking a position in futures equal and opposite to an existing or anticipated cash position, or (2) by shorting a security similar to one in which a long position has been established.

Hit: A dealer who agrees to sell at the bid price quoted by another dealer is said to *hit* that bid.

In the box: This means that a dealer has a wire receipt for securities indicating that effective delivery on them has been made. This jargon is a holdover from the time when Treasuries took the form of physical securities and were stored in a rack.

Indenture of a bond: A legal statement spelling out the obligations of the bond issuer and the rights of the bondholder.

Interest rate exposure: Risk of gain or loss to which an institution is exposed due to possible changes in interest rate levels.

Investment banker: A firm that engages in the origination, underwriting, and distribution of new issues.

Junk bonds: High-risk bonds that have low credit ratings or are in default.

Letter repo: Nondelivery repo confirmed by letter.

Letter repo: A term used to describe repo transactions, typically overnight or very short term, in which collateral is not delivered to the investor. In certain dealer shops, such repos go by the moniker of hold-in-custody repo or due bills. Letter repo is done typically against physical securities: commercial paper, Ginnie Maes, and so on.

Leverage: See **Debt leverage.**

LIBOR: The London Interbank Offered Rate on Eurodollar deposits traded between banks. There is a different LIBOR rate for each deposit maturity. Different banks may quote slightly different LIBOR rates because they use different reference banks.

Lifting a leg: Closing out one side of a long-short arbitrage before the other is closed.

Line of credit: An arrangement by which a bank agrees to lend to the line holder during some specified period any amount up to the full amount of the line.

Liquidity: A liquid asset is one that can be converted easily and rapidly into cash without a substantial loss of value. In the money market, a security is said to be liquid if the spread between bid and asked prices is narrow and reasonable size can be done at those quotes.

Liquidity diversification: Investing in a variety of maturities to reduce the price risk to which holding long bonds exposes the investor.

Liquidity risk: In banking, risk that monies needed to fund assets may not be available in sufficient quantities at some future date. Implies an imbalance in committed maturities of assets and liabilities.

Locked market: A market is said to be locked if the bid price equals the asked price. This can occur, for example, if the market is brokered and brokerage is paid by one side only, the initiator of the transaction.

Long: (1) Owning a debt security, stock, or other asset. (2) Owning more than one has contracted to deliver.

Long bonds: Bonds with long current maturity.

Long coupons: (1) Bonds or notes with a long current maturity. (2) A bond on which one of the coupon periods, usually the first, is longer than the others or than standard.

Long hedge: *Purchase* of a *futures* contract to lock in the yield at which an anticipated cash inflow can be invested.

Make a market: A dealer is said to make a market when he quotes bid and offered prices at which he stands ready to buy and sell.

Margin: (1) In a repo or a reverse repurchase transaction, the amount by which the market value of the securities collateralizing the transaction exceeds the amount lent. (2) In futures markets, money buyers and sellers must put up to ensure performance on the contracts. (3) In options, similar meaning as in futures for sellers of put and call options.

Marginal tax rate: The tax rate that would have to be paid on any additional dollars of taxable income earned.

Market value: The price at which a security is trading and could presumably be purchased or sold.

Marketability: A negotiable security is said to have good marketability if there is an active secondary market in which it can be easily resold.

Match fund: A bank is said to match fund a loan or other asset when it does so by buying (taking) a deposit of the same maturity. The term is commonly used in the Euromarket.

Matched book: If the distribution of the maturities of a bank's liabilities equals that of its assets, it is said to be running a *matched book*. The term is commonly used in the Euromarket.

MBSCC: Mortgage-Backed Securities Clearing Corporation.

Money market: The market in which short-term debt instruments (bills, commercial paper, bankers' acceptances, etc.) are issued and traded.

Money market (center) bank: A bank that is one of the nation's largest and consequently plays an active and important role in every sector of the money market.

Money market fund: Mutual fund that invests solely in money market instruments.

Money rate of return: Annual return as a percentage of asset value.

Mortgage bond: Bond secured by a lien on property, equipment, or other real assets.

Municipal (muni) notes: Short-term notes issued by municipalities in anticipation of tax receipts, proceeds from a bond issue, or other revenues.

Municipals: Securities issued by state and local governments and their agencies.

Naked position: An unhedged long or short position.

Negative carry: The net cost incurred when the cost of carry exceeds the yield on the securities being financed.

Negative fail ratio: A dealer is said to have a negative fail ratio if his fails to others exceed fails to him. In this case, the dealer is losing money on fails.

Negotiable certificate of deposit: A large-denomination (generally $1 million) CD that can be sold but cannot be cashed in before maturity.

Negotiated sale: Situation in which the terms of an offering are determined by negotiation between the issuer and the underwriter rather than through competitive bidding by underwriting groups.

New-issues market: The market in which a new issue of securities is first sold to investors.

New money: In a Treasury refunding, the amount by which the par value of the securities offered exceeds that of those at maturity.

Nominee: See **Street name.**

Noncompetitive bid: In a Treasury auction, bidding for a specific amount of securities at the price, whatever it may turn out to be, equal to the average price of the accepted competitive bids.

Note: Coupon issues with a relatively short original maturity are often called *notes.* Muni notes, however, have maturities ranging from a month to a year and pay interest only at maturity. Treasury notes are coupon securities that have an original maturity of up to 10 years.

NSCC: National Securities Clearing Corporation.

OD (Overdrawn): A bank that runs a daylight overdraft at the Fed is OD at the Fed.

Odd lot: Less than a round lot.

Off-the-run issue: In Treasuries and agencies, an issue that is not included in dealer or broker runs. With bills and notes, normally only current issues are quoted.

Offer: Price asked by a seller of securities.

One-man picture: The price quoted is said to be a one-man picture if both the bid and ask come from the same source.

One-sided (one-way) market: A market in which only one side, the bid or the asked, is quoted or firm.

Open book: See **Unmatched book.**

Open repo: A repo with no definite term. The agreement is made on a day-to-day basis and either the borrower or the lender may choose to terminate. The rate paid is higher than on overnight repo and is subject to adjustment if rates move.

OPM (Other People's Money): In the course of their varied transactions, dealers may end up holding temporarily balances of customers' money, OPM.

Opportunity cost: The cost of purchasing one course of action measured in terms of the forgone return offered by the most attractive alternative.

Option: (1) **Call option:** A contract sold for a price that gives the holder the right to buy from the writer of the option, over a specified period, a specified amount of securities at a specified price. (2) **Put option:** A contract sold for a price that gives the holder the right to sell to the writer of the contract, over a specified period, a specified amount of securities at a specified price.

Original maturity: Maturity at issue. For example, a 5-year note has an original maturity at issue of five years; 1 year later, it has a current maturity of four years.

Over-the-counter (OTC) market: Market created by dealer trading as opposed to the auction market prevailing on organized exchanges.

Paper: Money market instruments, commercial paper, and other.

Paper gain (loss): Unrealized capital gain (loss) on securities held in portfolio, based on a comparison of current market price and original cost.

Par: (1) Price of 100%. (2) The principal amount at which the issuer of a debt security contracts to redeem that security at maturity, *face value.*

Par bond: A bond selling at par.

Pass-throughs: Securities backed by a pool of mortgages that pass through monthly to the holders of the securities interest and principal payments made on the underlying pool of mortgages.

Paydown: In a Treasury refunding, the amount by which the par value of the securities maturing exceeds that of those sold.

Pay-up: (1) The loss of cash resulting from a swap into higher-price bonds. (2) The need (or willingness) of a bank or other borrower to pay a higher rate to get funds.

Perfected interest: Having an ownership interest that will stand up in court. State UCCs (Uniform Commercial Codes) state what steps a buyer must take to perfect his interest in an item he has purchased.

Pickup: The gain in yield that occurs when a block of bonds is swapped for another block of higher-coupon bonds.

Picture: The bid and asked prices quoted by a broker for a given security.

Play for fail: A dealer is said to play for fail when he leaves unfinanced some of the securities due to be delivered to him because he anticipates that some of these securities will fail to come in.

Plus: Dealers in governments normally quote bids and offers in 32nds. To quote a bid or offer in 64ths, they use pluses; for example, a dealer who bids 4+ is bidding the handle plus $4/32 + 1/64$, which equals the handle plus $9/64$.

Point: (1) 100 basis points = 1%. (2) One percent of the face value of a note or bond. (3) In the foreign exchange market, the lowest level at which the currency is priced. Example: "One point" is the difference between sterling prices of $1.8080 and $1.8081.

Portfolio: Collection of securities held by an investor.

Position: (1) To go long or short in a security. (2) The amount of securities owned (long position) or owed (short position).

Positive carry: The net gain earned when the cost of carry is less than the yield on the securities being financed.

Positive fail ratio: A dealer is said to have a positive fail ratio if fails to him exceed his fails to others. In that case, the dealer is earning money on fails.

Premium: (1) The amount by which the price at which an issue is trading exceeds the issue's par value. (2) The amount that must be paid in excess of par to call or refund an issue before maturity. (3) In money market parlance, the fact that a particular bank's CDs trade at a rate higher than others of its class, or that a bank has to pay up to acquire funds.

Premium bond: Bond selling above par.

Prepayment: A payment made ahead of the scheduled payment date.

Presold issue: An issue that is sold out before the coupon announcement.

Price risk: The risk that a debt security's price may change due to a rise or fall in the going level of interest rates.

Prime rate: The rate at which banks lend to their best (prime) customers. The all-in cost of a bank loan to a prime credit equals the prime rate plus the cost of holding compensating balances.

Principal: (1) The face amount or par value of a debt security. (2) One who acts as a dealer buying and selling for his own account.

Private placement: An issue that is offered to a single or a few investors as opposed to being publicly offered. Private placements do not have to be registered with the SEC.

Prospectus: A detailed statement prepared by an issuer and filed with the SEC prior to the sale of a new issue. The prospectus gives detailed information on the issue and on the issuer's condition and prospects.

Proving: Reconciling ins and outs of money and securities to a daily statement provided to a bank by the Fed, to a dealer by his clearing bank.

Put: An option that gives the holder the right to sell the underlying security at a specified price during a fixed time period.

PVD (Payment versus delivery): Method of clearing a securities trade.

RANs (Revenue anticipation notes): These are issued by states and municipalities to finance current expenditures in anticipation of the future receipt of nontax revenues.

Rate risk: In banking, the risk that profits may decline or losses occur because a rise in interest rates forces up the cost of funding fixed-rate loans or other fixed-rate assets.

Ratings: An evaluation given by Moody's, Standard & Poor's, Fitch, or other rating services of a security's creditworthiness.

Real market: The bid and offer prices at which a dealer could do size. Quotes in the brokers market may reflect not the real market, but pictures painted by dealers playing trading games.

Red herring: A preliminary prospectus containing all the information required by the Securities and Exchange Commission except the offering price and coupon of a new issue.

Refunding: Redemption of securities by funds raised through the sale of a new issue.

Registered bond: A bond whose owner is registered with the issuer.

Regular-way settlement: In the money and bond markets, the regular basis on which some security trades are settled is that delivery of the securities purchased is made against payment in Fed funds on the day following the transaction.

Reinvestment rate: (1) The rate at which an investor assumes interest payments made on a debt security can be reinvested over the life of that security. (2) Also, the rate at which funds from a maturity or sale of a security can be reinvested. Often used in comparison to *give up* yield.

Relative value: The attractiveness—measured in terms of risk, liquidity, and return—of one instrument relative to another, or for a given instrument, of one maturity relative to another.

Reopen an issue: The Treasury, when it wants to sell additional securities, will occasionally sell more of an existing issue (reopen it) rather than offer a new issue.

Repo: See **Repurchase agreement.**

Repurchase agreement (repo or RP): A holder of securities sells these securities to an investor with an agreement to repurchase them at a fixed price on a fixed date. The security "buyer" in effect lends the "seller" money for the period of the agreement, and the terms of the agreement are structured to compensate him for this. Dealers use repo extensively to finance their positions. Exception: When the Fed is said to be doing repo, it is lending money, that is, increasing bank reserves.

Reserve requirements: The percentages of different types of deposits that member banks are required to hold on deposit at the Fed.

Retail: Individual and institutional customers as opposed to dealers and brokers.

Revenue bond: A municipal bond secured by revenue from tolls, user charges, or rents derived from the facility financed.

Reverse: See Reverse repurchase agreement.

Reverse repurchase agreement: Most typically, a repurchase agreement initiated by the lender of funds. Reverses are used by dealers to borrow securities they have shorted. Exception: When the Fed is said to be doing reverses, it is borrowing money; that is, absorbing reserves.

Revolving line of credit: A bank line of credit on which the customer pays a commitment fee and can take down and repay funds according to his needs. Normally the line involves a firm commitment from the bank for a period of several years.

ROA: Return on assets.

ROE: Return on equity capital.

Roll over: Reinvest funds received from a maturing security in a new issue of the same or a similar security.

Round lot: In the money market, round lot refers to the minimum amount for which dealers' quotes are good. This may range from $100,000 to $5 million, depending on the size and liquidity of the issue traded.

RP: See Repurchase agreement.

Run: A run consists of a series of bid and asked quotes for different securities or maturities. Dealers give to and ask for runs from each other.

S&L: See Savings and loan association.

Safekeep: For a fee, banks will safekeep (i.e., hold in book-entry form or, in the case of physical securities, hold in their vault, clip coupons on, and present for payment at maturity) bonds and money market instruments belonging to customers.

Sale repurchase agreement: See Repurchase agreement.

Savings and loan association: Federal- or state-chartered institution that accepts savings deposits and invests the bulk of the funds thus received in mortgages.

Savings deposit: Interest-bearing deposit at a savings institution that has no specific maturity.

Scale: A bank that offers to pay different rates of interest on CDs of varying maturities is said to "post a scale." Commercial paper issuers also post scales.

Scalper: A speculator who actively trades a futures contract in the hope of making small profits off transitory upticks and downticks in price.

Seasoned issue: An issue that has been well distributed and trades well in the secondary market.

Secondary market: The market in which previously issued securities are traded.

Sector: Refers to a group of securities that are similar with respect to maturity, type, rating, and/or coupon.

Securities and Exchange Commission (SEC): Agency created by Congress to protect investors in securities transactions by administering securities legislation.

Serial bonds: A bond issue in which maturities are staggered over a number of years.

Settle: See Clear.

Settlement date: The date on which trade is cleared by delivery of securities against funds. The settlement date may be the trade date or a later date.

Shell branch: A foreign branch—usually in a tax haven—which engages in Eurocurrency business but is run out of a head office.

Shop: In Street jargon, a money market or bond dealership.

Shopping: Seeking to obtain the best bid or offer available by calling a number of dealers and/or brokers.

Short: A market participant assumes a short position by selling a security he does not own. The seller makes delivery by borrowing the security sold or reversing it in.

Short bonds: Bonds with a short current maturity.

Short book: See **Unmatched book.**

Short coupons: Bonds or notes with a short current maturity.

Short hedge: *Sale* of a *futures* contract to hedge, for example, a position in cash securities or an anticipated borrowing need.

Short sale: The sale of securities not owned by the seller in the expectation that the price of these securities will fall or as part of an arbitrage. A short sale must eventually be covered by a purchase of the securities sold.

Sinking fund: Indentures on corporate issues often require that the issuer make annual payments to a sinking fund, the proceeds of which are used to retire randomly selected bonds in the issue.

Size: Large in size, as in "size offering" or "in there for size." What constitutes size varies with the sector of the market.

Skip-day settlement: The trade is settled one business day beyond what is normal.

Specific issues market: The market in which dealers reverse in securities they want to short.

Spectail: A dealer that does business with retail but concentrates more on acquiring and financing its own speculative position.

Spot market: Market for immediate as opposed to future delivery. In the spot market for foreign exchange settlement is two business days ahead.

Spot rate: The price prevailing in the spot market.

Spread: (1) Difference between bid and asked prices on a security. (2) Difference between yields on or prices of two securities of differing sorts or differing maturities. (3) In underwriting, difference between price realized by the issuer and price paid by the investor. (4) Difference between two prices or two rates. What a commodities trader would refer to as the *basis*.

Stop: An owner of a physical security that has been mutilated, lost, or stolen will request the issuer to place a stop (transfer) on the security and to cancel and replace the security.

Stop-out price: The lowest price (highest yield) accepted by the Treasury in an auction of a new issue.

Street name: A security is said to be in *Street name* when it is registered in the name of a *nominee*. Nominees are shell partnerships whose sole function is to act as nominee, to pass through payments of interest and dividends, etc.

Sub right: Right of substitution—to change collateral—on a repo.

Subject: Refers to a bid or offer that cannot be executed without confirmation from the customer.

Subordinated debenture: The claims of holders of this issue rank after those of holders of various other unsecured debts incurred by the issuer.

Swap: (1) In securities, selling one issue and buying another. (2) In foreign exchange, buying a currency spot and simultaneously selling it forward.

TABs (tax anticipation bills): Special bills that the Treasury occasionally issues. They mature on corporate quarterly income tax dates and can be used at face value by corporations to pay their tax liabilities.

Tail: (1) The difference between the average price in Treasury auctions and the stop-out price. (2) A *future* money market instrument (one available some period hence) created by buying an existing instrument and financing the initial portion of its life with term repo.

Take: (1) A dealer or customer who agrees to buy at another dealer's offered price is said to take that offer. (2) Eurobankers speak of taking deposits rather than buying money.

Take-out: (1) A cash surplus generated by the sale of one block of securities and the purchase of another, for example, selling a block of bonds at 99 and buying another block at 95. (2) A bid made to a seller of a security that is designed (and generally agreed) to take him out of the market.

TANs: Tax anticipation notes issued by states or municipalities to finance current operations in anticipation of future tax receipts.

Technical condition of a market: Demand and supply factors affecting price, in particular the net position—long or short—of dealers.

Technicals: (1) Supply and demand factors influencing the cash market. (2) Value or shape of technical indicators.

Tenor: Maturity.

Term bonds: A bond issue in which all bonds mature at the same time.

Term Fed funds: Fed funds sold for a period of time longer than overnight.

Term loan: Loan extended by a bank for more than the normal 90-day period. A term loan might run five years or more.

Term repo (RP): Repo borrowings for a period longer than overnight, may be 30, 60, or even 90 days.

Thin market: A market in which trading volume is low and in which consequently bid and asked quotes are wide and the liquidity of the instrument traded is low.

Throttle: Slowing of the rate at which Fedwire processed incoming messages. Throttle was caused by heavy traffic on Fedwire.

Throughput: The number of transactions a computer system can handle per unit of time.

Tight: An issue is said to be tight when it is hard to obtain and expensive to borrow. Big shorts in an issue make it "tight."

Tight market: A tight market, as opposed to a thin market, is one in which volume is large, trading is active and highly competitive, and spreads between bid and ask prices are narrow.

Time deposit: Interest-bearing deposit at a savings institution that has a specific maturity.

Trade date: The date on which a transaction is initiated. The settlement date may be the trade date or a later date.

Trade on top of: Trade at a narrow or no spread in basis points to some other instrument.

Trading paper: CDs purchased by accounts that are likely to resell them. The term is commonly used in the Euromarket.

Treasurer's check: A check issued by a bank to make a payment. Treasurer's checks outstanding are counted as part of a bank's reservable deposits and as part of the money supply.

Treasury bill: A non–interest-bearing discount security issued by the U.S. Treasury to finance the national debt. Most bills are issued to mature in 3 months, 6 months, or 1 year.

TT&L account: Treasury tax and loan account at a bank.

Turnaround: Securities bought and sold for settlement on the same day.

Turnaround time: The time available or needed to effect a turnaround.

Two-sided market: A market in which both bid and asked prices, good for the standard unit of trading, are quoted.

Two-way market: Market in which both a bid and an asked price are quoted.

Underwriter: A dealer who purchases new issues from the issuer and distributes them to investors. Underwriting is one function of an investment banker.

Unmatched book: If the average maturity of a bank's liabilities is less than that of its assets, it is said to be running an unmatched book. The term is commonly used in the Euromarket. Equivalent expressions are **open book** and **short book.**

Variable-price security: A security, such as stocks or bonds, that sells at a fluctuating, market-determined price.

Variable-rate CDs: Short-term CDs that pay interest periodically on *roll* dates; on each roll date the coupon on the CD is adjusted to reflect current market rates.

Variable-rate loan: Loan made at an interest rate that fluctuates with the prime.

Visible supply: New muni bond issues scheduled to come to market within the next 30 days.

When-issued trades: Typically there is a lag between the time a new bond is announced and sold and the time it is actually issued. During this interval, the security trades, **wi,** "when, as, and if issued."

Wi: When, as, and if issued. See **When-issued trades.**

Wi wi: T bills trade on a wi basis between the day they are announced and the day they are settled. Late Tuesday and on Wednesday, two bills will trade wi, the bill just auctioned and the bill just announced. The latter used to be called the wi bill. However, now it is common for dealers to speak of the just auctioned bill as the 3-month bill and of the newly announced bill as the wi bill. This change in jargon resulted from a change in the way interdealer brokers of bills list bills on their screens. Cantor Fitz still lists a new bill as the wi bill until it is settled.

Without: If 70 were bid in the market and there was no offer, the quote would be "70 bid without." The expression *without* indicates a one-way market.

Write: To sell an option.

Yankee bond: A foreign bond issued in the U.S. market, payable in dollars, and registered with the SEC.

Yankee CD: A CD issued in the domestic market (typically in New York) by a branch of a foreign bank.

Yield curve: A graph showing, for securities that all expose the investor to the same credit risk, the relationship at a given point in time between yield and current maturity. Yield curves are typically drawn using yields on governments of various maturities.

Yield to maturity: The rate of return yielded by a debt security held to maturity when both interest payments and the investor's capital gain or loss on the security are taken into account.

Bibliography

Repos and reverses

REPO: GENERAL BACKGROUND AND HISTORY

Bowsher, N. *Instruments of the Money Market.* Federal Reserve Bank of Richmond, 1981.

Jones, M. T.; C. M. Lucas; and T. B. Thurston. "Federal Reserve Funds and Repurchase Agreements." *Quarterly Review* (Federal Reserve Bank of New York) 2 (Summer 1977), pp. 33–48.

McCarthy, E. J. *Reserve Position—Methods of Adjustment.* Federal Reserve Bank of Boston, Summer 1977, pp. 29–33.

Pence, B. "Repurchase Agreements: Their Dramatic Growth." *Economic Review* (Federal Reserve Bank of Cleveland), Winter 1979, pp. 2–12.

Peters, Ralph F. "The Repurchase Agreement: Its Position in Today's Money Market." Thesis, Stonier Graduate School of Banking, 1962.

Simpson, T. D. "The Market for Federal Funds and Repurchase Agreements." Staff Studies 106. Washington, D.C.: Board of Governors of the Federal Reserve System, 1979. Mimeo.

Smith, W. J. "Repurchase Agreements and Federal Funds." *Federal Reserve Bulletin* (Board of Governors of the Federal Reserve System) 64 (May 1978), pp. 353–60.

Stigum, Marcia. *Money Market Calculations: Yields, Break-Evens and Arbitrage.* Homewood, Ill.: Dow Jones-Irwin, 1981. See index for examples of repo and reverse trades.

————. *The Money Market.* Homewood, Ill.: Dow Jones-Irwin, 1978, chaps. 11 and 12.

Tucker, James F. *Buying Treasury Securities at Federal Reserve Banks.* Federal Reserve Bank of Richmond, 1985.

U.S. General Accounting Office. *Survey of the Federal Reserve System's Supervision of the Treasury Securities Market.* October 1984.

EDUCATIONAL PAMPHLETS AND ARTICLES FOR REPO INVESTORS

Carroll McEntee & McGinley, Inc. *A Handbook on Repurchase Agreements: A Guide to Doing Repos Safely.* New York: Carroll McEntee & McGinley, Inc., 1982.

Federal Reserve Bank of Atlanta. "Repurchase Agreements: Taking a Closer Look at Safety." *Economic Review,* 1985.

Federal Reserve Bank of Cleveland, Public Information Department. *Repurchase Agreements.* Undated.

Federal Reserve Bank of New York, Public Information Department. *It's 8:00 A.M. Do you know where your collateral is?* June 1985.

Samansky, Arthur W. *Statfacts* (Federal Reserve Bank of New York, Public Information Department, November 1981).

Stigum, Marcia. "Repo Deals: Know Thy Dealer, but Demand Delivery." *The Cash Manager* 8 (December 1985), pp. 8–9.

REPO AGREEMENTS

Bowsher, N. "Repurchase Agreements." *Review* (Federal Reserve Bank of St. Louis) 61 (September 1979), pp. 17–22.

Dunning, Alan S., and Martin E. Lowy. *Repurchase and Reverse Repurchase Agreements.* Commercial Law and Practice Course Handbook Series, no. 290. New York: Practising Law Institute, 1982.

Dunning, Alan S. *Repurchase and Reverse Repurchase Agreements Revisited 1984.* Commercial Law and Practice Course Handbook Series, no. 341. New York: Practising Law Institute, 1984.

Holland, David S. "Repurchase Agreements Everywhere." *Banking Expansion Reporter* 1 (October 4, 1982), pp. 1, 8–12.

Levin, Alisa F., and Harold S. Novikoff. *Repurchase and Reverse Repurchase Agreements 1985.* Commercial Law and Practice Course Handbook Series, no. 368. New York: Practising Law Institute, 1985.

REPO MARKET PARTICIPANTS

Banks

Stigum, Marcia, and Rene Branch, Jr. *Managing Bank Assets and Liabilities.* Homewood, III.: Dow Jones-Irwin, 1983. See index for use of repos in bank asset and liability management.

Dealers

"The Dealer Market for United States Government Securities." *Quarterly Review* (Federal Reserve Bank of New York), Winter 1977–78, pp. 35–45.

"Repurchase Agreements: Their Role in Dealer Financing and in Monetary Policy." *Economic Review* (Federal Reserve Bank of Cleveland), November–December 1969, pp. 3–15.

Zigas, David. "Free-Wheeling Treasury Market Troubled by Repo Problems and Threat of More Regulation." *Credit Markets,* June 18, 1984, pp. 1, 45.

The Fed

Meek, P. *Discount Policy and Open Market Operations.* Washington, D.C.: Board of Governors of the Federal Reserve System, 1971, pp. 171–82.

Melton, William C. *Inside the Fed: Making Monetary Policy.* New York: Dow Jones-Irwin, 1985. See chaps 2, 17, and appendix.

Roosa, Robert V. *Federal Reserve Operations in the Money Market and Government Securities Markets.* Federal Reserve Bank of New York, 1956.

S&Ls

Office of Finance, Federal Home Loan Banks; Department of Economic Analysis and Planning, Federal Home Loan Bank of Chicago; Office of Policy and Economic Research, Federal Home Loan Bank Board; and Office of District Banks, Federal Home Loan Bank Board. "Reverse Repurchase Agreements." Staff study, March 1985.

State and local governments

New York State Assembly, Committee on Ways and Means. "Gambling with Public Funds: The Lion Capital Bankruptcy and Its Implications for Government Investment Practice." A report edited by Dean A. Fuleihan and Janet Penska, March 1985.

Office of the State Comptroller, Division of Municipal Affairs. "Cash Management and Investment Policies for Use by Local Government Officials." New York: Office of the State Comptroller, 1984.

Retail repo

Kurucza, Robert M., and J. E. Shockey. *Retail Repurchase Agreements*. Commercial Law and Practice Course Handbook Series, no. 377. New York: Practising Law Institute, 1981, pp. 149–68.

Sigel, Gabrielle. "Retail Repurchase Agreements." *Annual Review of Banking Law* 2 (1983), pp. 257–79.

Repo regulatory rulings

Federal Financial Institutions Examination Council. "Repurchase Agreements of Depository Institutions with Securities Dealers and Others." Washington, D.C.: Federal Financial Institutions Examination Council, October 1985, mimeo.

REPO LITIGATION

SEC v. *Miller et al. CCH Law Reports,* 91, 145, Southern District of New York, 60 Civ. 2063, 1962.

Tew, Thomas. "Report on the Condition of the E.S.M. Companies." U.S. District Court, Southern District of Florida, Fort Lauderdale Division, Case No. 85-6190-Civ-Gonzalez. *SEC* v. *ESM Companies,* April 2, 1985.

————. "Second Report on the Condition of the E.S.M. Companies." U.S. District Court, Southern District of Florida, Fort Lauderdale Division, Case No. 85-6190-Civ-Gonzalez. *SEC* v. *ESM Companies,* November 4, 1985.

Wachtell, Lipton, Rosen & Katz. Letter (including copy of Lombard-Wall repo agreement) from WLR&K, Attorneys for Goldman Sachs & Co., to Hon. Edward J. Ryan, Judge in the *Lombard-Wall* case, September 21, 1982.

CHARACTERIZATION OF REPO: LEGAL ARTICLES

Haggerty, William F., IV. "Lifting the Cloud of Uncertainty over the Repo Market: Characterization of Repos as Separate Purchases and Sales of Securities." *Vanderbilt Law Review* 37 (1984), pp. 401–31.

Ketchum, Richard G.; A. B. Levenson; and R. B. Smith. *Government Securities: Counselling and Regulation*. New York/Washington, D.C.: Law & Business Inc./Harcourt Brace Jovanovich, 1985.

Mitchell, Clyde. "Banking—Repurchase Agreements." *New York Law Journal* 189 (January 1983).

Porter, H. Boone, III. "Repurchase Agreements Revisited." *The Banking Law Journal* 99 (1982), pp. 676–708.

BANKRUPTCY ACT AMENDMENT

U.S. Congress. House Committee of Conference. *Bankruptcy Amendments of 1984.* 98th Congress, 2nd session, 1984. Report no. 98-882.

U.S. Congress. Senate Committee on the Judiciary. *Omnibus Bankruptcy Improvements Act of 1983.* 98th Congress, 1st session, 1983. Report no. 98-65.

DEALER BANKRUPTCIES AND REGULATION OF DEALERS

Federal Reserve Bank of New York. "A Report on Drysdale and Other Recent Problems of Firms Involved in the Government Securities Market." September 1982.

Perlstein, William J. "When Government Securities Dealers *Fail*: An Overview of the Repo Insolvency Issue." *ABA Bank Compliance.* New York: American Bankers Association, September 1985, pp. 27–32.

"Repurchase Agreements and the Bankruptcy Code: The Need for Legislative Action." *Fordham Law Review* 52 (1984), pp. 828–49.

Securities and Exchange Commission. "Regulation of the Government Securities Market." Report submitted by John S. R. Shad to the Subcommittee on Domestic Monetary Policy of the House Committee on Banking, Finance and Urban Affairs, June 1985.

BOOK-ENTRY SECURITIES

Debs, Richard A. "The Program for the Automation of the Government Securities Market." *Monthly Review* (Federal Reserve Bank of New York) 54 (July 1972), pp. 178–82.

Federal Reserve Bank of New York. "Operating Circular No. 21. Revised December 12, 1977."

Hoey, Matthew J. "Automation of U.S. Government and Agency Securities Operations." Federal Reserve Bank of New York Presentation to the American Bankers Association, New Orleans, La., March 9–12, 1975.

————. "Summary of Opinions and Conclusions; *Wichita Federal Savings and Loan Association, et al.* v. *Comark and Marine Midland Bank, N.A.*" (N.p., n.d.)

Hoey, M. J., and J. J. Lubeley. "The Book Entry System: A Paperless Revolution." (N.p.,n.d.)

Hoey, M. J., and L. S. Rassnick. "Automation of Government Securities Operations." *Jurimetrics Journal,* Winter 1976, pp. 176–85. Reprint of paper presented to the American Bar Association, Section of Science and Technology, First National Institute, New York City, May 13, 1976.

Hoey, M. J., and R. Vollkommer. "Development of a Clearing Arrangement and Book-Entry Custody Procedure for U.S. Government Securities." *The Magazine of Bank Administration,* June 1971, pp. 21–29.

Martin, A. E., III. "The Book-Entry System for Treasury Securities." *Economic Review* (Federal Reserve Bank of Atlanta), September 1985, pp. 15–16.

CLEARING REPOS AND REVERSES

Stigum, Marcia. *After the Trade: Dealer and Clearing Bank Operations in Money Market and Government Securities.* Homewood, Ill.: Dow Jones-Irwin, 1987.

Index